THE INVENTOR AND THE TYCOON

The Inventor
and
The Tycoon

A GILDED AGE MURDER AND
THE BIRTH OF MOVING PICTURES

Edward Ball

DOUBLEDAY

New York   London   Toronto   Sydney   Auckland

Frontispiece photographs: (top) Eadweard Muybridge, self-portrait, swinging a railroad lineman's pickax, 1879; (bottom) Leland Stanford (center, a hammer in his right hand) during the "last spike" ceremony at the completion of the transcontinental railroad, Promontory Summit, Utah, May 10, 1869

Book design by Maria Carella
Jacket design by Michael J. Windsor
Jacket illustration © Wellcome Library, London

Library of Congress Cataloging-in-Publication Data
Ball, Edward
The inventor and the tycoon : a Gilded Age murder and the birth of moving pictures / Edward Ball. — 1st ed.
p. cm.
Includes bibliographical references.
(hardcover : alk. paper)
1. Muybridge, Eadweard, 1830–1904. 2. Muybridge, Eadweard, 1830–1904—Trials, litigation, etc. 3. Stanford, Leland, 1824–1893. 4. Trials (Murder)—California—San Francisco. 5. Cinematography—United States—History. 6. Motion pictures—United States—History. 7. Cinematographers—California—Biography. 8. Businesspeople—California—Biography. I. Title.
TR849.M84B35 2012
777—dc23   2012019977

ISBN 978-0-385-52575-6

MANUFACTURED IN THE UNITED STATES OF AMERICA

1 3 5 7 9 10 8 6 4 2

First Edition

for Candace

CONTENTS

PART THREE

Floodwaters

The man with beaten clothes could be forgiven for his crime, because he had invented a new way of seeing.

In the late 1800s, in California, the photographer Edward Muybridge and the railroad capitalist Leland Stanford, whose lives and personalities differed sharply, made a strange and unforgettable discovery. Using horses and cameras and speed, Muybridge, the creative one, and Stanford, the rich one, built a technology of vision. Together they married the camera to the railroad and became the inventors of moving pictures, the basis of our culture of screens—handheld ones and televisions, theater screens and screens on counters and desks. For this they stand at the headwaters of the visual media. From Stanford and Muybridge came the first spray of images that became the stream of pictures in which most of us bathe for half our waking hours.

There is another uncommon thing about Muybridge and Stanford, namely, one of them was a murderer. Muybridge, the photographer, killed coolly and in a meticulous way, with the expectation that he would die as he killed. As an artist and inventor, Muybridge helped turn the world into a community of spectators—people who watch, transfixed by screens. As a killer, he fascinated Americans with his story of sexual possession. The photographer's crime did not seem to trouble Stanford, his friend and patron, so common was murder in California during the frontier years, but the Muybridge killing became an early sensation, a fitting prelude to the technology he and Stanford loosed on the world. I should add that these things unfolded in a particular order. To be truthful about the sequence, Muybridge killed, and then came the invention of media.

PREFACE

The story of the people who improvised moving pictures and put them on a screen, during the 1870s, when everyone still rode horses and cut firewood, might be worth the trouble of telling by itself, but Edward Muybridge has an enigma to add to this feat, which is his crime. Muybridge—and his friend and patron, Leland Stanford (in the old sense, the moneyed man who pays for art)—brought visual media into the world, a kind of seeing that grew from the kernel idea of "motion studies." Thus began the source of distraction and pleasure that much of the world uses much of the time: moving pictures fill daily life and fascinate us. But the mystery that Muybridge carries is that he was a murderer—not an accidental killer, but a cool one, and remorseless.

Edward Muybridge's life as an artist and inventor who happened to be a killer means trouble for a biographer. Most accounts of artists' lives are admiring of their subject, whereas the crime of murder tends to put a man in a bad light. Many have talked about Muybridge, but no one knows quite what to do with his violence—the usual line is to focus on his photography and to box away the crime, hiding this embarrassing "mistake." At a distance of many years, the photographer looks to be a romantic hero, a soft glow haloing his wild hair, a lonely visionary at work in the fields of early industry. Gustave Flaubert said that writing history is like drinking an ocean and pissing a cupful, and that some historians do just the opposite. In this story about the strange partnership of an artist and a railroad magnate, in which I find the genesis of the media, I do not provide a roll call of the many other people who made the movies and their later child, our society of spectacle.[1] I don't tell the full tale of all the toys and tools, from the panorama to the zoetrope and magic lantern, that came together to make the cinema. Instead, I see the photography with which Muybridge shot animals and people performing daily tasks—and his projection of these on screens—as the genetic imprint of all the visual media. The strand that holds together all our ways of looking at screens is the fascination with what moves, which is satisfied by an apparatus that captures time and plays it back. This is the story of two difficult, important, and incompatible men who joined photography to the railroad, and in so doing opened an exit from the Machine Age and an entrance to our own virtual worlds.

———

There is one unusual obstacle to speaking about "Eadweard Muybridge," as he is usually called, namely that my subject's name cannot be pronounced. It can hardly be spelled. The best I can do, aloud, is "aid-weird my-bridge." It is a name that looks back at you and says, *Well, so?* And also, *I am.* Muybridge changed the spelling of his name every ten years or so; his many names float over his life like his dissolving pictures, and "Eadweard Muybridge" was merely the last version. He coined five spellings, using one and tossing it, choosing another and leaving that one behind. Although he called himself "Edward Muybridge" during the years of his most important work, I will use all of his names, as he himself did, attaching each to the time in his life that he assumed it.

Edward Muybridge—peripatetic, obsessed, murderous—was uncomfortable with renown and at the same time wanted it. And so to the first name, and to what happened.

PART ONE

Eadweard Muybridge, *Horses. Running. Phryne L., Plate 40*, 1879

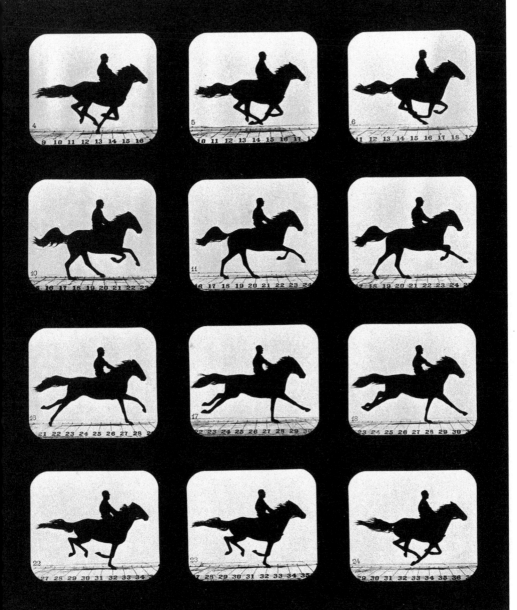

Chapter 1

THE STANFORD ENTERTAINMENT

The mansion in San Francisco had collapsed with the earthquake in 1906 and burned to nothing a day later in the fires. I walked up the face of Nob Hill to look at the place where it used to stand. Could there be a tiny remnant of this temple of money? The hill had been known as California Hill until Leland Stanford and family moved there in 1876, followed by their preposterously rich friends. After that it was Nob Hill. Stanford and the other nabobs (a word borrowed from Mughal India, trimmed in America to "nobs") built houses that showed their money and looked with a possessive gaze at the city below. The day after the earthquake the fire came, on a Thursday morning in April, and the two disasters took down all the big houses but one.

At the top of Nob Hill today are apartment buildings, hotels, a little park. The place that survived, the last sign of the sovereigns who had set themselves up on these blocks, was the Flood house. James Flood, a mining multimillionaire, was one of the men who exploited the Comstock Lode, a thick vein of silver in Nevada that ended up in most coins. The fire had somehow wrapped around and missed his house. When the silver man died, the Flood mansion went into the hands of the Pacific-Union Club, which seems fitting—a men's club whose members dote on money, the way the nabobs did. I looked at the Flood house, a megalith in brown stucco, and imagined it in its original setting, amid a colony of American palaces. The first and most ostentatious of them, the Stanford house, used to stand a block to the east, at California and Powell Streets. An eight-story hotel now occupied that site, planted over the ruins. Only the granite wall that used to frame the house remained.

Mark Twain's novel *The Gilded Age* gave its name to the late nineteenth century, a time of monopoly with its high tide of corruption and greed. Nob Hill was one of the age's capitals, and whatever went on here took shape on a Brobdingnagian scale. But one episode of those years, as far as I can see, has been overlooked. It could be said that the world of visual media got under way on this hill, amid the new money of California, in the late 1800s. It happened one night at a party at which the entertainment was a photographer called Edward Muybridge.

JANUARY 16, 1880
CALIFORNIA AND POWELL STREETS, SAN FRANCISCO

It was the night pictures began to move. Just what it was that happened that night could not be accurately described for many years. It would not be comprehensible until the movie theaters had spread and the television stations were built, or maybe even until screens appeared in most rooms and people carried them in their hands. That winter night in San Francisco pictures jumped into motion, someone captured time and played it back. A newspaperman noticed that something unusual

Edward Muybridge often photographed the property of Leland and Jane Stanford, particularly their horses and houses. In San Francisco, the Stanfords' home on California Hill (later Nob Hill), built in 1876, had some fifty rooms, depending on how you counted, and the showiest decor west of the Mississippi.

had happened, although he did not say anything about time. He noticed only that whatever it was that happened had taken place in the home of the best-known citizen of the state of California; he noticed these facts but missed the main event. The newspaperman pointed out that a photographer of angular shape named Edward Muybridge and his new machine had been the reason for the gathering, but he did not describe what Muybridge had done. Thanks to the paper (and notwithstanding the reporter's oversights), we know who was there, in the house. We know who came around to the stupendous mansion where Muybridge assembled his mechanism and put it in motion and carried it through its initial performance.

The event with the photographer took place in the home of an abnormally rich family. It was the end of the week. The family stayed in for the evening and invited some friends for a party and a show.

Their brown, stuccoed palazzo occupied the best site on California Hill, looking out to the flickering lights on San Francisco Bay and down at the streets of the rolling city. From a block away—and you had to get that far back to see the whole thing—the house looked to be a chunky, dark mass, Italianate in style. The owners of the house wanted it to exceed, if possible, the pomp of the European palaces, and to achieve this they had hired the New York design firm Pottier & Stymus, which had a record of extravagance, to ornament every square yard of its interior. When the decorators were finished, the place had a magnitude and pretense that no one in California had previously seen. Without rival, it was the most talked-up house west of the Mississippi.

The Stanford family lived here, just three people, a mother and father and their eleven-year-old son. The Stanfords employed about twelve servants, half of whom lived in the brown house and some of whom traveled with the family to serve them at their horse farm south of the city. Newspapers were soaked with ink about the Stanfords' outsized lives. The *San Francisco Daily Call* labeled tonight's event "The Stanford Entertainment," and from those three words everyone knew where and for whom the photographer Edward Muybridge was doing whatever it was he did with his picture machine.

This year he was Edward Muybridge, but the spelling of his name would soon change, as it had done on four previous occasions. Every few years, the photographer would move a vowel or switch a couple of consonants. He used to be Edward Muygridge, and before that, Edward Muggeridge. For a few years he used the professional name "Helios,"

Leland Stanford, his wife,
Jane Lathrop Stanford, and their
son, Leland Stanford Jr., 1881

the single moniker of an artist, borrowed in this case from the Greek
god of the sun.

Along with his name, his working life had already passed through
several metamorphoses. During his twenties Muybridge had been a
book and print salesman for a London publisher; he sold dictionaries
and encyclopedias and art books, engravings, and lithographs. In his
thirties he tried to make a living as an inventor but failed when buyers
showed indifference to his patents. After that, he put on the top hat of
a capitalist: he started a mining company, and then an investment firm.
Both ended badly. At age thirty-seven, he invented himself for the last
time, as an artist: he became a photographer. He had followed a wandering path and only came to a single road as a middle-aged man. The
choice of photography, at last, seemed to him to vindicate all the disap-
pointments and failures that had gone before.

Edward Muybridge wore a beard down to the middle of his chest,
a gray weave with a dark residue. Occasionally he might have combed
it. The hair on his head was white, swirling at the ears, tossed up from
his brow. His eyes were sharp blue. The crinkly beard and flowing hair
made him look antique, wizardlike. One newspaper said that Muybridge looked "at least ten years older" than his natural age, which was
forty-nine: a man in midlife wearing a mask of seniority.

After twelve years with the camera, he was the best-known photographer in San Francisco. Part of his renown came from his pictures, notably the ones he had taken in Yosemite Valley. The naturalist John Muir had explored and written about the seven-mile-long chasm in upper California, an extravagance of cliffs and depths and vistas. A photographer called Carleton Watkins had been one of the first to descend into Yosemite's hollows and come back with pictures. But Muybridge's photographs of the valley's flagrant rock faces and bridal-veil waterfalls had exceeded those of Watkins and helped to make Yosemite a part of national lore. The landscape of Yosemite, its wildness and excess, which Muybridge framed and made mythic, had come to represent the West to people in the eastern states.

Yosemite was part of Muybridge, but other parts of him were urban. Three years earlier he had made a panorama of San Francisco in photographs, the city in 360 degrees. To shoot it he had stood on the turret of the Mark Hopkins house, another mansion farther up the hill from the Stanford place. Muybridge had cranked the camera around on his tripod, measuring and panning, foot by foot, until the whole city went under the lens. He had given Leland Stanford and his wife, Jane, the biggest version of the panorama, an unrolling carpet of a picture, seventeen feet long and two feet high—an expensive thank-you gift for years of assignments and friendship.

The photographer who tramped the wilderness and scaled city summits had a thin, vigorous body. The same witness who called him "old" also wrote that Muybridge possessed the jauntiness of a twenty-five-year-old man. People knew his athleticism. He was the man who skipped down flights of stairs, the agile camera operator most conspicuous around San Francisco, a blur seen in continual movement from the Golden Gate to San Jose. The tripod went up—it must be Muybridge again—and it came down.

Edward Muybridge had another stroke of renown, outside of his work, which was the fame of his crime. Wherever he went, it followed the photographer. He was a murderer, and the aura of his violence lingered, stirring an atmosphere as palpable as his acclaim as an artist. Muybridge's crime had been reported throughout the United States, so strange were its details, so fascinating was its passion to so many people. The photographer had a reasonable claim to be the one citizen who pulled behind him the largest cloud of dark gossip in the state of California. Of course he pretended as though the talk about him did not buzz incessantly, that he was merely a member of San Francisco's small, vivid cultural establishment. Perhaps he had no other choice but to pretend. Certainly this pose worked more to his advantage than fully inhabiting the role of a killer.

Tonight Muybridge stood at a table in the middle of a giant room. In the Stanford mansion, the rooms had names. This one, in all probability, was the Pompeian Room, the showiest room, which the family used to entertain. About forty feet square, it had four walls of murals that replicated frescoes found in houses uncovered beneath the volcanic dirt at Pompeii. The Stanfords had paid Pottier & Stymus, the decorators, to create a showplace of replica history in their house. In the Pompeian Room they had placed gilded chairs and marble-topped tables with slender legs to make a pastiche of ancient Rome, and life-size marble nymphs to stand guard.

If not here, Muybridge may have stood in the Music and Art Room, a gallery twenty yards long whose wine-red walls were hung with fifty-some landscapes and portraits, and whose ceiling was painted with medallions depicting the faces of Rubens, Van Dyck, Beethoven, Mozart, Raphael, and Michelangelo. "Few palaces of Europe excel this house," said one newswriter, who may not have been to Europe but who knew the fantasies of Americans who looked up to the Old World.

Or he could have been in one of the other downstairs parlors, or in the library, the ballroom, or the aviary. Huge mantelpieces and elaborate rosewood fittings dominated each of them, and a grove of furnishing spread to the edges in leather, silk, brocade, or velvet. Wherever Muybridge was, he had to clear away the crush of decor and work around chandeliers heavy as cannon that dangled just above the head, because he needed a straight thirty feet for what he had to accomplish. Muybridge made pictures that were very different from the imagery that decorated the walls, ceilings, and floors of the Stanford mansion. His pictures were not massive, like most of the fixtures, and they were not imitations of art found in Europe. They were evanescent and thin, they were pictures flung on air.

A scattering of guests arrived in twos and threes, with buttons on bulges, lace on bosoms. Some were politicians, like the newly elected governor of California, George Perkins, and Reuben Fenton, U.S. senator from New York and former governor. Behind the lawmakers came a phalanx of rich people, a few of them as rich as their hosts, the Stanfords. In this group were the neighbors, Charles Crocker and his wife,

One of the downstairs salons of the Stanford house, the Pompeian Room,
in which every square foot of surface stalks the eyes

Mary Ann Deming, who lived two blocks away in a brown house only
a little less grand than the Stanfords' palazzo. There was also a young
woman, Jennie Flood, an heiress in the new California manner. She
came with her father, James Flood, a silver miner who had gotten rich
on specie metal from Nevada and built a supreme and impressive house
around the corner, at California and Mason Streets. Lesser elites and
their spouses filled out the invitation list—a judge here, a doctor there.

Servants brought in drink, gaslight drank the air. The woman of
the house, Mrs. Jane Stanford, presented herself, tall, ample, and bejew-
eled. Jane Stanford cultivated a gothic look. She liked to drape herself
in crimson velvet, with pools of hem and long trains behind, old lace
circling her neck. She was sure to be wearing an arm's length of opals
or a parure of diamonds consisting of necklace, bracelets, and earrings.

The night promised a pageant of some kind, but two men already
radiated something of the theater. Leland Stanford and Edward Muybridge were the best-known men at the party—Stanford for his money,
Muybridge for his pictures (as well as the other thing), and together
they inspired most of the hushed chatter. They had known each other
for almost ten years and had spent a lot of that time talking and wondering about a single subject: the gait of horses. A narrow topic, yes, but
one on the mind of many in the year 1880. Everyone knew that Stanford was horse-mad, and that he and Muybridge had formed a bond
over horses. It was Stanford's belief that during a gallop, horses at some

point in their stride lift all four hooves off the ground, that in effect, they become airborne. No one knew, really—the legs of a horse moved too fast to tell with the eye. Stanford had asked Muybridge to solve his problem, to prove or disprove his hypothesis, which horse people referred to as the theory of "unsupported transit."

Some of the talk that Stanford aroused would not have flattered him. At least some of the guests at the party, perhaps the politicians and the more middle-class group, inevitably regarded their hosts with ambivalence—envy would not be too strong a word, and maybe a touch of fear. Almost twenty years before, Leland Stanford and several others had founded the Central Pacific Railroad, with Stanford in the role of company president. The firm, using big government subsidies, and the sweat of perhaps twenty thousand Chinese immigrants, had built the western half of the transcontinental line, the 850-mile track over the Sierra Mountains that linked California to the eastern states. In the early years of the Central Pacific, Stanford had been an object of fealty. Newspaper accounts painted him as a great benefactor of California: he brought work and wealth and even glory to the West, his admirers said, justifying the stage name of California, the Golden State. But after a rosy flush, Stanford's reputation had fallen. The Central Pacific and its sister company, the Southern Pacific, which Stanford also ran, had built a transportation monopoly. The Central and Southern had acquired millions of acres of public land and looked at times to be bigger than the government of California, which they seemed to run to their liking. Stanford's railroads picked up a nickname: "the Octopus." Newspapers ran cartoons that showed Stanford and his partners as a watery beast, tentacles reaching out to strangle farmers, factories, and politicians. Stanford became the West's most famous symbol of greed. Not long before this evening's event, several thousand marchers, followers of the Workingmen's Party of California, had come up Nob Hill and surrounded his house, calling out for Stanford to be lynched.

Edward Muybridge was not quite equal to Stanford in the number of news items that trailed him, but his name was also in print throughout America. Seven years earlier, in 1873, Muybridge had made national headlines when his camera first brought motion to a halt. He had photographed a horse, one of Stanford's, in the middle of a full trot, making it stop in the air. In the forty years of photography, no one had done anything like it. Though the picture was blurry, no one had trapped such a tiny instant in an image. Five years later, in 1878, Muybridge had set up twelve cameras to catch twelve slices of a horse's run. It was while taking pictures of a mare called Sallie Gardner and a stallion named Occident that Muybridge had first split the gallop into many parts. His photographs were seen and admired around the world, his name and accomplishment published in scientific journals like *Nature*, popular magazines like *Harper's Weekly*, and in their counterparts in England, France, and Germany. The multiple-camera experiment made Muybridge into an international celebrity. Some saw him as an artist, others regarded him as a scientist, and he did not shy from playing either role. Some understood him to be a conjurer, because he had done something so very elusive as to appear impossible.

There was an uneasy balance to the relationship between the artist and Stanford, the Octopus. The two men helped each other, but to Stanford, Muybridge was something less than an equal: he was a friend, but also a subordinate. The photographer wasn't exactly an employee. To make the pictures on show tonight, Muybridge had worked on and off for eight years without a fee. Instead, Stanford had paid for the photographer's giant expenses—a mountain of equipment, several assistants, horses and a track, and mechanisms that added speed to the cameras. The two shared interests, but Stanford's money was in charge.

Both Stanford and Muybridge would have remembered the time almost ten years before when the photographer first worked for the family, taking pictures of their house in Sacramento, the California capital, one hundred miles upstate. As a commercial photographer, Muybridge dutifully made a portfolio of that Stanford residence, the place the family had lived before building the mansion with rooms that had names.

Muybridge had gone to some length to cultivate Stanford's attention, but their friendship looked off kilter in other ways. The two neither looked nor acted anything alike. Even in their choice of clothes, the host and his entertainer flaunted the separate worlds in which they lived. Unlike the silk-and-velvet-attired Stanfords, Muybridge conspicuously dressed down. Photographs from this period show him in rough outdoor gear—a loose and rumpled cotton jacket and weather-beaten pants with strings on the cuffs. He had another physical signature, a corncob pipe. People who knew him said he loaded up the pipe in the middle of conversation, sometimes at the midpoint of a sentence. The pipe helped Muybridge fill out the role of a rustic, the man with the floppy hat who didn't care what people thought.

There was also his speech. Everyone would have noticed that Muybridge had an English accent, a residue of his birth and upbringing near London. His diction was respectable, although not precious. He had not attended university, but his English was careful enough that he could compose an artful sentence in front of an audience and keep his consonants in line. The speech of Leland and Jane Stanford, notwithstanding their exorbitant surroundings, showed their plain American roots. Both had been born and raised in upper New York State, where Leland was the son of farmers and odd jobbers, and the former Jane Lathrop the daughter of merchants.

Their behavior also contrasted them. People who saw Muybridge and Stanford pointed out that the photographer was agitated and sharp, while the rail man was phlegmatic, almost wordless.

Stanford was nowhere near as nimble as Muybridge, his lithe artist-in-residence. Stanford was fifty-five, his body thick and thickening. He had begun to carry an ivory-inlaid, gold-tipped cane, perhaps for show as well as to manage his heavy trudge. At the top of his barrel-like body was an oval head and a face seemingly without angles, with a trim beard, groomed, dark and speckled gray, and a full run of straight, graying hair, much combed, on his head. In public Stanford was thoroughly adorned, often in tails, low vests, and white shirts starched wooden, with ribbon ties and mother-of-pearl studs. His black shoes shined into dark mirrors.

The slow-moving and formal Stanford played the accustomed host. He had been a politician for some time and spent a term as governor of California, so for him a reception was common as breakfast. But despite his practiced public life, he was taciturn, and a hundred words came from others for every syllable Stanford spoke. He could afford to listen, or perhaps he could do little else—his fortune meant he spent most days besieged with supplicants for his money.

Everyone called him "Governor" Stanford. His years in politics were long past, but he liked the honorific. He had quit politics for business, for the railroad. If you asked, however, Stanford might have said (adopting a pose) that actually he had quit politics for his horses. At the family estate, thirty-five miles south of San Francisco, he collected horses, not three or four, but one hundred, give or take—racers and bay mares, thoroughbreds and standardbreds, ponies and trotters. Stanford's love of horses rivaled that for his wife, Jane, and son, Leland Jr. The horse farm, at the place they had named Palo Alto (high tree, in Spanish), was the centerpoint of his life. The Palo Alto Stock Farm, as it was known, had begun as a diversion from business, but it had turned into an obsession—a riding and training laboratory. At Palo Alto, Stanford could imagine himself as a researcher in equestrian enigmas. In this scenario Edward Muybridge, the photographer who had set up an elaborate studio at Palo Alto, served as his investigator, the man assigned to the scientific study of movement—or, appropriately for a rail-powered fortune, "animal locomotion."

———

Tonight, Edward Muybridge would cease to be a photographer who framed up his client's possessions. From this point forward he would be an impresario, a man with a new and remarkable show. He could present himself as the builder of an apparatus, born from speed, that captured time. Edward Muybridge knew about acceleration: it was all around him in his world, in the telegraph and in Stanford's speeding railroad. Tonight he would introduce the element of speed to vision.

The photographer stood in the middle of the gaping and much decorated parlor, his hands on a machine. It was a modified "magic lantern," a projector of glass slides, which Muybridge had rebuilt to create his special effect. The projector stood on a large table, a boxy wooden device with brass fittings and a big lens, three feet tall and about as long. When the projector was up and running it blasted out light.* Muybridge the engineer touched the lens, turned a wheel, and adjusted a burning gas jet of hydrogen and oxygen on a brick of lime, the source of the piercing light. He aimed the lens at a screen placed at the far wall to catch the pictures. And, fiddling with his machine, the photographer cued the pictures that he had come to shove into motion.

Leland Stanford placed his guests in the room. Chairs were occupied, gaslight dimmed. Muybridge picked up a glass disk the size of a dinner plate and fitted it in his machine. And on the screen came a blinking of light, a throbbing of something, and finally a big trembling mass. The look of a horse, almost the size of life, which was running! A picture in motion of a galloping horse.

* Muybridge gave his machine the lovingly recondite name the "zoogyroscope." A year later he was calling it the zoopraxiscope, the name that stuck, after the tabletop toy (the zoetrope) and a projector popular in France (the praxinoscope). Once, when a census clerk asked his job, Muybridge said he was a "zoopraxographer," probably the only person of that profession in the country.

As Muybridge whirled the disk in his projector, the horse on the screen seemed to run along for two seconds—and then it started again, repeating the same two seconds, running them over and over. The machine released its flood of pictures, weightless, coming from nowhere, a lighted nothing jittering in space, in the clutter of the Pompeian Room. Muybridge stopped the device, and the ghost disappeared. He turned off the gas jets, and the blasting light went black.

Abe Edgington, a trotter owned by Leland Stanford, appears twelve times in one and a half seconds, starring in one of the first of many "serial photographs" that Muybridge made at the Palo Alto Stock Farm.

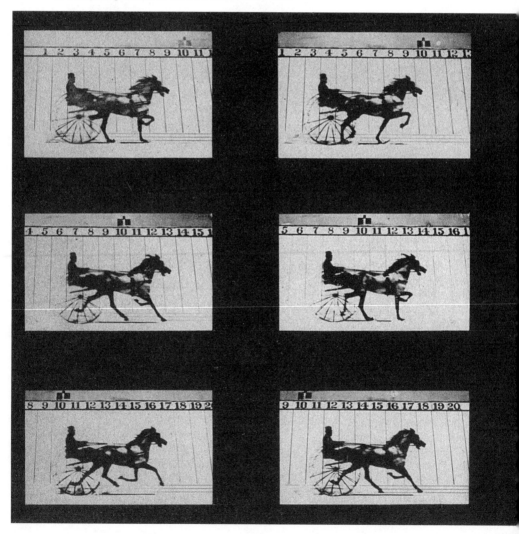

Muybridge's projector, the "zoopraxiscope"

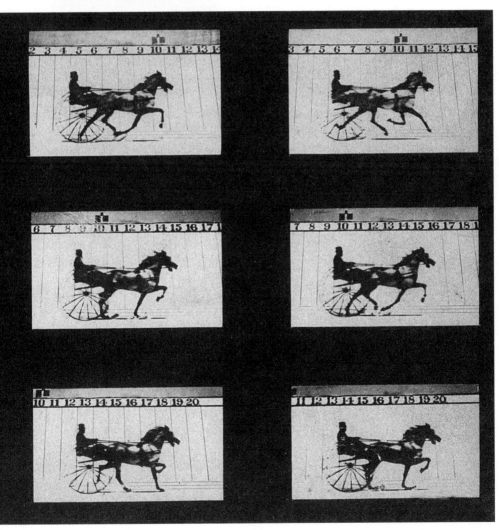

———

The idea of moving pictures had appeared in plenty of heads before this. Thanks to the zoetrope, a living room toy, the idea would have occurred countless times to thousands of people. The zoetrope, a popular gadget during the 1860s and '70s, looked like a little drum mounted on an axle. It worked like a cartoon flipbook, only the drawings were lined up side by side. If you spun it around and peered into it, an acrobat tumbled over and over, or a couple danced a short and endless waltz. Zoetropes were common amusements in homes around America and Europe. By this time, there were also one or two projecting machines that threw little comics and sketches on a wall, and showmen who made a living with them.

But the Muybridge apparatus was different from all that. Muybridge's pictures were not like a flipbook, and neither were they posed. He photographed live action, he captured and stored real time, and he played back the scene he had photographed. His cameras grabbed many pictures in a second, he had hired an artist to paint the pictures on a glass disk, and he showed this virtual world based in photographs to an audience. He took his audience out of their routine consciousness and made them into something they had not been—a crowd of mesmerized spectators. By doing these things, all at once, Muybridge brought a new thing into the world.

Only a single newspaper clipping documents this night at the Stanford mansion. And yet it is not too much to call this occasion the birth hour of the visual media. Movies, television, video games, the twitching images of the Internet user—Muybridge's pictures contain the primal DNA of all of them. All the media have at their crux images that move, and all of them have a spectator, frozen and fascinated.

If you had to choose a single trait to characterize everyday life in the twenty-first century, it could be our *screenophilia*, and the common obsession with moving pictures. The attraction to images that dance and play, the instinctual turn toward the lighted screen, in the hand or on the desk, or on the wall, the fascination with a piece of recorded time cut to shape—all this links the world's billions in a community of spectatorship. Edward Muybridge and Leland Stanford made the initial template of this visual life. They identified the genetic strand that threads through all media, the moving images that combine in endless mutations on every screen. And they introduced their connecting element, which is speed. The Muybridge pictures accelerated the eye, doubling and tripling and multiplying every glance, quickening vision and communication. After the fast-talking Muybridge and his laconic friend Stanford had finished, we became immobilized as spectators, fixed every day in silence and looking, propelled by screenophilia to attach ourselves to chains and networks of pictures.

———

The San Francisco papers made no reference to the reactions of Stanford's guests that night on Nob Hill, but it may be that some of them wondered about things. It might have happened that at least a few in the audience with a little wine in their stomachs looked over at Edward Muybridge and his projector and felt a flutter of anxiety—not at the invention, but at the inventor. Muybridge was well known to everyone in the room. Stanford's friends had heard about his photography. They had heard about the horse pictures, about Muybridge's trick of capturing time. But like everyone else in California, the well-heeled spectators in the parlor knew there was more to the thin photographer than his work. They knew about the crime.

When the murder happened, the newspapers indulged a period of frenzy around it, an early instance of a news media rush. California's papers covered the crime, and after that they followed the trial, and later on, the aftermath and all the stories that trickled out about the famous, and now infamous, photographer. Muybridge appeared in the papers for months, and not only in California. Thanks to the telegraph, another harbinger of speed, and the Associated Press, a clipping service that hastened the spread of news, he drew headlines in Chicago, New York, New Orleans, and around America.

On this night, as virtual worlds of all kinds first came into focus, more than a few people in this audience of viewers looked over at Muybridge and remembered all this. Years later, Muybridge would write about the night he showed his pictures and his projector, the night he cued up a stored memory and replayed it. He described it several times, and each time he wrote an almost identical version of the story. Muybridge remembered that after he threw the galloping horse onto the screen, he turned to Stanford and described what they were seeing.

"There are all the positions that a galloping horse will assume in making a complete stride, Governor," Muybridge said. "And I suppose you will recognize your horse, Hawthorn, galloping at a one-minute-forty-two gait."

Muybridge meant that Hawthorn was covering a mile in one min-ute, forty-two seconds. The photographer might have been jumpy and disheveled, but he knew to flatter the man with the money.

Stanford looked at the screen from his chair. "Well, Mr. Muy-bridge," he said, "you have a galloping horse there, but it is not Haw-thorn. It's Florence Anderson." (The name of another horse.)

"No, it is Hawthorn," Muybridge said. "The trainer sent the horse out to me, and my notes have it that way."

It was a peculiar exchange—strange that in the birth hour of a media-made world, the two partners most involved with bringing the thing alive should be disputing the names of horses.

Stanford looked again at the flying pictures. "I think you must be mistaken in the name of the animal, Mr. Muybridge. That is certainly not the gait of Hawthorn, but of Anderson."

The identity of the horse interested Stanford more than seeing the animal run across the room. And who was right?

At the Palo Alto Stock Farm, Muybridge's equipment had filled a barn, and he had photographed five or six animals a day, taking notes on the fillies and mares and stallions. They were his study subjects, and Muybridge's relationship to them was not that of a horse connoisseur. He did not know the animals as Stanford did, and so Muybridge relied on a written schedule. Stanford was right. On the day Muybridge made the pictures that he now projected on the screen, the horse called Haw-thorn had been scheduled for the photographer's cameras, and he had marked the name in his notebook. But that morning Stanford's trainer had substituted a different horse, Florence Anderson, which Muybridge did not know at the time.

Three months after "the Stanford entertainment," Muybridge repeated his show. The parlor banter was behind him, and he wanted press. On May 4, 1880, he hired a room at the San Francisco Art Asso-ciation, a members' society and art gallery, at 313 Pine Street, next door to the Bohemian Club, and advertised his appearances, his show. This time he charged for seats: fifty cents for a ticket. An audience came, and so did reporters, because Muybridge made good copy. The pic-ture machine transfixed the newsmen, and next day came the stories in the city press. An item in the *San Francisco Daily Call* singled out the feeling of fascination, the instant when the people in their chairs had become spectators, frozen and mesmerized.

"The moment that attracted the most attention," a reporter wrote,

Muybridge, self-portrait, ca. 1879

"which in fact aroused a pronounced flutter of enthusiasm from the audience, was the representation . . . of horses in motion. It placed upon the screen, apparently, the living, moving horse."

Whoever he was (there was no byline), the reporter also talked about what we might call the "reality effect" of the media. "Nothing was wanting but the clatter of the hooves upon the turf and an occasional breath of steam from the nostrils to make the spectator believe that he had before him genuine flesh-and-blood steeds," said the paper.

And the writer made a forecast that in retrospect seems perfectly uncanny.

"Mr. Muybridge has laid the foundation of a new method of entertaining the people, and we predict that his instantaneous, photographic magic-lantern zoetrope will make the rounds of the civilized world." This journalist thought he had glimpsed the beginnings of a new way of seeing.

The "screening" in May 1880 was the public curtain raiser, if you like, of visual media. If we live in a sensory world where images orbit and engulf us, Muybridge opened the door to it. He handed us our distractions as a magician gives out illusions. And this conjurer of horses that ran across the screen was a wizardlike, prematurely aged, disheveled, and murderous man.

At the end of the night, Edward Muybridge removed the glass disk from his projecting device and packed up his kit for the next show.[1]

Chapter 2

THE YELLOW JACKET MURDER

Six years earlier . . .
OCTOBER 17, 1874, SAN FRANCISCO

I t was a Saturday, and Edward Muybridge walked home at about noon, crossing Market Street and making his way in somewhat of a delirium to his house at the corner of Howard and Third Streets. He had spent the morning talking to a woman named Susan Smith in her rooms on Telegraph Hill, and their conversation had disturbed him. No, it had stunned him, reduced him to animal shaking. Susan Smith was paid help, a midwife and nurse who a year earlier had worked for Muybridge and his wife, the former Flora Downs. Smith had helped Flora give birth to her son, the Muybridge couple's only child, and Smith had also taken care of the baby. She had done so in part because Edward and Flora were badly matched in their marriage (although neither would have said so). Edward could live on rice and wear a few things out of a suitcase, Flora liked clothes and luxury. Edward wanted to travel for work and stay home when he was in town, Flora liked the theater and friends and going out. What is more, Edward was forty-four, and Flora was twenty-three.

On this day Muybridge had come home to an empty house. Flora had been away with their baby for several months, leaving the photographer alone, which at any rate he preferred. After visiting Smith, Muybridge retreated for an hour to decide what to do about Smith's stories, and among the things he had to decide was whether to take out his gun.

To own a gun in California was more common than owning a horse. It was cheaper, to start, thanks to the efficient gun makers in Massachu-

After their marriage in 1871, Muybridge and his wife, Flora, lived in a townhouse in the South Park section of San Francisco, a development that simulated a square in London.

setts and Connecticut, whose factories sent a stream of drop-forged, reliable, and not badly priced shooting gear out to the western states. California and the rest of the West, especially the glorious and strange and violent frontier parts, the underpopulated and contentious sprawl of Nevada, Utah, Colorado, and Oregon, gave the gun makers their most reliable customers. These parts of America were home to the most steadfast buyers of guns, at least since the conclusion of the Civil War had taken away that previous heavy consumer of personal firearms, the government of the United States, which had bought up a million Winchesters and Colts to settle its disagreement with the southern states.

Edward Muybridge's gun was the most ordinary of revolvers, a Smith & Wesson #2. The #2, from the Smith & Wesson Company of Springfield, Massachusetts, had turned into the most popular revolver to accompany the national push into the West, which was now in full flood, with tens of thousands picking up their lives in the eastern states and carrying them across the Mississippi every year. The #2 was an

Smith & Wesson #2 revolver, ca. 1866

instrument favored by lawmen and casual shooters, the gun of the boomtowns and the homesteaders and the traveling salesmen. It was a single-action six-shooter—you had to cock the hammer each time— and it took the medium bullets, .32-caliber ammunition. Just as the men in California's mining camps kept guns in their tents and cabins, Muybridge kept a pistol at home in the biggest city in the West, San Francisco, a would-be cosmopolitan capital that had not succeeded in restricting its ritual and frequent revenge killings, its I-am-a-man bloodiness, despite almost seasonal attempts to do so.

Edward Muybridge earned good money as a photographer, and he and Flora lived high. They had settled for two years at 3 South Park, which a reporter called their "fascinating address," one way of expressing envy at their stylish house. (It was no rival to the homes of Muybridge's friend, Leland Stanford, but no one could compete with the Stanfords.) In South Park, twenty-odd townhouses faced each other around an oval garden—to walk through it, you would think that San Francisco, the instant city of shacks and rooming houses and brothels, stood far away. You would think you were not in the West at all, but in a corner of London, maybe Grosvenor Square. Since then Muybridge and his wife had moved a few blocks north, and perhaps down a step on the social ladder, to a rented place where the Third Street trolley ran right past their window. (There again was Stanford, whose company, the Central Pacific Railroad, operated the streetcar.)

Arriving at home, Muybridge spent the hour dwelling on his choices before coming to a decision. It might have taken a few minutes to find the Smith & Wesson, which he did not use very much. Muybridge later told the papers that he had not fired his six-shooter in four months, although he did not say what he had previously shot at.

The photographer was in plain dress but high color—he wore his usual tattered gray jacket and wide-brimmed hat, a corncob pipe in his pocket. He had no reason to change clothes, and in his state of mind no ability to do so. When he let his mind go to the subject preoccupying him, he broke down weeping, until after two or three minutes he could again force composure on himself.

From his townhouse Muybridge walked across Market Street and made his way for fifteen minutes along Montgomery Street, three-quarters of a mile, arriving at number 429—the address of Bradley & Rulofson, a photography studio that was his art dealer. Bradley & Rulofson was one of a handful of decent art galleries in San Francisco, and Muybridge had the distinction of being the gallery's most prominent artist. The gallery's managing partner, a portrait photographer called William Rulofson, was a slight, good-looking man with a full head of light hair and mutton chops. Rulofson, age forty-eight, said to be keen and volatile by people who observed these things, showed Muybridge's photographs in the gallery, sold them to collectors, and found clients for the artist, taking a commission on all of this from Muybridge's sales, which were constant and considerable. Rulofson later said that when Muybridge came into the gallery during the early afternoon that Saturday, his state of mind was "the most intense and agonizing I have ever seen." It was about 2:00 p.m. when the Smith & Wesson #2 and its owner reached Bradley & Rulofson's, and they stayed for ninety minutes.

Muybridge appeared to his friend and dealer to be something more than manic but something less than deranged. The two men spent much of this visit in Rulofson's third-floor office, where Muybridge talked and then yelled, moaned, wept, and occasionally got out a sentence or two about what he was going to do. At some point Muybridge brought out a piece of paper on which he had written some instructions. He gave the piece of paper to Rulofson and told his friend to put its contents into action if circumstances made it necessary. By "if" and "necessary," conditional words, he intended to suggest that he might not survive the events of the day, that the photographer, who had made a good deal of money for the gallery, might have to have his affairs settled by his business manager, Rulofson, in probate.

———

The western slope of Mount St. Helena, in central California, looks from a distance like a rippling curtain of brown dirt. Here and there oak trees and conifers make islands of shadows. I drove seventy-five miles northeast of San Francisco to look for the cottage where Edward Muybridge had come only once, at night, on a Saturday in the fall of 1874. It was a place difficult for him to find, and it remained well hidden. Following a winding mile of road over scalps of bald foothills, I arrived at a gate, a house—and there was the man who owned the land. He said that he had retired to it from a career in oil in Texas. He asked if I knew the story about the photographer, and he said the wasps had gone for the season. He said that the little frame house—clapboard on the outside, five rooms within, propped off the ground on corner piers—had burned a few years before, and so we walked down the hill to look at the foundation, which did not tell much. The retired oilman said in addition that in those days, the days of that photographer, the place used to be known as the Yellow Jacket Mine. I noticed that the twenty-some acres of rolling brown fields and evergreens possessed exceptional light, light that a photographer might admire. It was a place known for nothing much before Edward Muybridge showed up there, and nothing much after. The story did not seem to age, and the man said that one or two people had come up the road to ask about it, but that was ten years before.

————

The twenty-five-mile-long gulley called Napa Valley runs south to north between two courses of the Sierra Nevada range. A railroad track goes up the middle most of the way, leaving off in the town of Calistoga, and the valley ends a bit further, at the barricade of Mount St. Helena. It was here that a speculator chose to try for mercury, in the 1870s.

The Yellow Jacket Mine sounded like a tunnel into earth, but it was not that, or not yet. The miners were looking for minerals and had not found them, and the Yellow Jacket was chiefly the cottage where the miners ate and slept and drank when they were not gouging randomly at a hollow of St. Helena called Pine Flat. The little house at the Yellow Jacket attached itself about halfway up the two-thousand-foot rise of the mountain. It had one decent room to sit in, and on Saturday night, October 17, 1874, four or five miners and two or three others, women from nearby Calistoga, smoked and played cards and talked.

There were miners at Yellow Jacket because a year before somebody in San Francisco with money had thought to send men over the ridge to dig for "quicksilver," as the element mercury was called. Mercury was one of the metals that California offered from its bosom to determined pickaxes, along with gold, silver, and copper, any of which would pay happy sums of money if you could get them out of the ground.

Prior to the quicksilver experiment, the Yellow Jacket Mine had been known, with some irony, as the Yellow Jacket Ranch. The name was a bit of a joke for the reason that far more than cattle or sheep, the most numerous animal on the ranch was a stinging variety of wasp— yellow jackets. The yellow jackets swarmed for two months every autumn. Now and then they killed a dog during that season, and one year they had killed an unlucky and drunken ranch hand who happened to fall on a horde's nest, but mainly they kept people indoors.

It was mid-October, the swarms were gone. At about 11:00 p.m. the men were playing cards and drinking; the women sat across the room and swatted at the men's chatter. (These glimpses of the scene, as well as the dialogue and choreography, are distilled from a thick folder of newspaper accounts.) The women did not live in the cottage, and although none of the news stories remarks on this, it would not have been unusual had the men paid the women to come see them that night. Outside the door were a thin moon, a road, pines, and outspreading oaks. Light from the oil lamps flickered at the windows.

One man in the group did not play cards much. His name was Harry Larkyns, the best-looking man, probably, and in the eyes of many observers the most charming and vain of the group. He sat with the women and was entertaining them. There are no photographs that might show us one way or the other how handsome he was; nevertheless, reporters went on about him. A news writer described Harry Larkyns as "a young man, not over thirty, with a quiet aristocratic air that rather impresses one." Larkyns was in fact forty years old, tall and graceful and lithe in form, with dirty blond hair. His diction pointed to his birthplace, which was Scotland. His manners and use of similes and artful talk reflected long schooling. Like most Californians, Harry Larkyns was new to California. He had arrived in San Francisco two years earlier, in November 1872, and within a few months, he had surfaced in the news, unpleasantly. The *San Francisco Chronicle* told the story of a monthlong transaction he had undertaken that had ended with Larkyns's arrest for "obtaining money on false pretenses." A confidence act, most likely.[1] In two days the accused was out of jail, however, having promised to repay money to the accuser, a young Englishman who had given Larkyns a long credit line.

Harry Larkyns's introduction to the West had the region's habitual stamp of invention and bluff. He told everyone he was rich, and so it was initially accepted—until his arrest. After he escaped prosecution, the well-schooled Larkyns found a job in the office of a publisher, Bancroft & Co., as a translator of French. Quitting that job, he moved on to journalism. Larkyns claimed to anyone who would listen that he was at home in theaters and around the stage, and so it came about that one of the city papers, the *Daily Evening Post*, hired him to write theater criticism. After a year, however, he had lost that job for handing in copy

someone else had written. Next Larkyns worked as a booking agent for
Wilson's Circus, a ten-year-old caravanserai in San Francisco, boosting
the show and trying to find road dates for its epauletted ringmaster and
leaping acrobats. Larkyns in other words did what was necessary—he
improvised, he sculpted himself, in the Western style. He was full of big
stories and bon mots, a handsome swain on the stinking streets.

At present Larkyns was in the pay of the speculators who were trying to turn the Yellow Jacket into a quicksilver strike. Their names have
been forgotten, but these investors, or gamblers, had hired Larkyns to
make a map of the mercury fields and to describe their prospects. (That
a confidence man would have such a job speaks to the mental resources
of California at this point in time.) Larkyns had been walking around
St. Helena and its lower slopes for three months, writing up his impres-
sions of the suitability of different sites for the placement of pickaxes.
Although little prior experience qualified him to make such judgments,
he allowed himself to imagine the money to be made and to publish his
thoughts in a mining bulletin called the *Weekly Stock Report*. His last
dispatch, published in August 1874, said the quicksilver fields north of
Napa Valley promised to be one of the next windfalls of California mining for those fortunate enough to recognize the opportunity.

———

Edward Muybridge left Bradley & Rulofson's at 3:56 p.m., as William Rulofson remembered it. From 429 Montgomery, at the corner of
Sacramento Street, Muybridge ran eight blocks north and east, sprint-
ing to reach a certain wharf on the waterfront. He arrived at the ferry
dock and jumped on the 4:00 p.m. steamboat as it fired up its boilers and
paddled out, aiming for Vallejo, a town at the north end of San Francisco Bay. At 6:00 p.m., he got off the boat and boarded a train headed
north. During the journey an interesting fact might have crossed his
inflamed mind, namely, that the train, like everything else, it seemed,
belonged to his friend Leland Stanford's company, the Central Pacific.
No matter. Muybridge made his way up the channel of the valley and
after an uncomfortably slow four-hour ride (railroads were supposed
to be about speed, but not the local trains) stepped down at the town of
Calistoga, population five hundred, the last stop. It was 10:00 p.m. He
looked for a buggy to take him the rest of the way around the thighs of
Mount St. Helena. The driver of the hack on the late shift that night was

an eighteen-year-old named George Wolf. Wolf remembered later that Muybridge got on the buggy and told him to drive north for ten miles. Wolf also remembered that the road that night was dark under the narrow moon, and that on the way, as the buggy's oil lamp threw a faint light, Muybridge asked whether there might be a danger of robbers. A fair question—the area had a reputation for bandits. Muybridge asked if he could fire his pistol as a warning shot, to frighten off any rough men who might be lying in wait in the gullies. The driver trotted the horse along in the near black, and Muybridge shot into the evergreens with his gun, because he had not used it in four months.

———

In the sitting room at the Yellow Jacket, Harry Larkyns offered a stream of stories to the women. People who knew him said Larkyns beguiled women, he had the charm of talk and powers of arousal. Larkyns told the women that while living in London he had been an impresario, a theatrical producer in the West End. He said, in fact, that it was the theater, or rather an error of judgment in the theater business, that had compelled him to come to the United States from England. Larkyns told whoever would listen that as a young man, he had invested some of his family's plentiful money in the theater, over the protest of his grandmother. His parents were dead, he said, which is why his grandmother had become his benefactor. In London, when his new and expensive and most favorite production failed to make money—as splendid as the company had been, as smart the staging—he had lost an irreplaceable sum of the family money. The mistake had thrown him into disgrace with his more conservative relations, grandmother included, and he had been forced to emigrate, he said, to escape the general humiliation. Larkyns held the women's open-eyed attention with this variety of story.

It was about midnight. The card game went along across the room, with no sign of folding. A knock came at the door, and one of the miners, Benjamin Pricket, got up from the table to answer. Pricket came back to say that someone wanted to speak with Harry Larkyns.

"I will see who this mysterious visitor is," Larkyns said.

Larkyns went to the door, which stood open, and looked into the black.

"I can't see you," he said. "Step into the light."

Edward Muybridge stood outside. In an interview with the *San Francisco Examiner* two months later, Muybridge remembered the night and described a precise little scene to the reporter.

"I said, 'My name is Muybridge, and I have received a message from my wife,'" he told the papers. "But before I could say more, Larkyns started to retreat into the house. I had made no attempt against him. I saw that he would be gone in a moment and that I must act on the instant, or he would escape."

Muybridge raised the Smith & Wesson #2 and shot Larkyns in the chest. Someone who saw the effect said the bullet went into his body "an inch above the left nipple." Harry Larkyns turned into the room, put his hand on his chest, and shouted, "Let me out! Let me out!" He ran away from Muybridge, through the cottage, and out the back door.

Muybridge walked into the house with the gun in his hand. One witness said that he turned to the women who had been talking with Larkyns and spoke to them. "I'm sorry for the disturbance," he said.

One of the men at the card table, a miner named James McArthur, stepped into a bedroom and came out with his own gun. Muybridge had started to follow Larkyns out the back door. "And as he passed the bedroom door I covered him with a pistol and made him surrender,"

At 11:00 p.m. on October 17, 1874, Muybridge knocked at this house—a cottage at the former Yellow Jacket Mine in northern California, near the town of Calistoga— asked for one of the men inside, Harry Larkyns, and shot him with a Smith & Wesson #2 revolver.

McArthur remembered. Muybridge put up no resistance and handed over his revolver.

One of the miners went out to Larkyns behind the house. There was a large oak tree near the door, which is where Larkyns fell dead. A physician who looked at him gave the opinion that he had lived "no more than twenty seconds" after the shot. The miner returned to the room to say that Larkyns was dead. Hearing this, Muybridge announced to the group, seven or eight people now on their feet, that this was a good outcome, and that he was glad for it.

Harry Larkyns's body was carried into the cottage and laid on a sofa, and somebody went on a horse to bring back a doctor. The nearest settlement was Calistoga, ten miles away, and at about 1:00 a.m. a Dr. Reed arrived. Reed examined the body and said that Larkyns was dead, which was known to everyone.

California had a reputation as the national center of gunplay, a place where shootings happened with the rhythm of the sunset. The Muybridge crime was a killing among miners out in the wilderness, which meant it was an event so ordinary as to seem commonplace. Notwithstanding its plainness, and far out of proportion to its remoteness, the murder of Harry Larkyns swelled into a national story. The shooting was reported in newspapers in New York, Chicago, Philadelphia, Baltimore, and Washington, D.C. It appeared in the press in Indiana, Nebraska, Idaho, Arizona, and in all likelihood in many other places whose newspapers did not survive to be taken care of, microfilmed, and scanned 150 years later by libraries.

The shooting created a brief national sensation. Most of the papers, west to east, had previously followed the doings of Edward Muybridge. They had run stories on his photographs of Yosemite Valley, some of the most beautiful images to come out of California. They had run stories the first time that he used his camera to stop the motion of a running horse. But Muybridge the killer was something different. Muybridge was not just an artist who happened to have shot a man. He was known to be the personal cameraman of Leland Stanford, the best-known and richest man west of the Mississippi—Stanford, who was something like the paterfamilias of California. That connection made the story especially newsworthy.

In San Francisco, people from all walks of life talked about Muybridge and the killing. They parsed it, defended it, took it apart, and ran through its inflections. It was interesting, wasn't it, that Muybridge had committed an instantaneous murder. The crime was precise and ecstatic, and therefore a shooting suited to the shooter. It was not unlike a running horse, a quick frame of an act like the impossible pictures the photographer had made. It was interesting, wasn't it, that there was a cognate in the crime.

In the Yellow Jacket cottage, the miners talked about what to do with the photographer. Muybridge said later that he thought he might be lynched. Gang rule did not lie far beneath the surface in California. Three years earlier, in 1871, a mob of five hundred had rioted and lynched some twenty Chinese immigrants, for the reason that immigrants did not belong in the state because they took away work from whites. Lynching was a familiar part of the miner's life in the mountains, far from a courthouse, and Harry Larkyns had made friends with this particular group of miners. The lynching idea in fact did come up for discussion, witnesses later said. Talk of killing Muybridge went around the room, but the man who had taken the photographer's gun, James McArthur (who now guarded the scene with his own revolver), persuaded the other men that bringing out the noose was a bad idea this

Muybridge at the base of the tree named U. S. Grant in the Mariposa Grove of sequoias, Yosemite Valley, 1872

time. If the men did it, it would not reflect well on them, and further-more none of them was particularly close to Harry Larkyns, who had airs. McArthur persuaded the others that the best thing to do would be to hand the shooter over to the law, down the valley in the county seat, the town of Napa.

The killing was done, and Muybridge was left in a clearer mind. He had survived and surrendered, surprising himself on both counts. Witnesses described a calm that came over him, which lasted for hours.

James McArthur used a rope to tie the photographer's ankles, and Muybridge was put into the back of a four-seat open buggy. McAr-thur sat next to him, and along with two other men they rode down the mountain toward Calistoga. The plan was to take Muybridge to the sheriff. However, it was the middle of the night, the road skirted the mountain, with drop-offs into brush, and the lamp was weak. Some-where on the way down, the carriage dropped a wheel off the edge of a little bridge and slipped. Muybridge and McArthur were thrown into the ditch beside the road. The prisoner was all right, but McArthur, badly hurt, couldn't move. Muybridge might have thought, This would be the right time to try to get away, but he climbed out of the ditch and plopped back into the carriage.[2]

Chapter 3

GOD OF THE SUN

Eight years before . . .
1866, MONTGOMERY STREET, SAN FRANCISCO

He called himself a "photograph-ic artist," although he had not yet sold any pictures. "Artist" was his new identity, the camera his new instrument. The last time he lived here he made a living as a book-seller. The last time he lived here he also had a different name—E. J. Muygridge. He arrived back in San Francisco sometime in 1866, no lon-ger Muygridge the book dealer, but the photographer known as Helios. A new living required a new identity. He thought highly enough of his new self to use a single name, borrowed from the Greek god of the sun. At age thirty-seven, a time when most people surrender to whatever circumstances trap them, Muygridge had discarded his previous life as a businessman and nominated himself an artist. *Helios.* He had a stage name, like that of a diva.

It was not at all uncommon, in the brand-new West, that while inventing a future a person might make up a past or use a new name. The emblem of California was the miner with a sieve and a knapsack, the man who came from nowhere and claimed to be whoever, his truth accepted as soon as he could trade a bag of ore for specie. Everyone in California came from somewhere else (except the Miwok, Hupa, Modoc, and ten other tribes, who did not come from somewhere else). More than a few blurred and touched up the past. But because personal history referred to a life back east, or in Europe, or for that matter China, it could not be said to be of importance.

San Francisco was Helios's adopted city, and he knew his way

A "bird's-eye view" drawing of San Francisco, ca. 1864

around. There was the little art district along Montgomery near California Street, with the photography and art galleries. Three blocks
away lay Chinatown, with its joss houses and their shrines, and smells
of opium. There were the wharfs east of Montgomery, where every
other clipper seemed to come from Hong Kong with another three hundred men on their way to swing sledgehammers for the railroad. (That
was new, they weren't laying tracks over the Sierras when he left.) And
there also at the dock rode the steamers, in from Panama, full of the
Irish from New York who had crossed the isthmus. That wasn't new.
Last time he was here, the Irish were already going to Nevada to dig for
silver in Virginia City. Helios knew the rhythms of the place because
he had lived in San Francisco during the 1850s, but then he had gone
home to England. Nothing unusual there—people came and went in
California, to and from the frontier, trying to cash in, going away, coming back, trying again. In those days, when he was E. J. Muygridge and
he sold books, he lived on Montgomery Street in a pair of rooms on the
second floor. He sold dictionaries then, and science books, and illustrated encyclopedias, and also some art. Mainly lithographs, pictures
of things far from the West, like Roman cities, good things for people
to hang above the fireplace. The book business had not been a crashing
success. Dignified books for libraries, Muygridge's specialty, did not

much interest Californians. These were people who wanted a stake in a mine or land, or had an appetite for anything having to do with money, but who did not particularly want literature. Discovering this fact took a long time, five years start to finish, but once he did, the artist formerly known as E. J. Muygridge had closed up shop and left for London, in 1860.

He had stayed away for six years. Those particular six years happened to have been exactly enough time for the United States to go to pieces and bleed itself out in the Civil War, and then come back together again. (Although he did not plan it this way, Helios was careful to stay away until the war was over.) Six years was an eternity in the far West, on the edge of America, where things changed annually. Montgomery Street might look familiar, but the photographer did not recognize many people. In six years, San Francisco had doubled in size, from 60,000 up to 120,000. Rents had gone up, the sound of construction was never-ending. There were more women on the street, but the ratio still ran low, about one woman for every two men. The numbers were so lopsided that women appeared to be foreigners invited from abroad.

While away in England, Helios had burned through two or three more lives and tossed them on the trash heap, on top of the bookseller. In London he had changed the spelling of his name again, becoming "E. J. Muybridge," and in that iteration he had tried his hand as an inventor and taken out a pair of patents. (As Muybridge, he designed a hand-crank washing machine, and he tried to perfect a method of printing illustrations—neither patent went anywhere.) After that, he had worked for three years in finance, wearing the spats and high collars of the London banking tribe. That was his worst memory, because he had failed miserably. But fortunately, during a stay in Paris, E. J. Muybridge had found his way into a photography studio, and that accident had given him a new pattern to follow—something he could try out in California, a place where you might keep trying on masks even after you reached middle age.

The evidence about the way Helios became a photographer is circumstantial but persuasive. It was at a photo studio called Maison Hélios, in Paris, that the businessman E. J. Muybridge remade himself into an artist, picking up another name, borrowing it like a piece of equipment, before heading to America for the second time.[1] Maison

Hélios, at number 9 rue Cadet, in the 9th arrondissement, belonged to three brothers named Berthaud—Michel, Jean, and "G." Berthaud. During a long visit to Paris in the fall of 1862, Muybridge, who was trying unsuccessfully to sell a patent for his printing process in the French market, used the Berthaud brothers' studio as his own address. Maison Hélios was booming. The Berthaud brothers would eventually have branch photography operations in eight cities in France, and with their expansion they had reason to take on an apprentice, in this case, an English inventor who used to sell books.

It seems the *frères* Berthaud and Maison Hélios not only gave the wayward E. J. Muybridge, a man dangling between one thing and another, a technical education in cameras, photo chemicals, and lenses; they also showed him how to sell himself in the business. The Berthaud brothers used as a trademark an emblem stamped with the word "Hélios," with rays of light emanating from the center. When E. J. Muybridge set himself up in San Francisco as the photographer called Helios, he designed a logo—a camera, the word "Helios," and emanating rays of light. The businessman knew to copy a successful formula.

Photographs of Helios himself from his first years as an artist show a man in hobnail boots and ragged jackets. He wears rumpled pants and floppy hats against the sun as he skitters through the streets decked in his anonymous, run-down drag. As a London businessman, he once tricked himself out in formal woolens and buttoned up in choking collars, but as an artist he dressed like a man who lived outdoors.

The clothes had changed during his time away; so had the manner. Friends who had known him before he left said something had shifted in the man. For most of his working life, E. J. Muybridge had been careful about presenting himself, keeping up a bland front, tiptoeing through business in a polite dance of sales calls and follow-up letters.

Helios logo, ca. 1872. A camera with wings, aloft under the sun—the logo used in California by the artist formerly known as E. J. Muygridge

Muybridge, self-portrait, San Francisco's North Point Dock, ca. 1868

Now, returning, he took no interest in his grooming. He was "very eccentric," said an old friend, "and so unlike his way before going, the change in his appearance was such that I could scarcely recognize him." Another who had known Helios in a previous incarnation said, "He was much less irritable before his return, and much more careless in dress when he came back—not the same man in any respect." An art dealer he knew said the photographer had become disorderly and often changed his mind. "He would take violent dislikes of people, utterly causeless," said the man. A news reporter added that Helios "was not a man of strong, or even of average social leanings." The photographer had a new profession and an altered personality. He raced toward things, surprising people with his intensity.[2]

From his viewpoint, Helios was just adopting the Western mode. Wasn't the West, for everyone, mainly a chase after something? Much of the West used to be Mexico anyway, before the American pursuit and takeover. Mexico occupied nearly half of the continent—if you drew a line from Texas to Oregon, Mexico was everything to the west and south. In those days, the western vastness meant mission outposts and a thin ribbon of haciendas, but the majority population was indigenous—the Apache, Arapaho, Cayuse, Cheyenne, Comanche, Hopi, Modoc, Mohave, Nez Perce, Navajo, Paiute, Shoshone, Sioux, Ute, Yakima, and Yuma tribes, among others. Maybe two million Indians lived between the Mississippi River and the Pacific. The invasion by U.S. infantry cut Mexico in half, and California and the Southwest came to Washington as spoils. The West, to Helios, with the clearer sight of an immigrant, was just the newest piece of land-grab America.

In 1848, two weeks after Mexico capitulated, white prospectors in California found gold in the foothills of the Sierra Nevada, and within a year, fifty thousand migrants arrived from the East Coast. Twenty-five thousand came the next year, and in 1850 California rode to immediate statehood on a fuel of nationalism and money. "We all understand the emotions connected with the word *California*," said the New York *Knickerbocker*. The feelings flying around gold dust. "Did not its discovery cause millions of hearts the feeling of avarice?" In Boston, Baltimore, Philadelphia, and Charleston, the West meant gold, freedom, rough justice, easy sex, and sometimes paid work. California was the main chance, and an antidote to boredom. The eastern states saw the West much as Europe had regarded its New World colonies—as a dangerous place where money could be made, where all desire found

its object. Which was why Helios had come the first time, during the
1850s.

Now he was back, his desires changed; this time he wanted room
to be an artist. Fortunately, he knew some of the earliest generation in
San Francisco, the Gold Rush migrants, the ones who had stayed—
like his friend Silas Selleck. Selleck was the American he had known
longer than any other. The two had become friends in New York City
fifteen years earlier, when Selleck was a young camera operator at the
Mathew Brady Gallery on Broadway, and Helios was a twenty-year-
old immigrant to New York named Edward Muggeridge. Selleck had
come to California, panned for gold like everyone else, but came to his
middle-class senses. He now lived in San Francisco and ran his own
photography studio, the Cosmopolitan Gallery of Photographic Art, at
415 Montgomery Street. Looking for a start as a photographer, Helios

Muybridge spent most of his years in San Francisco working on Montgomery Street
(pictured here about 1866). In 1867 he began his photography career in the studio
of Silas Selleck at 415 Montgomery, in the tall building painted on the side in large
letters "Selleck's Photographic Gallery."

tracked down his old friend Selleck, who invited him to set up in the gallery as a new freelancer. Selleck allowed Helios to use the gallery as his own and probably also shared his cameras and lenses and chemicals. And he made room for the beginner's prints on display tables where customers might see them.

When he started, Helios needed subjects that might give him an income. The most lucrative genre of photography had always been portraits. Silas Selleck had done them for years, beginning with the old image technology, daguerreotypes. After that, Selleck moved on to the newer visiting cards. A French invention, *cartes de visite* were four-by-six-inch calling cards with the client's photograph on them. There was another format selling well, which Helios could try—stereographs. "Stereos" were stiff cards, four by eight inches, with two nearly identical photographs on them, side by side. They fit into a viewer that looked like a pair of opera glasses on a handle, and the cards seen through the device produced a three-dimensional image. Stereos sold heavily in bookstores and at stationers, and families built collections of them, creating the first era of 3-D, the 1860s.

———

Photography had changed as rapidly as California. Some called it an art, some a science, but whatever its nature, the thing was just twenty-five years old. Henry Fox Talbot in England and Louis Daguerre in France have good but not sole claim to be the medium's inventors, during the 1830s. (The word *photography*, "light writing," came from a chemist and astronomer, John Herschel, in London, in the year 1840.)[3] Photochemistry uses silver halides, crystals of salt and silver that react when exposed to light. This was true from the medium's beginnings until about 2000, when digital light sensors displaced chemical ones. When a surface painted with a silver halide is exposed to light, some of the crystals convert to elemental silver, and with this reaction, light traces an image. Louis Daguerre spread silver solution on polished metal plates, Fox Talbot soaked paper in it. Daguerre, a painter of panoramas who stumbled into photochemistry, collaborating with a mentor who possessed a melodic name, Nicéphore Niépce, invented the positive image in photography, a one-time view that could not be reproduced. Talbot, a gentleman scientist, invented the negative, a template that could be struck into copies. Daguerre and Talbot announced their separate creations in 1839.[4]

After that came a strange turn of events. Daguerre patented his invention in France and England, whereupon the French government bought the Paris patent from him and made it public domain—anyone could use the Daguerre process if they bought a few pieces of equipment. Meanwhile, the British patent on daguerreotypes stayed in place. Daguerreotypes spread across Europe and America, but not to Britain, where the steep cost of a Daguerre license meant no one could operate a studio.

The second photo process, the *calotype*, came from Fox Talbot. Aside from the national polarity—Daguerre from France and Talbot from England—the two had personal disparities. Daguerre was an artist who worked in the theater, while Talbot had served five years in Parliament, possessed a fortune, belonged to the Royal Society, was the grandson of an earl, had published books of archaeology, and lived in a fifteenth-century manor, Lacock Abbey, where he converted a stone barn into a photography workshop. When he coined the word *calotype*, Talbot leaned on his classical education, using a Greek phrase he liked for "beautiful template." Talbot patented the calotype, but no government stepped in to give it away, so the upper-class inventor became a businessman and sold licenses as high as the market would bear.

In America, Helios's friend Silas Selleck and hundreds of others opened royalty-free daguerreotype studios, which delivered to customers a flinty, palm-sized picture of themselves that took three minutes to expose and came in a velvet case. In Britain, because of Daguerre's and Talbot's patent fees, photography went nowhere. In 1851, after a dozen years of photochemistry, only fifty people tried to eke out a living as "photographers."

Daguerreotypes became obsolete about 1855, pushed aside by a new negative process, "wet plate" photography (this one also free for the taking), that let you make copies of pictures. Portraits remained the moneymaking genre, although they now took the form of *cartes de visite*, full-body or upper-body shots in a studio against a painted backdrop.

It was probably with Silas Selleck's help that Helios found his first clients. The trouble was that the photographer Helios does not seem to have liked taking pictures of people. He did not care for the nice-family genre, showing nice couples with their nice possessions and nice children on hand. At the start of his professional life, in other words,

Muybridge, *Residence of James Rogers at Watsonville, California*, ca. 1879

Helios shut off much of his potential income. He would photograph you outside, in front of your house, but he would not photograph you alone, or indoors. Certainly he would not photograph you surrounded by the props a studio used to frame its customers—the backdrops, sculpture, and fake columns.

It would be difficult to find subjects who look less happy than those photographed by Helios in some of his early images. In one set of what we might call his "house" pictures, Helios depicted the Rogers family of Watsonville, California, posed next to their fine, freshly built Greek Revival home. The people in the pictures appear cowed. Helios has consigned them to sit in the horse paddock and obscured their house behind a tree. In his photograph of the Lent family house on San Francisco's Rincon Hill, a group of children wearing their Sunday best stand in front of a Gothic mansion; they look just about as comfortable and natural as the stone statuary that frames them. Helios seemed to have an aversion to the respectable class of Californians whom, a few years earlier, he might have seen living in a covered wagon and eating dried beef. And to be fair, to judge from his clients' faces and body language, the nice families that hired Helios did not seem to care for him as a man. He turned to landscapes.

———

In June 1867, Helios took a stagecoach to the folds of central California, into Yosemite Valley, to make his first commercial series, a group of photographs with a theme. The trip would either make him a success or show him to be just another talker in the big-mouthed West. Yosemite Valley, two hundred miles east of San Francisco, was a seven-mile-long gash in the mountains, a strange and ravishing geo-formation with vertical rock faces, gauze waterfalls, and mirroring lagoons. Some regarded Yosemite as proof California was an Eden. Helios had been there once before, and this time he would not let the beauty of Yosemite paralyze him.

Only a few white people, trekking out from San Francisco, had seen Yosemite—240 tourists in 1864, 360 the next year, 450 in 1867.[5] And yet through word of mouth, engravings, and big paintings by landscape artists like Albert Bierstadt, Yosemite had acquired a large aura. It was becoming, already, something like a trademark of the West. Depending on who wrote about it, the valley could appear to be either a peaceful enclave or nonnegotiable majesty, indifferent or welcoming, a sign of American empire or an index finger that pointed to democracy. Yosemite was a projection screen that took on what you threw at it.*

It did not add to the sublime reputation of Yosemite that miners and militiamen had entered the valley and clashed with native people, a tribe called the Ahwanichee, scattering their villages on a murderous raid. But since then, Congress itself had consecrated Yosemite as the untouchable symbol of the state of California.

And now, if only someone could make sense of it, using photography. Two photographers had already been out to Yosemite from San Francisco, trying to represent the enigma of the valley and elevate it to myth. Helios was the third, and at minimum, the most energetic. He rented rooms in the Yosemite Hotel, at the north end of the valley, the single place to sleep when you were not on the ground (although he also slept there), and the only place to store his gear. The money for the trip

---

* In her book about Eadweard Muybridge, *River of Shadows*, Rebecca Solnit describes the national curiosity about Yosemite this way: "The United States rooted its identity in its landscapes, as though to suggest that its identity was itself natural, in contrast to the much denounced artificiality of European culture."

probably came from a publisher. In San Francisco, a man called John Hittell was working up the first book-length guide to Yosemite, and he wanted to illustrate it with photographs, which would be "tipped in," or pasted to the page. (This was before half-tone printing let you print photographs on paper.) Helios had received the assignment.

He might have borrowed the hardware from Silas Selleck. He brought a "half plate" camera, which made a six-by-eight-inch negative. (A "full plate" made negatives not quite double this, measuring eight by ten inches.) He brought a "stereo camera," which had two lenses protruding from it, to make the hugely popular stereographs, which would be the moneymaker, if anything made money. He carried canned food, and probably a gun. With all the apparatus, he was like a machine invading the wilderness.

For at least five months he roamed the valley. In November 1867, the *Mariposa Gazette* reported the journeyman photographer was "still at Yosemite, after this long time."[6] Helios put on the mask of unaccommodated man, disappearing into the remoteness of nature, throwing off culture, shedding its skin. During the day he hired men and mules to carry his gear. He hired guides, possibly Indians whose villages had been broken up. He photographed landmarks Californians were starting to know—Glacier Point, Sentinel Dome, and Taft Point—and he went to upper Yosemite Fall. He photographed one of his own campsites. The image shows a clearing in the woods, scattered with crates and bottles, and in the middle, a tent with the dimensions of a closet (his darkroom). His floppy hat, the sign of a wanderer, sits somewhere. The name "Helios" appears on a tree limb, like graffiti—it has been scratched into the negative.

Yosemite was known to surveyors. In summer 1866 a team came from Sacramento led by Josiah Whitney, the state geologist, and in 1867, a party exploring the fortieth parallel arrived, led by the surveyor Clarence King and accompanied by a former Civil War photographer, Timothy O'Sullivan. These were among many expeditions through the West, some of which combined military maneuvers and mapping, like those under the command of General A. A. Humphreys, head of the federal Corps of Engineers. America had grown vastly in thirty years, and the people back east, especially in Washington, D.C., had persistent questions: What are these giant pieces of land that America has grabbed up, and bought up, and taken by war? What are our "territories"?

Muybridge, *The Flying Studio, Photographer's Equipment in the Field*, 1867. On his trip to Yosemite Valley, Muybridge created a darkroom (a shower-like tent to hide negatives from light), poured ample chemicals (including the flammable syrup known as collodion, seen here in bottles), and, to judge from the title of this picture, saw himself as a new kind of location photographer.

Muybridge, *Little Grizzly Fall*, 1867. Stereograph. Many photographs in Muybridge's Yosemite series show an attachment to rushing waters, swollen rivers, whitewater runs, and waterfalls, as though the photographer is obsessed with motion.

American landscape photography began at Yosemite, and Helios was at the start of it. The year before he came, photographer Carleton Watkins, a New Yorker transplanted to California, made pictures of the peaks and gorges, as had Charles Leander Weed, a photographer who made serene, static compositions from the outlines of the rock faces and pools. Helios took a different approach. He was drawn to the watercourses, staying close along the Merced River, photographing its whitewater runs, its cool, still flows, the water spewing out from crevices. When you look at his later pictures, the ones that capture motion, it does not appear to be a coincidence that he was attracted to moving water. Rivers and waterfalls clock the passage of time, and the photographer Helios returned obsessively to the seeping and sprays, visual markers of time wheeling ahead, as though he wanted to seize them.

The Watkins and Weed pictures had sold, but both had photographed the voids of the valley, attaching the eye to vistas and vanish-

Muybridge, *Kahchoomah, Wild Cat Fall, 30 Feet High*, 1868. Muybridge preferred Native American names for sites in Yosemite Valley, during the same period when whites were erasing Indian designations.

ing points. Their subject at Yosemite was space, but Helios's subject, in many photographs, was time.

The experimental filmmaker Hollis Frampton, one hundred years after Muybridge, described how Helios's pictures at Yosemite gathered up duration, giving it the form of a tesseract, the extension of three dimensions into the fourth one, time. The waterfall photos "produce images of a strange ghostly substance that is in fact the *tesseract* of water," Frampton said of the liquid's geometry. "What is to be seen is not water itself, but the virtual volume it occupies during the whole time interval of the exposures."

His most literary photograph of water is a self-portrait, an image about the passage of time, and about death, he called *Charon at the Ferry.* While walking deep at the base of the valley, Helios made this image, which shows the photographer himself standing on a dock beside the slow-moving Merced, the habitual hat on his head, and in his left hand, a heavy rope that droops into the water. The title refers to Charon, the ferryman of death in Greek myth, the enigmatic boatman who carries the souls of the dead across the River Styx to Hades. The Merced has become the Styx and Helios the messenger of death, the messenger of time's end.

To prepare a single image took time, many minutes of the messen-

Muybridge, self-portrait, *Charon at the Ferry*, 1868. In a stereograph, the photographer depicted himself as a figure from Greek myth, Charon, the ferryman of death who conveys souls across the River Styx to the afterlife in the underworld of Hades.

In Yosemite, Muybridge encountered not only nature and the sublime, but also lumbermen cutting down the ancient trees in the Mariposa Grove of sequoias at the southern end of the valley.

ger's time. First he chose the site, which might require a half day on foot and on the back of a mule, then he set the tripod and aimed the camera. The exposure itself involved a graceful choreography peculiar to wet-plate photography. The photographer poured the flammable syrup called collodion—which would become the base of the light-sensitive emulsion—evenly across a glass plate, immersed the glass covered with goo in a bath of solution that contained the silver halide (while hiding it from light under a black hood), inserted the drippy plate in the camera, removed the lens cover and then replaced it, withdrew the plate and bathed it, still hidden, in a solution of acetic acid and iron sulfate, which developed the image, and finally washed the glass plate in a solution of sodium hyposulfite, or "fixer," to stop the silver reaction. One negative came out of this minuet.

It sounds cumbersome, but wet plate actually sped up the photography market. With negatives on glass, photos spread everywhere, because paper prints could be mass-produced from them, and the 3-D stereograph spread the fastest. In Britain, a man called George Nottage

The type of stereo camera that Muybridge probably took to Yosemite, made by the Scovill Company of New York

set up the London Stereoscopic Company in 1854; after five years the company had a stock of 100,000 different stereos, the majority of them of buildings and landscapes, the kind of photography Helios wanted to do.[7]

At some point during these months Helios took another revealing picture of himself, or rather he told an assistant to take it. He sat on a precipice, dangling his legs over a thousand-foot drop in a death-mocking stunt, and signaled to a helper to get the shot. The picture possesses a mania, an unmistakable ecstasy. He had no reason to risk his life for a photograph, and yet he did. Everyone who saw the picture had a similar reaction and took note of the artist's curious death drive. The photograph would come up again, after the murder.

———

Helios lowered himself into the wilderness—other than a mule driver he might not see another face for two days. He was alone, which he preferred, but he had his cameras and chemicals.

During these same months, in the state capital at Sacramento, 150 miles away, Leland Stanford was never alone. Much the opposite. Stanford was beset, which he preferred—he was the person that everyone swarmed around. The former governor of California, age forty-four, Stanford sat on top of and gave the convincing impression that he ran the Central Pacific Railroad, an enterprise that involved some fifteen thousand workers, the largest workforce in America. Stanford's apparatus, if you like, was somewhat larger than Helios's. Stanford's apparatus was a grinding, exploding machine for the conquest of nature that was at this particular moment trying to chip and bomb a 1,700-foot-long hole through granite at the summit of the Sierra Nevada, a place called Donner Pass.

Muybridge and Stanford had never met. The photographer knew about Stanford, as did everyone in California, but the railroad president probably did not know about Muybridge as yet.

Thick, slow-moving Leland Stanford spent most of his days in a second-floor office on K Street in the Sacramento headquarters of the Central Pacific. His six-year-old company had on its balance sheet one hundred miles of track, six locomotives, six passenger cars, two baggage cars, twenty-five flat freight cars, and fifteen boxcars.[8] Stanford knew his train speculation would make an immeasurable fortune if he (helped by thousands of Chinese men) could find a way to drag

Muybridge, self-portrait, 1872. Muybridge asked an assistant to photograph him tempting death, dangling on a precipice above a thousand-foot drop, a picture that would be introduced as evidence of his insanity at the murder trial.

his machines over the Sierras. "We are crawling up the mountains," he called the track laying. It was a Sisyphus-like scheme that nobody thought would work, not even Stanford and his partners, at least on some days. Except that this year they had a new piece of equipment to add to his kit and speed things up—nitroglycerine.

Stanford might have found it hard to remember he was once only a grocer.

Chapter 4

HARNESSING THE ELEPHANT

Interstate 80 was routed during the 1960s, following the path of the old Central Pacific Railroad through Nevada and California. If you drive west on I-80 from Utah, the road takes you over the Sierras along the same route the train once did and deposits you in the same place, Sacramento, in central California. Sacramento erupted during the Gold Rush as a frontier post, then as a settlement on the banks of the Sacramento River, which flows north to south, at the confluence with the American River, which runs east to west. In 2010, the city counted 460,000 people. Downtown, several blocks of nineteenth-century buildings survive, squeezed against the river levee by another 1960s highway, Interstate 5. Within this thin strip of the past an idea of the Old West, although it is not entirely clear whose idea, has been quarantined in order to make a tourist district.

I paid a visit, in the make-believe settler strip, to the California State Railroad Museum on I Street. The museum has a library that houses some of the paper records of the Central Pacific, its reading room all paneled walls and dark shelving, like an apothecary. Here the patrons are men older than sixty with a liking for flannel. It is the only library I have ever been in where men can be found who possess a gentle kind of fetish, the one for old trains.

With its wooden sidewalks and shed porches, the California capital of Sacramento was much the frontier town. Leland Stanford's grocery occupied one of the brick buildings on these blocks of K Street, the main commercial strip, photographed in 1865.

In the fall of 1860 Theodore Judah, a railroad engineer living in California, placed a notice in the *Sacramento Union* newspaper calling an open meeting of whoever might be interested in a new railroad scheme. It was a sales pitch; he wanted investors. Judah appears in one photograph, dressed in checked vest and slanted hat, like a supreme dude, his body language more than a little vain. Leland Stanford, a Sacramento grocer with a store on K Street, had probably already heard about Judah. The garrulous, somewhat manic engineer from upstate New York had helped to design the only rail line that then existed in California, the twenty-four-mile-long Sacramento Valley line. Judah had lately been ricocheting around with a new and preposterous scheme, a plan for a "Pacific railroad" that would cross the United States. Railroads had already spidered inland from the Eastern Seaboard as far as the Missouri River, a third of the way across the continent. The idea of continuing the link all the way west to California had floated around Washington, D.C., for fifteen years. But in part because of regional

In 1860 Theodore Judah, railroad engineer and obsessive personality, recruited store owner Leland Stanford and other shopkeepers for his scheme to build a railroad to the Pacific. (He is shown here in 1848.)

divisions—where to put the route—in part because the scheme was too vast, it died frequent deaths in Congress. Judah had tried to sell his version of the Pacific railroad to rich men in San Francisco but had found no one to put down money (maybe his frenzied personal manner scared them), so he had come to California's second city, Sacramento, population twelve thousand. Some say twelve people came to his sales pitch, some say thirty, but the most likely story is that Collis Huntington, a hardware dealer on K Street, came, and more shopkeepers fell into place. A lanky, ostrichlike man with a squeaky voice, Huntington persuaded other small businessmen to listen. To hear more from Judah, Huntington recruited his partner, the meticulous and brittle Mark Hopkins, plus the grocer a couple of doors down K Street, Leland Stanford, and finally the dry goods dealer Charles Crocker, bibulous and barrel-shaped at 250 pounds. This group and two or three others gave Judah a second and third meeting, after which they presented him with enough money to survey a route for his train over the Sierra range to Nevada, a task of several months on horseback.[1]

Judah came down from the rocks and peaks and made a huge map, sixty feet long, that showed a hypothetical train route of many switchbacks up the western hills, cutaways that wrapped the road around each mountain, four tunnels through granite, ravines to be leveled with infill, a route over the crest of Donner Pass (elevation seven thousand feet), the placement of creaky wooden trestles, and a wheeling descent to the east. He called the 115-mile track "my little road."

Leland Stanford, in his mid-thirties, owned a busy and profitable store on K Street in Sacramento, and, unusual for his time and place, he was active in the Republican Party. Stanford's politics were probusiness and antislavery, which made him a rarity in California, a state run by Democrats, some of them proslavery, the rest indifferent to it. He had tried for several offices, including that of governor (which one could do as a grocer in a full-length apron if your state had only 120,000 voters), losing in the last election by a margin of ten votes to one but always going back to party meetings. In March 1861, Stanford went to Washington to attend the inaugural of the new president, Abraham Lincoln. Republicans had national power for the first time, and although the party had not carried California, Stanford had reason to lobby Lincoln about the West and ask for party spoils, perhaps a few appointments he could manage. He also had reason to talk about the railroad.

The timing of Theodore Judah's scheme was good, perversely, thanks to the disaster of the Civil War; the Southern states had just seceded, and the War of Rebellion was about to begin. Despite earlier promoters with train plans before Judah and two federal surveys for a coast-to-coast train, the idea of funding a railroad with tax money had gone nowhere in Washington, due to the sectional split that divided North and South. Southern lawmakers wanted a southern route through Louisiana and Texas, and northern politicians wanted a track that ran anywhere but through the South. Suddenly, with the South in revolt in 1861, half the senators and congressmen had disappeared from Capitol Hill and gone home to work for the new Confederate States of America. By the rule of crisis politics—do not let a calamity pass without exploiting it—this meant an opportunity. There is no direct evidence that Stanford talked to Lincoln about Theodore Judah's train, but the circumstances point to it.

In mid-June of 1861, California's Republican Party, for the second time, named Stanford its candidate for governor. Nine days later, on June 28, Theodore Judah, the four shopkeepers—Huntington, Stanford, Hopkins, and Crocker—and four others incorporated the Central Pacific Railroad of California. The nine speculators named Stanford president of the company; he had met Lincoln, and if he became governor he could push the train. The would-be train executives were small-town rich, with combined personal assets of $118,000, whereas Judah's estimate put the cost of a track over the mountains at $12 million. Stock went on sale at $100 a share, and the first tally of returns came to an unpromising 1,580 shares, which, at 10 percent down, resulted in $15,000 cash in hand.

Aside from Judah, the train investors looked at the railroad as a gamble. They could conceivably trim back plans, perhaps building a short line that took advantage of the silver rush up to the Comstock Lode in Nevada and get Congress to pay for it, and that by itself would be a boondoggle.

Stanford seems to have been confident things would happen, at least for him. In July he and his wife bought a big brick house on Eighth Street in Sacramento, and he announced to her that this would be their governor's mansion. He was right: Stanford won the election in September, thanks to the crisis back east. In California Republicans usually lost, but when the South seceded, the Democrats split the poll, running two candidates for governor, one pro-South, the other pro-Union, and the divided ticket gave the victory to Stanford.

A month later, Theodore Judah packed his map and sailed from San Francisco on the steamship *St. Louis* for Washington, D.C., to sell the train to Congress. On Capitol Hill, Judah restarted his sales machinery—a pitch to anyone who would listen, handshakes in the corridors, the map brandished in committee. If Congress funded it, a train across the West would defeat the Indians, he said. If Congress funded it, a train would send Easterners into the empty western half of the country and ignite the economy, he said. Building the Central Pacific would keep California in the Union during the fight between North and South, he said, if Congress funded it.

The Pacific Railroad Act was written in the spring, passed in June, and signed by President Lincoln on July 1, 1862. It chartered two companies—the Union Pacific Railroad, to build west from the Missouri River, and the Central Pacific, to build east from California. The act told the builders to string telegraph lines alongside the track, extending those already in place, in effect spreading physical and virtual networks at the same time. The law—"an act to aid in the construction of a railroad and telegraph line from the Missouri River to the Pacific Ocean"—provided for two links between New York and San Francisco, one physical, one mental, the telegraph being the line for the mind.

When the Railroad Act went through, Theodore Judah sent a fifteen-word dispatch that zigzagged from Washington along still-patchy lines to California.

"We have drawn the elephant," he wrote Governor Stanford. "Now let us see if we can harness him up."

————

Rain threatened to wash the crowd gathered at First and K Streets in Sacramento on January 8, 1863, but clouds drifted off in time for the ceremony at noon. It was a Thursday. A thousand people shuffled in the dirt street beside the Sacramento River levee, and more clustered on the wood plank sidewalks. All eyes went to the man in formal clothes standing behind bunting on a makeshift wooden stage, Governor Leland Stanford. A band played patriotic songs and ministers stood around, awaiting permission to pray.[2]

Stanford had always been uneasy in speechmaking, and his remarks began with a bromide.

"Fellow citizens, I congratulate you upon the commencement of the great work which we this day inaugurate—the Pacific Railroad." His hands felt for the shovel as his eyes went down the speech. The railroad "will form an iron bond that shall strengthen the ties of nationality," he said. Stanford was referring to the Civil War that had pulled America apart for two years. It was an unlikely time for declarations of national unity. One week earlier, President Lincoln had issued the Emancipation Proclamation, a 250-word executive order that freed, on paper though not in fact, four million people enslaved in the South. And three weeks before this date, at Fredericksburg, Virginia, 114,000 Union troops had turned out against 72,000 Confederates and lost, with 12,000 killed or wounded.

The railroad, Stanford went on, would "vanquish the untutored native." In other words, the train would defeat the Indian nations, perhaps a million people between California and Missouri who did not want the coasts to be united by an "iron bond" and who suspected the rail line would bring a fresh round of wars, treaties, and deportations. The previous month, in Minnesota, the United States Army had put down some of the "untutored natives," crushing an uprising of the Sioux and staging a mass execution of thirty-six Dakota Indians. Stanford acknowledged these things in a few words that conveyed much.

The choice of Sacramento as the terminus of the national rail line made another odd feature of this groundbreaking ceremony. The capital of California was barely two miles square, with a population that had risen to just fifteen thousand, not quite a counterbalance to the million-plus of New York City at the other end.

For all the national conflict and other drawbacks, "the wealth and the commerce of the East and the West is to float upon this rail line," said Stanford from the platform. He might have been referring to the payout from the Railroad Act. If he and his partners could actually build the train, they would receive government bonds at the rate of $16,000 per mile of track over flat country, $32,000 per mile in the foothills, and $48,000 per mile through the Sierra peaks. They would also acquire vast stretches of land, five tracts per mile on alternating sides, amounting to 6,400 acres for every mile of railroad. If they could build, the rail operators would immediately become, after the federal government, the biggest landlords in the country.

Stanford would have thought that all this was much to be thankful for, so he wound up his speech and turned things over to a minister. "It is meet and proper that we should invoke God's blessing upon the undertaking," he said, as he stepped back and one Reverend J. Benton stepped forward. The clergyman requested bowed heads, offered a prayer, and retreated.

Two wagons full of dirt pulled up to the platform—the first mounds of earth for the railroad bed. Governor Stanford shoveled "with a zeal," according to the newspaper, and the dirt hit the road to applause and huzzahs.

———

The Central Pacific investors divided up their work. The public face of the company would be Stanford, polished, unsmiling, and not incidentally the governor of the state. Stanford had the second-floor warehouse of his brick, two-story grocery on K Street renovated to create offices for the train company. His governor's desk stayed in the capitol, the train desk above the grocery, but the new president of a railroad with no track walked the five blocks between them once or twice a day, blending the government's and the company's fortunes.

At the train company's loftlike headquarters, Stanford shared space with the careful and withdrawn Mark Hopkins, the designated accountant. Meanwhile, Charles Crocker, the dry goods dealer, by several accounts a loud and crude man, became the contractor. Occasionally Crocker appeared in Sacramento, but for months at a time he played the barnstorming crew captain, riding out on horseback to drop in along the building line, distributing bags of gold coin to pay the men, yelling orders and riding on.

The fourth speculator, Collis Huntington, possessed a will to power as strong as that of the other three combined. It would be an understatement to describe Huntington, a cranelike man whose voice creaked, as severe. Huntington was the cashier who ended the day with more money than sales would strictly account for, the tally man with his thumb always on the scale. He moved to New York in 1863 to raise construction funds for the train—selling bonds, bonds, bonds, and more bonds for the company—while also arranging the shipment of the hardware that would make the track happen.

The Sacramento shopkeepers edged out the rest of the company's investors during construction, until only Stanford, Crocker, Hopkins, and Huntington remained. (No one yet called them "the Big Four"—that label would wait until a 1935 book of that title about them and their train.) They referred to themselves as "the associates." There was a fifth associate, Charles Crocker's brother, Edwin Crocker, a lawyer who was cut in with stock and given a job as the train company's attorney, but the balance of power stayed with the quartet.

When Stanford was California governor, his term of office extended for only two years. During his first twelve months, in 1862–63, Stanford signed seven bills to subsidize the Central Pacific and persuaded two county governments to buy stock outright. No one doubted his self-dealing, no one complained about conflict of interest, although in a few years many would. Californians wanted the train and did not yet object to one man running both the state and the company that would cash in. When Governor Stanford had to fill an open seat on the California Supreme Court, he appointed one of the associates, Edwin Crocker, knowing Crocker would rule for the railroad in every case. Crocker served out the two-year justiceship and then returned to the train company, picking up the honorific "Judge Crocker," which he wore for the rest of his life. (Judge Crocker had another distinction: several years later he would be the instrument for the introduction of Leland Stanford to Helios, the landscape photographer.)

It was said that Governor Stanford used so much energy to push the Central Pacific that he was able to levitate the mountains and move them closer to Sacramento. The subsidy from Washington went up per mile as the grade rose into the Sierras, starting with the foothills. The conventional view put the first hills thirty miles east of Sacramento, but Stanford telegraphed President Lincoln with a question: "Will you please inform me what evidence you will require to fix the western base of Sierra Nevada?"[3] The governor recruited the help of his friend Josiah Whitney, geologist for the state, and with Stanford's nod Whitney placed the western line of the mountains at Arcade Creek, a stream just east of Sacramento with no hills in sight. Revising the map to move the mountains released an additional $300,000 for the train. Lincoln acquiesced—he was more worried about the Civil War.

———

The manic promoter Theodore Judah had brought all the interests to the table, but he fell to fighting with the four associates. They were businesspeople, local and wired into Sacramento—a contract for a friend here, a right-of-way deal for one there. Judah, the engineer, turned his back on politics to study rail widths and spikes and tempers of iron. At one point he changed the route of the first mile of track through Sacramento to bring it closer to the wharfs. Huntington, the sharpest of the group, was away; returning to town, Huntington threw a fit. Within a few weeks, he and the other associates turned against Judah. The shopkeepers told the railroad engineer to buy them out, at $100,000 per head, or to leave the company.

Theodore Judah got a San Francisco bank to back him, but the bank changed its mind. He reached new investors in New York, and in October 1863 Judah and his wife, Anna Judah, took a steamship from California to meet the sources of their new money. From their stateroom Judah wrote to the small shareholder with whom he was still on good terms—Daniel Strong, with whom he had ridden up the Sierras to make the first survey. "The Central Pacific will pass into the hands of men of experience and capital," he told Strong, and the grocer Stanford and hardware man Huntington "will rue the day they ever embarked" on the train. Anna Judah, in a memoir, claimed that her husband "had secured the right and had the power to buy out the men opposed to him," and that "everything was arranged for a meeting in New York City on his arrival." The deal, if it existed, was probably with New York's most senior dealer in railroads, Cornelius Vanderbilt.

Anna and Theodore Judah took the Central American route to the

East Coast—a steamer to Panama, a hard road across the isthmus, a steamer to New York. On the overland leg in Panama, Judah caught yellow fever, or perhaps typhoid, and spent the remainder of the trip semiconscious. In New York, he was carried to the Metropolitan Hotel, delirious. He died a day later, at age thirty-seven.

Theodore Judah had laid the train franchise at Stanford's door. The associates, who already made decent money selling pickaxes and bags of rice to miners, would become a founding clique of the Gilded Age, the first circle in American life of the poisonously rich. When Judah died, Stanford and the others sent flowers to Anna Judah, his widow, and enclosed the condolences of the investors, professing their "unfeigned sorrow" that he was out of their way.

———

"Occasionally the newspapers find fault and slander and impugn my motives but less so than I expected," Stanford said in a letter to his mother. He was governor of California and president of its most devouring company; while his mother, Elizabeth Stanford, age seventy-one, lived alone in a farmhouse in upstate New York, widowed for several years. "I manage to pursue very steadily the even tenor of my way despite the clamor of enemies," Stanford told her, an understated boast. Two weeks later, on Christmas Eve, Stanford wrote his mother again, this time to reminisce about winter sleigh rides they used to take through snowbound fields and to apologize that he had not visited her in seven or eight years. The governor offered his mother a grand but wooden excuse—"The building of a railroad over the Sierra Nevada Mountains with as much rapidity as possible is an enterprise that is very exacting in its requirements of time." Stanford seems to have felt guilty about neglecting his mother, about having left, as a young man, the peaceable modesty of the family farm near Albany for the dream of California, and having never returned. "How many sacrifices you have made for us all," he said, referring to his brothers, who had also gone to follow money in the West, "and comparatively how little we have been able to make return." Easing his conscience, Stanford promised to come home to upstate New York one final time to retrieve his mother and bring her to California. "If I am able to visit you during the year I shall hope to have you return with me," he said. "I am sure that once here we could make your stay happy." In a couple of years, he would persuade his mother to follow him west, and Elizabeth Stanford would live out her

Leland and Jane Stanford on the porch of their house on N Street in Sacramento, ca. 1868

days with her successful son, on the third floor of his house, the dowager matron who had produced the most powerful man west of Chicago.[4]

———

Stanford sent Collis Huntington to Washington to lobby for more subsidies, and Huntington in effect bought his way through Congress. Exactly how he did so would emerge years later, when his correspondence, full of talk of bribes, became public. It was 1863, the Civil War was peaking. To Stanford, back in California, the catastrophe of the Battle of Gettysburg (July 1863, fifty-one thousand casualties) looked understandably distant from the task, 2,700 miles away, of laying track with a 105-foot rise in grade for each mile up into the mountains. But to Huntington, the man in Washington, the slaughter of the war made a kind of background music. In the first month of summer 1864, a second Railroad Act emerged from committee. During early June, as Huntington marked up the draft of the bill, the Union lost twelve thousand men at the Battle of Cold Harbor, Virginia, one hundred miles from Washington. In late June, with Huntington's notes appended, Congress passed the Railroad Act of 1864; President Lincoln signed it on July 2.

The ink was drying when the Union began its long siege of Petersburg, south of the Confederate capital of Richmond. The siege would last ten months and cost the Confederacy twenty-eight thousand men. It is not clear how much the rising lake of blood meant to Huntington and the associates. It is entirely clear they wanted their railroad to go on the ground.

The Railroad Act of 1864 doubled the payout in bonds for Stanford's company. The valleys were enriched to $24,000 per mile, the foothills to $48,000, and the high mountains to $96,000. In an additional part, the federal government was now subordinated as the debtor on the bonds, giving up the first mortgage, which meant the Central Pacific could borrow money on them easily, important within capital markets in London. This simple change, finagled by Huntington in a room rank with cigars, hugely increased the flow of capital to the building and grading sites.

With money streaming in, Stanford stepped off the uneasy boat of politics. When his two-year term as governor ended, he declined to run again, and he was out of his office in the capitol by early 1864. Although the Central Pacific would turn into the company that ran California, Stanford told everyone that he was no longer a politician, but a businessman. He liked it, however, that people still called him Governor Stanford.

———

Railroads were thirty years old in the eastern states, and foundries had been developed to build them, but west of the Mississippi no metal works, no rails, and certainly no locomotives could be found. From New York, Huntington shipped the hardware. In his first purchases he bought sixty miles of iron rails, plus the necessary spikes and chairs. A chair was a six-by-nine-inch iron plate, bolted to the wood crosstie, on which the iron rail could sit without slipping; spikes were the fat seven-inch nails that held the rail to the tie. From McKay & Aldus Iron Works in Boston, Huntington bought the first rolling stock: locomotives, passenger and baggage cars, flat cars and boxcars. He bought "frogs," X-shaped iron plates the size of a table that guided a train from one track to another. He bought turntables, iron disks as big as a train car that wheeled it around 180 degrees so a locomotive might go the other way. Seat springs came from Delaware, engine oil from Pennsylvania, brakes from Pittsburgh, telegraph wire from Boston, and plate glass from New York City. A glazing company in Manhattan got the contract to make the embossed signs, in silver leaf, for "Ladies" and "Gentlemen."[5]

Everything went by ship around the Horn. People traveling to California from the east might cross the isthmus at Panama, but hardware in multi-ton loads had to go from New York south to the bottom of South America and back up west and north to San Francisco, a distance of eighteen thousand miles and three months.

Construction gear came from the east, raw materials from the west. Stanford in his office in Sacramento kept up the delivery of timber for rail ties and trestles. Timber went into the furnaces that drove the locomotives, it went into the snow sheds that covered the tracks in the blizzard-prone Sierras. (Thirty-seven miles of roof were built to keep snowdrifts off the rail.) And California had rags. A used clothing dealer in Sacramento, Charles Harley, got a contract for "wiping rags," and in one month he sent 1,584 of them to rail depots.

Theodore Judah's survey had picked out places where tunnels were meant to go through rock, the longest being a 1,660-foot-long hole through a mountain near the peak of the Sierras, the Summit Tunnel. In 1866, crews with hand tools and black gunpowder chipped at the mountain, advancing at a rate of six inches a day. That April a new explosive arrived, nitroglycerine, or "Nobel's Patent Blasting Oil." Devised by a Swede of gentle temperament named Alfred Nobel, nitroglycerine possessed much more destructive power than the powder Charles Crocker's crews had been using. The volatile gelatin might speed up the tunnel at the summit, but the trouble with the explosive goo was that it tended to blow up in transit. After half of a wharf in San Francisco disappeared as one shipload jostled its mooring and exploded, Crocker hired an English chemist named James Howden to make nitroglycerine at the construction site in the mountains, avoiding the need to ship the material. It also escaped the necessity of reimbursing Mr. Nobel for his patent, which Stanford and Crocker thought cost too much. With nitroglycerine, crews blasted a twelve-foot hole in the mountain at a rate of three feet a day, faster by five-fold than the initial method. The death rate also multiplied. The company ordered fresh caskets for the increased numbers of men killed. In November 1867 the Summit Tunnel, the most arduous half mile of the 1,800-mile route, was finished,

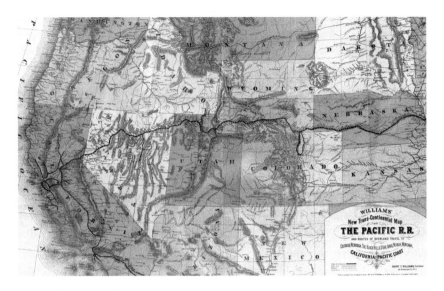

The route of the transcontinental railroad, in a map from 1877. The Central Pacific portion reached from western California, east over the Sierras, nearly to Salt Lake City, Utah.

The eastern portal of Summit Tunnel, a 1,660-foot-long aperture at the peak of the mountains just west of Truckee, California just as Helios, the photographer, ended his excursion in Yosemite Valley. The tunnel had taken a year to cut.

――――

For six years an army of men clamored around the roadbed, inching the track forward, but no list of their names survives. There is not even a dependable estimate of their numbers. Were there fifteen thousand? Twenty-five thousand? The men (and perhaps a thousand women) came from Guangdong province, China. They built 742 miles of track over the Sierras, and after three or five years, most went back to Asia. The Central Pacific kept memos when the Chinese crews went on strike, yet notes about who was maimed by dynamite or crushed by a loose car were tossed or never existed.[6]

In his first speech as governor, in January 1862, Stanford mentioned the lowly decadence of the Chinese. "An inferior race," he said at his inauguration, on the steps of the capitol building in Sacramento, in the basso voice that pleased people. "China is sending the dregs of its society to California." By this time, one in six Californians had emigrated from southern China. By this time many whites thought that their state was too full of colored obstacles to their moneymaking—Indians, Mexicans, Negroes, and especially Chinese. Stanford promised voters he would stop the Asian flood and enlarge the stream of white Americans immigrating from the East—the "superior race," as he put it.[7] Follow-through came quickly. Three months into office, Governor Stanford signed House bill 201, which laid a head tax on Chinese residents. (The state's supreme court later threw out the law.)*

Migrants from Guangdong, in southeast China, came to California in debt. Chinese brokers in San Francisco or in Hong Kong bought passage and loaned the cost to immigrants, who stayed under the broker's thumb until the money was repaid; meanwhile the lender hired out his debtors to anyone. Immigrants sent money home—the Cantonese called it "sojourn work."

Charles Crocker, the dry goods man, resigned from the Central Pacific board to form Charles Crocker & Co., a contractor with

―――――――――

* Helios looked on Chinese immigration as a photography subject—nonwhites were California's exotics, whose pictures might sell like landscapes. He photographed the temples, or joss houses, where ancestors and deities shared an altar, and he photographed people—Chinese miners, priests, and performers.

Muybridge, *The "Heathen Chinee" Prospecting*, ca. 1868. Muybridge looked for subjects among Chinese people, marketable because they were exotic and "heathen" in the eyes of the white photograph-buying mainstream.

a monopoly on the train's construction. He claimed to have been the nonracist who broke ranks to hire Chinese after Irish-born workers asked for more money. The Central Pacific put down track beginning in October 1863, and the first Chinese crews went on the line in early 1864. "We increased them very rapidly, and in six months we averaged 3000," Crocker said, remembering the time. By June, the company had trains running on thirty-one miles of track, from Sacramento to the town of Newcastle, as it kept building east. At the peak, in 1866, some 14,500 Cantonese ("Chinamen") lived next to the tracks, working six-day weeks to shovel and cart, blast and hammer, spike and straighten, for thirty-one dollars a month.[8] The *Alta California* newspaper said the Chinese crews looked to be "in these dreary solitudes, the presiding genius."[9]

In January 1865 Crocker advertised in the *Sacramento Union* for more linemen—"Wanted, 5,000 men for permanent work." Labor companies, run from San Francisco by Chinese bosses, sent workers in teams, twenty-five to thirty men, each with a leader. Crocker gave each crew a white overseer. A handful of payroll sheets in the Central Pacific files sketch the story. Payroll 288 for September 1866 lists about fifty crews, but not individual linemen, using the name of a single headman for each group. That month, Ah Sing's company was the biggest with thirty-four men, followed by Ah Fong's (twenty-eight) and Ah Wing's (twenty-six). Crocker's supervisors were mostly Irishmen, who paid the headman a lump sum in gold coin for the number of days a company worked. White workers like carpenters, cooks, and woodchoppers earned $1.60 a day, Chinese laborers a dollar. Deductions thinned the wage. Payrolls show penalties for "fighting the foreman" (fifty dollars deducted from a crew) and for each lost (two dollars) or broken (one

Chinese linemen traveling on wood cars through a sixty-three-foot-deep crease in the Sierra rock known as Bloomer Cut

dollar) hammer, shovel, or pickax. There were makeshift jails—notes on "detention" appear many times.[10]

When the crews shifted from Irish to Chinese, Governor Stanford changed his melody about the "inferiors." As company president he wrote the White House to praise the linemen—"As a class they are quiet, peaceable, patient, industrious and economical [and] as efficient as white laborers." Chinese workers were "more prudent and economical" than whites whom the railroad employed. Happily, they were also "contented with less wages."[11]

Throughout the 1860s anyone who rode along the Central Pacific line would rattle past a string of tent villages and look out on the dwellings of many thousands of linemen. Under each tented or ramshackle wooden roof, a dozen or two men lived together, with every crew employing a cook to feed them. An entire workers' village of five hundred would have drinking sheds and a gambling hall—sometimes a theater for music and comedy, sometimes a brothel. There were no women on the roadbed gangs, but in their sex work, women also helped build the train.

An item appeared in the *Sacramento Reporter* as construction was ending. "The accumulated bones of perhaps 1200 Chinamen came in by the eastern train from along the line of the Central Pacific," the paper said. "Nearly all of them are the remains of employees of the company, who were engaged in building the road." The paper published no figures for injury or death, nothing but this observation, merely stating that the bodies were going back to Guangdong.[12]

———

Stations opened on the finished track as the crews built out, and the train spewed money. In 1864, 49,375 passengers and 13,902 tons of freight went by rail, with a profit margin for the associates approaching 50 percent.[13] In Sacramento, Stanford and Mark Hopkins, the company accountant, perhaps with some astonishment, counted the income. Revenue as well as work on the train swelled just as Stanford's two-year term as governor was ending.

The associates set up an outfit to enlarge the money flow—the Contract and Finance Company, which appears on paper in 1867. By this time, 150 miles of track had gone down, but the majority, 550 miles (and the vault of subsidies they held), remained to be laid. In November, the associates awarded all contracts for construction to the new company, which they owned. The Contract and Finance Company named its prices for work and materials, while subcontracting construction at a fraction of the sum. Government money accruing to the Stanford train at the front end exceeded by five or six times what the train actually cost to put on the ground. The construction deal looks to have been a classic two-sets-of-books accounting scheme, and the overbilling appears to be the first well of Stanford's fortune—I say *appears* because the company's rigging of costs, hidden at the time, can barely be deciphered a century and a half later. The usual figure cited is $47 million—the bonds taken from Washington and pocketed by the associates. (The Union Pacific used a similar shell company, the Crédit Mobilier, to harvest its own subsidies.) Collis Huntington and Charles Crocker later told Congress in hearings that their books, fifteen volumes of ledgers, had been destroyed, and both claimed ignorance about who might have burned them. The four associates emerged as the richest men in the West, and Leland Stanford became first among equals.[14]

Stanford assembled a monopoly on train tracks throughout the rest of California. Since the start of the Central Pacific, many short train lines had grown up around the state. The Yuba Railroad had twenty-five miles of rail running north from Sacramento, the California and Oregon line was building from San Francisco toward Oregon Territory, and the San Francisco and Oakland Railroad went around San Francisco Bay. Stanford picked them up, one by one. Four others—the San Francisco and Alameda line, the Sacramento Valley Railroad, the California Central line, and the San Francisco and San Jose Railroad—had combined track running three hundred miles. All fell under Stanford's control, typically without a transfer of capital. The associates used a promise of stock, on the one hand, and threats, on the other.

The most important section of rail was a line from San Francisco to Sacramento, the mid-state hub of the Central Pacific, in the plains. Without it, the biggest revenue would escape, and the "transcontinental" label itself would be a fiction. The Western Pacific Railroad controlled the 121-mile route, and in 1867, Stanford made that company an offer it could not refuse. Give us control, or we will build track parallel to yours. The smaller company acquiesced, and Stanford's company ingested it, promising stock for its owners, only some of which materialized.[15]

If you take the long view, the Central Pacific does not look uniquely voracious but appears to be part of a trend. In the five years between 1868 and 1873, around America, more than twenty-eight thousand miles of track were laid, according to *Poor's Manual of Railroads*, nine times the width of the continent, amounting to an orgy of railroad building after the Civil War. For every short line Stanford added to the company, revenues went up, until the Central Pacific counted 293,880 passengers and 276,324 tons of freight traveling its tracks in 1869, quadrupling its income in five years.[16]

Despite rivers of money that washed over the associates, relations between the men cracked. Charles Crocker, the contractor among the four, described Stanford as lazy. In a letter to a friend, Crocker complained, "As to work, Stanford absolutely succeeds in doing nothing, as near a man can. He spends an hour or two per day at the office if we send for him." It was spring 1869. Crocker wanted Stanford to go to Utah to help cut deals for the end of the train line, near Salt Lake City, but Stanford had resisted. "If it was Washington, N.Y., London or Paris," Crocker wrote, "all would be right, he would go immediately and stay indefinitely."

Notwithstanding his personal flood of cash, Stanford was sullen. Under pressure, he went to Utah in January 1869 to meet with Mormon politicians in Salt Lake City in an attempt to arrange better terms. By this time Stanford had done a thousand deals, and, with Huntington in the lead, made a thousand payoffs. So much money had passed through his hands that gold in the palm no longer served to comfort. From his hotel room Stanford wrote his friend and partner Mark Hopkins. "I have no pleasure in the thought of the Railroad," Stanford said. "It is mortification. I tell you Hopkins the thought makes me feel like a dog."

———

In early 1868 Helios reappeared in San Francisco—he took his Yosemite negatives and went to work printing and editing the photographs. Helios had not seen the newspapers for months, and they were full of stories about Stanford, his train, and the Chinese who crossed the mountains. The way the newspapers treated the ex-governor, as though he was a miracle worker, might have surprised Helios. The photographer was at the bottom of his work life, starting a new profession, while Stanford stood at the top. At some point they might have equal footing. Did the photographer let himself imagine it?

He printed a brochure and stacked it around the city: "Helios is prepared to accept commissions to photograph private residences, ranches, mills, views, animals, ships, etc., anywhere in the city, or any portion of the Pacific coast." Let me photograph anything, he meant—or at any rate, anything but people.

Helios thought some day he might photograph the train, the new landscape machine. To ride the train and look out the window was to be a spectator on the western sprawl. To ride the train was to put the eye in motion in a way that it had never before been—mobile, continuous, smooth. He knew the Central Pacific had a staff photographer, Alfred Hart. He also knew that Hart did not possess a franchise on the trestles and machines, the shocks and speed of the rail, the land it crossed and penetrated. Helios knew that anyone could make them a subject.

In the back room at Silas Selleck's studio, the photographer bent to his printing and touching up.

Chapter 5

THE PHOTOGRAPHER

Helios floated from one assignment to another and one address to the next for five years. He became the cameraman who went anywhere, running from the bottom of Yosemite to the coast of Alaska, five hundred miles this way, five hundred miles that, from the lighthouses on the Pacific coast to the train tracks in Utah. His output grew from a dribble to a gush of thousands of images. Around San Francisco, he could hardly keep sheets on the same bed, changing rooms every six to ten months, his signature never drying on a lease. As an artist, Helios could not stay put with one gallery; he moved from dealer to dealer. He made himself into a commercial machine, working for any client and putting his lens in front of anything. Except people—he disliked photographing people.

He wanted a portable life, and he built one with a darkroom. "The Flying Studio," he called it. It consisted of a four-wheeled cargo wagon, about five by eight feet, framed with walls and covered with a black canvas roof—the covered wagon of the settlers, retooled as a machine to produce images.* The black tent of canvas made a dark closet where the photographer could prepare wet plates and develop them. Inside

---

* One of the limits of wet-plate photography was that you had to develop the negative fast, or lose the image. Your pictures went into the developing bath on site, or they disappeared, which meant that a photographer who worked outdoors like Helios had to have an obsessive bent, so much greater was the labor.

the wagon were a tripod, cameras, lenses, chemicals, glass plates, light screens, miscellany (notebooks, food, a gun?). A single horse pulled the thing around town. A painted sign, THE FLYING STUDIO, appeared on the back, accompanied by the Helios logo—the camera with wings sprouting from its sides and light beams shooting out. The man with the flying, radiant camera rode through San Francisco in his strange wagon, his studio itself rattling for attention, an advertisement for the abnormally skilled location artist you should hire.

Without waiting for commissions, Helios took the Flying Studio and made another series, "San Francisco Views," documenting what one might see of the city if, like him, you were a person who could not stay put. He photographed houses, schools, ships, prisons, gardens, banks, military forts, hotels, stores, orphanages, and the water. He photographed the rich sections on Rincon Hill, squalor on Russian Hill, the water view streets on Telegraph Hill. The new series numbered about four hundred images, many of them in stereo prints, easy to sell in bookstores, gift shops, and at Selleck's. He printed "Helios" on the back, added the winged camera, and copyrighted them.

At one time, after years of failures in business, he might have felt like a mediocrity. Now he made a living, and good money. Who said life as an artist was impossible?

The Flying Studio wagon, the photographer's portable darkroom, parked on Clay Street in San Francisco, 1869

San Francisco, twenty years old, population almost 150,000, was the tenth-largest city in the country. In 1868 Helios took the Flying Studio up Rincon Hill, at the southern edge of town, to make a panorama of the city. A panorama—a cityscape in multiple images, what in filmmaking became the "pan"—swept the camera from left to right. Other photographers had made panoramas of San Francisco; the hilltops made them practical. This one looked different. Where other panorama artists raced against time, shooting as quickly as possible, Helios took a day, his camera lingering through an elapsing afternoon, the shadows creeping, turning out a twisted, impossible, simultaneous view of many hours. He planted the tripod, pointed the stereo camera north, and took seven images, left to right, 180 degrees of the streets and hills and waterfront. (His later panoramas would run all the way round, 360 degrees.) The subject was not only space, but once again, time. A panorama made a piece of time-lapse photography, the eyes slowly panning over the scene.*

Looking for a fresh market, Helios made his panorama to suit a tabletop device that itself showed the passage of time, the Alexander Beckers Viewer. The machine, made in New York, occupied an eighteen-by-twenty-four-inch cabinet, plopped on a table, and held between thirty and fifty stereo cards. The viewer peered into it through a pair of eyepieces and turned a knob to flip between views. The Beckers Viewer gave the impression of panning, the smooth movement of the eye through space, like a railroad through landscape.[1]

Wherever he photographed, Helios seemed to aim for time. He went to San Quentin State Prison, twenty miles north of the city by ferry, where a thousand prisoners sweated for no wages in factories, and returned with pictures that made the inmates look like cogs on a wheel. He went to the Napa Valley vineyards, now five or six years old, and photographed workers bottling the harvest. He went to Cliff House, a hotel on a Pacific bluff, and made pictures of the waves and bathers.

Helios became known for time, especially for his speed to the job

---

* In Paris during the 1970s, Roland Barthes thought he heard the wind of time passing in and throughout the camera, which he called "a clock for seeing." Barthes called the mechanical clicks and snaps, the "metallic shifting of the plates" associated with the making of photographs, "the noise of Time, which is not sad." The sounds of the apparatus, for that matter, are voluptuous, because they "break through the mortiferous layer of the Pose."

Muybridge photographed the streets of San Francisco . . .

. . . after the earthquake of October 21, 1868.

and fast turnaround. Just before 8:00 a.m. on October 21, 1868, the city shook with an earthquake. This was a time before seismometers recorded things, but the papers called the quake the worst the city had experienced—"it continued nearly one minute, being the longest ever known," said one paper. "Men, women, and children rushed into the streets—some in a state of semi-nudity—and all in the wildest state of excitement." The temblor destroyed City Hall and wrecked and tilted dozens of wooden storefronts and brick warehouses. By midday Helios was out with the Flying Studio to photograph the broken buildings and cracked streets. No doubt the earthquake was an event Californians and people in the eastern states would pay to see, but there's an added detail. Is an earthquake not also a signature of some kind, a marker of time? A cracked building captures in one image the three dimensions of space—and the fourth, time. Within a week Helios had printed an earthquake series and had his stereographs of the broken and devolved city in stores around town.[2]

———

Helios printed the Yosemite negatives and from Selleck's gallery offered 260 of the pictures for sale. You notice, if you browse them, that when he gave his pictures titles the photographer used native place names. The stringlike waterfalls and naked rock shelves of Yosemite, with their idiosyncratic shapes and sprays, had acquired English names, but Helios preferred the Indian labels. When most people visited Yosemite they saw Bridal Veil Fall, a 940-foot waterfall that emerged from a crease in the mountain, or they encountered Sentinel Rock and Half-Dome. But Helios's stereograph #1173 was the 3,300-foot stone forehead called Tulochahnulah ("the great chief") instead of its English name, the Captain, and his stereo #1147 was Pohono ("spirit of the wind"), not Bridal Veil. Other shots depicted Pompompasus ("leaping frogs") instead of Three Brothers; Poosenachucka ("large acorn cache"), not Cathedral Rocks; Kekootoyem ("water asleep") versus Mirror Lake; and Tocoya ("baby basket shade"), not North Dome. It was as though Helios thought the tribes had not been vanquished, or at least not yet.[3]

America might be a giant but its photographic life remained small. California had did not have any magazines for people with cameras, and taste in art remained in the hands of people back east. Helios wanted press, so he sent some prints to *The Philadelphia Photographer*, the jour-

Muybridge, *Pom-pom-pa-sus* (Leaping Frogs), 1868. Most whites labeled this mountain at Yosemite "Three Brothers," while Muybridge often held to native names.

Muybridge, *Tu-loch-ah-nu-lah* (The Great Chief), 1868

nal that led the field. An endorsement came back when the editor of that tiny but influential journal tipped four of the pictures into the magazine and told readers, " 'Helios' has outdone all competitors. As a photographer, he might vie with the great Wilson of Scotland."[4] The Scottish photographer George W. Wilson was best known for his images of lakes, in which he sometimes aimed the lens into the sun behind a cloud, rather than away from it. Helios also shot with the sun behind a cloud curtain, creating a burning orb whose light fell on water and splashed up a mirror.

From other pictures in the series, it looked as though Helios had also seen images by the English landscape photographer Roger Fenton. Fenton had shown his pictures in London in 1862, when Helios was living there; he treated nature like a painter, composing a scene with trees and hedgerows, shooting down a river to create a vanishing point. Like Fenton, Helios used atmospherics that wrapped cliffs in haze and the device of a single figure in the frame to mark scale.

The photographer looked to the newspapers to push his work. In the past he had been a book publisher, and from his previous dealings

Muybridge, *Yo-wi-ye (Nevada Fall), 600 Feet Fall*, 1868

with the city's journalists he knew some of the writers at the three daily papers, the *San Francisco Bulletin*, the *Call*, and the *Alta California*. Helios apparently took a folio of his Yosemite prints from newspaper office to newspaper office, because the city's press ran similar items during the same week. On February 12, the *Bulletin* said, "The plunging movement and half vapory look of cataracts leaping 1000 or 1500 feet at a bound, are wonderfully realized." The *Call*, on February 17: "The views surpass, in artistic excellence, anything that has yet been published in San Francisco."[5] The *Alta California*: "The view of the Yu-wi-hah or Nevada Fall is a fine piece of instantaneous photographing. It seems as though the artist had arrested the descending sheet of water until its mottled and foamy surface had paid tribute to his genius."

Instantaneous photographing.

In 1868, "instantaneous photography" meant the avant-garde of the profession. It involved just a few dozen people who made attempts to arrest motion: these photographers of the instant tried to freeze a sneeze in a split second, or a crashing wave. They often failed because exposure times ran too long, resulting in image blur. The earliest photographs of city streets showed empty avenues in the middle of the day because slow-to-react emulsions could not register people in motion. Yet Helios had grabbed a frame of the waterfall, like stopping a running man. It was not twenty-four pictures in a second, his later threshold, but it was a gesture. Was this the beginning of Helios's obsession with speed, with capturing time?

A writer passing through San Francisco, Helen Hunt Jackson, saw the Yosemite photos, and in her book *Bits of Travel at Home*, she made a recommendation to tourists. "Go and see Mr. Muybridge's photographs. . . . I am not sure, after all, that there is anything so good to do as to spend a forenoon in Mr. Muybridge's little upper chamber, looking over his marvelous pictures."[6] She declined to call him by his stage name.

Helios finished the assignment for John Hittell, the publisher who had hired him to illustrate a guidebook, and Hittell had a batch of the photographs pasted into copies of *Yosemite: Its Wonders and Its Beauties*. The book fueled the Romantic aura of the American West. Helios's America was noble and savage, with racks of dead trees strewn in the rivers and rashes of waterfalls. The rawness of the pictures made them sell. America was ingesting the new machines—awful beasts like the locomotive, telegraph systems with their drapery of wires, production lines at factories, and the camera itself. Helios's pictures provided an antidote to this alien clatter—his Yosemite was a Xanadu with no intruders, no human presence at all. The stereographs sold and sold. From California to New York to Europe, people bought them up, and the pictures won prizes at shows in Paris and Vienna, cities where nature lived in domestic chains. The landscapes pulled him into his life in photography, and the wager he had made to throw away business and become Helios, the artist, paid and paid, like a criminal gamble.

———

He looked for more wilderness to shoot, a follow-up to Yosemite, and found it in the growing American empire. The United States grew by war, but also by cash purchase; in 1867 Secretary of State William Seward made a deal with the Russian Empire to buy Alaska. For $7.3 million, or two cents an acre, Alaska added 663,000 square miles to the swollen column of the national mass, which released a flood of derision in the papers. While the absorption of Sioux land might promise valleys and contented farmland soon peopled with voters, and while the taking of mountains from Mexico suggested a fountain of minerals from mines, the newspapers called frigid Alaska "Seward's folly," an ice-hard nothing "not worth taking as a gift," in the words of Horace Greeley of the *New York Tribune*. The executive branch in Washington, D.C., saw a public relations problem, and to answer it, the White House assigned the case to an army man named Henry Halleck. General Henry Halleck was a former Civil War soldier and old rival of Ulysses Grant who had been sent to the West and named Military Director of the Pacific, where he was now tasked with responding to the mockery that met the new territory. Halleck searched for a photographer who could make Alaska appear worth the price, or at least interesting, settled on Helios, and gave him the assignment.

On July 29, 1868, two weeks after Congress approved the Alaska deal, Halleck and Helios left San Francisco on the steamer *Pacific*.[7] They stopped for provisions in British Columbia, one hundred miles north of Seattle, then steamed six hundred miles farther north to the Queen Charlotte Islands. The lower coast of Alaska was home to perhaps ten thousand Tlingit people, Native Americans who had lived there for centuries, plus a few thousand Russian settlers of recent

Muybridge, *Fort Tongass, Alaska*, 1868

arrival. Finding his subjects by alternating between the two, almost by accident Helios produced, with his camera, some of the first ethnography in North America.

On the islands (which the Tlingit called Xaadala Gwayee), he photographed some Tlingit as well as a Russian fishing village. The *Pacific* weighed anchor and sailed another eight hundred miles north (the distances were undeniably vast) to Tongass Island, off the southern Alaska panhandle, where Helios photographed the new outpost of the U.S. Army, Fort Tongass. General Halleck wanted him to get pictures of military sites, so the pair sailed fifty miles to the old Russian outpost of Fort Stikine, renamed Fort Wrangell by the Americans.

Pulling in his subjects, Helios photographed the fishermen's harbors, wintry floes with barely a building on them, and unpeopled nature. He shot Russian Orthodox clergymen waiting their turn to go back to Vladivostok, and he photographed the Tlingit.

The Tlingit did not welcome what they saw as the new white bosses arriving from California, any more than Indians to the south had welcomed gold-diggers onto the Sacramento River. It had not been many years since Tlingit warriors wearing animal-headed helmets destroyed the Russian settlement at the town of Sitka, killing four hundred settlers and kidnapping the rest. But the Russians had reconquered Sitka and "pacified" the natives before selling their land to America.

In the Tlingit, Helios found another commercial niche. The market for pictures of Indians was a new one, but its genre traits could already be seen. Helios photographed near-naked women and men draped head to toe in caribou hides, and he included totem poles in the background. He photographed the aborigines not in close-up or as individuals, but full figure and in groups, ethnic strangers presenting themselves to the camera with eye contact, available to curious inspection.

Three months later Helios was back in San Francisco, promoting his pictures. He sent around to the papers a letter from Henry Halleck in which the general praised the Alaska photographs, and he printed up a stack of new stereo views that showed the Indians of Alaska, America's newest and most colorful subjects.

And to this you have to add mention of his clouds. Helios developed a style marker in his treatment of the sky. If he had scant love for people and a strong affinity for both land and city, on the evidence of his early pictures he loved the sky, especially its clouds and moon. He began printing into many photographs an extra canopy of clouds. The writer Helen Hunt Jackson said in the *New York Independent* that Helios had a thing for clouds. "The skies are always most exquisitely rendered," Jackson said. "His cloud photographs alone fill a volume; and many of them remind one vividly of Turner's studies of skies."[8]

The technical limitations of wet-plate photography, the universal negatives of the day, meant that most landscapes from this period have washed-out skies. Skies look like white bedsheets in photographs because blue light, the most intense in the spectrum, possesses the shortest wavelength; it blasts the sensitive silver halide and causes overexposure. For Helios, to acquiesce to a blank sky was like leaving one-third of his canvas untouched, and so he added clouds above the horizon in his landscapes, sometimes also a moon. He made dozens of pictures of cloudbanks and printed them in. He photographed the sun behind clouds, a white orb, passing off the result as moonlight.

The problem of the white sky led Helios to design an invention he called the "Sky Shade."[9] In 1869, he patented a device that blocked some of the intense blue light, keeping it off the negative to avoid wash-out. The May 1869 issue of the *Philadelphia Photographer* described the Sky Shade, which could be attached to the front of a camera. It worked like a miniature guillotine. During a three-second exposure, the lens

Muybridge, *Cemetery with cloud effect*, 1875

. . . and *Cemetery without cloud effect*, 1875

Muybridge, *Moonlight Effect on Bay*, 1868

Muybridge, *A Study of Clouds*, 1868

would be opened, and on a trigger a wooden shutter or curtain fell half-way over the aperture, dropping to the horizon line and screening the sky above to allow the landscape below a longer exposure. The Sky Shade was yet another piece of time-lapse tampering with the camera.

He loved his clouds and his moon.* While most photographers aimed their lens at well-dressed sitters, Helios turned his camera at the sky, which bewitched him.

———

The Civil War had ended; Abraham Lincoln was dead. The national disaster had thrown blood across the eastern states, and Reconstruction still commanded the attention of everyone from Boston to New Orleans. But in California the war and its aftermath seemed far away. Few had seen the decimation, and most felt only vicarious grief, through families affected back east. The war mattered not terribly much to new artists like Helios. It mattered to Leland Stanford mainly as the business climate that had launched his fortune.

The West was soon to be linked to the East, and the finish of the transcontinental line looked within reach. In spring 1869, an avalanche of news stories fell around the train, and Helios thought to catch some of the rush by photographing the great machine. He paid his fare, got on one of Stanford's Central Pacific cars, and took the train from San Francisco, up the Sierras, out to the last hundred miles of the route, in Utah, near the meeting point with the track from the east. His Central Pacific series would be another stack of plates, another speculation to make money from stereo cards, the picture medium for armchair travelers. And it was the last group of pictures he would make as the man with a single name, Helios.

In April 1869, Leland Stanford was in Utah for the last months of construction. As Helios went up and down the line, he and the rail president might have passed each other, but they didn't meet.

The final miles were still under the grading rakes of the Chinese linemen near Ogden, Utah. Helios crept along the route, got out of the train to shoot, crept along some more. He photographed the boxcars penetrating the valleys in distant plains in a way that made them

———

* The many moonlight settings, all of them shot during the day and under-printed, anticipate what in the movies would become "day for night," the use of afternoon light and a darkened print to simulate nighttime in a scene.

Muybridge, *Long Ravine Trestle and Bridge—113 Feet High, 878 Feet Long—Looking East,* 1869

look like worms on a table. He photographed the bridges over ravines, making their new, latticed wood beautiful, and at the same time rickety and temporary. He photographed the tunnels and cuts, the trestles and snow sheds, the summits, buttes, and lakes. And when it came time to print, he inserted clouds, and sometimes moonlight and fog, on the horizon.

The Central Pacific had its own photographer, Alfred Hart, who for six years had been documenting the construction of the beast over the mountains. Helios was a freelancer, but Stanford and the associates did not mind more publicity. They did not mind that another photographer spread more images of their organizational genius.[10]

Was it coincidence that Helios also photographed Indians? As promised by Stanford, bloody standoffs with the "untutored native" had erupted along the train line, lately with the Shoshone. In the Bear River Massacre of 1863, the U.S. Army had killed three hundred Shoshone, and in the Snake War of the last four years several hundred more. By the time the train crept across their land in Utah, the evicted Shoshone were starving and stealing food from Mormon settlements. At Corinne, Utah, Helios photographed the destitute tribe, making their unhappiness look interesting, the same thing he had done with the Tlingit in Alaska. For one photo he persuaded, or more likely paid, a group of Shoshone to stand together and look at the camera. In that picture, a

Muybridge, San Jose, California, train depot with the shadow of the photographer, ca. 1869

Muybridge, *Buffalo Skulls Beside Central Pacific Track*, ca. 1869. The shooting of buffalo herds from moving trains became a pastime of male travelers on the transcontinental line.

Muybridge, *Shoshone Indians at Corinne, Utah*, 1869

man trains his bow and arrow on the lens, a disdainful witness to the coming of Stanford's train.

———

Helios had outgrown his friend Silas Selleck's gallery—his business was too big. For a time he moved his sales to the showroom of an optician named Ewing, who sold zoetropes and stereo viewers in his store at 138 Montgomery, then he sold through the gallery of an importer of prints and photographs called Adrien Gensoul. In April 1869, Helios moved up to the top of the market, taking his business to the best art dealers in the city.

Charles and Arthur Nahl, who operated a gallery at 121 Montgomery, were the most glamorous of art retailers.[11] The "Nahl brothers," as everyone called them, both made art and sold it—oil paintings, photographs, and oddities like porcelain printed with photos. They were flamboyant, athletic, and not least, European. Charles Nahl, age fifty, and his stepbrother Arthur, thirty-five, had been born in Kassel, Germany, learned to paint and began work in Paris, and had moved together to California during the Gold Rush. It was one of their eccentricities that the Nahls, in addition to being painters and art dealers, were also gymnasts, and that the house they shared at 611 Clay Street was one of the city's hangouts for athletes. The brothers wrote and illustrated a training manual, *Instructions in Gymnastics*, and founded the Olympic Club, whose athletes could preen with each other and compete.

The Nahl brothers favored melodrama and exaggeration in their own art. When they made photographs, they loaded them down with ink and paint, both to add color and to turn them into framable decor for living rooms. When they painted—Charles Nahl did the heads, Arthur the bodies—they invented action scenes and mild erotica. In a "Western" scene, an Indian brave poses with his busty, half-naked squaw, the couple appearing as a pair of noble, but sexual savages. The Nahls' paintings were beautifully finished, heavily varnished, hyper-realist, and sentimental.

When Helios walked in the door at the Nahl gallery, the brothers were exhibiting their newest, most garish history picture, a painting of the famous Mexican bandit Joaquín Murieta, nemesis of Anglo settlers. Hanging prominently in the front room, the painting showed Murieta as a manic man on a black horse charging up a stone path, brandish-

Muybridge, ca. 1869

ing a knife and shrieking. It was a picture to feed California's appetite for myth about itself.

For Helios to associate himself with the Nahl brothers, and they with him, sent a message to San Francisco's little art world. It meant that the journeyman photographer was one of five or six artists who deserved the city's attention. The Nahls gave Helios the use of their darkroom. They began to sell his pictures and take a commission, to hang his photographs on display, and to keep behind the desk, in reserve drawers, a little group of Helios images to show their walk-in clients.

When he joined the Nahl brothers, Helios did not know how much his arrangement with these new art dealers, his fourth or fifth, would change things for him. The Nahl brothers' gallery would deflect his life from its pleasantly successful track. He did not know the German brothers would lead him to his most important client, Leland Stanford. He did not know that through the Nahls he would meet a young woman and have an affair with her, with disastrous results. As it happened, the Nahls were close to the rich men who ran the railroad. As it also happened, among the three employees on the gallery's payroll was a young woman. She was a photo retoucher, and she worked in the back room, brushing away scratches and filling in little gaps in photographs. She was eighteen, less than half the age of Helios, and her name was Flora Downs.

Chapter 6

FLORA DOWNS

Men thought she was fascinating and troublesome in equal parts. Flora Downs left traces of her life in the reports of witnesses and in news stories, but little about her survives in her own voice. A pair of letters she wrote, some overheard talk—the rest comes from others. Nevertheless, this wordless woman burned in the imagination of a lot of people who never met her.

In 1869, Flora Downs was eighteen years old, and she lived alone in a boardinghouse at 6 Montgomery Street, near the corner of Market, a busy, big, noisy road she could probably hear from the window.[1] She was married but separated from her husband. She had wed, at age sixteen, a twenty-four-year-old man called Lucius Stone. To marry at sixteen implies a desire to leap off a sinking boat, and then she had leaped again: after eighteen months Flora moved out of her husband's handsome and comfortable house, and she now occupied a single room. The boardinghouse had five other tenants. She told the census enumerator that she was an artist, although in fact she was a retoucher of photographs. A retoucher of photographs is not an artist. She told the census taker that she was twenty-one, although she was younger. She said she had $700 in the bank, a claim that if true made her the richest tenant both within her building and on much of the block. In 1869, $700 was a considerable sum for an artist, even a successful artist, and she was not a successful artist in the way the older man whom she had recently met was successful. Flora Downs worked a block away from the boarding-

Flora Downs, ca. 1868

house in the art gallery belonging to Charles and Arthur Nahl, at 121 Montgomery, and it was there she had met the artist who used to call himself Helios, and who now used the plainer name Edward Muybridge.

A photograph taken two or three years later shows Flora to have been a diminutive woman with an oval face, alabaster skin, and a loft of brown curls. She sometimes wore a floral arrangement on her head and often a billowing dress, but amid the adornment, her mouth appears fixed and her cheeks emotionless, and little feeling seems present in her almost spherical eyes. Flora's eyes withhold feeling. She seems to hold out her decorated appearance as an alternative to it.

A newspaperman said she was "voluptuous, with a sweet face and large, lustrous eyes." Another described "a handsome woman of petite but plump figure with a profusion of beautiful wavy brown hair." She made an impression on male newsmen, and also on women. One woman said Flora was "impulsive, given to fine dress and flirting."[2] That was at the murder trial.

On a workday Flora Downs, fitted out in petticoats and an ankle-length dress, ruffles at the breast and cuffs, with a hat and maybe a parasol, walked from her boardinghouse to the Nahls' gallery, where she went to a room at the back and deposited herself at the retouching table. The Nahl brothers paid Flora to doctor their photographs. In wet-plate photography, a scratch or dent on the collodion negative resulted in a white line or blur. Flora's job was to paint a liquid on the picture base to mask the defect. Sometimes she also did wax work. The

Nahls tinted their pictures with paint, and Flora had learned the skill of using wax to guide the liquid pigment. She manipulated a pool of hot wax into the shape of the figures on a photograph and used it to channel paint into place, making white skies blue and gray faces pink. Muybridge said that he considered Flora's wax work some of the best he had seen. It's also likely that in addition to his attraction to her work, he was attracted to Flora, an eighteen-year-old woman married to another man.

Muybridge testified at the trial that he and Flora had met at the Nahl brothers' gallery. They probably started seeing each other in mid-1869, and they continued seeing each other for two years while she was still married. Muybridge said that he and Flora did not have sex during this time. His words were opaque: "I was acquainted with her in this way, but not intimately."

———

Jane Stanford, wife of Leland, went by "Mrs. Stanford" for most of her life, but her husband and friends called her Jenny. Jenny Stanford was a large and tall woman, and to judge from her photographs, uncomfortable with her body, but her letters show off her mind. When she wrote to friends, even strangers, Jenny became loquacious and opinionated, literate and devout. She could not be chatty or trivial. Although her husband was nearly godless, except for the earthbound god of Mammon, and she knew it, Jenny's letters talk often of her attempt to help God's plan.

After eighteen years of marriage, she was childless. She may have miscarried once, or several times—impossible to say. Few women of her era wrote down their menstrual cycles and lost pregnancies and then left such a diary to posterity. In August 1867, Jenny turned thirty-nine. Her hair was still dark, but she was past the expected age for mothering. And so it probably came as a surprise to her when in October of that year she realized she was pregnant. She had a physician to talk to, a Dr. H. K. Harkness, and Leland Stanford's wife was his most prominent patient. Harkness prescribed bed rest for Jenny's middle-aged pregnancy, but she would not be confined. In the spring she gave a tea party to celebrate her imminent motherhood. She was full and round—the party came sometime during her third trimester—as she welcomed the other rich couples of Sacramento to her house, the grandest in town. Amid canapés and tea and little speeches about being a mother, Jenny Stanford slipped off the front porch and fell into the flowerbed. Her husband froze in his chair in fear, and others jumped to pull her up. Despite the embarrassment, she was all right, as was the baby. In May 1868, Dr. Harkness delivered the Stanfords' healthy boy, their first child.

A few weeks later the new parents celebrated in the way their copious money allowed, hosting an elaborate dinner. They now had a cook and several servants, who produced everything in exaggerated style, using large pieces of silver the Stanfords had bought. Jenny Stanford had a secretary who described a little dinner performance with the baby.

"When the guests were seated the waiter brought in a large silver platter with a cover and placed it in the center of the table," Jenny's assistant, Bertha Berner, remembered. Leland Stanford acknowledged the new dish and dismissed the waiter, then stood up and said that he wanted to introduce a new guest who had arrived late. The cover of the silver dish was lifted, and there was the new baby, Leland Stanford Jr., a tiny thing lying on a bed of flowers. He was carried around the table on the platter and shown to each guest. It was said the baby was smiling and went through his introductions well.[3]

———

Flora Downs was born in March 1851—in Ohio, according to one witness, in Alabama, according to another, or, by a third account, in Kentucky, across the Ohio River from Cincinnati. Her mother had died young, it was said. Her father remarried, and Flora was delivered into the hands of a stepmother, who raised her for a while and then decided not to. Her father and stepmother did not want her, and so at age twelve the motherless Flora went to the care of her mother's sister in Kentucky, Flora Downs Stump, the woman for whom she had been named. This aunt was married to a riverboat captain, Thomas Stump, and the couple had two children of their own. When in short order the family decided to go to California, about 1863, they took young Flora with them.

At a certain point the group came to the town of Marysville, one of the biggest mining settlements in California, in the north Central Valley, where they deposited young Flora with another of her mother's sisters, Sarah Downs Shallcross. Leaving Flora Downs behind with this aunt and her husband, William Shallcross, the Stump couple, who

Muybridge, *View of Mills Seminary (now Mills College), Oakland, California*, 1873

had brought Flora to California, moved five hundred miles north, to Portland, Oregon, where Thomas Stump proceeded to run steamboats on the Columbia River.

Growing up motherless, Flora, now twice abandoned, was uprooted, fourteen years old, and two thousand miles from home. One witness states that a year later Flora Downs moved again, this time to Mills Seminary, a school for girls on the east side of San Francisco Bay, in Oakland. Mills Seminary wanted to be a finishing school for California's comfortable daughters, girls with money and a good family, yet for Flora, who had known only caregivers who passed her along the chain, it cannot be taken for granted that a boarding school supplied much comfort. Flora had no family in California beyond her aunt and uncle, and no one knew Flora well enough to speak of the vortex of her life with anything like empathy, or even curiosity. She was a California artifact, washed up in the West, like thousands of others.

While still in school Flora, age sixteen, met a twenty-four-year-old named Lucius Stone. In frontier terms, Stone, the son of a family of saddle-makers, was something of a merchant prince. His parents owned the biggest saddlery in San Francisco, Stone & Hayden, a maker of reins and bridles, stirrups and saddles. The Stone family was rich—a

census assigns them $110,000 in property, fifty times that of other fami-
lies in their neighborhood. The horse leather business threw off money
in part because Stone & Hayden had a factory at San Quentin Prison
and employed convicts on the production line, 150 felons who did not
receive wages. The company paid the prison forty cents a day for each
man, and the warden pocketed the token salaries. From such dubious
business arrangements Lucius Stone was heir to easy money. Flora
Downs dropped out of school, married him, and moved in with her
husband at his parents' big house.[4]

Flora lived "very unhappily" during the marriage, she said during
the divorce trial, calling her mother-in-law, Sophie Stone, "cruel" and
"tyrannical." Perhaps Sophie Stone, age sixty-two, thought the teenage Flora was digging at the family riches, or perhaps Lucius Stone had
abused her. (Flora made another observation: her husband, in his early
twenties, was "too old.") For various reasons, Flora moved out, apparently with an inducement of money, rented a room in a boardinghouse,
and hoped her divorce would be easy. She was eighteen.

Flora Downs had not had much of a childhood. She had a little
education and a good face, and when she looked for work she found

Muybridge, *Convicts Quitting Work, State Prison, San Quentin*, ca. 1870

a clerk's job at a shop called Kearney's Dollar Store. From there she seems to have walked into the Nahl brothers' gallery, detouring into the world of artists and art. The Nahls hired her to retouch photographs.

Sometime in 1869, Flora looked up from her retouching table and saw Edward Muybridge, the photographer the Nahls had just taken on as a client. He was thirty-nine, with a gray beard and brown and gray hair. He looked at what she was doing, and although he did not like to use his camera with people, he asked her if she would let him photograph her.

———

A jeweler in San Francisco, Schulz & Fischer, had finished engraving the golden spikes.[5] The invoice went to the Central Pacific Railroad—$25.24 to etch 381 letters onto two five-pound souvenir rail spikes made of eighteen-carat gold, alloyed with copper. On one of them, a homily: "May God continue the unity of our country, as this railroad unites the two great oceans of the world." And in a larger font, the name LELAND STANFORD.

Stanford was the man picked from the lot (or he picked himself) to tap a final spike into a final railroad tie. He had an appetite for publicity, and he accepted the role of showman on behalf of his comrades, the other associates. To see his own name jostle down into the wood must have given Stanford a vain pleasure. The golden spike would be pulled up after the ceremony, replaced with the usual iron, and the spike, along with other shiny souvenirs, like a silver shovel, would be sent home with the governor.

It was May 10, 1868, a Monday morning, and cloudy. The completion ceremony had been arranged at Promontory Summit, Utah Territory, a non-place in dry flatland seventy miles northwest of Salt Lake City. The Central Pacific was joining its track with that of its partner and rival, the Union Pacific Railroad, which had built the eastern half of the line. The Union Pacific had been laying rail for seven years, starting in Omaha, Nebraska, and going west, throwing down 1,032 miles of track across the plains to the Rocky Mountains. Meanwhile the Central Pacific had built eastward, laying 742 miles of rail through California, over the Sierras, across Nevada, into Utah, to the edge of the Rockies. The locomotives surfaced on the horizon in the dust and dirt. Stanford arrived with other top hats from California in a two-car train pulled by Central Pacific's locomotive 60, an engine the company called the Jupiter. (The railroads meant something like the destruction of time and space, and the names of planets fit the scale of their ambition.) Thomas Clark Durant, who ran the Union Pacific, came on the track from the east, his car pulled by the Union's locomotive 119. (The Union Pacific people did not name their machines, preferring numbers.) The companies' two locomotives came face to face, cowcatcher to cowcatcher. From photographs it appears that about three hundred people (all men except for three or four women) stood around the locomotives and on top of them, to shout down the future.[6]

The Reverend Dr. Todd, from Massachusetts, offered a prayer. "And now we ask thee that this great work, so auspiciously begun and so magnificently completed, may remain a monument to our faith and good works," he said. "We here consecrate this great highway for the good of thy people. O God, we implore thy blessings upon it and upon those that may direct its operations. Through Jesus, the Redeemed, Amen."

Stanford, holding a hammer made of silver—workers knew it as a

Promontory Summit, Utah, May 10, 1869. Leland Stanford, center stage, a hammer in his right hand and hat in his left, just before he drove the gold spike into the last railroad tie. Holding a hammer in his left hand is Union Pacific Railroad vice president Thomas Durant.

"maul"—stepped onto the rails to give a speech. "I'm here to express the hope that the great importance which you are pleased to attach to our undertaking may be in all respects fully realized," he said. The ponderousness of his style kept his sentences from spilling at a normal pace. Stanford said nothing about the Chinese Americans who had built the rail and nothing about those who would profit from it (himself and his partners), but he said a considerable amount about freight rates. "We will transport coarse, heavy, and cheap products over all distances at living rates to the trade," he told the crowd, half or more of whom had been drinking. "We will render practicable the transportation of freights for a much less rate than is possible under any system which has thus far anywhere been adopted," he added woodenly. And with the hammer he tapped, but did not slam, the spike, which was gold after all.

The spike had been wired to a telegraph line, and the hammer blow sent an instantaneous buzz around the country to depots of the Western Union Company, signaling the crescendo of east–west unity with a telegraphed message. Stanford had composed the three-word telegram to send with the deed—LAST SPIKE DRIVEN. Laconic, like the man himself. A telegraph operator tapped the words over the network, from an outpost in the desert to cities on both coasts.

In California, the celebrations and drinking had already run for two days. The ceremony, because of bad weather, had been postponed from an initial date of Saturday, May 8, to the following Monday. No matter to the waiting masses. Newspapers reported that by Saturday night, carousers drank their way through the streets of Oakland, San Francisco, and Sacramento. In Chicago came a big parade, in New York a hundred-gun salute at City Hall, and in Philadelphia the pealing of bells at Independence Hall.

In Sacramento, a crowd gathered outside the California State Assembly building to hear music and speeches. From the rostrum, one politician compared the finishing of the railroad to the battle at Waterloo in 1815 as well as the invention of the printing press during the fifteenth century. Judge Edwin Crocker, one of the associates, stepped to the podium. Crocker was a heavy man who wore a long white beard with no mustache. In his speech, rather unexpectedly, he praised the Chinese men who had sweated and groaned to lay the track.

"I wish to call to your minds that the early completion of this railroad we have built has been in a great measure due to the poor, despised class of laborers called the Chinese," said Crocker, "and to the fidelity and industry they have shown." It was a surprise tribute, although Crocker did not bother to recall the scene two years before when two thousand Chinese linemen went on strike for better pay and found their camps surrounded by armed militia. (The strike ended in a week, with no pay raise.)

Stanford, speaking to a reporter years later, said his cross-country railroad had changed the country. "It was the commercial opening of practically a new world," he told the *San Francisco Examiner.* "The hardships of the pioneer settlers were ended and a stop was put to the Indian wars." All of this by the railroad. The track, as Stanford saw it, was the suture that laced a nation of parts into a whole. (A different version of the story would be that the train squeezed out the last resistance of the native people and tightened America into a commercial empire.)

Sometime after the completion of the rail line, the California artist Thomas Hill began painting a canvas he called *The Last Spike.* The giant picture, eight feet by twelve, took the Thomas Hart photo as a model—a railroad track in the plain, a locomotive, a mass of people, and at the center, holding a hammer, Leland Stanford, flanked by

Thomas Hill, *The Last Spike*, 1881. Oil on canvas, 96 x 144 inches. Leland Stanford (center) commissioned a painting of his moment of apotheosis involving the train and insisted that no one in the crowd of heroes hold a hammer but him.

executives and politicians in grim hurrah. Stanford commissioned the painting after seeing some of Thomas Hill's landscapes (and buying one of them, a picture of Yosemite Valley). As Hill developed *The Last Spike*—it was the size of a small room, and so it took time—Stanford would pay occasional visits to his studio. He was not interested in a documentary account; the photograph existed, but it need not be consulted. Instead, the picture was to represent Stanford's friends and business partners, many of whom had not been present at the scene, and according to their degree of importance. Stanford told Hill who would appear and where they might be placed—seventy-one people altogether, and they had to be recognizable. Stanford told Hill that only he could hold a hammer in the picture, despite others having also driven several spikes. Hill finished a version of the painting, after which Stanford ordered the artist to behead a number of figures and repaint them with different faces, giving the artist a new list of names. Hill later wrote of these events, "I swallowed my bile at this, for what was I but a slave, needing friends, not enemies." Having taken out some and painted over others, Hill was left with several headless silhouettes. For one of them he substituted a sad-looking figure, a symbolic and plausible Indian, standing feather-dressed and withdrawn. The picture was done, but unfortunately, Hill had placed Stanford's partner, Charles Crocker, too far from the center of the scene. The contractor who had built the train saw the painting and was enraged. Stanford, embarrassed, refused to take delivery of the picture, and the sale was off. He never paid Hill's fee, a year's income. The painting hangs in the California State Railroad Museum, in Sacramento.[7]

Stanford wanted to edit the present for the benefit of the future. Or, maybe he needed to benefit his own present. Photography and its realism could not do that job. It was a paradoxical view for a man who would soon be intent on cameras, but that was just for his horses.

———

Sometime in 1869 Edward Muybridge and Flora Downs took a trip out of San Francisco and into Sonoma County, seventy-five miles north. They boarded the ferry across the bay to Vallejo, and then rode a train up Napa Valley as far as the town of Calistoga. Muybridge would repeat this itinerary in a few years, on the night of the murder. The ostensible reason for this trip, however, was so Muybridge could photograph two strange ecosystems—a petrified forest, on the one hand, and on the other, a place known as the Geysers, where freshets of steam spewed from rocky ground around the Russian River. Another reason was so he and Flora could be alone out of town.

The petrified forest, a scattering of trees that had turned to stone after ten thousand years, stood on a ranch near Calistoga, and the Geysers lay twenty miles away. A tour guide named Clark Foss ran a stagecoach excursion that carried day-trippers out from the train to both sites.[8]

Several of Muybridge's photographs from the junket show Flora in the middle of things, looking with boredom at the natural curiosities. She wears a parachute-like white dress and high hat, a glimpse of city femininity teetering amid the rocks, the steam gathering around her. The couple is not alone: other tourists linger in the dead forest with its stone trunks, in street clothes. Muybridge was used to camping out, but with Flora he had taken the cushioned path, with nicely dressed sightseers and a tour guide.

Back in San Francisco, continuing their courtship, and the seduction, the couple went to an amusement park called Woodward's Gardens. Robert Woodward, a hotel owner and impresario, had turned the grounds of his mansion on Market Street into a pleasure park. (It appears to have been the very first of California's fantasy settings, its first theme

Muybridge photographed Flora Downs (left) at a petrified forest near the town of Calistoga, California.

park, admission price thirty-five cents.) Woodward's Gardens had a zoo with motley animals and a village with human attractions—acrobats from Japan, Hawaiians, Native Americans. A Chinese giant named Chang Woo Gow, eight feet, three inches tall, walked around the grounds wearing silk brocade. There were four museums, a boat for children that churned around a circular moat, and taxidermied animals strewn around the grass.[9] Muybridge and Flora did not go to Woodward's Gardens strictly for entertainment. About this time Muybridge opened a retail stand near the front gate of the amusement park, where he or a counter clerk sold his prints to the streams of tourists.

On a visit Muybridge photographed himself in one of the art galleries, or rather, he photographed his back. In the picture, he is an art lover at the end of the room, facing away from the camera, staring at a painting two feet from his nose.

Perhaps it was on the same visit that he photographed Flora. In several pictures she sits on a lawn, flanked by various taxidermied animals—a stuffed tiger in one picture, a pair of stuffed deer in another—appearing somewhat ridiculous. Flora is turned out in an elaborate dress and decorated hair, yet the expression on her face is blank and

Muybridge (standing), self-portrait, in an art gallery at Woodward's Gardens, ca. 1870

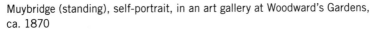

Woodward's Gardens in San Francisco, California's first theme park

An eight-foot-tall man called Chang Woo Gow, billed as "the Chinese giant," worked as a living attraction, walking around the grounds to arouse fascination.

Flora Downs on the lawn of the theme park, surrounded by taxidermied animals, ca. 1870

detached, as though she is accustomed to being looked at and puts up
with it.

———

Flora divorced the saddle-maker Lucius Stone in December 1870.
Probably she recruited Muybridge to help her find a lawyer and make
her case. She was an abused wife, she told the court.

The lovers had a wedding five months later, on May 20, 1871.
"Married—Edward J. Muybridge to Flora E. Downs," said the paper.
Muybridge was not religious, and there is no sign Flora cared about
church, but nevertheless they hired a Baptist preacher, Reverend
H. A. Sawtelle, to marry them. Sawtelle was an old-timer in California terms—ten years in San Francisco—and his Union Square Baptist
Church stood on Post Street, near the corner of Powell. Sawtelle had
been active in the temperance movement and was known for his enthusiastic antidrinking rallies. The church vows for the Muybridge wedding must have been followed by an abstemious reception.[10]

———

The only evidence that Edward Muybridge loved women appears
in his relationship with Flora Downs, whom he desired. In order to
say anything more about his sexuality you have to speculate. The first
American during the 1800s to write down when and how he had sex,
the first to place this information in public view, was possibly Walt
Whitman, who in *Leaves of Grass* describes his desire for skin, and his
lovers. Few if any of Whitman's contemporaries (Muybridge was ten
years younger than the poet) talked about sex in the garrulous way of
the late twentieth and early twenty-first centuries, and those who did,
Whitman included, found themselves ostracized. Edward Muybridge
did not write about his sex life. The mode of behavior in which people
confessed their sexuality to diaries and to willing or paid listeners took
shape after the first years of psychiatry. Because of these period varia-
tions in the history of sex, Muybridge's sexual life looks to be a riddle.

His letters imply that he treated women with diffidence. He wrote
to women carefully, politely; if his desire surfaced, he hid it beneath a
blanket of etiquette. Professional men were expected to use the deco-
rous style, and he did.

And yet, if Muybridge followed the habits of many, if not most, single men, he visited prostitutes. Unmarried people during Muybridge's

Muybridge and his wife, Flora, lived in a townhouse in the South Park neighborhood of San Francisco. This photograph by Muybridge was probably taken from the balcony of their house, which, one assumes, resembled the one across the street.

day had sex often enough, but the sex was policed to take place away from middle-class home life. There is no evidence that he did or did not hire prostitutes, but he was almost forty when he met Flora. The conjecture that Muybridge belonged for much of his adult life to the group of men who avail themselves of sex for hire becomes more plausible when you consider that he lived in a city whose pamphlets and newspapers bristled with items on brothels and commercial sex, and men greatly outnumbered women.

What was Muybridge's sex life before Flora Downs? It is possible to imagine the intent photographer arriving at a hotel or brothel. It is possible to imagine the photographer with an obsessive streak devouring one woman or another for the house fee. It is possible also to imagine him, as a client, not having much to say around sex, a laconic man who silently brings out his appetites, all but speechless.

———

Edward Muybridge did not much care for possessions. He did not mind living like a miner, out of a trunk. He often rented just one or two rooms, which he left after six months or a year for other rooms. After the wedding, he seems to have given in somewhat to comfort. Muybridge and Flora moved into a posh townhouse at the square called South Park. For the bride the new house, with its tiers of rooms and an oval garden that the neighborhood shared out front, was a big improvement on the single room with a washbasin that she had gotten used to at her boardinghouse. It was also, in a way, her return to what she thought she deserved. Flora had lived well during her first marriage, to the saddle-maker with his rich family. To live high again was one of the reasons, perhaps, that Flora had married, at age twenty, the forty-one-year-old Muybridge. He was making good money. He was the most conspicuous photographer in the city, a man with energy and connections to rich clients. Flora had seen this herself at the Nahl brothers' gallery.

The townhouse at South Park turned by degrees from something like a comfortable cushion for Flora Muybridge into her golden cage. Just as they married, Muybridge started traveling. The peripatetic camera man with the flying studio had lobbied the government for more work, perhaps another Alaska project, and a big job had come through, this time from a different agency, the Lighthouse Board. The federal government was building lighthouses along the coast, and photographs had to be sent to Washington to show the results. For six weeks before the wedding, Muybridge left Flora in San Francisco and went along the coast on the steamship *Shubrick*, stopping to photograph lighthouses as far north as Cape Flattery, at the border with Canada, and down south to Point Loma, at San Diego, near the border with Mexico. The whole thing paid well—a per diem, plus expenses, plus a charge for prints. He came home in May 1871 and married Flora. The couple spent June and July together, and then Muybridge was gone a second time, back aboard the *Shubrick*, up and down the coast, for more lighthouses. A period of fresh abandonment marked the beginning of Flora's marriage.[11]

The lighthouse photographs are empty, formal, and alienated. High cliffs fall off to abyss, and the spaces of waterfront look abandoned. Muybridge photographed twenty-three lighthouses, but in many pictures the point of view is unstable and the ocean a glass fog with atmospheric clouds, the waters a tissue of pale light, and the rocks a difficult mass. He seemed to be collecting a chronicle from the world's end, or at least the ends of the West and the continent.

Muybridge was mobile and driven, flinging himself through the world like a hummingbird, alighting on projects and touching ground only to get more supplies. During the first year of his marriage to Flora, he found himself at home with her in San Francisco less than half the time.

A midwife named Susan Smith, who came to work for the couple,

Muybridge, *Lighthouse at Punta de los Reyes, Coast of California*, 1871

Muybridge, *Sea Lion Islet*,
ca. 1872

and who testified at the murder trial, said that soon after Flora married Muybridge, she got pregnant, but the child was stillborn. Susan Smith said Flora became pregnant a second time, and that the second baby was also stillborn. To have a child born dead was not uncommon at this time, but this was before medicine could warn a mother that the child she was carrying was no longer alive. These were Flora's first children, and the mental cost can easily be imagined. Muybridge was traveling—he might have been at home for the births, but chances are good that he was not.

Chapter 7

OCCIDENT

The parties continued on a scale not many had seen in California. A gala to pay tribute to Stanford and the other associates was scheduled for September 28 in a ballroom in Sacramento, where, dressed in ribbon tie and silk vest, his shoes bright and no longer dusted by Utah desert, the ex-governor got up to speak to a dinner for several hundred. "We have grown with you. We have shared with you in all the various vicissitudes of the California experience." Whether Stanford's "California experience" had much in common with the linemen's tents and the exploding cliffs of the Summit tunnel remains unclear, but he nonetheless took pleasure in the adoration that flowed from businessmen and their nodding spouses. He took pleasure in winning the biggest wager yet put down on the roulette wheel of the West, a casino that paid off some bettors while turning out the rest. The work product, all the track plus the monopoly on transport he had put together, was, in his words, "the result of a great American sentiment."

Jenny Stanford and her husband decided to enlarge their home on Eighth and N Streets, already the least modest house in Sacramento. The train had created a new elite in the state, contractors and suppliers and politicians and retailers dependent on the rail, and the couple needed a place to entertain them. Jenny and Leland had builders add a third floor and a bulging new mansard roof, build an addition to the rear, and then raise their house ten feet and slide a basement underneath it. "We like the substantial," Leland had written his mother at

Leland Stanford, ca. 1880

one point, before he got rich. They added dozens of rooms, and, in a series of parties and dinners, won first place in the social columns growing up in the state's newspapers. To readers around California, mention of "Stanford's palace" and the "Prince of Central" became standard morning fare.

The Central Pacific had finished its immediate business. The trains were running, the revenue flowing. Stanford now entered a new stage of life in which he became a showman of money. From this point forward he would dole out (as one paper put it) "wealth and beauty at the shrine of Terpsichore."

The Stanfords' house in Sacramento, after enlargements, photographed by Muybridge in 1872

Muybridge photographed the house on N Street almost empty of people, including the windswept space of the ninety-four-foot-long ballroom.

Typical parties at the big, rebuilt house were themed. A "white" party saw the grounds covered in white sand and the trees hung with white lanterns, with ten rooms covered in a floor of white canvas, and chandeliers and mantelpieces wreathed with pale flowers. Dinner guests were met with a menu in French, a gold basket at each setting filled with roses, and place cards on white satin with a monogram in gold: L.S. Dance cards show that after dinner the guests were put through the quadrille, the polka, the waltz, the gallop, the lancers, a Royal Horse Guard dance, and finally, a Virginia reel.

On top of the comforts and trappings and whiteness and gold, there was one more thing—the automatons. The two hundred guests at this or that reception would have noticed that Stanford was allowing himself an indulgence not available to anyone else. In addition to his love for gold, Stanford had a passion for gadgets and machines. The governor's liking for devices extended to automatons, mechanical puppets that moved about like people, which he distributed around the house. Mechanical birds, hidden in the greenery, chirped when a button was pressed. (The Gilded Age overlapped the Machine Age.) A reporter at one party described the "band of automaton singers in the parlor, wonderfully real in appearance, perfected in concerted vocalization."[1] He was a man with his toys, perhaps, who liked the uncanny way that machines could appear to sing. It was a time before the invention of the phonograph, before recorded music. Stanford's musical puppets answered the desire for music—they played string instruments and danced to crank organs. The Prince of Central showed flesh-and-blood people his automatons—two feet tall, metal, creaking, their jaws working. Stanford liked the way machines could capture something in the living body and play it back. It was not unlike the way a photographer could capture a scene and give it back to you.

———

When he was young, Stanford looked down on horse racing. "A disreputable business," he wrote his brother, "for all its tendencies are evil." Racetracks were places where "gamblers pickpockets bullies and all kinds of low characters assemble." They contained enough human bad news "as to make them hateful."[2] He wrote those opinions when he was twenty and something of a prude. At forty-five, he had forgotten his contempt and started buying horses to race.

He bought three trotters—General Benton, Sontag, and Mohawk Chief— stabling them at the Union Race Track in Sacramento. His first "notable equine purchase," as one observer called it, came in July 1870, when he bought a trotting horse that had raced well, managing a half mile in one minute, twelve and a half seconds. The horse was a six-year-old gelding named Charlie.

"I bought a little horse that turned out to be remarkably fast," Stanford told a newsman, referring to Charlie. "It was in the using of it that I became interested in the study of the horse and its actions."[3]

In middle age, Stanford picked up a fascination with horses that settled inside him like a delirium. Charlie, a brown horse with slight haunches, had meager credentials and no thoroughbred "blood." A horse named Doc had sired him, but nobody knew the name of Doc's dame, the mare that had produced Charlie. Despite his shaky family history, the horse would become famous both as a racer and as a subject of art—a star of the track and of Edward Muybridge's camera.

Foaled in 1861 a few miles from Sacramento, Charlie is said to have run in a wild state until he was three, when his owner, a rancher named Shaw, sold him to a butcher called Lorenz, who broke him before selling the horse to a barber named Fred George, for $95. Charlie had two other owners, a dirt hauler and a chicken dealer, who both used him to pull their wagons, until he caught the eye of a horseman called Sid Eldred, in 1869. It was this man who recognized the racer in the horse (and who happened to know Stanford). Eldred bought Charlie for $300 and hitched him to a sulky, the flimsy, two-wheeled carriage that trotting horses pull in a race. He trained the animal for six months, until July 1, 1870, when Charlie trotted that half a mile at 1:12, a very fast shot around the track. He was ten years old at the time.

Late that month, Stanford bought Charlie, paying $4,000 in gold, plus another horse worth $500. With the change of ownership came a change in name: Stanford renamed the horse Occident. The source seems to be that the Central Pacific Company had just acquired a steamship line, the Occident and Orient Company.[4]

The Union Park racetrack in Sacramento was a mile-long oval on twenty acres with stables to one side. In 1870 the railroad president stopped going to the office so much and started spending days with his horses. He housed Occident and his growing equine collection at Union Park and made the place a second home.

There are two possible explanations for Stanford's late conversion to horse fanatic. The first involves his physician, Dr. Harkness, the man who had delivered the baby boy, Leland Jr. According to one writer, not long after he tapped in the last spike, the Prince of Central suffered some kind of physical breakdown. Seven years of building had exhausted him—the lobbying, money-raising, and enemy-making, the near-bankruptcies and crosscurrents of greed, the need to manage company politics and put a stable face on chaos. Harkness, the physician, advised a long vacation and complete absence from business. So Stanford struck a compromise: as a distraction he would take up horses, a gentleman's sport. This would allow him to spend more time outside.

The "doctor's order" explanation feels like a too-neat formula. Another explanation for Stanford's attachment to horses is more abstract. For thousands of years horses had been the mainstay of human transport, and now the railroad was pushing them aside. After a generation of coexistence with the train lines, horses were becoming objects of nostalgia and decoration. Stanford fell in love with horses because they were the beings, and a way of life, that his train system was destroying. The rail networks that spidered out from the cities, accelerating travel and turning the land into views out the window for passengers, promised the end of the stagecoach and covered wagon. Stanford became a horse aficionado in the way a maker of plastics might become a lover of craft and of antiques. Who better than the president of the railroad to appreciate horses not as work animals, but as leisure and diversion?

And maybe there was a further reason. Back on the East Coast, another railroad family, the Vanderbilts, had devoted themselves to horses. The Vanderbilts were leaders among the very rich; Leland and Jenny had lately become their social equals, and what the Vanderbilts did three thousand miles away in New York mattered more than anyone would say.

At any rate, Stanford made himself into something like a spectator, a viewer. He brought a swivel chair out to the infield of the track and sat, slowly turning, watching jockeys run his horses 360 degrees around the field. The horses were divided between trotters and sprinters; trotters pulled sulkies, sprinters ran with jockeys astride them, and both competed against Stanford's stopwatch. Stanford wanted to know how to make the animals run faster, how to improve their gait. He hired several grooms and a trainer named James Eoff, putting them to work with his animals and consulting with them every afternoon.

Within a year of becoming a horse connoisseur, Stanford got interested in the nature of the animals' gait, one of the old questions of the equestrian world. A horse's legs moved too fast to be observed with any accuracy, and so at the heart of the horse culture stood an enigma: how do the limbs rise and fall during a fast trot? In what order do the hooves hit the ground in a gallop? Does one hoof touch down, or two simultaneously?

One aspect of the trot and gallop, talked through by trainers and jockeys, involved "unsupported transit," a mystery with a scientific-sounding name. This was the presumed ability of a horse to hurl itself forward with all hooves off the ground. Since no one could see it, no one could prove it. Some horse people thought there was a phase in the stride during which an animal lifted up entirely from the earth, pulling up limbs, and, in effect, flying. Others said this was ridiculous, that one hoof had to remain in contact with turf. Stanford believed there was unsupported transit, but from his swivel chair he couldn't see it. Neither could anyone else. Now there was that new thing—"instantaneous photography." Maybe a camera could see it.

———

Judge Edwin Crocker, lawyer for the Central Pacific, limped through the door of the Nahl brothers' gallery, leaning on a crutch. He was the fifth of the railroad "princes," less rich than the others but still flush with stock and payouts and groaning under the weight of his

Judge Edwin Crocker, brother of Charles
and lawyer for the Central Pacific
Railroad, by a San Francisco society
painter, Steven William Shaw, 1873

houses and art collection. He used a crutch because in July 1869 he had
suffered a stroke that paralyzed some of his right side, which caused
him to withdraw from daily work at the train company. Despite his
condition, Crocker still possessed his mind as well as his money, and
now that he had extra time, he wanted to spend it on art.

The debilitated former judge looked a bit like his brother Charles—
they both had wide faces, white hair, and long goatees—but Judge
Crocker was considerably more polished than the crude, beery Charles,
who was known to hike his feet onto tables and eat all of anything put
out on a table. Judge Crocker professed an interest in "old California,"
the pioneer state of just twenty years ago, and he had come to the Nahl
brothers because they painted history scenes. He wanted them to paint
a mythic scene from the gold mines.

Charles and Arthur Nahl made Judge Crocker a big painting, six
by nine feet, called *Sunday Morning in the Mines*, a tableau of a miners'
camp in the Sierras from the rough glory years. The mining camps
were cruel, dirty, violent places, remote little hells where men fought
over gravel sluices that might contain flecks of gold. *Sunday Morning
in the Mines* improves on them. The painting shows a village bathed in
yellow light, with cabins and porches all around. In one corner, three
drunks stagger together, in another two riders race their horses, and in
a third, groggy miners argue and gamble. The scene, glossy and sentimental, is an idyll of rule and misrule, but with its vignettes of dejection
and folly, the picture retains some bite, like a William Hogarth satire
of rural life.[5]

Charles Nahl, *Sunday Morning in the Mines*, 1872. Oil on canvas, 6 x 9 feet

Sunday Morning in the Mines became the best-known picture the Nahl brothers ever made, and it turned Judge Crocker into a regular customer. In two years he would commission six other pictures from the German-born history painters. Crocker returned to the gallery often enough to be recognized limping along Montgomery Street. There's the railroad lawyer again, down from Sacramento and on his way to the showroom.

Edward Muybridge probably met Judge Crocker on one of the art collector's visits to the Nahls, in 1870 or 1871. The photographer would have been hanging around the gallery to follow his sales, and for that matter to see his girlfriend, Flora Downs. There is no direct evidence, but what happened next makes this accidental meeting the likely thing. Like a good nouveau riche, Judge Crocker owned a mansion in Sacramento—his house was one of the most beautiful in that plain city—and outfitted it with an art gallery. In 1871 Judge Crocker hired Muybridge to photograph his house. Muybridge took the train from San Francisco to the capital, did the job, and returned to the coast to make his prints.

Among the Central Pacific associates, Mark Hopkins and Collis Huntington were friends, and the two brothers, Edwin and Charles Crocker, were friends with Stanford, who always put them on his guest lists, which were published in the papers. It seems that Stanford heard of Muybridge's photos of Judge Crocker's place and decided that he too, having doubled the size of his house, had to have a portfolio of his real estate.

And now Stanford and Muybridge meet.

Stanford said years later that he met Muybridge when his wife, Jenny, hired the photographer to document their house. It's likely Judge Crocker introduced Muybridge to the Stanfords during one of the artist's Sacramento trips, because in the spring of 1872 the Stanfords asked him to photograph their place, as he had just photographed the judge's.[6]

In April that year, Muybridge made twenty-three pictures, inside and out, showing off the rooms and the exterior. Inside Muybridge posed Jenny Stanford and her sister, Anna Lathrop, who lived with the family, along with the little boy, Leland Jr. As always with the people in his pictures, they appear wooden, emotionless. He photographed the dining room, the aviary, and the library. He photographed the new grand staircase in wedding-cake stone that rose from the sidewalk to the front door. There is a faintly ridiculous photograph of Jenny Stanford playing billiards. And with this stock at-home-with assignment, the Stanford family acquired a personal photographer.

Jane Stanford aims a shot at the billiards table in her Sacramento house, with her sister, Anna Lathrop, looking on and her son, Leland Jr., in a blur at her elbow, photographed by Muybridge in 1872.

Muybridge had done this kind of work before when he was first getting started in photography, over at his friend Silas Selleck's studio, but he never liked the house-and-home trade. Now he had two supremely rich clients who wanted the same thing. As though to show his distaste, after finishing the job for Judge Crocker, Muybridge submitted an invoice for $700. The railroad lawyer thought this was exorbitant and refused to pay. Rather than fight about the money, Muybridge let it go and never collected his fee. This kind of behavior would be used against him during the murder trial, when witnesses said that his indifference to money could be taken as a sign of insanity.

As for Stanford, in the Central Pacific clique he had the reputation of being the most lavish with his money. Mark Hopkins and Collis Huntington were said to be misers: both lived in plain houses and dressed down, long after they could afford to live high. Stanford rarely questioned an invoice, and when he could, he always bought the most expensive thing available. Unlike Judge Crocker, Stanford paid Muybridge's bill. He might have had more in mind for the photographer.

The two started to spend time together. Stanford was forty-eight, Muybridge forty-one. Both men were "old Californians"—Stanford had come west in 1852, Muybridge three years later. As the railroad was being finished, Muybridge had photographed the Central Pacific, and maybe he shared some of his stereo prints with the former governor. For his part, Stanford liked mechanisms of all kinds, as seen in his fetish for automatons, and he might have taken an interest in the gear of Muybridge's so-called Flying Studio. Their friendship did not make the best sense: Muybridge was unkempt and on edge, a fast-talking man in boots in constant need of a haircut, while Stanford put forward the face of rectitude, grooming, and wordless restraint. But for whatever reason, the two men found a plane on which they could connect.

Stanford and his wife must have liked the photographs Muybridge made, which he put in an album with an embossed cover. The photographer had had enough clients to know how to push for the next assignment. By the way, was Governor Stanford not a lover of horses?

When Stanford looked to photograph his horses, he turned to the artist he knew. Muybridge said that his new client startled him when in 1872 he asked for photographs of Occident "taken while the horse was at full speed." Muybridge said he was "perfectly amazed at the boldness and originality of the proposition" and that he did not think it was possible.

"At that date, the only attempts that had ever been made to photograph objects in motion had been made only in London and Paris," Muybridge wrote, "only by the most conspicuous masters of the art. Occident was then admittedly the fastest trotter in the whole world. I therefore plainly told Mr. Stanford that such a thing had never been heard of—that photography had not yet arrived at such wonderful perfection as would enable it to depict a trotting horse."[7]

Muybridge remembered Stanford's answer. The lethargic and stubborn capitalist said, "I think if you give your attention to the subject, you will be able to do it, and I want you to try."

At this, Muybridge remembered, "I had nothing to do but 'try.'"

———

Later that spring, in May of 1872 at the Union Race Track in Sacramento, Muybridge took photographs of Occident that seemed to stop him in the middle of a fast trot, all his hooves off the ground, but the pictures have not survived. We can speculate that Muybridge destroyed them years later, when he got better results. The only thing left of these first freeze-frame images is talk, on the one hand, and two artworks, on the other.

The *Alta California* newspaper ran the first report, describing a theatrical scene involving bedsheets and a cross-eyed camera.[8]

Stanford wanted Occident photographed pulling a sulky at full

The racetrack at Sacramento where Muybridge began his motion studies of horses and made the first stop-motion pictures of Occident in 1872, before moving the experiments to Palo Alto

trot, some thirty-eight feet per second. Because wet-plate photography required generous light, Muybridge looked to increase the glare on the turf, and he asked for sheets. "All the sheets in the neighborhoods of the stable were procured to make a white ground to reflect the object," said a reporter for the paper. Trouble arose when Occident balked at trotting over the bedclothes strewn around, but Stanford's trainer, James Eoff, somehow persuaded the horse on the second or third try.

At this stage of photography, there were no shutters, no f-stops, no exposure times. Taking a photograph meant removing the cap over the lens for a second or two and then replacing it. "The first experiment of opening and closing the camera on the first day left no result," said the *Alta California*. "The second day, with increased velocity in opening and closing, a shadow was caught. On the third day, Mr. Muybridge, having studied the matter thoroughly, contrived to have two boards slip past each other by touching a spring and in so doing to leave an eighth of an inch opening for the five-hundredth part of a second, as the horse passed, and by an arrangement of double lenses, crossed, secured a negative that shows 'Occident' in full motion—a perfect likeness of the celebrated horse. The space of time was so small that the spokes of the sulky were caught as if they were not in motion."

What Muybridge did was peculiar enough. He used a stereo camera, with two lenses, doubling the light that reached the negative, positioned like a pair of crossed eyes to focus on a center point. He then devised a handmade shutter, mounted in front of the lenses, consisting of two slats of wood pulled back on rubber bands and latched, cocked to slide across one another when Muybridge tripped the latch. These tricks, plus the trick of the sheets, produced the photograph Stanford wanted. Muybridge said that the pictures that resulted were "sufficiently sharp to give a recognizable silhouette portrait of the driver, and some of them exhibited the horse with all four of his feet clearly lifted . . . above the surface of the ground." Still, the result was "shadowy and indistinct"—good enough to satisfy Stanford's curiosity, but not good enough to print and distribute.

There were some other things going on. Ever since these first freeze-frame photos, the story of a bet has attached itself to Stanford and Muybridge. A film historian, Terry Ramsaye, and others have it that Stanford bet another horse owner about the unsupported-transit theory—the amount varies in the story from $10,000 to $25,000—Stanford having taken the position that horses do leave the ground. The bet might have happened, but I doubt it. Stanford had a disdain for gambling, and although he liked his horses to win, he developed the habit of giving away the purse. There's no sign he put down money on his or anyone else's animals. The idea that Muybridge was brought in to settle a bet appeared as a legend around a rumor, and the legend became famous.

Muybridge tried to freeze the horses' movements at the Sacramento track during part of 1872, and he seems to have moved the experiment the following spring to San Francisco, apparently because the pictures weren't good enough. Stanford had started boarding some of his horses on the coast at the Bay District Track, which had just been laid out on Geary Boulevard, near the Presidio. In San Francisco, Muybridge stopped springing his shutter by hand and devised instead a trigger attached to a thread that stretched across the track, so the horses at contact would trip the pictures themselves. He also acquired a young assistant, sixteen or seventeen years old, named Sherman Blake, who remembered some things about these first pictures.

"It was necessary to improvise a temporary dark room out at the Bay District Track, and we took along with us an express wagon, a heavy orange and red cloth tent, and an improvised ruby light containing a lit candle," Blake said years later. "I carried six buckets of water into the dark room, and when the horse sprang the instantaneous shutter, by means of the thread across the track, Muybridge immediately took the plate holder from the camera, went into the dark room, and developed it."[9]

The news reporter who wrote the first story had not been at either the Sacramento or San Francisco track to see Muybridge and his camera. Instead the photographer seems to have brought the pictures to editors' offices and said what he had done, ten months later. A few days after the first report, the *New York Times* picked up the story—"A San Francisco photographer is declared to have obtained a perfect likeness of the horse Occident going at full speed." The *Atlanta Constitution* ran the headline A WONDERFUL PHOTOGRAPHIC FEAT. Next a Paris photography journal ran a story, and ten thousand miles away, a newspaper in New Zealand ran its report. That a man who photographed a horse became a piece of national, and then international, news shows something of the widespread desire for the fleetness of photography, the craving for movement, for speed and acceleration in horses, railroads, emulsions.[10]

The pictures themselves, from 1872 and 1873, of Occident and

In 1873 *The California Wonder Occident, Owned by Gov. L. Stanford* became a popular print by Currier & Ives, the purveyor of mass art for middle-class American living rooms.

Thomas Kirby van Zandt, *Goldsmith Maid Driven by Budd Doble*, 1876

another horse called Abe Edgington, have not survived. Nevertheless, a kind of secondary evidence of their existence remains. The popular printmaker Currier and Ives took an interest in Muybridge and Occident. Currier and Ives had one of their house artists, John Cameron, make a lithograph after one of the Muybridge photos. The color print, entitled *The California Wonder Occident, Owned by Gov. L. Stanford*, depicted the horse trotting left to right in the frame and flying above the ground. It went on sale in 1873.

Stanford, too, wanted art to hang on his walls, but not photographs, and not lithographs. He hired an artist called Thomas Kirby van Zandt, who made a canvas that copied one of the Muybridge photographs. Van Zandt's 1876 painting, *Goldsmith Maid Driven by Budd Doble*, this time showed the horse trotting right to left. The painting had all four hooves of the horse elevated above the track and the spokes of the sulky wheel frozen.[11]

And so we leave Stanford and Muybridge after their meeting and with their first collaboration, the freeze-frame photos of horses trotting, good enough to make but apparently not good enough to keep.

By the time van Zandt made his painting, four years had passed since the initial photographs. Why the delay? Maybe Muybridge never liked the results he had gotten. And maybe there was another reason for the delay. At the later date Muybridge was something of a household name in California. He was known for his pictures, but equally for his personal life. He was known for his revenge killing, a different kind of ecstatic moment.

Part Two

Chapter 8

HARRY LARKYNS

L et me refresh the facts about Harry Larkyns. They claimed he was a good-looking man with sandy hair, although no photographs survive that might prove it. One reporter wrote, "He is tall, sinewy and well built, of fine personal appearance, and graceful in manner and speech." When he arrived in San Francisco for the first time, in fall 1872, Harry Larkyns spread the rumor that he was rich, and many believed him. He said he had schooling, probably true, to judge from his jobs as a writer and translator. He played cricket superbly, which people could see because soon after coming to town he captained a team, and when he didn't play, he refereed. By the testimony of at least some of San Francisco's women, he was said to be genteel, with stories and one-liners. Genteel men stood out, a memorable minority on the grasping frontier. Such characterizations of the man called Harry Larkyns come from newswriters, who enjoyed him, counted him one of theirs, and followed him to the end.

His residence in California did not begin well, however. In March 1873, a reporter went to the city jail to interview Larkyns, who had left San Francisco briefly, returned to town, and been arrested. Behind bars, the *San Francisco Chronicle* reported, "He was dressed in the height of fashion having on a nobby suit of clothes and an English hat with a peacock feather."[1] The prisoner in the peacock hat said he was Scottish but also expatriated from England.

The name "Larkins" is common in Ireland, less so in Scotland, but

"Larkyns" seems to have been an invention. Like Edward Muybridge, he had probably tinkered with his name. Was he the man called Harry Larkin who arrived in New York from Ireland in May 1859, at age eighteen, aboard the steamship *Emerald Isle*? (That Harry traveled in steerage.) Or was he the immigrant recorded as "Mr. Larkins" who docked in New York in April 1864, age twenty-six, having come from England via Havana, on the *Corsica*? (A Larkins who had his own cabin on that voyage.) Or was he the Henry Larkins cited in customs records for July 1865, a twenty-five-year-old Irishman who came to New York aboard the steamer *Constantine*?[2] Many years distant, no one can say, and even in California's early days such questions were moot.

Harry Larkyns told the jailhouse interviewer that as a young man in England he found himself thrown out on the street by his rich, proper family. His parents were dead, his grandmother replacing them. She and other relatives had shunned him, he said, for having stooped to invest some of his inheritance in the theater, in London. His attempts to establish himself as an impresario went awry, he lost money, and he fled England in disgrace for France. This much formed the beginning of his story.

Larkyns filled the ears of many listeners with his grandiose biography. Here are some other parts of it. In 1870, during the Franco-Prussian War, he had joined the French ranks as an aide to General Charles Bourbaki, whose efforts to repel German armies from southern France had won glory. Larkyns said that under Bourbaki, he had risen to the rank of major, and as a result he wished to be referred to—here in California—as "Major Larkyns." He said the French government had awarded him the cross of the Legion of Honor. He said when the war ended, with the unfortunate surrender of France, he had decamped to Paris to take in the city's pleasures.

Major Larkyns, one writer said, "spoke French with the true Parisian accent, Spanish with the sweetness of a muleteer, and German with the resonance of a bullfrog."

While in Paris, Larkyns had met and befriended one Arthur Neil, another young English traveler who possessed both cash and a sense of adventure. Here Larkyns's story gets easier to nail down, because Neil, filing a complaint with the San Francisco police, corroborates some of it. With Arthur Neil, Larkyns "danced at the Mabille, rode on the Boulevards, and strolled on the Bois." After some weeks at this, said Larkyns, he and Arthur Neil parted company.

Harry Larkyns and Arthur Neil had both come to America, although separately, and upon arriving both had gone west. In Salt Lake City, Utah, where each went to take an interest in the mines, they bumped into each other again. Once the high greetings and reunion toasts were behind them, Larkyns, who was out of money, noticed that Neil was still possessed of a good store of cash. Larkyns informed Neil, whom he had impressed before, that he was en route to Yokohama, and that his bags, including credit instruments, had been sent ahead. He added that his grandmother in London was good for his expenses. Neil sympathized, loaned him clothes and money, and began writing checks. The pair decided to come together to San Francisco, with Neil paying all the bills.

The two arrived in San Francisco in November 1872 and checked into one of the city's stylish transit points, the Occidental Hotel, where Larkyns soon indulged "a riotous, extravagant course," giving champagne dinners, to which he invited a dozen new friends, including Arthur Neil, who was asked to pay for everything. Larkyns hired "a notorious lady in this city named Fanny ———" and spent heavily with her—flowers, opera tickets, carriages, and special meetings. Arthur Neil, reality now dawning on him, decided to escape his friend and told Larkyns that he was obliged to leave for Honolulu, in the Sandwich Islands—known as Hawaii after 1895. Larkyns informed Neil that he would accompany him, especially since his own money was imminent. Neil seemed dubious but remained enamored, and they sailed. In Honolulu, Neil rented a house and hired servants and a cook, and Larkyns resumed his spending on dinners and entertainment. A week passed, and Neil finally saw he was being taken, so he threw Larkyns out.

Larkyns sailed back to California in January 1873, on the SS *Nevada*. In San Francisco, said the paper, he once again "cut a terrible dash, ran up bills everywhere, and managed to have himself considered, for a time, a gentleman. All the young men about town knew him, and many believed him." When Arthur Neil arrived in the city on the next steamship, he was presented with a stack of invoices. Neil filed a complaint accusing Larkyns of obtaining money on false pretenses—$3,000 was the figure he gave. A warrant was issued, and Larkyns was jailed.

The man in the nobby suit, on the day after he spoke to the papers, promised to pay back some of the money and somehow talked his way out of jail. Arthur Neil left San Francisco and did not return. Larkyns was free to make his way, and to bank on his seductive powers.

In spring 1872 Muybridge went to Sacramento, leaving Flora behind in San Francisco. He left to photograph the Stanford house in April, and then, for the first time, Stanford's horses, including Occident, in May.

About this time Muybridge's dealers, the Nahl brothers, decided to sell their gallery and get out of retail art. When the Nahl gallery closed, Muybridge lost a distributor, and Flora was put out of her job as a photo retoucher. The married couple went as a pair over to another art dealer, a bigger operation called Bradley & Rulofson.

Bradley & Rulofson comprised two photographers—Henry Bradley, from Virginia, and William Rulofson, of New Brunswick, Canada. Rulofson made all the decisions, and like everyone in the art world, he and his partner did business on Montgomery Street. William Rulofson had come to California during the Gold Rush, and twenty-five years later, his gallery had thirty-four employees (six of them Chinese American) and occupied twenty-nine rooms on three floors of a building at 429 Montgomery, on the corner of Sacramento. Bradley & Rulofson advertised itself as the biggest art dealer in San Francisco, and the most

William Rulofson and his family at their San Francisco home, ca. 1880

progressive. As proof, the gallery boasted of a strange new machine it had installed, an elevator. (The elevator, another nod to speed, was water-powered. A pump attached to the city's water main filled a tank that acted as a counterweight to raise and lower the cage.) When he made arrangements to sell his photographs through Rulofson, Muybridge made sure his new dealers gave his wife, Flora, a part-time job retouching pictures, as she had done at the Nahl gallery. Despite his own attachment to velocity, Muybridge disliked the elevator and always took the stairs, a fact that came out at the murder trial.

To mark the acquisition—a new artist! the famous Helios!—Bradley & Rulofson printed a catalog of Muybridge's work, describing all his photographs for customers to buy. It ran to fifty pages and listed more than a thousand images.[3]

Back in San Francisco after a stint with the Stanfords, Muybridge packed for another trip that would take him away from his wife, Flora. In June he went to Yosemite. He had first made his reputation as a photographer, five years earlier, with turbulent pictures of Yosemite Valley, the state's natural spectacle. Most of those had been stereo cards, not much bigger than the human hand. This time he would make big pictures, seventeen by twenty-two inches—the scale of a small table—known as "mammoth plates." The operation required a big camera, the size of an oven. Before the invention of the enlarger, a darkroom device that could stretch a negative up to any scale, the photographic print was the same size as its glass negative: to make a big photograph you needed a big camera.

As he had done before, Muybridge spent five months at Yosemite. The writer Helen Hunt Jackson, a fan of the photographer, described running into him on a narrow path.

"As we slowly climbed the trail, a long line of pack-mules met us. We drew aside to let them pass. They were loaded with a photographer's apparatus, lenses, plates, camera, carefully packed boxes of chemicals. Their owner, Mr. Muybridge, has just established himself in the valley for the purpose of taking a series of views, larger and more perfect than any heretofore attempted."[4]

Between June and November Muybridge made his mammoth plates. According to one paper, to take his pictures, Muybridge "cut down trees by the score that interfered with the cameras from the best point of sight; he had himself lowered by ropes down precipices to establish his instruments in places where the full beauty of the object to be

Muybridge, in a publicity photo for
the Bradley & Rulofson Gallery in
San Francisco, 1872

photographed could be transferred to the negative, and he went to
points where his packers refused to follow." Muybridge was good at
publicity—there might have been 50 percent truth in that.[5]

The logistical problem of transporting the negatives—large rect-
angles of glass—two hundred miles along rattling roads back to San
Francisco must have been daunting, but Muybridge preferred this to
the alternative, which was to photograph people in their nicest clothes
and tightest expressions, like every other cameraman in the Bradley &
Rulofson studio.

Muybridge, *Leland Stanford*,
1872. Stereograph

On this trip he did not overlook his new patrons, the Stanfords, and went out of his way to flatter them. Muybridge made a point of going to the Mariposa Grove of giant sequoias, where many trees had stood for a thousand years. The trees had Indian names, but Californians had discarded these, and this time the photographer accepted the change. He photographed the tree known as "Jane L. Stanford" (244 feet high and sixty-five feet in circumference), as well as the "Leland Stanford" (248 feet high, eighty-two feet around). He gave the pictures to his new clients, making sure they would see that their names had inflated, along with their money, to the scale of natural monuments.

———

Released from jail, Harry Larkyns published a letter in a newspaper, the *Daily Register*, hoping to deflect some of the gossip about him that ricocheted through town. He said that his incarceration, his first California experience, had humiliated him. He said that people who did not know him had maligned his character and that he would remain in the state until he had vindicated himself. For a couple of months Larkyns worked as a stevedore, loading ships on the wharfs. When the book publisher Hubert Bancroft met him and took pity, he hired Larkyns as a translator of some French text his company planned to bring out. In summer 1873, Larkyns, the man the *Chronicle* had called "the prince of confidence men," joined the *San Francisco Evening Post* as an art and theater critic. That a duke of deception like Harry Larkyns would be a judge of anyone's artwork suggests something, though it's not clear what, about the state of culture commentary in the West.

After the artistic drought of the frontier decades, San Francisco now possessed a number of theaters, which put on stage shows that rolled into California from the eastern states by train. The perquisites of Larkyns's job took him frequently to see farces, melodramas, and opera. (The burlesque shows that put women on stage in bloomers, and also minstrel acts in which white men wearing blackface sang "Negro music," did not warrant coverage by the papers, though they sold twice the tickets of the legitimate theaters.) To file copy for the *Post*, Larkyns made his way every week to Maguire's Opera House, a three-story theater on Washington Street, west of Montgomery; the Metropolitan Theatre, on Montgomery between Washington and Jackson; the New Alhambra, on Bush Street near Kearny; the California Theatre, also on Bush; and the Amphitheatre, at the corner of Post and Stockton Streets.

Larkyns mingled with the best of the city's art world, including its photographers. When a production came to town it was expected that its actresses and singers would sit for photographs, and Bradley & Rulofson had a strong position in that trade. William Rulofson made portraits of romantic leads, famous faces of the day, from Edwin Booth to Sarah Bernhardt, who trod the boards of the theater district, and sold these pictures as "cabinet cards," the equivalent of celebrity head shots. For his part, Larkyns had reason to drop in on occasion at Rulofson's to pick up a picture of an actress and to talk to the performers themselves.

Flora Muybridge was now on the staff at Bradley & Rulofson. It might have happened that Harry Larkyns met Flora on one of these drop-ins; they would have come face-to-face without going out of their way to do so. Edward Muybridge, at any rate, remembered it that way. "In early 1873, Harry Larkyns came up to the gallery," he told a writer. "My wife was present, and she introduced him to me. I had frequently heard her speak of Major Larkyns before, but did not know that she was much acquainted with him." By the summer, Larkyns was coming around the gallery a lot, Muybridge said, "and I often gave him points in regard to art matters, which he was then writing about."[6]

A writer who knew him described Larkyns as a man whose "fascinating manners and pleasing address made him a great favorite among the female sex," which is perhaps a nineteenth-century way of saying that he seduced whoever came within range.

Muybridge went along obliviously as Flora became fascinated by Larkyns. "He was always trying to get me to take passes to the theater," Muybridge remembered, "but I seldom went to the theater and did not fancy the Major's style of man." Even the photographer called Larkyns "the Major."

One day Muybridge accepted the offer of theater tickets and went with Flora and Larkyns to the California Theatre. The three had drinks after the show, or probably, the men had whiskey as Flora looked on. In a few days Larkyns came to Muybridge's house "on some matter of business," and for the photographer that marked the end of his desire to indulge a friendship with the theater critic. Afterwards, Muybridge stopped answering Larkyns's supplications.

A day came when a popular English actress named Adelaide Neilson arrived from the East Coast for a monthlong booking. William

The California Theatre, a haunt of Harry Larkyns and the place where
Flora Muybridge and Larkyns began their affair, in a signed photograph by
Helios (Muybridge), ca. 1870

Rulofson photographed Neilson, then his gallery printed an adver-
tising card with a picture of the actress and, next to it, a Muybridge
photograph from Yosemite. Adelaide Neilson was on stage at the California Theatre in *Romeo and Juliet*. (At age twenty-six, a somewhat old
Juliet, but the role had made her famous.) Muybridge remembered that
when he came home one night Flora was out, and she did not come in
until late. He asked her where she had been. "To the theater with Major
Larkyns," she said. Larkyns, a fascinating dilettante, was also a fine
physical specimen and an athlete. A brief touch between Larkyns and
Flora at *Romeo and Juliet* would not have attracted notice.[7]

For her part, Flora Muybridge had an effect on men, including her
employer, William Rulofson, who asked her to sit for his portrait camera. Rulofson sent one picture of Flora out to the *Philadelphia Photogra-*

pher, which had previously flattered Muybridge for his landscapes. The journal inserted the portrait in its pages and praised Rulofson for it.

The picture of Flora, framed from her waist at the bottom to just above her pile of hair woven with flowers at the top, shows her in a white dress, which is squared around the neck with lace. (She wears enormous white outfits in nearly all of her pictures.) Her waist is cinched to a wasp circumference by a corset. A stack of light-brown hair weighs on her head, braided into a turban shape, while a crucifix hangs from a heavy necklace, and earrings dangle low. She stares to her right, making her profile into the subject. As in other pictures of her, it is the eyes that pull the attention: they look away from the camera, half-lidded, almost weary. Flora's eyes seem to make her unreachable.

Flora Muybridge, whom Larkyns called "Flo," saw much of her lover. Larkyns rented a room on Montgomery Street, and it became their rendezvous point. A second trysting place seems to have been the

The Cliff House Hotel, San Francisco, a trysting place for Harry Larkyns and his lover, Flora, photographed by Muybridge

Cliff House, a hotel on a bluff overlooking the Pacific. Muybridge had once photographed it.

———

When they had been married for two years, in spring 1873, Muybridge went away again to do a new kind of journalism: he photographed a war. The occupation of war cameraman had little precedent. Only since the Englishman Roger Fenton photographed the Crimean War, fifteen years before, had anyone brought a camera to a shooting field. In America during the Civil War, photographers Mathew Brady, Alexander Gardner, and George Barnard had deprived the theater of war of its perennial romance by taking pictures of actual bodies, barracks, and bomb sites. And now, during the Modoc War, just as he had been one of the first photographers of Native Americans in Alaska, Muybridge became the first to photograph America's fight with its indigenous people. It was known at the time by the euphemism "Indian removal." The Modoc War was a monthlong campaign, one of dozens over decades, distinguished now mainly because Muybridge photographed it.

The Modocs had lived for centuries in northern California at Tule Lake, near the border with Oregon, until the 1860s, when they were pushed by white settlement (and by the U.S. Army) one hundred miles north, onto the Klamath Reservation. A native leader named Kientpoos—called "Captain Jack" by whites for the blue military jacket he sometimes wore—defied the deportation and brought several hundred Modocs back to Tule Lake. When an army party attacked them in November 1872, Kientpoos and his band killed a dozen whites, fled to a rocky plain they knew well (whites called it the Lava Beds), and waited. Perhaps the army hired Muybridge to document its campaign against the Modocs because officers had seen his pictures of the Tlingit. Or maybe he was California's "adventure photographer," and everyone knew he would go anywhere. For whatever reason, at the beginning of May 1873, Muybridge left Flora at home in San Francisco and went four hundred miles north, to the fringe of Tule Lake, where he made his first war pictures.[8]

The Lava Beds, a craggy plain serrated with caves and crevasses, helped fifty Modoc fighters to hold off five hundred army infantry. Throughout May the Modocs killed dozens of soldiers in ambush, to the astonishment of Americans following the fight in *Harper's Weekly*, which covered events. Muybridge photographed the army camps, mak-

As an early war photographer, Muybridge took this picture of
the cave used by Kientpoos, or "Captain Jack," leader of a native
revolt against "Indian removal" during the Modoc War of 1873.

ing them look like fifty tents erected on the moon. He photographed the
sites of firefights, like "Captain Jack's Cave," which looked more oth-
erworldly than even Muybridge's lighthouses. He photographed a tent
where Modocs ambushed a party of officers. He photographed Indian
scouts, taken from the ranks of the Modocs' enemies, who worked for
the army. His images of Modocs themselves, hiding in the lava redoubts,
are limited to just one: a picture of four women.

Harper's Weekly published engravings of five of Muybridge's pictures.[9] When they weren't being asked to play the role of savages, Indians had become a curiosity to white readers. A ditty writer sent a few
lines to the Yreka Journal, the newspaper nearest the war zone, summa-
rizing the fight as it appeared to many Californians:

> In truth it was a gallant sight,
> To see a thousand men of might.
> With gun and cannons, day and night
> Fight fifty dirty Indians.[10]

Modoc women, photographed by Muybridge during the war,
1873

When the Modocs capitulated in early June, Kientpoos/Captain
Jack and three others were hanged, and the remaining 150 native sur-
vivors were sent into exile on the Quapaw reservation in Oklahoma.
They rode on a Central Pacific train owned by Leland Stanford.

————

Muybridge veered between subjects and clients. He photographed
skittish thoroughbreds and aboriginal outsiders, he worked for prince-
capitalists and cursing army colonels. An intoxicating workload, and it
had to be enough to keep him in a state of distraction. Occasionally, he
arrived home to his young wife, fitted out and frustrated in their nice
townhouse.

He was surprised to discover that Flora had been going to the theater with Harry Larkyns, and Muybridge told his wife to stop doing it.
Then he went to his wife's boyfriend. "The next morning I went to see
Larkyns," he remembered later, "and he greeted me gaily with a 'Good
morning.' I said, 'You know very well that as a married woman it is not
proper for her to be running about at night with you, and I want you

to let her alone. I do not request it of you, but I command you to keep away from her. You know my rights as a married man. So do I, and I shall defend them. If you transgress after this morning I shall hold you to the consequences, and I suppose you know what that means in California.'"

Muybridge meant that in California the rules of marriage could be enforced more harshly than elsewhere, with beatings or duels, and the authorities would look the other way. Larkyns groveled to Muybridge. "If there is any objection on your part I will take her out no more," he said to his rival.[11]

In summer 1873 Flora, age twenty-two, was pregnant. She had had two pregnancies before, both ending with stillborn infants. The couple hired a nurse and midwife, Susan Smith, to deliver the new baby when it came. Smith was a simple woman, excitable, prone to raise her voice, but she was loyal to her clients, the new mothers and mothers-to-be. Smith later told her version of what happened between Flora and her two men.

Harry Larkyns and Flora Muybridge started writing each other letters, Smith said, "two and three times a day." They hired a courier to take the letters back and forth between them ("a Negro," Smith remembered). Smith said she witnessed several things while working for Flora Muybridge. Once, Larkyns stopped at the South Park house in the

Flora Muybridge, pregnant, photographed by her husband, Edward, in 1874

morning, while Flora was still in bed. "He went into her room," Smith said. "I also went into the room, and she lay on the bed with the clothes down to her waist, and Larkyns sat on the bedside." Smith said she saw Flora and Larkyns go into Flora's bedroom and lock the door "as many as three times a week."

In the midst of the affair, Larkyns never stopped wanting to look good. Some of his shirts needed repair, according to Smith, but he did not have much money, and so he gave them to Flora, who sent the shirts out with her husband's laundry to be cleaned and mended. The same black man who delivered the couple's letters brought Larkyns's shirts back to him when they were sewn and starched, Smith said.

When Flora's third baby was born, Muybridge was traveling. The midwife told the story. At 2:00 a.m. on the morning of April 16, 1874, a carriage rattled up to her door, at 2116 Powell Street, and someone rang the bell. It was Larkyns, who was wearing a high white hat. Larkyns said that Flora had gone into labor and was lying down in the carriage. "I said that she must be brought into the house," Smith remembered, "but he said no, and half lifted me across the sidewalk. We drove rapidly, I half clothed." They went to the Muybridge house in South Park. There, Smith said, "Larkyns held Flora in his arms and kissed and caressed her. He stooped over the bed, kissed Mrs. Muybridge, and said, 'Never mind baby, it will soon be over.' "

Larkyns went for a doctor and brought him back about 3:00 a.m. Smith said that before the baby was born, Flora "was afraid it would have sandy hair, like Larkyns's." The midwife and obstetrician delivered a son to Flora at 4:00 a.m. Smith said that Flora "asked me if it had sandy hair, and I replied, 'Its hair is light.' "

Flora told Susan Smith that Larkyns was going to take her to England as his wife. Flora said, "It is too bad I treat old Muybridge so badly, but I love Harry Larkyns."

Smith telegraphed Muybridge, who was out of town, and he came home the day after the delivery. He stayed for a week or ten days, "until all danger was past," said Smith. Then he went away again, oblivious, to take photographs of a rich man's house in the town of Belmont, twenty-five miles south of the city.

The day after he left, Flora wrote a note and told Smith to take it to the *San Francisco Evening Post*, where Larkyns had an office. Muybridge stayed out of town for several more weeks, and during that time Larkyns visited Flora "frequently," according to Smith. On one occasion Larkyns was standing at the bedside, and Flora said, looking at the baby, "Harry, we will remember the thirteenth of July. We have something to show for it." July 13 was nine months before the birth.

When the baby was four weeks old, Muybridge came home. "He always seemed affectionate and attentive," Smith remembered, but this time the photographer was disturbed by what he saw.

Chapter 9

THE OCTOPUS

Usually when Leland Stanford opened the paper or one of the periodicals cropping up in California, he found an item or two extolling him. The more rails that went on the ground, the more writers sketched the portrait of a benign Western monarch who happened to be a businessman. "Stanford's genius and energy are so conspicuous," said one profile, he "possesses the sign and signet of the Almighty to command." To tell the story of the West without Stanford, said another, "would be like staging Hamlet without the prince." The encomia flowed, and the monarch sometimes turned into a musician. "The vast railroad organization obeys Stanford's gentlest touch, as the keys of a piano obey every pulsation of the master's hand."[1] And so forth.

Edward Muybridge had been clipping news stories about himself and saving them in a big scrapbook. Stanford did the same, only he told his secretaries to make the selection.

Two years passed, however, and the adoration thinned. When Muybridge photographed Occident and Abe Edgington in 1872 and 1873, Stanford found it hard to keep his collection of flattery current. The golden spike in Utah had flooded the plain with praise of the former grocer, but those waters receded, and the Central Pacific turned from savior of the people into its enemy. Stanford became the brain of a hydra-headed beast, the thinking organ of a creature not seen before, an industrial monopoly.

Farmers were the first to feel the grip of the railroad and the first to revile it. After the Civil War, as the cash crops of gold and silver dwindled, the economy of California turned away from mining and toward agriculture. Wheat moved from the margins to the center and by the 1870s counted as the state's biggest staple. Two variables pushed the change: giant tracts amassed by early Gold Rush migrants allowed one crop to spread across millions of acres, and the railroad itself opened the out-of-state food market. Stanford saw it happening and watched the price of grain. California wheat and other staples could not get to the Chicago commodities market and the eastern states without the Central Pacific, so why shouldn't the company milk farmers? If prices go up in the East, why can't freight rates go up for California crops heading that direction?

From the start the Central Pacific made 90 percent of its revenue from freight, only 10 percent from passengers, and from the first, freight meant crops. In 1873, the company moved 122,431 tons of wheat, 14,505 tons of wool, 6,362 tons of tea, 2,050 tons of coffee, 2,488 tons of tobacco, and smaller amounts of flour, butter, and oysters.[2] Farmers thought it mysterious that rail prices kept going up until they approached the cost of raising the crop, shaving their margins, leaving them with little profit and a geyser of resentment that they were working for the train.

In 1872, to push back, growers set up the California Farmers Union and started lobbying for legislation. Train systems back east and all around the farm states came in for similar loathing. The Granger movement, a farmers' cooperative that started in Kentucky and went national, pushed for laws to limit freight rates as well as fees at grain elevators, often owned by railroads. The Grangers came to the West in the early 1870s, and their influence in Sacramento challenged that of Stanford and the associates.

"I know the mistrust there is abroad in the community against myself and the management of this great railroad enterprise," said Stanford in an interview. He missed being treated like a saint. "Nothing but jealousies and misunderstanding," he said, tossing aside complaints against his power to make or break whole towns with a change in rates.[3]

The associates spent a good bit of time defending their monopoly, not only buying smaller carriers, but keeping the competition off balance. During the 1870s, the Southern Pacific blocked an attempt by a rival train prince in the East, the investor Tom Scott, to build a second transcontinental line on a southern route from Louisiana to Los Angeles. Within a few years, the associates built the line themselves, from southern California across Arizona, New Mexico, and Texas to New Orleans.

Financial manipulations by the railroad also gave off a bad odor. Stanford made only part of his fortune from the train's revenue, and better than half the wealth of the associates came from paper—bond sales to investors, enormous and ever-growing bank loans, and beautifully corrupt transactions. An example of the last: about the time Muybridge photographed Occident, in 1872, Stanford started to deposit Central Pacific money into a sinking fund, as the law required, to pay off federal construction subsidies, the bond debt of about $50 million that would come due in twenty-five years. But the associates wanted that money, so the Central Pacific began lending the cash from the sinking fund to a subsidiary, the Western Development Corporation, which the associates also owned. As collateral for the loans, Stanford and company transferred from their accounts 17,500 shares of train stock, which they owned, to the Central Pacific, also theirs. The Central Pacific kept the stock collateral and canceled the debt. The associates wound up with cash for their securities and still had the securities themselves.[4]

A railroad bubble of sorts burst in 1873, when many train companies, heavy with debt from these kinds of deals, went under during a financial panic that rolled from the eastern states to the Pacific. It began on September 18, when Jay Cooke & Company, a financial house in Philadelphia, closed its doors, groaning from giant, overvalued railroad investments. Tens of thousands of businesses failed in the cascade, and unemployment went to 14 percent. Of the railroads, one quarter of the country's 350 train companies went bankrupt, but Stanford's operation stayed alive. Monopolists, east and west, looked to be the villains in charge, and in the eyes of millions Stanford traded the role of benevolent Caesar for that of criminal-in-chief.[5]

"The Octopus" came to life when California saw the new kind of power that four men held (or five, including the stroke-impaired Judge Crocker). For years, Stanford, Collis Huntington, Mark Hopkins, and the Crocker brothers, Charles and Edwin, controlled all track west of the Rockies and held almost all of the stock in the company. The *San Francisco Wasp*, a paper edited by the novelist and muckraking journalist Ambrose Bierce, ran a cartoon about what that reality meant. The illustration, by an artist named Edward Keller, depicted Stanford and partners as a pink octopus, its tentacles reaching out to strangle farmers, factories, and politicians.

The name "Octopus" stuck (and it would follow the associates to their graves). An investor fleeced by the associates, John Robinson, complained about the company in a modestly titled book, *The Octopus: A History of the Construction, Conspiracies, Extortions, Robberies, and Villainous Acts of the Central Pacific*. A big-selling novel with the same disdainful tone, *The Octopus: A Story of California*, made writer Frank Norris, in 1901, a prophet of the West. Norris wrote: "The galloping monster, the terror of steel and steam, with its single eye, Cyclopian, red, shooting from horizon to horizon . . . symbol of a vast power,

THE CURSE OF CALIFORNIA.

"The Curse of California," *San Francisco Wasp*, August 19, 1882. Here the Octopus sees with the faces of Stanford (in its right eye) and his partner Charles Crocker (in its left). With bags of money blocking City Hall, and over the graves of families killed resisting the railroad at the town of Mussel Slough, the Octopus strangles (among others) farmers, miners, vintners, timber companies, telegraph operators, shipping, and the superannuated stagecoach.

huge, terrible, flinging the echo of its thunder over all reaches of the valley, leaving blood and destruction in its path; the Leviathan, with tentacles of steel clutching into the soil, the soulless Force, the iron hearted Power, the monster, the Colossus, the Octopus." And further: "The whole map was gridironed by a vast, complicated network of red lines . . . to every quarter of the state . . . ran the plexus of red, a veritable system of blood circulation, complicated, dividing, and reuniting, branching, splitting, extending, throwing out feelers, offshoots, tap roots, feeders—diminutive little blood suckers that shot out from the main jugular . . . in . . . a hundred tentacles."

The smell of corruption circled the train company like a discharge from the watery beast. The Central Pacific had its hands on the legislatures of all the western states from an early date. "Send copy of California railroad law with such amendments as you think ought to be made," Stanford telegraphed Charles Crocker from Utah, where he met and manipulated the political class. "I want it to be introduced here."[6] In December 1872, Huntington, from Washington, D.C., telegraphed Hopkins in California to say he had just sent along some land bills coming up in the House of Representatives. "Which do you desire passed and which defeated?" Huntington asked, leaving unspoken the assumption that the company checkbook could make the difference.[7]

People had seen nothing like this kind of business before the trains, no capitalist with this kind of grip. The scale and intrusions of the operation exceeded those of the state government. In one of its muscular policies, the railroad gave different rates to different shippers, making would-be customers show their books to Stanford's accountants before the train accepted their freight, so the company could calculate the maximum to charge. In meetings banked with fake smiles, the railroad men told customers that if they shipped anything by another carrier, a steamboat or a stagecoach, their rates on the train would run 100 percent higher than if the railroad took all the freight.[8]

Californians' loathing for the train grew like a weed. Ambrose Bierce, the *Wasp* editor, followed his "Octopus" label by pinning a new name on the railroad president, whose company had picked up free acreage with the dimensions of a small state—"Stealing Landford."

The news media of the day, along with newspapers, included political pamphlets. Writers dashed off these ten-page items, little speech bombs, and tossed them into circulation in print runs of a thousand or two, for sale at newsstands and stationers and shops. In one such

harangue, "The California King: His Conquests, Crimes, Confederates, Counselors, Courtiers and Vassals"—a short story with Stanford
as its antihero, published anonymously and scattered around San Francisco in 1876—a fictitious Stanford says cheerfully to an audience of
sycophants, "I have California pretty well at my mercy" and "I and my
associates go for grand cash and political power."[9]

The *Sacramento Union* had been a pro-railroad newspaper for years,
until 1869, when the trains started to run, after which its editors felt an
attack of bad conscience and flipped. Stanford's hometown paper then
generated a stream of invective against the train company. In answer,
the associates bought a competing newspaper, the *Record*, and made it
into a mouthpiece for train-friendly stories. Circulation for the *Record*
disappointed, however, so the Central Pacific bought the *Sacramento
Union* itself and closed it down.

The most pungent jeers against the train, and the most personal,
came from an insider, a lawyer called Alfred A. Cohen, whom the
associates had tried to manipulate. During the 1860s, Cohen, a former banker, had gotten up two short train lines running into the cities
of Oakland and Alameda; Stanford acquired them by threatening to
put Cohen out of business. The associates thought they had purchased
Cohen's loyalty by paying him a $10,000-a-year retainer and giving
him the job of in-house counsel (Huntington called Cohen "our Isra-
elite friend"), but they neglected to pay their new partner a promised
several million dollars in railroad stock. In retaliation, Cohen went to
the state legislature, where he pushed for ceilings on freight rates, lobbying for a railroad regulation package known as the Archer Bill. The
Central Pacific sued Cohen, its own insider, accusing him of embezzle-
ment, which had the unintended effect of giving this artful speaker a
megaphone in the Twelfth District Court, where all the papers reported
on his fulminations.

In one courtroom speech, Cohen painted verbal portraits of the
train partners. Collis Huntington he called "the diner and winer of the
Washington department of this devilfish, the railroad." (The devilfish, or manta ray, a giant, winged sea creature, fit nicely alongside the
Octopus.) Charles Crocker amounted to what Cohen called "a living,
breathing, waddling monument of the triumph of vulgarity, vicious-
ness and dishonesty."

The former insider kept back his most delicate embroidery for Stanford, who sat listening in the courtroom. "In common with the whole

people of the state of California, it was an unfortunate hour in which I first saw Stanford," he began. "With him, the play has been elaborately cast, and Stanford is the heavy character of the plot. Sullen and saturnine, he is remorseless, grand, gloomy, and peculiar. Stanford stalks across this courtroom to ascend to the witness box, where he speaks his part in a basso-profundo growl and departs, while the attendant actors hold their breath in awe. He has the ambition of an emperor and the spite of a peanut vendor."[10]

———

In the fall of 1873, their power having outgrown little Sacramento—and maybe to escape the poison that gripped them in their hometown—Stanford and his partners decided to move their business, and themselves, to San Francisco.[11] The move began when Stanford bought sixty acres around the intersection of Fourth and Townsend Streets, near the Bay, building rail yards and a four-story brick headquarters. Stanford's office had the biggest footprint, with a vast Persian rug and sprawling oak desk (curiously empty, people noticed), the walls decorated with engravings of Washington and Lincoln.

The associates simultaneously built new houses for themselves at the top of California Hill, the highest point in the city. Stanford and Mark Hopkins bought a city block and divided it in half, with Stanford's portion to the east, with the grand view of the Bay. Charles Crocker bought a half block for himself, next to his partners' stake. (Collis Huntington might have joined them, but he still lived in New York.) Stanford added a small lot on the corner of California and Powell Streets to build a separate, two-story stable for some of his horses.

Leland and Jenny Stanford moved into the Grand Hotel, on Market Street, while they planned what to build. In late 1874, as construction started, they rented a house a block away from the site of their new mansion, which inched upward at the corner of California and Powell Streets. In April 1876, one paper remarked that the extraordinary house was nearly done, and that it had the ordinary address of 901 California Street.[12] The couple moved in that summer with their six-year-old son, Leland Jr.

The associates built the grandest houses in town, fine and garish, using the contracting arm of the railroad, the Western Development Company, which ran the train's hundreds of buildings. Charles Crocker ran into a problem with his mansion, a somber, brown balloon of a house, and the trouble followed him for years. Crocker had picked up nearly an acre, and to make it square he had bought out several home-owners and torn down their houses—excepting the house of a German American family called Yung. The title holder, the undertaker Nicholas Yung, refused to sell his two-story cottage at the northwest corner of Crocker's tract at the price Crocker wanted to pay. In a show of pique, Crocker had his builders put up a forty-foot fence, as tall as the Yung family's house, that wrapped around three sides of it, entirely cutting off its light and air. Yung replied by staking a flagpole on his house, flying a skull-and-bones banner, and laying out an empty coffin on his roof. Crocker's "spite fence," his intent to strangle a neighbor, became a symbol of the railroad's greed. Tourists by the thousands visited it in order to marvel at the avarice and venality of the train princes. Nicholas Yung and his family moved out, but they left their house standing, sur-rounded by its wooden cocoon. Eventually the undertaker died, but his widow kept up their defiance, and the fence and empty, rotting house stood for thirty years—until 1904, when, Crocker and the Yung couple now dead, the property went to new owners, who leveled it.[13]

The Charles Crocker "spite fence" (behind the white house), forty feet tall, encasing the home of a neighbor who refused to sell his land to Crocker, one of the associates of the Central Pacific

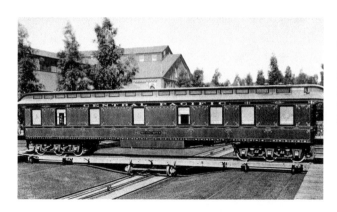

One year Jane Stanford "surprised" her husband with a birthday gift, a private railroad car ordered up from the Central Pacific yards.

No one had seen this kind of money before; Leland and Jenny found it a full-time occupation just trying to spend it. Jenny decided to give her husband a private railroad car for his birthday, and the Central Pacific shops spent months on the design. Fueled with gaslight and steam heat, it had two bedrooms, a living room, dining room, and kitchen, plus servant quarters. The couple used it as a virtual second home for many years. Leland encouraged his wife to help herself to diamonds, and over the years she acquired a pound or two. The jewels turned into her fetishes after a time, so much so that one year she commissioned a painter to collect them all on one canvas, so she could look at them in a picture.

Jane Stanford, in a photograph retouched with paint, ca. 1870

Astley David Middleton Cooper, *Mrs. Stanford's Jewel Collection*, 1898. Oil on canvas, 50 x 75 inches. The artist was hired by Jane Stanford to inventory her stock of diamonds in a six-foot-wide painting.

Stanford liked to impress people with his house; he took pleasure in his excess. One day, a British shipping company executive visited the rail builder at his office; after the meeting, his wife being away with Leland Jr., Stanford invited the man to dinner. The Englishman wrote about the night in his diary. "The house I heard spoken of as the finest in the western part of America," he remembered, "and in San Francisco I saw no others that rivaled it in size."[14] Stanford showed his guest around the fifty rooms, but silently; then he took his company to the stables, where in further silence they looked over horses and carriages. The two men had dinner, alone, in the sixty-foot dining room. Following a multicourse and largely wordless meal, Stanford brought his guest into the library, where life-size portraits of himself and his wife hung on the walls.

"For the next half hour," the visitor remembered, "we talked. That is, I talked and Mr. Stanford sat silent. I do not say that he listened, for that I had no means of knowing. He merely sat, regarding me not impolitely but with a face from which all expression had been erased. He may have heard every word I uttered, or he may have heard nothing. I began by feeling that I must be boring him, then by wondering if I had perhaps given him cause for great offense. Next, it occurred to me that he might be sleepy; finally I became certain that he was ill." The host led his dinner company out and thanked him for the visit.

Many remarked on Stanford's impassive manner, and he grew more cryptic as he aged. He surrendered to his possessions the task of communicating with people.

Chapter 10

LITTLE HARRY

Flora and Edward Muybridge gave their son an invented name—Florado Helios Muybridge. It came from his mother, Flora (with a masculine suffix attached—*do*). It borrowed the whole-cloth name of his father, Helios, and also his father's made-up surname, Muybridge.

In late 1873, when Flora was pregnant, Muybridge suspected Flora and Harry Larkyns might be lovers. Susan Smith, the midwife, who would soon deliver the baby, had witnessed a scene at the house. Flora had given Smith a letter to take to Larkyns, and Smith had done it. While Smith stood with Larkyns in the doorway of the *Post* newspaper, having just handed him the note, Muybridge walked past. That night at 9:00 p.m. Muybridge came into Flora's room, where Flora sat talking to Smith; he asked Smith if she had seen Larkyns that afternoon.

"I was just going to say yes," Smith remembered, "when I caught sight of Mrs. Muybridge. Her face was white as death. And she held her finger up warningly. As her love affairs were none of my business, I passed it off by saying that I had gone to the newspaper office about an advertisement, and thought I had seen him." Muybridge turned to Flora and pulled an envelope from his pocket, which he had apparently found, and which contained a different, unsigned letter. Muybridge asked if Larkyns had written it to her. Flora said he had not. Muybridge tossed the letter at Flora. She laughed and said the note was a joke, and that she knew who had written it.

Flora Muybridge and her son, Florado, in the petrified forest near Calistoga, California, photographed by Edward Muybridge, 1874

Susan Smith remembered, "He was pale and said he hoped to God that what she said was true. He asked her to swear to it."

Muybridge wondered what happened to the money that he gave his wife. "I was always a man of very simple tastes and few wants," he told a reporter, "and I did not spend much money. What I had left after paying my expenses, I gave to my wife, and yet she was always wanting more. I could never see what she did with it."

Harry Larkyns lived generously, often buying meals for people, and dressing like a rake. He found ample use for cash from the man he was cuckolding.

In early 1874, Muybridge talked to managers at the Pacific Mail Steamship Company, a possible client. He hoped they might hire him and send him to Central America to photograph the carrier's ports of call. If so, Muybridge would be able to get away again for another five or six months—and he felt happiest alone, on the road. Flora Muybridge had an uncle and aunt in Oregon, Thomas and Flora Stump, the steamboat captain and his wife, whom she had lived with as a young girl. Muybridge asked Flora whether she would stay for a while with her relatives in Oregon after the baby was born. "I told her I would send her up to Oregon to her uncle and give her money to pay her expenses there while I was away, if she would go," Muybridge remembered. Flora said she would.

Florado was born April 16. Maybe Muybridge hoped to end his wife's love affair by putting Harry Larkyns out of reach. Or maybe his first act as a father was to put Flora and the baby aside so he could travel. In June 1874 Flora took a steamship from San Francisco north to Oregon with two-month-old Florado.

The Stump family lived at a place called The Dalles, near Portland, and from here Flora resumed writing letters to Larkyns. On July 11, she wrote Susan Smith, the nurse, "I wish I had a nice little home with you-know-who . . . I'm not ashamed to say I love him better than anyone else upon this earth, and no one can change my mind."[1]

———

Harry Larkyns made a meager living from his newspaper items about the shows and starlets of San Francisco's theaters. At one point he tried to save himself some work by subcontracting his writing job. The scheme involved another journalist, a man called Edward Ellis, who used a made-up name in print, "Coppinger."

The story goes that one night Larkyns met a man in the street, "shivering and hungry," an Englishman who gave his name as Edward Ellis. Ellis leaned on Larkyns for help, and the Scotland native took pity. Larkyns brought Ellis home, cleaned him up, and nursed his hangover. Ellis made good company, Larkyns discovered, and as a writer he knew a surprising amount about theater. When Ellis had recovered, he and Larkyns struck a deal. Edward Ellis/Coppinger would write items for Larkyns's paper, the *Evening Post*; Larkyns would submit them as his own, and they would split the money. The scheme worked for some months, Ellis/Coppinger reviewing shows and Larkyns getting credit, but Ellis grew tired of writing in the dark. He sent an anonymous letter to the editor of the *Post* claiming Larkyns did not write his own copy. Larkyns's editor confronted him, the writer admitted the fraud, and he was fired. Edward Ellis/Coppinger took over Larkyns's job, going to work for a rival paper, the *Chronicle*, writing about theater and art.

Larkyns failed to take pleasure from this turn of events. After losing his job, whenever Larkyns saw Ellis/Coppinger on the street, he extracted from his former protégé a strange, ritual punishment. Larkyns would grab Coppinger by the nose and jaw, pull open his mouth, and spit into it. Word about this treatment got around, and Ellis acquired a nickname—"Cuspidor Coppinger."[2]

———

With Flora five hundred miles away in Oregon, unable to provide handouts, Harry Larkyns looked for better work. He found a job as an agent of John Wilson's Circus, a San Francisco company trying to drum up appearances out of town. John Wilson was a forty-five-year-old impresario and a native of Scotland. He might have empathized with Larkyns, who called himself "an Inverness man." Wilson had run a circus in San Francisco for fifteen years—minstrels, tumblers, acrobats, contortionists, the performing elephant Albert, and two trick mules known as Pete and Barney. In January 1874, Wilson had opened a new venue in San Francisco on a lot that fronted New Montgomery Street, and he wanted to take his act on the road. He hired Larkyns, with his lovely speech, to get the bookings.[3]

Larkyns probably had a hand in a contract that sent a group of Wilson's performers to Portland, Oregon, where Flora had retreated with her baby. He regretted it. In San Francisco, Larkyns heard rumors that Flora was sleeping with someone from Wilson's show. He got jealous and wrote a letter to Susan Smith, the nurse.

> *Wednesday*
> *Dear Mrs. Smith:*
> *You will be surprised to hear from me . . . but I have been so uneasy and worried about that poor girl that I cannot rest, and it is a relief to talk or write about her. . . . I want you to be perfectly frank, open and honest with me. If you hear anything of that little lady, no matter what, tell me right out. She may return to the city and beg you not to let me know; but do not, pray do not, listen to her. Do not be afraid that I shall get angry with her. I will never say a harsh word to her, and even if things turn out as badly as possible, and I find she has been deceiving me all along, I can only be grieved and sorry, but I can never be angry with her. I ascertained today that all the minstrels will return from Portland on the next steamer, which will arrive on Tuesday. I cannot and will not believe anything so bad as that rumor. . . . I have written to the morning and evening papers in Portland today, and advertised in the "personals," as so—"Flora and Georgie: If you have a heart you will write to H. Have you forgotten that April night*

when we were both so pale?" She will understand this. Mrs. Smith,
I assure you, I am sick with anxiety and doubt, the whole thing is so
incomprehensible and I am so helpless. If an angel had come and told
me she was false to me, I would not have believed it. I cannot attend
to my work, nor sleep. I cannot help thinking of that speech of hers to
you the day before she left, when she begged you not to think ill of her,
whatever you might hear. And yet Mrs. Smith, after all that has come
and gone, would she be so utterly untrue to me, so utterly false? If she
had nothing to conceal from me, why does she not write?

Harry Larkyns

Larkyns wrote Flora in Oregon and accused her vaguely of sleeping with another man. She wrote to a friend, Sarah Smith, daughter of the nurse Susan Smith, to complain.

The Dalles [Oregon]

July 11, 1874
Dear Sarah,
I received such a letter from H.L. I was so provoked. He ought to
know me better than to accuse me of such a thing, but I may forgive
him. I am not ashamed to say I love him . . . unless with his own lips
he tells me that he does not care for me any more. I don't want Harry
to come up here, as much as I would like to see him, for this is a small
place, and people cannot hold their tongues.

Mrs. Muybridge

P.S. Destroy my letters after reading them, for you might lose one,
and it might get picked up.[4]

Harry Larkyns quit his job promoting Wilson's Circus, perhaps over his jealousy about "the minstrels," the company musicians who had seen Flora. He needed money. Larkyns next tried his hand in the small corner of the mining trade that depended on writers. He wrote items for a newsletter about mining called the *Weekly Stock Report* and at the same time struck a deal with some speculators to work on a map of the mercury mines in Napa County, north of San Francisco.

In July 1874, Larkyns started traveling back and forth from San Francisco to the town of Calistoga, seventy-five miles upcountry.

From scrub hills near Calistoga, at a place called Pine Flat, Larkyns

wrote a friend to complain about the dirty work he was doing survey-
ing the mines.

> *Pine Flat*
>
> *August 29, 1874*
> *Dear Old L——,*
>   *Up in the mountains, riding twenty and thirty miles a day, groping
> along tunnels, clambering up and down shafts; nothing but mines,
> mines, mines; everybody making money, apparently, except the poor
> devils who work hardest, myself and the pick-and-hammer men to wit.
> The country up here is very pretty. The weather is hot and if I only
> had a companion I might have a very pleasant trip; but I'm as blue
> as the sky and lakes. This situation sticks to me tighter than poverty.
> Sleep and I are strangers, and if I could get along without eating I'd
> prefer it, for feeding is hard labor. The thing is that the last two years
> have broken me down terribly; the undeserved disgrace where I was
> unknown, and the uphill fight ever since have been too much to carry. I
> laugh off everything, and have the reputation of being the most devil-
> may-care, jovial case; but I feel my position every hour in every day,
> as I do not think there lives a bitterer man than myself. All my life
> had been a holiday; I was admired, courted and respected everywhere,
> and from holding up my head as an equal among the proudest people
> in the world, I dropped in a day to the level—at least in the eyes
> of others—of riff-raff terms. I tell you, it's hard to bear. This map
> business is making me gray-haired.*[5]
>
>   *H. Larkyns*

———

Susan Smith felt abused by Flora and Muybridge—they owed her
for two months of work, and they had not paid. Smith brought up the
money to Muybridge, and he said that he had given cash for her wages
to Flora. Smith then went to Larkyns, asking him to help her write an
invoice and an appeal for the money. He did, and in early fall 1874 she
took these papers to municipal court to see about filing a suit in order to
collect. When the hearing came, in October, the judge told Smith that
in order to prove her claim she had to produce a letter from Flora Muybridge documenting Smith's employment and services. Smith com-
plied, turning in such a letter, and on October 13, represented by one

Samuel Harding, of Harding & Co., collectors, Smith won a judgment against the Muybridge couple for back pay plus court costs.

The next day, Muybridge spoke to Smith about the court decision—he would pay, but he asked her for a little time to get the money together. As they talked, Smith mentioned the letter she had shown to the judge at the hearing. Muybridge asked to see it, and Smith handed him a letter from Flora. Muybridge read it and became agitated— evidently Harry Larkyns's name came up several times in the letter. "He said it was strange that his wife should mention Larkyns so familiarly," Smith remembered.

Smith must have been angry, or maybe she was tired of acting as the go-between, because she began to talk to Muybridge about Flora and Larkyns.

"I told him that his wife slept out of the house for ten nights when he was at Belmont," she remembered, mentioning the weeks after the birth of Florado. "I also told him that his wife once sent me to Larkyns's room, and that Larkyns said to me, 'Why doesn't the old man go away to take pictures, so that Flora and I can do as we wish?'"

Muybridge, who thought Smith only wanted money, now saw her as a cruel messenger. He asked her whether she possessed any other letters from Flora, and Smith said yes. He asked whether Smith would give them to him. Smith said yes. Smith wanted her back pay, but she also wanted to see who would be injured by her stories.

On the morning of October 15, a Thursday, Smith went to the office of Muybridge's attorney, a man called Sawyer, carrying two letters written by Larkyns and two written by Flora. When she arrived, Muybridge was pacing up and down in front of Sawyer's office "looking wild and excited," as she put it. Smith had come to be paid, Muybridge had come for the letters.

Smith said, "I have come to see about getting my money." Muybridge asked whether she had any proof of Flora's infidelity. "I don't know," Smith answered. The two went upstairs to Sawyer's office, where Smith handed the four letters to the lawyer and then left. "As I closed the door I heard a scream and fall," Smith later said, the sound of Muybridge dropping to the floor.

A few hours later, in the afternoon, Muybridge went to Smith's rooms on Powell Street to question her again. What was she doing with Larkyns the day he saw her talking to him if she had not carried a note to Larkyns from Flora? Smith admitted she had taken a message to

Larkyns's office. Why had she not told him the truth about it when he brought it up? Smith said that she had seen Flora standing behind him, pale, and that Flora had silenced her with a shake of the finger.

"Mrs. Smith, you know more than you tell me. How could the woman I loved so dearly treat me so cruelly?" Smith remembered him saying. Muybridge stamped on the floor, went white in the face, and trembled. She recalled that Muybridge "talked incoherently for a while," and then he left.

———

Two days later, October 17, 1874, a Saturday morning, Muybridge again went to Smith's apartment on Powell Street, at 11:00 a.m., and knocked.

"He looked more terrible than I had ever seen him," said Smith. "He appeared as though he had had no sleep the night before." In the sitting room, Muybridge picked up a photograph that he saw on a table. A photograph of an infant. Florado was six months old that week. Either the picture had not been on the table two days before, on his last visit, or Smith had recently put it there.

"Who is this?" Muybridge said.

"It is your baby," said Smith.

"I have never seen this picture before. Where did you get it and where was it taken?"

"Your wife sent it to me from Oregon. It was taken at Rulofson's"— Bradley & Rulofson, Muybridge's art dealer, Flora's employer. Muybridge turned the photograph over.

"My God! What is this—'Little Harry!'—on the back of this picture in my wife's handwriting!"

Smith described Muybridge's behavior.

"He exhibited the wildest excitement. His appearance was that of a madman. He was haggard and pale, his eyes glassy—his lower jaw hung down, showing his teeth—he trembled from head to foot, and gasped for breath."

"Great God! Tell me all!" Muybridge came toward Smith with his arm raised, as though to hit her.

"I thought he was insane," Smith said later, "and would kill me or himself if I did not answer him. And so I told him all I knew."

Muybridge stayed for more than an hour, talking to Smith. She told him how, on the night Florado was born, after Flora had gone into labor, Larkyns and Flora had come to her at 2:00 a.m. to wake her up. She told him how Larkyns had gone out for a doctor to help deliver the boy, and how after the birth he had held Flora in his arms and kissed her, calling her "my baby." She told Muybridge that Larkyns often went into Flora's bedroom and locked the door. She told him that Flora had asked her to take care of Florado for several weeks so that she and Larkyns could travel together, but Smith had said she would not. Smith told Muybridge that Flora had said Larkyns was going to take her to England as his wife—that she had said it was "too bad to treat old Muybridge this way," but she was in love.

Muybridge asked whether Smith thought Flora was, as he put it, "guilty."

"I have seen it," she said.

"This is more than I can bear," Muybridge answered.

Muybridge walked to the door. He muttered, Smith said, and turned as though he had awakened from a trance.

"Flora, Flora, my heart is broken," he said. "I would have given my heart's best blood for you."

———

Muybridge left Susan Smith's apartment and found the way to his own house. He spent an hour weeping. He took out his Smith & Wesson #2 six-shooter, loaded a little bag with it and a short statement of last wishes, and walked to 429 Montgomery, the Bradley & Rulofson gallery. In the past he had never taken the elevator, but this time he stepped inside the cage. It was 2:30 p.m.

The photographer wore his customary tattered gray jacket and wide-brimmed felt hat. His beard stretched this way and that, and when he raised his chin, it stuck out horizontally. He carried his corncob pipe. Breathing hard, he could not smoke.[6]

By chance William Rulofson appeared and boarded the elevator. Rulofson told a reporter, "I was at once struck with the singularity of his appearance, and not a little alarmed. Muybridge's lower jaw was chattering against his upper, as if he was seized with an ague, while his upper lip was drawn up to expose his teeth and as rigidly fixed as if he were paralyzed. His face was as pale as marble, and his eyes glazed like those of a madman. He was laboring under the most intense excitement, and when the elevator reached the landing he did not know which door to take, but seemed to be entirely bewildered."

Rulofson asked Muybridge the reason for his anxiety, and the photographer answered that he wanted to speak in private. The art dealer walked Muybridge to a dressing room, a place where customers waited before having their portraits taken. The room had a chair and a sofa.

"He threw himself on the lounge and wept bitterly, moaning like a man in great distress of mind," Rulofson remembered. "He finally became sufficiently calm to speak, and he said, 'Rulofson, you have been a good friend to me. I want you to promise me that in case of my death you will uphold the good name of my wife, and that you will settle our business affairs with her as you would with me.'" Muybridge pulled out the piece of paper containing this and other instructions and asked his dealer whether he would carry them out.

"Yes, I will," said Rulofson. "Now, what is wrong?"

"It is too horrible to tell," Muybridge said.

Some in his position might have had trouble handling Muybridge, but William Rulofson stayed cool, possibly because he had family experience with this sort of thing. Four years earlier, Rulofson's brother, Edward Ruloff, a linguist who lived in New York, had gone into a rage and, under mysterious circumstances, killed a shopkeeper. Ruloff was convicted and hanged. Muybridge's dealer, with a killer in his own family, knew the value of calm.

Rulofson thought Muybridge might be capable of killing himself. He told Muybridge it would be a mistake, that suicide would rob the world of an important artist and leave more questions than answers.

"That isn't my intention," Muybridge said.

Rulofson later remembered that during this time, "Muybridge would frequently throw himself on the lounge and burst into paroxysms of grief." At one point Muybridge got up off the sofa to leave, and Rulofson put his back against the door to prevent him exiting the room.

"You shouldn't go out in this frame of mind," Rulofson said. Muybridge grabbed him, and, as the art dealer remembered it, "with almost superhuman strength he literally hurled me across the room, and then started down the stairs." Rulofson ran after him and caught Muybridge in the well of the stairs, on the ground floor.

"If you leave the building in this condition you will be arrested," Rulofson said, or shouted. Rulofson persuaded Muybridge to talk some more, and they went into another empty room.

"I again attempted to calm him and to ascertain what it was that had so affected him," Rulofson told a newspaper. Muybridge said he had been "dishonored" by Harry Larkyns. "I tried to convince him that there might be some mistake—that the whole story was perhaps only the effect of idle gossip, and that such things were difficult to prove. Muybridge said he had the proof. He showed me with great reluctance, and many tears, a letter from his wife to Larkyns"—a letter Susan Smith had given him. He then produced one of Larkyns's letters to Flora. One letter begged Flora to come back to San Francisco. Larkyns said that he had heard she had been unfaithful to him, but he did not and could not believe the mother of his child would betray him.

Rulofson went silent at this turn in Muybridge's story. He asked Muybridge what he proposed to do. The photographer looked at his pocket watch. He answered that Larkyns was at Calistoga, and that he planned to go.

"And one of us will be shot."

"For God's sake, don't kill him," Rulofson said.

Muybridge put his letters in an envelope and gave them to Rulofson, telling him not to show them to anyone, telling him to destroy them if he was killed. Rulofson told Muybridge that he looked in no shape to do anything. "You are in no condition of mind," he said. "The task requires the greatest coolness and judgment."

It was four minutes before four o'clock. To get to Calistoga, Muybridge would have to take a ferry to Vallejo, and Rulofson knew the last ferry left at four. If Muybridge missed it, the shooting would be off. The art dealer kept arguing, prevaricating. "I talked against time," Rulofson remembered.

Muybridge "had been looking at his watch at intervals, and he sprang out of the room and ran down the street like a deer." Eight blocks away, at the waterfront, the Vallejo ferry took on its passengers. Rulofson said the distance took ten minutes to walk, and that only a person touched by madness could have sprinted to the boat in time.

———

Muybridge had been to Calistoga before. He had come to upper Napa Valley to photograph the geysers (including one that shot up every fifteen minutes). He had come to photograph some of the vineyards, which had started to spread through the valley, turning it into wine country. He had photographed the petrified forest of trees at least twice, with Flora, before and after they married. On this Saturday, Muybridge came for the last time. He took the ferry to Vallejo and there boarded a train that brought him to the northern end of Napa. He got off at Calistoga and took a buggy across the spurs of Mount St. Helena. It was an hour before midnight when he reached the Yellow Jacket Mine.

Muybridge told the story to a reporter.[7]

"I had no idea that I would come back alive. I thought that I would find him armed. I expected that a fight would ensue, and that I would probably be shot by him, even if I killed him too. I went to the door of the house, knocked and asked to see him. As soon as he came to the door I said to him, 'My name is Muybridge. I have received a message about my wife——.' Before I could say more he started to retreat into the house, so I fired on him. I did not intend to shoot him so quickly, but thought to talk with him and hear what he had to say, to hear his excuses, but he turned to run like a guilty craven when I pronounced my name, and I had to shoot him. The only thing I am sorry for is that he died so quickly."[8]

Muybridge had no regrets, no shame, no remorse.

———

Larkyns's body was sent back to San Francisco, where it arrived Sunday night.[9] The undertakers Lockhart & Porter took charge of it, and someone made the decision not to change the bloodied shirt. They dressed Larkyns in a suit that he had among his belongings and placed him in a rosewood casket with silver-plated screws and handles. Altogether a quick turnaround, especially considering it was Sunday. The undertakers set up the casket, open, in the visiting room at 11:00 p.m.

The dead man had one enemy other than Muybridge, Cuspidor Coppinger. Edward Ellis/Coppinger was drinking in a saloon when someone came in with news of Larkyns's body. Standing at the bar, Ellis ordered a glass of whiskey in celebration. "There is a special providence in the killing of that man," he said. "I drink to the special providence." According to one paper, Ellis, "who had trembled before the deceased while he lived," left the bar and walked to Lockhart & Porter, at 39 Third Street, where Larkyns lay in his coffin. He stood over the body and stared at the face, "long and maliciously," then walked out, rubbing his hands together, "grinning like a human jackal." Outside, Ellis turned to his friends. "I'd walk twenty miles the stormiest night that was ever seen to gaze on that sight," he said.

On Monday, a stream of people from the worlds of journalism and theater visited Larkyns. His face looked natural, but his forehead and nose showed bruises, made when he fell after being shot.

One of Larkyns's friends referred to Ellis's gloating as "a refined and brilliant exhibition of depravity";[10] another, a man called Gerald Darcy, took it upon himself to defend the memory of the dead man. On Monday, Darcy went to Ellis's office at the *Chronicle*, told him loudly that he had insulted the corpse of Larkyns, and threatened to kill him. Darcy challenged Ellis to a duel, the two arranged to meet the next day, and Darcy left.[11] After a few minutes Darcy returned to the drama critic's desk and said he wanted to kill him on the spot. At this, the paper's editors surrounded Larkyns's friend and physically ejected him from the building. On Tuesday, Ellis skipped the 1:00 p.m. showdown appointment and instead went to the city sheriff, who arrested Darcy for slander and for attempting a duel. Despite being condoned in much of California, dueling violated section 229 in the penal code, a little-heeded provision outlawing guns at private disputes.[12]

Larkyns's funeral took place Tuesday, October 20, at the Church of the Advent on Howard Street, with grand flourishes. A choir sang "Rock of Ages," after which a baritone from McGuire's Opera House, one of Larkyns's haunts, sang solo another hymn, "Flee as a Bird to Your Mountain." From the pews crowded with theater people, Larkyns's eulogist, Henry Edwards, stepped to the pulpit. An English-born actor and theater director, Henry Edwards, thick and jowly, with wavy hair and a walrus mustache, cut a wide swath in the cultural life of the city. He was president of the Bohemian Club, a circle of artists and journalists; he had founded the acting company of the California Theatre, where Larkyns had spent nights out with Flora; and he was an expert entomologist—he sat on the board of the California Academy of Sciences and possessed the most exquisite butterfly collection west of Chicago.

In his eulogy, Edwards dressed a tale of Harry Larkyns that went beyond his fame as a confidence man and seducer.

"It is good for us to linger for a moment about his remains," Edwards began, "and from the plain which soon will cover them to pluck a blade of memory, greener than the grass, to weave it into a chaplet of sorrow lighter than the air. He sleeps in peace, for gentle and loving hands have laid him in his grave." Larkyns should be remembered as "an admirable linguist, familiar with the literature of most continental nations—a brilliant writer, to whom no theme appeared to come amiss—a musician of culture—an artist of refined and polished taste—and, as a conversationalist rarely excelled." And yet, "poverty always hung like a gaunt specter about his footsteps, and the generous fountains of his nature were dried up by her touch." Edwards had no time for Muybridge. "The grandest and most heroic struggles of Larkyns's life," he said, "were the hand-to-hand conflict which he waged against those who reviled him here and who were far beneath him in every point of manliness and truth and honor."[13]

A hearse carried Harry Larkyns's coffin to the Masonic Cemetery, where his friends placed it in the vault pending instructions from Larkyns's relatives in England. These apparently never came. No record of his burial can be found.

———

The day before the funeral, two bailiffs put Edward Muybridge on the train in Calistoga and brought him twenty-five miles to the town of Napa, the county seat, where a Sheriff Corwin took charge of the perpetrator. A crowd watched the prisoner transfer. One said, "Muybridge is a man of fine appearance, with sprightly, elastic tread, and he tripped lightly down the steps and onto the sidewalk." The sheriff gave Muybridge a standard cell, and the photographer, known to be ascetic, made no complaint. Corwin gave the prisoner books and stationery, plus a menu from the Napa Hotel across the street. Prisoners had to pay for their own meals. Muybridge didn't mind ordering from the kitchen of the four-story brick inn that had just opened adjacent to the courthouse—the plates were still warm when Corwin carried them in.[14]

For days before and after the murder, as usual, Leland Stanford had been preoccupied with horses. His star gelding, Occident, had a big race scheduled at the end of October, and several hours a day Stanford watched his trainers put the horse through exercise. Occident was to meet a stallion called Fullerton, whose owners had sent him from the East Coast to challenge Stanford's dominance in harness racing. The horses would run three heats at the Bay District Track for a purse of $3,500. Stanford liked these single matches—he had put Occident through several. They generated good press, something the unpopular man needed.[15]

One day during training, although there's no direct evidence, Stanford seems to have interrupted his regime to send a message to a friend, a lawyer. Wirt Pendegast, age thirty-two, practiced law in the town of Napa, but Stanford knew him from his previous life in Sacramento.[16] During six years as a California senator, Pendegast had defended the Central Pacific and pushed laws in its favor. Stanford knew Pendegast because the rail president kept track of which lawmakers stood with him and which had to be brought over with an envelope containing an inducement. Stanford apparently told Pendegast that someone he knew had gotten into trouble in Napa, and that man needed an attorney. It wouldn't have been the first time Stanford had come to the aid of one of "his people" who had collided with the law. He once wrote the governor to ask for a pardon for a railroad lineman sent up to San Quentin.[17] There is no proof in Muybridge's case that Stanford intervened, no paper trail (why would he want his handprints on a murder case?), but the rich man probably sent word to Pendegast that "my photographer" needed help, and to get over to the courthouse.

A handler called Budd Doble drove Occident on the day of the race against Fullerton. Stanford's horse won two out of the three heats against the challenger, running the middle heat in the fastest time ever recorded in California, 2:18 for a mile. For good publicity, Stanford turned down the prize money—the Palo Alto Stock Farm and its owner both looked better for it.

Some days after being jailed, Muybridge hired a lawyer, the former state senator Wirt Pendegast. The attorney had an office in the courthouse, downstairs from the jail: to consult with his client he would merely take the staircase. Muybridge had heard of Pendegast—they said he had a reputation for oratory. They said he usually got his clients off. Pendegast came to see Muybridge in jail. The grand jury had not indicted yet, Pendegast said, but would do so in about a month. The charge would be capital murder, the lawyer said, which carried the penalty of death by hanging. (The lawyer knew that his client knew these things—both the client and the lawyer also understood that they had to be said out loud.) Pendegast told Muybridge he could expect to stay in jail until the trial. In a case like this, three months, maybe four.

Chapter 11

KING EADWEARD

At Waterloo Station in London, I bought a train ticket out to the hometown of Edward James Muggeridge. It cost five pounds. Muggeridge grew up in Kingston-upon-Thames, fifteen miles southwest of central London, eight stops and twenty-eight minutes on a commuter line. When he lived there, Kingston was one of England's thousand hermetical villages; then the railroad came. Now the town sits under the London canopy, another piece in the city's sprawl.

He was born in Kingston, lived in America for nearly fifty years, and went back to England in his late sixties. He died in Kingston in 1904—as Eadweard Muybridge, age seventy-four—and in his will left his remaining negatives and photographs, as well as some of his equipment, to his hometown. He also left the projector that put the first moving pictures on screens. (Or at any rate a second version, built to replace the one he used at Leland Stanford's house.) I wanted to have a look at the machine that had started the revolution in vision, the device he grandly named the zoopraxiscope.

Kingston-upon-Thames sits on the river upstream from London, and its history goes back about 1,300 years. For most of that time, the River Thames made the only way in and out, but the railroad arrived during Muggeridge's childhood and turned the old town into a station stop. Lately Kingston has become a heritage town. Like many ancient places in England it sells the past, antiquity being one of the few brands that small places can make money on. Day-trippers come from London to shoulder down crooked medieval alleys and look at half-timbered Tudor houses in the thousand-year-old market square, to row a bit on the Thames and drink the ale at waterfront pubs. The river, sluggish and bending, measures about fifty yards across at Kingston. Get into a boat, push downstream, and you come to London. The trip was one Edward Muggeridge would have made often as a boy, shuttling between his antique birthplace and the coal-blackened metropolis, but it takes five or six hours.

I walked through the oldest part of Kingston and came to his house. A tasteful green plaque on the front reads: CHILDHOOD HOME OF EADWEARD MUYBRIDGE, PIONEER PHOTOGRAPHER, 1830–1904. It's a two-story brick merchant's townhouse on a busy commercial street, just as it was almost two centuries ago, with a door that opens directly onto the sidewalk. The house shares its walls with the neighboring townhouses. Each house also possesses a storefront, the Muggeridge place with a carriageway leading to the back. There is a curve in the narrow street at this point; the back of the house faces the Thames, thirty yards away, and you can see that the curve of the street follows the bend in the river. The Muggeridge place was the kind of house where people worked and lived before the industrial tide came in and swept everything before it, turning the idea of business done at home into a useless husk.

Kingston is old even by creaky English standards. The tourist literature calls it the "Royal Borough of Kingston-upon-Thames," part of the heritage spin and a reference to a royal backstory. The "royal"

The childhood home of Ted Muggeridge— 30 High Street (then called West-by-Thames) in Kingston, England, fifteen miles southwest of the center of London. John and Susannah Muggeridge and their four sons occupied the upper floors of the commercial townhouse, and a hatmaker rented the store below.

trademark, which came alive during Edward Muggeridge's youth, seems to have awakened in him personally during midlife, prompting the photographer, at age fifty, to change the spelling of his first name to the medieval "Eadweard." That name dates from the Saxons, and one of the curious things about the man who was arguably the inventor of moving pictures, a modern man if you like, is that he felt attracted to a thing so old and dead as the name of a Saxon king.

A record shows a settlement at Kingston, on the banks of the River Thames, in 838. For a thousand years it served as the region's market town, farm life coming and going. About the year 1200, a bridge went over the river at Kingston, the only bridge upstream from London, and hundreds of carriages and wagons and stagecoaches crossed the water every day, adding the role of highway station to that of river town. Another six hundred years passed, the river and the bridge framing village life. Kingston was already a changeless relic when the Muggeridge family, during the 1820s, moved into their house, the one on the bend in the river, with the nice enameled plaque.

———

Edward James Muggeridge, born April 9, 1830, left few traces of his feelings and thoughts. He left no diaries. The confessional style, in which artists write down the names of their lovers and leave journals to be collected by posterity, came later. His surviving letters talk about his photographs and how to sell them. He did not write a memoir or otherwise disburden himself of what it was to be a boy growing up in an old place outside the capital. One of his cousins, however, in a memoir she wrote, recorded some observations about him from the time they were both children. The cousin said he went by the name of "Ted."[1]

A photograph of Ted Muggeridge, probably at age twenty, shows a plump and dressed-up boy, scrubbed bright. He wears a vested suit and a tie in a way that says he has put them on before, occasionally. The face is clean-shaven, the cheeks buxom and the lips thick. He has strong eyebrows and straight brown hair. Muggeridge looks chunky and fresh, not yet burned by anything, apparently not yet disappointed, but there seems to be uncertainty at the eyes.

His family was comfortable but not wealthy. England had a small elite and a mass of farmers and workers, and the Muggeridges occupied the lower part of the slender middle. They left more copious records than most lower-middle-class people, because a handful of their in-

Ted Muggeridge, ca. 1850. Probably taken when he was twenty—just before he emigrated from England to America—for the benefit of his family, who did not know whether they would see him again. It is the only photograph of Muggeridge at an age younger than thirty-five, and the sole picture that shows his face without his lifelong, substantial beard.

laws owned real estate. Ted was the second of four sons—his father was twenty-four at the time of Ted's birth, his mother twenty-three. They gave him the name of his mother's father, Edward, and the middle name of his father's brother, James.

When Edward James Muggeridge was born, his parents lived in the house with its back to the river, at what is now 30 High Street. (The street runs west from the center of town, beside the water—during his childhood it was called West-by-Thames Street.) The Muggeridge family lived upstairs, renting their floors from the landlord, one Daniel Dacombe. Downstairs was a hatmaker, Mrs. Phillips, who rented the storefront. Maybe you could smell the millinery as you walked past. Street life around the Muggeridge house was beery. Two doors one way stood a pub, the Ram Inn, two doors the other way a drunks' alley, where boatmen staggered and leaned.

His parents baptized Ted beneath the thirteenth-century Gothic arches of All Saints Church, three blocks from their doorstep. As a boy Ted might have been made to go to services. The stone church was the town's venerable landmark, a building with a past that reaches almost to the time of St. Augustine's mission to the Saxons, with additions and changes made every few hundred years, and walls studded with marble memorials to long-dead parishioners.

John Muggeridge, Ted's father, sold corn and coal for a living, according to a census. He lived on commissions, which meant the family money went up and down. John Muggeridge had married up in class, rising from people who made ends meet to join his wife's clan of small business owners. John Muggeridge's parents, Ted's grandparents, had moved to Kingston from the village of Banstead, ten miles south by a winding road, where most of the Muggeridges had been tenant farmers. After their move Ted's grandparents had found a living in Kingston as makers of malt, the first step in beer brewing. Malt making was a process that went on in scores of houses and barns—the huge beer thirst of the people was such that many had to be recruited to it, so-called maltsters. Ted's grandparents used to buy a barrel of barley at a time, stew it, and when it sprouted spread it out on the floor of an empty room to dry. Fires in the basement helped the parching, and the malt was then sold to a brewer. Kingston shared its hunger for beer with every other English town. At a time when public water sources ranged from unreliable to unclean, and epidemics came and went, beer gave people fluids and calories free of disease, while it soothed psychic injury.

Ted's uncle, Charles Muggeridge, had followed Ted's grandfather into malt making. When Ted was a boy Uncle Charles lived with his wife and four children a few doors away. Thus there were at least two Muggeridge households in Kingston. Added to these were two houses where his mother's siblings lived with their families. A network of cousins, aunts, and uncles surrounded Ted, as it did many village people.

His mother was one Susannah Smith, and of his two parents, her family was the more posh. The Smiths owned a venerable business that

Susanna Smith, Ted Muggeridge's maternal grandmother, ca. 1860

ran barges on the Thames. For some fifty years they had been sending their flatboats loaded with farm goods or coal or timber down to
London and bringing them back with city stuffs. Horses moved the
barge traffic. One end of a rope was tied to the prow of a flatboat and
the other end to horses on land—the animals pulled from a towpath
that ran beside the river, heaving the boats at walking speed. The family of Ted's mother employed some ten bargemen, and these so-called
bargees lived in shacks by the water at the foot of the Smiths' backyard.
The colony of workmen, many with families of their own, imparted to
the Smiths a feudal glow, with the bargees in the role of serfs and their
employers as minor-key lords. The Smiths lived a quarter mile from
the Muggeridges, five minutes by foot along the river, in a big house
with two servants living in, on Old Bridge Street (the place where
the first bridge had stood a thousand years earlier). They made good
money most years and had one foot conspicuously planted in the drawing room. But the barge trade had an enemy, the railroad, which was
appearing on the horizon.

Susannah Muggeridge, Ted's mother, seems to have lived under the
shadow of her own mother, a woman named Susanna Smith (minus the
h she gave to her daughter). This was Ted's grandmother, who played
up the role of a matriarch, doling out favors and cash and running the
lives of her three grown children, not to mention her ten grandchildren.
Grandmother Susanna Smith had been widowed during her thirties
and raised her children alone while running the family barge business,
inherited from her husband. She eventually brought into the business
her oldest son, Joseph Smith. Ted's uncle Joseph lived in the house on
Old Bridge Street, and he appeared to people in town to be a young
eminence—a wife and three children, plus the servants. But the house
belonged to his mother, the forbidding Susanna Smith; she occupied
the second floor, still owned the barge business, and vetted her son's
decisions. At one point she had a run-in with another of her sons, who
was thirty at the time, and added a codicil to her will that stripped him
of his inheritance "until he shall be outlawed or be found bankrupt."[2]

By her photograph, Susanna Smith looks to have been about five
feet six and stout. She wore floor-length black dresses in lifelong public
mourning for her husband. To lighten the black she put on a white lace
collar. Susanna Smith was grand in her hands-on-the-till way. In addition to the boats, she owned several houses that she rented to simpler

people. The memoir by Ted's cousin calls her "the family autocrat" and says she dominated her family and her workers, the bargemen, treating the latter like peasants who depended on her.

Her husband, Ted's grandfather Edward Smith, had died before Ted was born, and since Ted was named after him, he became something like a memento mori, and it is possible the grandmother had a special zone in her heart for young Ted, the boy who stood in for her husband. The Smith family had some airs—wineglasses and silver, stuffed chairs, rugs, mahogany furniture. Susanna Smith presided at grandish dinners, as Ted's cousin described them. The matriarch sat at the head of the table, flanked on one side by Ted with his brothers and parents, while the other cousins and aunts and uncles formed similar clusters. After a dinner of some formality came a performance of strange artifice, directed by the grandmother and featuring Ted and the other grandchildren. Smith made each of them stand and "recite, or tell of work done, or answer pointed questions on varied subjects," and in general account for themselves. She went around the room, and each child had to speak to the group, sum up their life and doings, and say what they had planned. It was a performance that everyone studied for, "preparation which included every detail of health, conduct and dress which might attract the careful oversight of the head of the clan." Ted like the others steadied his nerves and announced something about his record at school, maybe a word about what work he hoped to get into. It was the song the grandchildren had to sing for handouts.[3]

To judge from the way they did business, the Smith family, Ted's maternal clan, seems to have been a living antique. As telegraph lines were being strung here and there and railroad beds laid, the Smiths still used carrier pigeons for their correspondence. From Kingston, the River Thames runs downstream to London in a meandering path. When the barges went to the capital, they had to cross three different locks, the filling and draining of which slowed the trip, extending it to most of a day. To communicate with home, one of the Smith men brought along a cage containing a messenger bird. In London, the barges were unloaded, and the bargees looked for new cargo to take back upriver—furniture, iron, liquor, clothes, machines. The goods went on board, and the boatman scribbled a note to describe the freight returning that night. The note went into a thimble, and one of the Smith family pigeons carried it back to Kingston.

When Ted Muggeridge was a boy, five thousand people lived in Kingston and two million in London, the biggest city in Europe, as well as the command post of the British Empire. London threw a long and dark shadow, with its factories that provided new forms of wage serfdom and epidemics that swept thousands from the slums into mass graves. This was the urban hell described by Friedrich Engels in *The Condition of the Working Class in England in 1844*, a chronicle of despair from the early 1840s. London would have pressed itself into Ted's world—the industrial storm creeping toward his town, the strict ways of the Regency fading and in retreat. As the city came closer, it both frightened the outlying places as well as teased their desires. For many, the big adventure would have been to go into the capital. To get there Ted had an advantage, since the boats belonging to his mother's family went back and forth to the docks. It might have been his habit to go to London for a day, the riverboat men his chaperones, and take a dose of the stinking, trembling metropolis.

If he paddled in the other direction on the river, not downstream but up, and around the first bend, Ted would have come to another blast of power, Hampton Court Palace. This ancient and stupendous royal residence overlooked the river near Kingston as indifferently as the Pentagon, and on nearly the same scale. What Ted would have seen, after twenty minutes in a rowboat, was two palaces, a sixteenth-century red-brick fortress with turrets and a serenely square, white addition built in the eighteenth century. He would have seen the grounds along the river teeming with gardeners and retainers. The people of Kingston were keenly aware of Hampton Court—many worked there as servants and factotums. Ted, like the rest, would have felt the radiating heat that comes from living near a place of power, the sense that important people are at hand and in some way difficult to express they have you in their grasp.

The year Ted Muggeridge was born, the first trains in England started service—the Liverpool and Manchester Railway—and when he was eight years old a second train system, which came directly to Kingston, went into service. This was the Great Western Railway, which ran from Waterloo Station in London to southwest England, with Ted's town one of its brand-new stations. The advent of the rail stirred excitement and fear. It represented the future, and speed, but also something dangerous, filthy, and loud. To placate opposition, the company was forced to put the Kingston rail station outside of town. (It was later moved to the center.) From a clue in later life, it is likely Ted Muggeridge, the boy, paid close attention to the train. The Great Western was the feat of an engineer named Isambard Brunel, a man featured in the newspapers as a hero, a machine-age impresario. Years later, as a photographer, Ted would publish pictures of Brunel's other engineering work, showing that he never forgot the man who brought the train to Kingston. It seems likely that after the rail service began, in 1838, Ted Muggeridge traded his barge rides to London for train rides.

The telegraph came at the same time. When the Great Western Railway went in, its developers strung telegraph wires along the track route, and on them the first telegraph service to go into commercial operation in England went live, extending from London to towns in the west. The coming all at once of these two life-changing machines, the locomotive and the telegraph, would have shaken perceptions. They would have made Ted's hometown feel weaker, more provincial. They would have tied it to a network that originated in the city and made every place it touched into a dependent node on the line. The railroad changed the land, cutting through centuries of settlement and across property lines; the telegraph seemed to destroy time, reducing distance and the difficulty of getting out a message to nothing. Prior to the railroad, Kingston was one of England's antiques. After it, the town became a destination on the branch from the capital, a stopping place for dots and dashes sent on the wire.

As a boy Ted saw firsthand that traditions like his family's barge business, which stood in the path of the machine, turned obsolete and went into decline. Eventually he began building little machines of his own. The cousin who wrote about him, Maybanke Anderson, said that Ted, during his childhood, was something of a tinkerer— she described his appetite for making little gadgets and toys to impress other kids. Later in life Ted would patent his own equipment and place it on show in industrial exhibitions. And forty years after the rail came to his hometown, Edward Muybridge would photograph the horses of Leland Stanford, the train monopolist, closing a circle of some kind.

———

Ted Muggeridge was "an eccentric boy, rather mischievous, always doing something or saying something unusual or inventing a new toy or a fresh trick," his cousin said. He sounds like the kid known in the family for entertaining the others, and for getting up stunts to attract attention. He seemed to like persuading younger children to fetch things for him and do him favors. Anderson wrote down her memories after Edward Muybridge had become famous—in fact, after he had died. But if you adjust for the dressing-up that's done by old memory, you come away with Ted Muggeridge as a boy who had the mind of a prankwise child, a boy perhaps skeptical if not devious. Some of this remained in the personality of the grown-up, at any rate, the artist and shape shifter of photo-technology.

His parents could not send him to an exclusive school, so according to most sources they sent Ted to the next best, a place called Queen Elizabeth's Grammar. An upright institute, no dithering allowed, this place for the better boys in town was housed in a four-hundred-year-old church, known as Lovekyn Chapel, remade into a school. With decent teachers and a steady family life, Ted was on the way to mapping a life, maybe a role in the barge business, or something in trade. But soon after he had enrolled, just when his voice was breaking, all this changed.

Ted Muggeridge's school, Queen Elizabeth's Grammar, operated out of a fifteenth-century church known as Lovekyn Chapel.

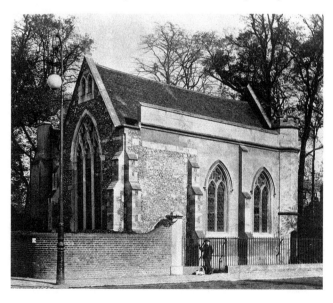

Ted's uncle Charles Muggeridge, the malt maker, age thirty, was the first to die. There is no record of the cause, but the year Charles died, 1842, an epidemic of typhus killed some sixteen thousand people in England and Wales.[4] Ted would have gone to his uncle's funeral and seen his four young cousins, Charles's children, in the front pew. A year later Charles's widow, Ted's aunt Ann Muggeridge, possibly short of money, moved away with her children—she disappears from Kingston records.

The second to die, in March 1843, was Ted's father, John Muggeridge. Again there is no record, but medical histories cite that month as one when an epidemic of influenza broke out in England, killing many thousands before it crossed the Atlantic and killed many more in America. John Muggeridge probably died in the sweep of this virus, age thirty-seven.

Ted was twelve years old. The cull that took away his father and uncle in a period of a little more than a year would have been, at that time, a common experience, when waves of disease flooded the population, and children lost adults to sudden death. But there is nothing routine about the mental injury Ted would have experienced. His father's people were gone from town, and three of his four grandparents were dead. When Ted's father died, he took away from his son some kind of an ideal. It may have burned Ted in a way that caused him to withdraw, might have made him even more irregular, or "mischievous," as his cousin put it.

———

The death of Ted's father erased most of the family's income and left his mother with four young sons. Susannah Muggeridge had to worry about money, but less than other women in the same place because her own mother had extra. The widow was thirty-five. Her circumstances would have been familiar to her mother, the matriarch, who was also once a young widow with a house full of children. It seems the grand Susanna Smith stepped in, paid the bills, and padded things for Ted, softening his fatherless world.

Ted was the second of the four boys. The oldest by two years was the father's namesake, John Muggeridge. Ted may have looked up to him, the more so when the older boy found his way into a venerable boarding school in London. It was 1846. The academy known as Christ's Hospital was a three-hundred-year-old school at Newgate, in the old city center, which subsidized tuition for the sons of workers and so gave plainer boys a chance at university. The school took the sons of certain tradesmen as scholarship students, and among the favored guilds, a union of riverboat hands called the Company of Watermen had the right to send a few boys. John Muggeridge Jr. seems to have gotten into the school thanks to his grandmother's barges. At a time when one in a hundred boys went beyond high school, a place at Christ's Hospital meant university might lie over the horizon, and Ted's brother could end up with a profession and a great leap in class.

John Jr. left Kingston for school, spent a year there, came home. He returned for his second year and started studying, but in October 1847, he fell sick and died. He was nineteen. As usual, the record gives no cause, but 1847 was yet another year of pandemic. This one was known as the "Irish fever," an eruption of typhus that killed thirty thousand around the country.[5]

The spasms of natural selection arranged Ted's childhood. First his uncle's funeral, then his father's, now his brother's. Ted was sixteen when his brother died. Historians say this kind of loss happened all the time, but Ted Muggeridge could count more than the average number of family members gone missing, all of them men. What is it like, behind the eyes, as your closest ones disappear into the churchyard? What kind of self remains? Is it the personality of a survivor? Ted's childhood does not have ample documentation, but if you look at what evidence does exist, you might conclude that the shocks he experienced with death correspond with later patterns of alienation (if that is the right word). As an adult, Edward Muybridge, the photographer, relied on few people. He changed his relationships often and made not many friends, and he seemed most content alone. Solitary, peripatetic, Muybridge lived like a castaway, deracinated and drifting. Are the sources of his isolation to be found in the time when the men in his family vanished?

The boy Ted Muggeridge also felt the plain fragility of status. When his father died, he saw success and social standing collapse between one year and the next; when his brother died, the same. I imagine that from these things the understanding might have entered his mind how nothing really remains, how you remake yourself as you go. If Ted took a message from all these deaths, it might have been to make his life more available to self-styling, to improvisation, a tactic of getting by that he eventually put into action in America.

———

As a child he lived in a rooted place, but the storm of industrialization was all around. Britain embraced the machine—factories and mass production, coal and urbanization—and its center was London. A list of the city's industries, all of them adult but still growing, would include engineering, shipbuilding, papermaking, and leather. (The textile mills, the biggest industrial drivers, were in Manchester.) The experience of England during Muggeridge's youth was not unlike that of China during its industrialization in the late twentieth and early-twenty-first centuries: masses of people moved from farmland to cities to shoehorn themselves into crowded rooms and neighborhoods. As they did, the rural experience of time itself disappeared, replaced by the inflexible clock, the measured hour. With it came new forms of degradation—child labor and the twelve-hour day, slums and epidemic disease, the exhaustion of being tethered to machines.

Muggeridge as a boy saw these things from the relative calm of his river town. Looking at his later life, it is obvious that technology interested him, how to build a better machine. As a boy he seems to have admired the iron bridges, the machines that sped up life and made it more standard. He seems to have admired the steam engine that made possible the great "overland ship" of the railroad. Muggeridge was a practical boy from an impractically old place. His mother's family, the comfortable ones, may not have seen that their prosperity would be wiped away by the railroad, but maybe Ted Muggeridge did.

———

The patronymic "Muggeridge" had been around for centuries. For some reason, around the middle of the 1800s, it presented a problem to many of the family's men. Ted would not be the only one who changed his name. He had two brothers who survived into adulthood, and it turns out that they, too, would change their last name. And the brothers also had a male cousin who did the same. All this relabeling adds up.

You can speculate about what prompted it. The name Muggeridge happens to rhyme with "bugger." The Oxford English Dictionary, so thorough with a million other etymologies, defines *buggery* pretty obscurely as "a technical term in criminal law" and cites an 1861 statute that criminalized "the abominable crime of buggery, committed either with mankind or with any animal." The apparently wild and indefensible act of anal sex was criminalized. It may have been that the act of buggery, during the famously anti-sexual Victorian decades, grew from merely furtive behavior into a crime. It may have been that the word *buggery* (and jokes at the family's expense) got pretty hot around this time. In the end, many Muggeridge men took steps to ditch their surname, as though they wanted to get away from something. Was it this sort of adolescent boy trouble that made Ted begin to tinker with his name, a habit he kept up throughout his life? It seemed easier to change the family handle than to carry it.

As for his first name, the metamorphosis into Eadweard links up with local history. According to a legend (few papers exist to back it up), during the tenth century, Kingston became the coronation place for seven Saxon kings. The kings demonstrably lived, but whether they came to this place to be crowned is another matter. The first of them, in the year 900, was King Eadweard. A bit later you find a sovereign called Eadwig, coronation date 955, and then another like the first, Eadweard the Martyr, crowned 975. When Ted Muggeridge was a teenager, the burghers of Kingston, in a show of civic pride, dusted off the legend of the Saxon rulers. A great stumplike boulder was produced from the yard of All Saints Church, where Ted had been baptized, and designated the Coronation Stone—the flat, round rock was said to have been the place on which the rulers sat to be crowned. Not wishing truth to stand in the way of a story, the town placed the stone in the market square and chiseled the names of the kings on a large plinth. It was 1850. That year, gossip and storytelling about the stone preoccupied Kingston, and suitable ceremony accompanied the placement of the flat rock—a dais with bunting, music, and speeches.

In hindsight, it seems more than a coincidence that local excitement about the town's ancient royal roots grew just after the appearance of the rail line and the telegraph. When Kingston became a London afterthought, with the hint of irrelevance, it suddenly discovered its fancy history. The stone and its plinth remain, since moved next to the guildhall, and if you have a look, you will see prominently on the base the medieval spelling of the name: EADWEARD.

Ted Muggeridge, who was nineteen when Kingston reclaimed the story of its Saxon king, took the name "Eadweard" from his hometown's tale about itself. But this part is curious: he was fifty-two years

Coronation Stone, Kingston

old, and living abroad, when he finally did so. He knew the story, but waited a long time before dressing himself in the unpronounceable name, Eadweard.

He might have been aware of another thing, namely, the association of King Eadweard with murder. As it happened, two kings called Eadweard reigned, and the second of them, Eadweard the Martyr, ruled for just three years before he was murdered, in the year 975, by his stepmother and stepbrother—leading posterity to give him the cheery epithet "the Martyr." No evidence exists, though, that these facts played a role when Edward Muybridge, lately a murderer himself, took up the king's name.

———

He was about five foot ten, age sixteen. He came from deep tradition and tight family, but at some point during his teens these things ceased to give him what he wanted. His brother John Jr. had gone to the fancy boarding school, Christ's Hospital, and there was not another place for the Muggeridges, not another chance at Oxford or Cambridge. The barge business would go into the hands of his cousins, boys named Smith, grandsons of the matriarch, Susanna Smith. (He was also a grandson, but through his mother, a different matter.) The English pattern caused most boys who had run out of other prospects to leave the classroom before age sixteen and apprentice to a company or trade. Despite having a bit of cash, the Muggeridges and Smiths kept to this line. A record shows that Ted's brother Thomas left school at sixteen to apprentice to a shipper in Carmarthen, Wales, a step he took before joining the merchant marine, and although there is no direct evidence for Ted, an apprenticeship someplace would have been the only path open.[6]

It seems that in the year 1846, Ted Muggeridge was taken from his books and made to support himself. When it happened, circumstances suggest that he would have looked to his father's people. There were no Muggeridges left in Kingston, but a lot of them elsewhere. Ten miles away, in the village of Banstead, were the Muggeridges who farmed (but there was not much to offer there). More Muggeridges lived in London itself, on the south side of the Thames, and these were better off. This big-city branch kept up with Ted's mother, and in later years she would move to London and live with some of them in the neighborhood of Camberwell.

At least two Muggeridge families in London ran businesses in publishing. A stationer called Muggeridge & Sprague had two offices, a showplace in the center city, and a printing operation in Camberwell. Another stationer named Muggeridge did business two miles from Camberwell in Southwark. Stationers did not merely sell paper (although they did that, too). By long tradition, stationers published books and pamphlets, and they printed art. Muggeridge & Sprague had been in business for fifty years at 61 Queen Street, near St. Paul's Cathedral, in the center of the legal and money nexus, the City. An established stationer like Muggeridge & Sprague operated as a publisher of literature as well as a dealer in engravings and full-color prints you could frame. It employed salesmen to drum up subscribers, people who might put down money for books before publication date, and it ran an art printing operation. From its substantial office in central London, Muggeridge & Sprague published encyclopedias and other reference books, and folios of art, and sold all of them on site.[7]

It may have been that either Muggeridge & Sprague or the stationer in Southwark, Nathaniel & John Muggeridge, belonged to cousins of Ted's dead father. What Ted Muggeridge did later in America—selling reference books, publishing art—implies that he apprenticed to one of these two. Both would have used young men who signed up to the trade and suffered what abuse and long hours and bad pay were necessary in order to leave in three or four years, having learned how things were done. Books and pamphlets were old trades, so this would have been regarded as a conservative path for Ted. But machines, as everywhere, were changing things. Chromolithography, or mass-produced color printing, came in around 1840, and the rotary press about 1850, both of them boosting print runs and pushing the public to read and to look, more and faster. The technology made stationers grow and brought more young men like Ted to the training bench.

His letters contain another bit of circumstantial evidence. The business mail Ted wrote, years later, displays the style that Victorian gentlemen used with one another—polite and high, full of mannerisms like "your obedient servant," a writing voice that flourished in an office staffed with scriveners, like a stationer's.

Ted Muggeridge might have lived at the publishing house, might have taken the train back and forth from Kingston. He would have gotten the feel of books and their varieties, learned about quartos and engraving plates and thirty-six-page duodecimos. He would have learned announcements and tombstone ads and layout, cardstock and engravings and pamphlets. He would also have been hitting the streets of stinking and euphoric London and picking up a taste for the metropolis.

One firm in downtown London stood a notch in status above the stationers—the London Printing & Publishing Company. It had offices on St. John's Street, a mile from Muggeridge & Sprague, and Ted Muggeridge, when he came to the city, would have walked past it. London Printing & Publishing produced thick, ponderous books—encyclopedias, multivolume histories, science monographs—titles aimed at the deep libraries of rich people and institutions. The company also put out travel books, art reproductions, etchings, and engravings. It happened that London Printing & Publishing had designs on America. The company wanted to increase its sales in the United States and was opening an office in New York. For this overseas operation, the book publisher needed a salesman—a "merchant," as Ted would put it on his travel papers.

It was the spring of 1850, and Ted had just turned twenty. It may have been that London Printing & Publishing offered him a job if he would go to New York; it may have been something more. Whatever the source of his desire (and he never wrote about it), things came to a head in early 1850. Ted's cousin Maybanke, in her memoir, puts a romantic spin on the moment he left. "He wanted to see the world and 'to make a name for himself' and at last he came to say 'Goodbye,' he was going to America." Ted went to his grandmother Susanna Smith, the autocrat, who offered him money. "With her usual kindliness, she put a little pile of sovereigns beside him and said, 'you may be glad to have them Ted.' He pushed them back to her and said 'No, thank you, Grandma, I'm going to make a name for myself. If I fail, you will never hear of me again.' "[8]

If he had come from a richer family, Ted might have made a different exit. The British Empire, with its colonies, trading companies, and military, extended around the world. A young man from the gentry who wanted to leave home might become a naval officer or join the diplomatic corps. These routes did not open to a boy who fell below the threshold of entitlement, a boy from bargemen and maltsters.

In June he packed three trunks and took one of the new trains to Liverpool. Ted made an unusual emigrant to America. He was not poor. He was not going to California to find gold. The steamship *Liverpool*, moored at the dock, would fill up with Irish passengers. Ted was English, another anomaly. His trunks went onto the luggage wagon.

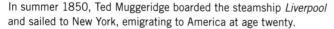

In summer 1850, Ted Muggeridge boarded the steamship *Liverpool* and sailed to New York, emigrating to America at age twenty.

On the water it looked like a hybrid beast, a steam-powered ship fitted on the sides with paddlewheels and with two smokestacks, but also three masts planted in the deck and sails. The steamship *Liverpool*, like many long-distance carriers of the time, used sail power to bolster its feeble steam. Unfortunately for its passengers, the *Liverpool* had a spotty record. Four years earlier, it had run aground off Spain, after which the Peninsular and Oriental Line had patched the hull and sent it back out. On this crossing from England to America, however, there were no incidents. Captain John Eldridge had taken particulars from every passenger, 414 immigrants slotted, squeezed, and jammed into his 225-foot ship, and written them into the manifest. Passenger 91 said he was twenty years old. He said his name was Edward Muggeridge.[9]

Almost all the *Liverpool*'s passengers were Irish refugees, like the passengers on most ships from Britain to America during these years. The great potato famine had killed close to a million people in Ireland, and nearly a million more were in the midst of emptying the island's western counties. Plenty aboard the *Liverpool* were single men, at least some of them on the first leg of a journey to California. The previous year someone had found gold in the American West at a place called Sutter's Mill, and it was common belief, based on the best hearsay, that young men who could make it to California would be rich soon after arrival. Ted Muggeridge was one of the few passengers not from Ireland. He had boarded the *Liverpool* in the city of the same name, after which the ship had stopped in Ireland to load everybody else.

At the slow pace of the ship, less than eight knots, the crossing to New York took about three weeks. One of the Irish passengers, a forty-year-old woman named Ellen Dunn, eight months pregnant, had come aboard with her five young children. In the middle of the ocean, Dunn's six-year-old daughter Mary fell sick of something and died; a week later Dunn gave birth to a new baby. Captain Eldridge wrote it all down in his report to customs. On the passenger list, Eldridge had labeled nearly everyone a "laborer," "servant," or "farmer." There were two "gentlemen." Ted Muggeridge told the captain he was a "merchant," a salesman of merchandise. The *Liverpool* docked near the southern tip of Manhattan on July 16, 1850—another cargo of immigrants, the diet of America.

Most of his fellow passengers would have marked Ted Muggeridge, the Englishman, as the comparatively rich one among them. Whereas nearly everyone else had registered a single bag, the Englishman carried three trunks. Most passengers did not know what awaited them, but Muggeridge had a job lined up in New York. He would be a sales representative for a British publishing company. Perhaps the trunks carried inventory, samples of the books and engravings he was coming to America to sell.

Muggeridge wrote down many things over the next fifty years, but in his letters and published articles, he never spoke about immigrating to the United States. He never wrote about his decision to leave behind an antique village west of London, where he had grown up, or about his feelings of being an expatriate. His reticence might have been part of his culture, but perhaps the episode itself had too little form to remember. He was young, with raw appetites. Like everyone else aboard, he would soon become wood for the blaze of the American marketplace.

In New York, Muggeridge would be a salesman of books and art. After ten years, he would renounce this life and become an inventor, and after that an artist, before rebranding himself as a murderer, and then as a scientist. He would be many different men, but on the *Liverpool*, he was not yet any of them. His bags hurtling onto the dock, Ted Muggeridge stepped off to the customs house.

Chapter 12

MARITAL RIGHTS

Edward Muybridge sat in jail far from his adopted city, San Francisco. The town of Napa, no more than three thousand people and just incorporated, stood at the center of the long, narrow valley of the same name. Tanneries lay outside of it, plus a swirl of vineyards and farms. Thanks to the train line, which Leland Stanford had lately bought, you could get to San Francisco in five hours. It would have occurred to Muybridge, awaiting his trial, that he might not see it again.

He now had three lawyers—Wirt Pendegast, Stanford's friend, who had a reputation for blinding the courtroom with clouds of metaphor; Pendegast's partner F. E. Johnston; and a San Francisco attorney, Cameron King. Pendegast visited often, King came to the jail when he could. William Wirt Pendegast had been born in Kentucky, the son of an attorney who had given up the law to become an evangelist with a fundamentalist sect, the Disciples of Christ. Pendegast had grown up hearing his father preach and push crowds close to weeping, and he drew lessons from it. His parents had named him after William Wirt, attorney general under presidents James Monroe and John Quincy Adams, and a man famous for his courtroom soliloquies. After his parents moved their family west, to Sacramento, Wirt Pendegast studied law and then went into politics, becoming the youngest legislator elected to the California Senate. Cameron King, Muybridge's other lawyer, was another attorney with political connections. A solo practitioner in San Francisco, age thirty, King had trained in the law firm of his uncle, Governor Henry Haight, the man who succeeded Stanford in that office.[1]

Pendegast and King told Muybridge that they would prefer not to get him out on bail before the trial. If Muybridge posted bail, then his lawyers would be obliged to share their evidence and the substance of their case with the prosecutor, and Pendegast and King preferred to keep all that hidden. As for a defense, there could be no denying the killing. Not only had several people witnessed it, and not only had Muybridge admitted shooting Larkyns, he had gone out of his way to take credit for it. When the *Chronicle* ran a story that said Muybridge had merely wanted to maim Harry Larkyns and not to kill him, two days later the paper had to run a retraction, because Muybridge had written the editor to complain. ("The defendant," said the paper, "denies that he intended only to maim the deceased, but avers that his intention was to kill him.") Muybridge liked people to know he was meticulous.[2]

His lawyers wanted to keep Muybridge off the gallows, but how? They could try "justifiable homicide." A killing shown to be an act of justice meant a verdict of not guilty. Justifiable homicide worked, most often, in cases of self-defense: a murder might be justified if the accused could show, for example, he had been threatened with a gun. The justifiable argument, which also went under another name, the "provocation defense," allowed a killer to admit the act and still be absolved. With Muybridge, the provocation defense looked like a difficult fit. Harry Larkyns had been unarmed; Muybridge had traveled seventy-five miles to find him, and he had shot without giving Larkyns a chance to defend himself. On the other hand, lawyers like Pendegast and King knew that juries sometimes accepted a version of the provocation defense not readily acknowledged by the law—the "marital rights" argument. For many men (and juries were all male), the fact that Flora Muybridge had been sleeping with Harry Larkyns could be construed as a provocation. In this view, self-defense translated into the husband's prerogative to retaliate, because he was "provoked" by his sexual rival. When adultery was involved, juries sometimes let men go free for killings.

The marital rights defense appeared nowhere in the legal code, and it had dubious standing. Judges didn't care for it. The argument forced them to tell juries that seduction did not constitute a mortal threat, that a stronger warrant for self-defense was necessary. And there was another fact about the marital rights claim. It worked for men but did not commonly apply to women. If a wife discovered her husband having sex with another woman, she did not, by custom, have the go-ahead to kill her competitor in defense of the marriage bed. No jury, at least, had ever seen it that way. You could say the precedent favored men and not women, but that was neither Muybridge's nor his lawyers' problem.

Talking it through, Pendegast and King decided they would tread lightly around the argument for justifiable homicide. Pendegast suspected the judge in the case, likely to be a man called William Wallace, would not let the adultery argument in the front door of his courtroom. On the other hand, the lawyers could play on the feelings of the jury. To begin with, they could try to stack the jury with sympathetic men—married men, if possible, who might identify with the defendant. And perhaps Pendegast could *insinuate* that his client had the right to kill Larkyns, without claiming it.

The only other defense that came to mind, disagreeable and not much used, was insanity. Pendegast and King could argue that Muybridge had been in a mad fugue when he tracked down and shot Larkyns. The insanity argument had two problems, however, the first being that the defendant objected to it. Not only did Muybridge *not* think of himself as mad; to be called insane by his lawyer (and presumably by witnesses), even as a piece of theater in the courtroom, would be an insult he did not want to entertain. The second problem with the insanity defense involved a hypothetical. Suppose it worked? Suppose a jury found Muybridge not guilty by reason of insanity—would he not then have to submit to treatment meted out to the insane? As it happened, one mile from the county courthouse where the trial was to take place, the state of California had begun to erect the new Napa State Asylum for the Insane. The redbrick building, a giant castle of a compound with four corner turrets, would be ready to receive inmates in a few months, just as the trial ended. Everyone knew that jail in an asylum did not differ much from jail in a prison. If a jury pronounced him mad and California's new asylum was finished, Muybridge might have to check into it. Another insult he did not want to entertain.

———

In early December 1874, a grand jury indicted Edward Muybridge for murder. A few days later, on December 14, Flora Muybridge filed for divorce from her husband, accusing him of "extreme cruelty" and demanding alimony and child support. The murder case was referred to the district court and a trial date set for the first week of February

1875. Following these developments, the *Chronicle* sent a reporter from San Francisco to Napa to conduct a jailhouse interview with Edward Muybridge and to pick his mind.

The photographer had been in jail two months when the reporter, George H. Smith, arrived to talk. It was five days before Christmas. In a full-page story published December 21, Smith's descriptions of the prisoner depict a man pleased with himself. Muybridge was "in excellent spirits," Smith said, though "confinement and care have made him paler than usual." With his "quiet and reserved manner," his "unkempt beard and mild blue eyes," the reporter thought the photographer "looked like a good-natured old farmer." There was one often-noticed problem. Muybridge's "plain clothes" seemed "somewhat out of keeping with his profession and standing."[3]

Muybridge knew how to work the press and for years had befriended newspaper editors, so it is possible to read his appearance in the *Chronicle* as something of a performance, maybe an audition for the murder trial. "Many of my friends have visited me," he told Smith, "and I have received a great many letters from others—piles of them—expressing sympathy with me, and many offers of assistance." Muybridge spun out his story. People were not surprised by what he had done, he said. They understood it. Furthermore, they approved of it. His corncob pipe in his hand, his beard shaking as he nodded for emphasis, Muybridge made his case in the papers before the court convened. Referring to Harry Larkyns, who had died within a minute of being shot, he said, "I would have wished that he could have lived long enough at least to acknowledge the wrong he had done me—that his punishment was deserved, and that my act was a justifiable defense of my marital rights." It was a calculated reference, the mention of marriage, the allusion to "justification" and "rights." Muybridge knew the traditional notion of self-defense would not be part of the trial.

He was proud of what he had done with himself since immigrating to America, and easy with his conscience. "I have lived in California over twenty years, and am well known. They may ransack my record as much as they please, and I defy them to bring anything against me," he said.

At first Muybridge showed himself to be cold about his wife. He and Flora were "completely estranged," he said, "and I do not desire to see her again." Then he reversed direction, letting himself look vulnerable. "I loved the woman with all my heart and soul," he said about Flora, "and the revelation of her infidelity was a cruel, prostrating blow to me, shattering my idol and blighting the bright affection of my life." It was a fine performance, a scene from the playbook of a man who knew how to use the mass medium of the newspaper. Muybridge understood that he was talking to all of California, and for that matter, to readers who might include members of his jury.

"I have no fear of the result of the trial," Muybridge said, guiding the reporter back to the marital rights defense. "I feel I was justified in what I did, that all right-minded people will justify my action."

———

Since the early summer, Flora Muybridge and her son, Florado, had been staying in Oregon with Flora's aunt and uncle, the closest thing she had to parents of her own. When her husband killed her lover, five hundred miles to the south, the news went up and down the West—she probably read about it in the Portland newspaper. Harry Larkyns was "the only one I love," she had said. We can imagine that Flora, a twenty-three-year-old mother, felt panic and revulsion when she heard the news. She would have been stunned by grief and helplessness, perhaps filled with self-pity and, before long, loathing for her husband. Then, when her own name appeared in the news stories—when she was called a central character in the murder drama—the small Oregon town of The Dalles would have heated up with gossip. Flora would have been the subject of speculation and muttering, and she would have found it difficult to go out of the house. It is less easy to imagine what she might have said to her aunt and uncle. Whatever that script, Flora decided she had to leave Oregon and get back to California. In San Francisco she had a few friends but no family, and her world had just collapsed.

Several weeks after the murder, taking Florado with her, Flora returned to San Francisco. Except a few words from her divorce pleadings, asking for alimony, nothing she said or wrote during this period survives. Her life could not have been simple. She would have been recognized and talked about around the city. She was the adulteress. She was the wife of the killer. She was the victim of a seducer, a fallen woman, undone by her desire for love.

There is evidence she saw some friends, but it is possible that Flora spent much of her time out of sight, in hiding from gossip. The prosecutor in Muybridge's case, Napa district attorney Daniel Spencer, paid a visit to her. The two talked about the upcoming trial, but in the end Flora did not participate in it. Those who knew her said she sympathized with the prosecution, but by law she could testify neither against Muybridge nor in his behalf. She occupied an impossible position: supporting her husband, she was damned; condemning him, she was also damned.

From court filings it is possible to guess at her feelings. Flora sued Muybridge for divorce, and later, several times, she asked a judge for alimony. She appears to have turned her grief at losing her lover into contempt for her husband. She appears also to have turned her sadness into some kind of illness. It would surface months later—nature's justice, people said.

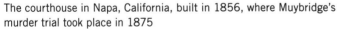

The county courthouse should be replaced, people said. (A year later, it was judged too far gone to repair, and torn down.) The beat-up brick building, with its nearly square footprint, stood in the center of a square in the center of Napa. Two stories high, it had four pilas-

The courthouse in Napa, California, built in 1856, where Muybridge's murder trial took place in 1875

ters on its face and a cupola on the roof. Muybridge occupied a jail cell on the second floor; he was brought downstairs, through the crowded hall, and entered a courtroom in which every seat had a spectator. A full house, with spillover out onto the street. In a county where the entire practicing bar consisted of ten lawyers, including the judge, the prosecutor, and the defense attorney, it was an unprecedented sight, as was the special section of the courtroom set aside for newswriters, who were inclined to jump from their seats and trot down to the Western Union office every so often to dictate a story that might end up in the *Chicago Tribune* or *New York Times*.[4]

At 11:00 a.m. on Monday, February 3, 1875, Judge William C. Wallace made the call to order. Wallace had presided over the Seventh District Court for five years. He was married, with three children. (In the case of *People vs. Edward J. Muybridge*, which involved a cuckolded husband, family status seems relevant.) Everyone knew everyone in the courtroom, or so it seemed, everyone but the defendant—Edward Muybridge looked like the single outsider. But in keeping with the California paradox, no one was truly local. Judge Wallace came from Missouri, Muybridge from England, his chief lawyer had been born in Kentucky, and the prosecutor came from South Carolina. In different ways, all had washed up in the West.[5]

Muybridge wore a light woolen suit, "the same that he has worn since his arrest," said a reporter. He showed "nervousness," at the same time that "he strived to appear cool and collected." At Muybridge's table sat three lawyers, two from Napa and one from San Francisco. His lead counsel was the very composed Wirt Pendegast. Next to Pendegast sat his law partner, F. E. Johnston, with whom he practiced in Napa, and Cameron King, the San Francisco lawyer and nephew of a former governor.[6]

At the prosecutor's table sat Daniel Spencer, the district attorney, and, next to him, Thomas P. Stoney, age forty, a native of Charleston, South Carolina. Stoney, who in his usual role served as a county judge, was new to the case. Judge Wallace seems to have felt that Spencer had gotten in over his head, so Wallace had assigned Stoney to lead the prosecution. Because of his day job, everyone called him Judge Stoney, a fact that led to some confusion with the presiding judge.

As soon as Judge Wallace made the call to order, Judge Stoney of the prosecution moved to ask for a continuance to a later date because two witnesses had not turned up, both of them being sick. The first was eighteen-year-old George Wolf, who had driven Muybridge in a hired buggy from Calistoga to the scene of the murder. Wolf had submitted an affidavit, but the eighteen-year-old was said to be in bed with the measles. James McArthur, the other man, had not only witnessed the shooting but had taken the gun away from Muybridge. The presiding judge said the witnesses might show up in the afternoon, and the case must go ahead without them. He ruled that a jury be impaneled in the meantime.

From a box full of slips of paper, a bailiff pulled the names, and as each was called, a man emerged from the crowded courtroom and stepped into the witness box to be examined. The defense wanted jurors who empathized with Muybridge—a married man who had a runaway wife, on the one hand, and a man who confronted a sexual rival, on the other. The prosecution wanted jurors who neither put themselves in Muybridge's place nor objected to the death penalty.

As each prospective juror took a seat, each answered a question about capital punishment. Did he have scruples about hanging a man? If so, would he be willing to render a guilty verdict? In the first draft of the jury, two men out of twelve said they objected to the death penalty. A farmer called D. O. Hunt "had conscientious scruples about hanging a man," and another named A. F. Rony "objected to hanging a man, growing out of human sympathy." Both were excused.

The prosecution and the defense each challenged six prospects, but a jury came together in two hours, after three drafts. Their names— Pratt, Garfield, Hallet, Greenwood, Klam, Sterling, Chapson, New- comer, Connery, Smith, Forester, and Kruze—showed a mix of Irish, German, and English ancestry. (The law excluded Chinese and Mexi- cans from serving.) A newswriter called the jury "with two exceptions, bronzed and sturdy farmers of middle age." The exceptions were both carpenters. The defense got the better of the pre-selection: eleven of the jurors had wives, which made them perhaps more likely to sympathize with Muybridge, the enraged husband. On the other hand, farmers and carpenters might have found it hard to identify with Muybridge, the artist.

A bailiff read the indictment for the jury, and the trial began at 4:00 p.m., when Judge Stoney made the opening address for the prosecution.

"I feel as though I should say, in the language of the old law, with regard to the prisoner, if he is innocent, then may God give him good deliverance," said Stoney in his coastal Carolina dialect, with its long vowels. "But there is no doubt in this case. There is no doubt that on the 17th day of October Harry Larkyns, who was unarmed, was shot down and murdered without cause. There is no question that Muybridge killed Larkyns, that he assassinated him."

Stoney turned away from the circumstances of the crime, toward the shooting itself.

"Larkyns is dead, and his voice cannot be heard. And so now there are just two parties involved in the question of guilt—the people and the prisoner. In this case there is no question of the rights or wrongs of the two men with regard to their relations with one another," he said. Stoney wanted to push the idea that it did not matter what Harry Larkyns had gotten up to—the affair with Flora meant nothing, set next to the killing.

"The question is this," Stoney went on, "has the defendant violated the law? Larkyns's blood was not demanded at the hands of the prisoner, whatever Larkyns might have done." Several reporters commented on the feeling in the room of sympathy for the defendant. From the start the prosecutor had to oppose a strain of favor for Muybridge, emerging from the idea that what Harry Larkyns had done mattered very much. Nevertheless, Stoney did not want conviction on a lesser charge, saying that he and the district attorney wanted the case to end with the gallows or with nothing at all. "The prosecution holds that this man is guilty of murder in the first degree, or he is guilty of nothing." He read aloud the statute for murder, and concluded, "The defendant is just as guilty as possible!" He then took aim at the arguments he knew were coming. "Nothing but actual self-defense authorizes a man to take the life of another—no other provocation justifies such an act." Infidelity, in other words, does not constitute provocation. Stoney sat down.

Muybridge's defense lawyers opened with an argument by attorney Cameron King. At thirty, King was the youngest lawyer in the room. He opened with the provocation angle, testing Judge Wallace to see if he would let the argument out into the open. "We will prove that Harry Larkyns was a man of bad character," King said. "We will prove that he pursued the wife of the prisoner, and that he rented rooms on Montgomery Street by representing himself as a married man, that he induced her to accompany him there, and that he boasted of the fact to his friends." King turned to the madness explanation. "We will also prove insanity," he went on. "The circumstances that aroused the defendant's suspicions were ones that drove him to mania. When

Mr. Muybridge discovered the photograph with the name of the man whom he had forbidden his wife to speak to, and when he then learned everything about her adultery—from that moment, he was not himself. Strung up to the pitch of insanity, the defendant made up his mind that he must slay the destroyer of his happiness, the man who had debauched his home! The prisoner went to kill that man. He would have followed him to the ends of the earth for that purpose!" Insanity, the argument Muybridge detested, was a fallback claim. The defendant, seated stiffly at the table, let his eyes shift left and right.

"We claim a verdict of not guilty both on the grounds of justifiable homicide, and on the grounds of insanity! We shall prove that years ago the prisoner was thrown from a stagecoach, receiving a concussion of the brain, which turned his hair from black to gray, and that he has never been the same since. We shall show you the depth of his impassioned love of his wife—that he was wrapped up in her and lived only for her. Having shown all this, we shall ask you, as the law does, to look upon his acts with mercy."

Having brought in insanity and mixed it up with provocation, Muybridge's lawyer finished with a set of rhetorical questions.

"I ask you, if these facts be so, was this man guilty of a crime? I do not believe he could be. Who is the man, even though he be of the soundest mind, that can say he would have acted differently? I assert that he who would not shoot the seducer of his wife, even if he were to suffer ten thousand deaths, is a coward and a cur. Better—far better, death!—than that the seducer should boast his conquest and a wife's dishonor with drunken companions over the flowing bowl, and point out the wretched man who walks the streets, a cuckold."

A vindication, even a celebration of the killing—this was the way Muybridge hoped to get off.

What Leland Stanford thought of all this remains an enigma. His papers are silent on the subject, and he never spoke of it—at least in public. We can imagine he spoke about it plenty of times, maybe at home, with his wife, Jenny. Maybe, in one or another of their gilded rooms, he spoke about Muybridge with the railroad associates, who could not fathom how Stanford had gotten involved with such a morally dubious character.

Chapter 13

THE GROCER

His parents named him Amasa, after his mother's father. An Old Testament name popular among devout people. Amasa Leland Stanford. His mother was a Presbyterian from church people, New England ministers going back to the 1600s, but his father followed no flock. His father had little feeling for divines; he was a work-for-money man.

Amasa Stanford was born 150 miles north of New York City in a tavern on a dirt road in farm country, in March 1824. When he was about sixteen, Amasa threw in his lot with his worldly father, dropping his first name and its pious trappings. He started signing his letters "Leland"—his middle name, the family name of a great-grandmother.

Leland Stanford's parents had eight children in seventeen years. The first was a girl, dead when she was born, and the eighth was a boy who would die at age nine. (Parents expected a sifting of this kind—at that time, one in four children died before age ten.) The Stanford couple did not own their place, the Bull's Head Tavern, but leased it. Albany, the capital of New York, lay six miles south of the tavern. The road that passed directly in front of the Bull's Head took carriages ten miles west to the next town, Schenectady—thus a good place for an inn. Crops and meadows spread in most directions, woods in the near distance. The rattling of wagons and the shouts of drivers rushing their animals must have risen from the road much of the day. The Stanford couple sold beer and food and a bed to the team drivers on the wagons, the truckers of the era.

Leland Stanford as a boy would have seen the teamsters boot into the house, reeking of horse. A nickel and his father tied up and watered the animals, two bits and his mother changed the sheets and filled a bowl of stew. The Bull's Head Tavern stood on a farm where the Stanfords also grew things to eat and to feed their customers. This was a family that pieced together income. They bought and sold livestock, and most winters they sold firewood that the Stanford sons cut from forests near the farm.[1]

Leland's father, Josiah Stanford, was a big man. More income arrived when Josiah got contracts from road builders to cut through old forest, to dig ditches and drain the route, and to grade the beds for the carriage traffic.

When Leland was fourteen, his nine-year-old brother Jerome died of some disease (no records specify it). Leland would have seen his brother on his deathbed, his body in the casket. As a teenager, Leland wrote letters to his younger siblings, preaching to them the rewards of self-possession and control over their feelings. In his writings and interviews from decades later, the ones that survive, he does not mention any trouble during his childhood. Instead, Leland would paint a rose-tinted picture of toil and comradeship, hard work and moneymaking with his brothers. He was one of the boys who fitted a carapace over himself so as not to feel too much.

The Stanfords had six children who lived, all boys—Leland was fourth in line. One of his brothers said that Leland was built like a barrel, just under six feet, and reluctant to talk. Throughout his life, whoever met him commented that he was genial but silent. He seems to have kept his desires in retreat. When he was twenty-five and starting work as a lawyer, Leland wrote his seventeen-year-old brother, Thomas, with advice about how to carry himself. "Do not be too ready to speak," he said. "Everyone is most inclined to hear himself talk. Everyone loves a good listener in conversation."[2]

The wagon traffic out of Albany was in decline, which meant the Stanford tavern saw dwindling business. The Erie Canal had opened the year Leland was born, and on its run from the Hudson River at Albany and northwest across the state, the canal cut through fields a few miles from the Stanford place, taking much of the freight traffic that used to

run on the roads and guaranteeing a slow economic death for innkeep-
ers. The Stanfords compensated using the muscles of their sons. One of
Leland's brothers remembered how their father used to buy timberland
in hundred-acre lots and make his sons cut tons of firewood to sell into
the fireplaces of Albany. With his two hundred pounds, Leland in his
teens could certainly swing an ax, although whether he did so remained
a point of family dispute. When he was old and rich, Leland told newspaper reporters a story. His father had gotten a contract to provide firewood to a dealer in Albany—2,500 cords. (A cord was a stack of wood
eight feet long and four feet high and wide, enough to heat a house for
a winter.) The contract meant that five men chopped trees full time for
two years, and the teenage Leland got the assignment to execute it. He
told reporters he hired day workers, showed them what to do, and made
$2,500 profit.

Another version of the story paints Leland as an indolent woodcut-
ter. "I never called Leland a good worker," said Josiah Stanford Jr.,
one of his brothers. Josiah remembered that Leland used to disappear
at key times. "While we would be fixing our teams and tools, he would
go around a corner, and when the time came to go to work, we would
have to call him."

Another run-in between Leland and his brothers had to do with
manure. Leland and the other Stanford boys often went to a slaughterhouse to collect manure for the farm. They put on aprons down to
their shins, stuffed their pants into their boots, and shoveled the shit.
"We hauled manure when there was nothing else of importance going
on," said Josiah, who added that the manure was full of water and piss.
"Leland used to dislike hauling the slaughterhouse manure because it
was so slushy, and because we left a horrible smell all along the road."
This was a big, reticent boy—pleasant, but restrained about hard work.

———

A photograph of Leland at age twenty-four shows a long-faced
and fine-complexioned man with a wave of black hair and with plump,
sensuous lips. He looks sullen, but sends a sexual pulse. People often
remarked on his uncomfortable style of friendliness—people said it
seemed made up and awkward. Leland's body, strongly masculine,
failed him in some ways. He was said (years later, by a person who
remembered Stanford in his twenties) to have had difficulty with

Leland Stanford in 1848, at age twenty-four, after he had apprenticed as an attorney for three years at a law firm in Albany, New York

speech—not an impediment, but a halting manner. It caused social trouble and made him bashful.

The silent Leland must have given at least an impression of seriousness, because his parents chose him alone from among their many sons for extra schooling. At sixteen Stanford left home and went one hundred miles west to enroll in the Oneida Institute, a private school in the village of Whitesboro, New York. (His brothers had finished their education after basic reading and writing, having studied in public schools. When the Stanford boys came of age to attend, free common public schools had lately opened in New York State.) To get to his boarding school, Leland would have taken a steamship from Albany and up the Erie Canal to the town of Utica, a daylong trip. The day after he arrived, he wrote his parents to describe what he had seen.

"I landed at whitesbouroug [*sic*] on wednesday evening. I proceeded to the institute immediately and saw one of the teachers, And he informed me that it was a thorough abolition school."[3]

The fact that his school tended toward abolition at a time when most of the country remained in favor of slavery, or indifferent to it, was a bit much. So was the shocking discovery that the Oneida Institute was integrated.

"One of the teachers . . . said that the whites and blacks all ate at one table," he wrote home.

One of the students at Oneida, at this point, was an escaped slave from Tennessee named Jermain Loguen. In later life, Loguen published an autobiography about his flight from slavery; he also founded schools for black students in upstate New York. Leland thought the Oneida Institute was not right for him. Even at sixteen he understood that a school where whites and former slaves sat together to eat was a subversive place, and the laconic, obedient Leland did not consider himself a subversive.

After spending one day at the "thorough abolition school," Stanford went seven miles southwest, stopped, and enrolled at the Clinton Liberal Institute, an academy run by the Universalist Church. The Universalists were liberal in a way different from the Oneida group: rather than admitting whites with blacks, the Clinton school admitted only whites, but both sexes. At a time when women were educated separately, if at all, the idea of bringing together men with women in a classroom felt intoxicatingly strange.[4]

Stanford might not have known it, but his choice of schools in Oneida County in upper New York State was limited to radical experiments in curriculum and dissident principles. This was because Oneida County lay within the "burned-over district," a swath of the Northeast crisscrossed by traveling preachers, many of whom sprayed fire and brimstone rhetoric from beneath their giant revival tents. Like many, Leland felt pressure to go to revivals, which seemed constant and ubiquitous. He wrote home about one religious meeting where students were expected to come forward to be saved. "I was a hard prospect for that preacher," he said, admitting his godlessness. Ministers in Stanford's corner of America pushed radical causes like the abolition of slavery. Some even advocated "complex marriage," or mass adultery. Upper New York State was as radical as anyplace in America. A few years after Leland left, a few hundred utopian followers of Christ set up the Oneida Community, a proto-communist village that abolished private property and called for anytime, anywhere sex.

The Clinton Institute, Stanford's school, had two small buildings, for women and for men, and enrolled just thirty-five students. Lecturers taught that slavery was immoral, and when Stanford arrived, in 1841, this placed the school on the fringe in the national discourse. But in the curious politics of abolition, the school had no black students.

Leland wrote his father that he was elected to an honor society and that he'd joined a debating group, but money was also on his mind. "Here are the things you would want to know," he said in a letter home. "We pay for our board 12 shillings and for our bed two shillings more."[5]

Stanford studied at the Clinton Institute, went home to work, chopping wood and shoveling manure, and came back. In 1844, when he was nineteen, he wrote home with a question—"I should like particularly to know about the contract on the R. Road." The Mohawk & Hudson Railroad was ten years old, one of the earliest tracks in America. It ran just sixteen miles in upstate New York, between Albany and Schenectady, but it passed near the Bull's Head Tavern. Leland's father, Josiah, had gotten the job of digging ditches along the track and grading an extension of the roadbed, and his son wanted details. "The settlement . . . is full as equitable as I expected," he wrote two weeks later, after someone had answered. "I have an idea that there will be a store built on the premises in consequence, the advantages of which you will readily perceive."[6]

A short time later Stanford left the Clinton Academy and enrolled in a third school, thirty miles further west in the town of Cazenovia— the eponymous Cazenovia Seminary. (None of Stanford's several schools were colleges or universities—all were academies, advanced high schools designed as endpoints of middle-class aspiration.) An engraving from the period shows Cazenovia to possess a physical plant of three brick buildings, each three stories tall, joined end to end. Founded by the Methodist Episcopal Church, the school had 160 students and enrolled women and men together, making it yet another progressive school that pressured Leland's hesitant mind.[7]

He wrote home about women. "If I should get lonesome, I will solace myself with visiting some two or three pretty girls who live in the village, and with whom I am on pretty good terms; or at least might be. But I am almost afraid of them for they are not only the prettiest girls that attend the school but also the most intelligent." He mentioned a woman he was interested in. "She took a notion to go riding with me because I suppose she knew nothing bad of me." And fortunately, he added, "I am not encumbered by a very horrible face."[8]

While riding around with girlfriends, Leland complained he was falling behind the other students in Latin. He wrote home to say he wanted to delay his pleasures until after his youth. "With that ambition which the whole family of us have naturally," he said, "I am in hopes it will prevent me from being contented with a mediocrity or rather from not striving after something higher."

Another time he put it more plainly, writing home with a joke about his hopes for money. The school held frequent revival campaigns, and Stanford saw that these ran headlong into his desire to get rich. "They are holding a protracted meeting here," he told his brother DeWitt, "and I think I must go over this evening to see if I cannot be made to set a less value upon this world's goods." He tipped his hand, slightly, showing that making money was his reason for going to school.[9]

Gradually the progressive trend of Leland's teachers had an impact on him. In October, he wrote his brother Philip with some excitement about Cassius Clay, the antislavery politician from Kentucky, whom Leland had gone to hear speak. Cassius Clay was born to a slaveholding family and rebelled against it, and when he won a seat in the Kentucky legislature, his constituents quickly voted him out because he called for a general emancipation. While still a lawmaker, he came to the Cazenovia Seminary to speak in favor of his cousin, Henry Clay, who was running on the Whig ticket for U.S. president. Leland went to listen and was moved.

"Clay is known throughout the world for having liberated his own slaves and for having given up all political hopes on account of his humanity in ardently advocating the cause of the slave," Leland told his brother. "His position is truly an envious one. Clay forms a glorious example for all to imitate and if he continues in the path in which he now trips his name will descend to posterity." Stanford's leanings toward freedom and a clear path to class advancement for black people seem to date from this time. A dozen years later, in California, Leland would join the Republican Party, which rose up in opposition to slavery.[10]

Stanford's pain at public speaking can be seen in his teens, when he complained about rehearsals in oratory that his teachers demanded. One class required him to speak "in public and in the church," and he told his brothers that he was afraid of the experiment. "I shall have to address an assembled multitude," he said. "Sympathise with me. My heart flutters now when I think of it."[11] Leland may have admired Cassius Clay, but to imagine himself in front of a crowd was too much. His fear of speeches never left him. He never addressed a room extemporaneously, always carrying his text, always reading from it.

Stanford went home at the end of 1844, age twenty, his schooling finished. Thirty years later, using a droplet of his fortune, he sent Caze-novia Seminary a life-size portrait of himself. He asked that it be hung in the school chapel. It must have seemed a strange request, coming as it did from an agnostic who was frightened of the pulpit.

As the favored son chosen for a white collar, Leland wanted to practice law, but there were only a few law schools in the country. The commoner's path to a career in law was apprenticeship in a law firm, not school. In 1845 he enlisted at the law office of Wheaton, Doolittle and Hadley, in Albany. He would work at the firm for three years, until he learned his trade. During this time, Stanford lived at 42 Washington Avenue in Albany—and after the requisite three years, the Wheaton firm asked him to join its practice.[12]

———

In 1848, a new migrant arrived in the town of Port Washington, Wisconsin, the twenty-four-year-old lawyer Leland Stanford. Wiscon-sin had just become the thirtieth of the United States: America pushed on into the continent, picking up colonies, calling them territories, then renaming them states. Stanford had taken a train west from New York, joining a labor stream that was fleeing the East by the thousands. Something had led him to trade the sure thing of a city law firm in Albany for the random grab of a move out. Wisconsin was growing fast. Many immigrants from Germany picked up their things and made directly for the Great Lakes. Perhaps it was merely the moment. Had it been ten years before, Stanford might have gone to Ohio, the previous destination for twentysomethings from New York.

He took a train to Chicago and then a ferry north on Lake Michi-gan. The town called Port Washington, Wisconsin, sometimes used the name Ozaukee, the label applied by Algonquin natives who lived in the dense forests along Lake Michigan. Ozaukee would have liked to rival Milwaukee and Chicago, small but growing cities that shared the same western bank of the lake, but Ozaukee had only 1,500 people, and it was not growing. It lacked something, perhaps the appetites that those other places possessed. Stanford didn't see this yet, not when he first arrived.[13]

In his adopted town, Stanford partnered with another lawyer already in practice, Wesley Pierce, and the two opened for business as Pierce & Stanford. Leland was the new attorney in Port Washington, the one with no clients. But he brought at least one thing Pierce did not have—a shelf of leather-bound law books bought for him by his parents.

While he waited to join the Wisconsin bar, Stanford did the office work. He joined the Ozaukee Lodge of the Masons. In a year, he passed the bar, after which he broke up the partnership with Pierce and went into business on his own. It turned out to be a thin living—some real estate deals, some petty crime, a few lawsuits. He felt irritated about the number of German immigrants, complaining in a letter to his parents (maybe half jokingly) that he would do better in the law if only he spoke German.

Stanford had five brothers. After the Gold Rush in 1849, one at a time they moved to California. The brothers were rough—Leland was the only one with any education beyond the age of sixteen, the only one with a job that gave him a desk and not a shovel. Josiah Stanford Jr., the oldest, went to California first, followed by the middle brother, Charles, and then the other three. Leland stayed in Wisconsin and traded letters with all of them. (Think of the parents. They raised six boys, and then all of them left.)

From California the brothers wrote Leland that gold could be had, the money was good if not great, and if you did not want to swing a pickax you could make money by selling supplies to miners. Leland preferred the prestige and comfort of the desk to the sluices of a mining camp, and as his brothers went to the frontier to gamble their lives, he stood fast for a while with his barrister's fantasy.

He kept trying to rise in his little town. In 1850 Stanford got on the ballot for district attorney of Washington County, the entity that wrapped around Port Washington. He ran as a Whig, the liberal party of the day, but the more conservative Democrats outnumbered Whigs three to one, and he lost.

Stanford wanted to make money straight, with a profession. The next step of the climb, he thought, would be to marry. In summer 1850 Stanford took a train back to Albany, a thousand miles east, and started visiting a woman there named Jane Lathrop. They had known each other during his apprenticeship at the Wheaton firm. Twenty-six, like Stanford, Jane Lathrop lived with her parents on the same street where the young lawyer had rented a room as a legal apprentice three years before. They had met when Stanford pressured Jane's brother to have him over for tea so he could talk to the sister. The Lathrop family had more money and education than the Stanfords. Leland's people were woodcutters and ditchdiggers and farmers, while the Lathrops had accountants in the current generation and ministers in their past. From their dating days he called her Jenny.

In the end, Stanford married up. He and Jenny Lathrop married on September 30, 1850, at North Pearl Baptist Church in Albany, and left soon after for Wisconsin.

In a photograph of the couple made for the wedding, Jenny Lathrop appears tall and big-boned. She wears a black satin dress with a white lace collar. She has an oval face and shining black hair, parted in the middle and pulled behind, and appears to have a drifting eye—her left eye stares at the camera, while her right turns away. A flaw to add to her husband's halting speech. She would complain, years later, that she had trouble reading for any length of time, because of her "weak eyes."

The couple rented a one-room apartment over a saloon in Port Washington. When Stanford's fees came in more reliably, they moved to a one-and-a-half-story cottage next to a stream, furnished with things sent from their parents. Years later, when she and her husband were supremely rich, and with the nostalgia felt by a woman thronged with servants, Jenny remembered the years in Wisconsin as the time

Jane Lathrop and Leland Stanford, newly married, in 1850

when she did her happiest homemaking. But even then, the couple liked it when others did the work. They hired a black woman to come once a week for a twelve-hour day. (Although Jenny Stanford remembered her, no one seems to have written down her name.) The woman did the housecleaning, the laundry and ironing for the week, the firewood cutting, and half of the cooking, including stews and pies that would keep for the week. When Jenny reminisced, it was sometimes about her first, unnamed servant.

The town did not grow, the small change from Stanford's clients did not turn into big fees. Meanwhile, his brothers wrote a stream of letters about the high days in California. In January 1852 Leland felt aroused by the golden stories. He wrote his brother Thomas: "Judging from what you have written home I expect to see you in California in the spring."

Two months later, in March 1852, a fire destroyed the frame building on Franklin Street where Stanford had his office. It started in the grocery store, below him, and continued up to the second floor to consume the office, his records, his law books. No one was hurt but all was cinders. Stanford wrote his parents, "I hope you are in good spirits, for I am afraid mine approach very near the blues." He was already a man who did not take possession of his emotions: to say he was "near the blues" might have meant he felt a wretched depression.

After the fire, his brothers' stories about the munificence of the Golden State sounded better. In California, even farm boys who had shoveled manure could now dig out gold, or more reliably—the thing the brothers were doing—they could flip a profit by selling pickaxes and boots and oil lamps to gold diggers. Leland wrote his mother and father, who did not want to lose their last son to the far West, "You speak in your letters somewhat it seems to me as if you would prefer that I should not go to California. Now that my library is burned I make no doubt that you would say to me go though I had said nothing upon the subject."[14]

Stanford estimated his clients owed him $2,000 in fees, but he guessed he could collect only a tenth of it. He owned twenty acres of land and some town lots, neither worth much. "The recent fire together with the fact of the passage of a law removing the county seat has put a perfect damper upon real estate here," he told his parents. "I shall probably be able to settle up everything here and have something upwards of $200."

At age twenty-eight and married, Stanford lowered his gaze and asked his parents for money. "You have kindly offered to furnish me with the means necessary to take me to California," he wrote. "It will be with great reluctance that I can receive assistance from you." He took the money.

Of Leland's brothers in California, three were younger than thirty, two older. Like everyone, they had tried digging for gold, choosing a place on the American River called Mormon Island, twenty-five miles east of Sacramento. Coming up with some gold, but not enough, the five brothers decided instead to sell provisions and tools to other miners. In spring 1851, Charles and Josiah Stanford opened a general store in Sacramento. "We made a great deal of money," Josiah later remembered, "$2000 clear every month."[15]

Leland Stanford and his wife initially went home to Albany. It was May 1852. There, Stanford deposited Jenny with her parents, with the excuse that they were getting old. (Jenny Stanford always regretted having been stabled, like a horse, while her husband had his first western adventure.) Stanford got on a boat down the Hudson River to New York City, and from there on June 5 he boarded a steamship, the *Northern Light*. He arrived in Nicaragua and traveled over the mountains to the Pacific side of the isthmus, boarded a steamer called the *Independence*, and reached San Francisco on July 12. The trip from New York to San Francisco took thirty-seven days.

"He came out here without a dollar," his brother Josiah remembered. Stanford's brothers loaned him, at interest, some goods to sell. Leland took the groceries and dry goods and hardware and fuel to a mining camp called Cold Springs, a muddy settlement of six hundred men in tents and shanties near a big gold strike at the town of Placerville, fifty miles east of Sacramento. He opened a store in a tent. Like all frontier stores of the time, it had canvas for the roof and walls, except for one wooden wall, which faced the street. There shoppers passed through a genuine wooden door, which made the storefront look like a building. Stanford joined with a partner who knew the area, Nicholas Smith, and put up the shop sign, SMITH & STANFORD.

There had been a lynching at Placerville—two Frenchmen and a Mexican, accused of stealing, were killed by other miners—thus the nickname of the area was "Hangtown."[16] One of the locals, a man called George Mull, had brought several slaves with him from the South and put them to work on his claims. Lynching and slaves—for Stanford, it was a cold introduction to the frontier. As a teenager Stanford had attended a school in upstate New York with abolitionist leanings, and he detested slavery, but with his caution about things, there is no evidence he tried to help black workers in the hills. In 1852, the California census recorded a new arrival in Hangtown, a "laborer" called Leland Stanford. In fact, he was a lawyer who had given up the law and now tried to make his way as a shopkeeper, a grocer.

————

Miners drifted off when the mines did not pay, and Hangtown thinned out. After ten months Stanford and Smith took down their store and followed the prospecting herd, moving thirty miles north to a new mining camp, Michigan Bluff. The slapdash cluster of tents and cabins stood half a mile from a fork in the Sacramento River and 1,500 feet up the side of a gorge. Gold came strong from the sluices, but Stanford kept away from the roulette of claims and strikes because he preferred the dull money in dry goods. At least as a start.

Late in life Stanford remembered that for two years, as a trader on the frontier, he had slept on the countertop of his store, blankets beneath and on top of him, his arms wrapped around the cash box. (Although he never mentioned it, he might have had a gun in the bundle, too.) His brother Josiah, who ran the bigger Stanford Brothers store in Sacramento, said that he and his siblings used to man their shops wearing a full apron down to the ankles. Leland probably did the same, measuring pounds of rice in the hollow of his apron, taking an I.O.U. for potatoes or for a shovel. There is a photograph from about 1854 that shows the store in Michigan Bluff, a rickety shack next to a ditch, with two big signs hanging above. The smaller reads SMITH & STANFORD. The larger sign lists the contents of the store, in Cantonese. About a quarter of the miners came from China, and Stanford wanted their business.

Chinese miners in the Sierra camps lived about twenty men to a cabin and took orders from a foreman who had brought the group from San Francisco—a Chinese boss who guided the digging and took most of the profit. By contrast, white miners worked alone or in pairs and did not mingle with their Chinese rivals. But Leland Stanford sold anything to everyone.

Native Americans stayed out of the mining boom. They weren't inclined to chase gold, and anyway episodes of warfare with whites often flared. The year after Stanford moved to California, settlers mas-

The Stanford store at the mining camp of Michigan Bluff, California, ca. 1853

sacred some twenty-five Indians in the village of Tehama, one hundred miles northwest of Michigan Bluff. A native group the papers called only "the Indians of Colusa County" had been trying to move American ranchers off their land by killing their livestock and vandalizing fences. "The mountains are alive with these red devils," as the reporter neutrally put it. White ranchers retaliated by capturing and killing two Indian men. They tortured a third captive, who then led the ranchers to a cave where his people lived. The ranchers smoked out the cave with fires and shot ten men and three women as they fled. Five children survived. The leader of the attack took one child, whose parents he had killed, home with him. Four others younger than ten years "were disposed in the same charitable manner among the party," as the paper explained. Mile by mile (child by child?), California was made safe for white possession.[17]

Michigan Bluff lacked a church, but instead it had four saloons where the miners drank, gambled, and paid for sex. Stanford probably had the best education in town. He got himself named justice of the peace, his first political office, and simultaneously he bought one of the barrooms, the Empire Saloon, for $575, on October 18, 1854. Justice Stanford's saloon differed from the other barrooms in that women, and not men, paid out the money from the gambling operation, a gimmick probably taken from the bar's previous owner. Stanford used his tavern to hold court proceedings during the day. Most cases involved assault, but he heard one murder case, which he sent to the next town, claiming the right jurisdiction rested there. Another thing comes to mind: no evidence suggests that Stanford's Empire Saloon might also have been a brothel, but the fact remains that most saloons at this place and time were also brothels, and there is the curious detail of women running the gaming till. The absence of evidence of prostitution is not evidence of absence.[18] With his wife three thousand miles away, did Justice Stanford operate a bordello?

Stanford was thirty. He and his wife, Jenny, had lived apart for three years, with Jenny sequestered in New York State with her parents. In May 1855, Stanford received a letter that his wife's father, Dyer Lathrop, had died. Within a week, he sold his half of the grocery business to his partner, Nicholas Smith, and resigned his justiceship. (There is no record of what he did with the Empire Saloon.) In June, Stanford arrived back in Albany, where he found his wife in a serious depression. Jenny's father had died, but apparently worse than this, she later remembered, she had been the victim of intense gossip. For a long time, people in her church and social circle had referred to her as "the deserted wife." She would resent this piece of condescension for the rest of her life. After leaving Albany, she gave it as a reason why she never went back.

He had expected to move home to New York State and set up in business, Stanford said later. He said his California stores had given him a big bankroll and that he even looked for a house to buy in Albany. Stanford later pointed out that his wife, Jenny, had been the one to talk him out of moving home. Because of the gossip, which had hurt her, she wanted the two of them to go to California. There may be some truth here, although the explanations that people give for what they do usually amount to less than half the whole.

Leland and Jenny Stanford left Albany behind, arriving in California in November 1855. They rented a house in Sacramento, 92 Second Street. Stanford's oldest brother, Josiah, had built the Stanford Brothers store at 56–58 K Street, and now Leland bought it from him. Next door to it stood a larger retail operation, Huntington & Hopkins, purveyors of hardware. Within a few days Stanford was friendly with its owners,

Collis Huntington and Mark Hopkins, two men with whom he would later build and run the railroad.

Stanford wrote his mother and father: "I suppose you all feel anxious to know how my business progresses. I think I shall be able to nurse it into a flourishing state. I sell my goods low and intend to continue doing so. I deal on the square with all, I shall try to be content with moderate gains." He wrote of himself as a modest man, happy to have less, and yet he was not. Stanford had appetites. A clue appears in another letter.

"We are very comfortable," he told his parents. "Jane does her own work, and has the neatest house in town. We live well, have plenty of good coffee, bread, meat and potatoes and such other things as we want, but we are both fond of the substantial."[19]

In his understated way, Stanford showed his grit, plus his greed. *We are fond of the substantial.*

In 1856 Stanford built a new store in Sacramento at 64 Front Street, at the corner of L Street. An idea of the inventory comes from a news-

The hardware store belonging to Collis Huntington and Mark Hopkins, at 54 K Street, Sacramento, ca. 1855. Leland Stanford, a grocer, went into business next door, at number 56, and the three future railroad associates met.

paper ad: groceries, wine, liquor, cigars, camphene (fuel oil), flour, grains, produce, and mining tools. The two-story brick building had a footprint of forty-two feet in frontage, with a deep awning, and 150 feet in length. Stanford did well in business and quickly saved tens of thousands, but he still wore an apron.

About the time the new store went up, Leland made an uncharacteristically rash investment, which turned out to be the smartest move of anything he'd tried. The boom economy of California had grown up on mines and options to extract minerals from the Sierra foothills. Both mineral rights and options went for sale all the time, with the usual result that buyers came up with nothing. Stanford didn't gamble and preferred to watch other people buy up their stakes and take the fall, except this one time. In 1856 he bought a piece of a dead gold strike, the so-called Amador mine, near the town of Placer City. The wager didn't fit his character: he liked to build his bank balance with no setbacks of the impulse and remorse variety. But two years later, to Stanford's and everyone else's surprise, a new vein of gold turned up at Amador, and the mine started paying in a gush. He decided to cash in, selling his claim for one hundred times what he had paid for it.

The Amador mine gave Stanford his first windfall. It raised him and Jenny to the upper ranks of the local rich, and it paid for a big new house, one of the finest in town, or one of the most ostentatious, depending on your view of it.

————

During his year as justice of the peace with a courtroom saloon, Stanford had tasted public office. After the Amador mine deal, he seems to have decided to go back to politics: he wanted to add influence to the money he now had in hand. When he lived in Wisconsin and worked as a lawyer, he had run for the office of county prosecutor as the Whig Party candidate and lost. Now, living in the California state capital, with extra cash for nice clothes and entertaining, and with literacy from his lawyering days, Stanford had the outward credentials to become a politician. It could also be said that the bar for entering politics in Sacramento tended to hang pretty low. Elections attracted thin public interest and thinner turnout. About 42 percent of white men—the only eligible group, blacks and Chinese men being barred—voted. (Put another way: 20 percent of the population decided the government.) The list of parties could be long and confusing, with six appearing on most ballots:

Citizen's Reform (the so-called Know-Nothings), Whig, Independent Citizen's, Custom House Whig, Democratic, and Ciudad.[20]

One problem for Stanford, as a would-be rookie politician, was that his old party had rapidly fallen from favor. The Whigs had been defeated in several national races, including the federal election of 1854, and as a result, the party had dwindled. To claim the Whig banner at this point would be to call yourself something of a loser. With the demise of the Whigs, however, the Republican Party, formed back east in 1854, comprised a new movement of liberals. Republicans, in a radical stand, opposed slavery. This position put them on the left fringe of national politics, but it also appealed to Stanford, who idolized the antislavery activist Cassius Clay and had been educated in the abolitionist terrain of upstate New York.

In California, the first meeting of Republican agitators took place in San Francisco, in April 1856. Five months later, another small group came together in Sacramento, and Stanford saw this as a moment to join the party's ranks. He and his brother Philip attended the meeting. At this stage, to be a Republican meant running some risks. The *Democratic State Journal*, a Sacramento newspaper that supported the proslavery Democrats, called the meeting that Stanford attended a "convention of nigger worshipers." The Republican Party's slogan for the year 1856 was "Freedom, Fremont, and the Railroad." (Freedom meant "free soil," or a stand against slavery in the West; Fremont was John C. Fremont, the Republican candidate for president; and the railroad meant a scheme to lay track from California to the Mississippi.)

In April 1857, Stanford went into politics as a Republican, running for a seat as an alderman in Sacramento. He won 87 votes of the 3,068 cast. Two things sabotaged him: the proslavery Democrats who dominated California disdained Republicans, seen as the party of liberal people who had too much money. The second handicap was Stanford's speaking style. He bored crowds. "Stanford is no orator," one paper said, "a fact patent to all who hear him."[21]

Three months later he was running again, this time for state treasurer. He accepted the nomination in the most awkward terms possible. "It is with unfeigned regret that I have to thank the convention," Stanford said, addressing a small rally. "I do not know precisely what chance there is for my election. I think our ticket may succeed."[22] In the election, in September, he ran third in a field of three.

Stanford went back to his grocery, thinking himself unelectable.

Two years passed, but in June 1859, he spoke at another Republican convention. There was talk in the press that the Southern states might secede if a Republican administration replaced the proslavery government in Washington. Abolitionist speakers had aroused him when he was a young man, and "free labor" seems to have been one of the issues that pulled him into politics. In the late 1850s, slavery had become a dividing knife in California, and sometimes people got shot for their views. On September 13, 1859, the chief justice of the California Supreme Court, David S. Terry, a Kentuckian who had come to California with enslaved people to serve him, shot to death U.S. senator David C. Broderick in a duel. Broderick had made speeches against slavery that the chief justice could not tolerate.

Stanford was a moderate opponent—he did not call for abolition—and he made it clear that he wouldn't break up the racial order. The Republicans named him as their candidate for governor in the 1859 race. He had never won an election, and he knew he would lose this one. Accepting the nomination, he said, "Were I an aspiring man, I might hesitate about allowing myself to be placed in this position. Now, I stand for the cause of the white man—the cause of free labor, of justice and of equal rights." He talked liberal, but he would go slowly on slavery, he said. So that no one could mistake him, he added this: "I prefer the white man to the Negro as an inhabitant of our country."[23] Stanford crisscrossed the state in the month before the election, appearing at small meetings in thirty towns. On election day, September 7, 1859, he lost by a margin of ten votes to one, finishing third in a field of three.

He'd run for office four times, always losing, but he consoled himself that he still made money. He sent home thousands of dollars to his parents and gave money to his brothers in San Francisco, Josiah and Charles, to keep their businesses afloat. (In letters home to Albany, he complained to his parents about having to do this.)

Yet another election came, in fall 1860, and this one brought Leland his long-needed stroke of luck. Among the Republicans running for president that year, U.S. senator William Seward was a former Whig who had led the antislavery faction of that party, now defunct. He had won the governor's office in New York State and then a senator's seat. Seward was expected to win the Republican nomination for president at the party convention in May 1860, and he did win a plurality of delegate votes on the first ballot. But Abraham Lincoln had been working the convention, and after three more ballots, Seward's support thinned. The nomination went to Lincoln. Stanford wrote his parents that he had hoped Lincoln would lose.

Stanford might have been as mystified as anyone on Election Day, November 6, 1860. Lincoln won in the East, and surprisingly, he also won in California. Although proslavery Democrats comprised the majority of white voters, they were split between their party's two candidates, Stephen Douglas and John Breckenridge.

After the election, the California Republicans decided to send someone to Washington to talk to Lincoln, the new president. A party stalwart now, Stanford received the nod. He went east to collect the spoils—to measure the scale of patronage for the West and to discuss the names of those who might get the handouts, the appointments, the jobs, the western distribution. In February 1861, Leland and Jenny left for Washington to attend the inauguration in March and shake the president's hand.

Lincoln had been in office two weeks when, on April 12, militias in Charleston, South Carolina, fired on Fort Sumter, the event that put the Civil War in motion. California was impossibly far from the East and South—it seemed to most Americans to be practically a separate country—but a backlash nevertheless rolled across the country and Stanford's fortunes picked up. When the South seceded, people in the West, isolated from Washington but feeling a national urge, swung to the Union cause and backed the Northern side.

Although the Republicans had lost with Stanford multiple times, in June 1861 the party convention in Sacramento named him its candidate for governor, his second run at the office. He accepted with a studied blandness that crowds by now recognized. "I believe in the people; I believe in the democracy; I believe in the elevation of the masses," he said, emphatically vague. This time he knew he had a chance. The Democratic vote had split in two during the last election; if it split again, he would be governor.

In advance of the election Mr. and Mrs. Stanford used the windfall from the Amador mine to buy their big house in Sacramento, on Eighth Street. The house was grand enough to serve as a governor's mansion, should it be necessary.

At the same time, Stanford was cutting a deal with his friends, the other Sacramento shopkeepers, to invest in the unlikely train scheme brought to market by a railroad engineer with a manic personality

Governor Leland Stanford (in a top hat on the balcony) reviewing troops on DuPont Street in San Francisco, July 4, 1863

named Theodore Judah. On June 28, 1861, a week after he accepted the Republican nomination for governor, Stanford was named president of the Central Pacific Railroad, a company that existed only on paper. And on September 4, Stanford cast a ballot for himself. He received fifty-six thousand votes, and another sixty-four thousand were divided between two Democratic candidates. Stanford, at age thirty-six, became California's governor.

Chapter 14

THE IMMIGRANT

When Edward Muggeridge was growing up in England, he went by the name of Ted.[1] America tried to be a more casual place than Britain, so in the States, he probably kept his nickname.

Ted Muggeridge turned up in New York in 1850, landing in a city that shined and seethed and stank. New York was ancient by the American clock, two hundred years old, and the biggest city in the republic. About half a million people lived on Manhattan Island, a quarter of them coming from Ireland. With the influx of mostly desperate people escaping the Irish famine, the city had doubled in size in twenty years, and it was growing faster than anywhere on the continent except San Francisco. The edge of New York had moved north from Twenty-third Street to Forty-second in about a decade—conferring on many neighborhoods a thrown-together appearance. City Hall's plan for a grid of streets justified the cutting and chewing through farms and hills, and immigration fueled the build-out, but so did the Erie Canal. A 360-mile-long ditch upstate, the Erie Canal meant that barges could leave Manhattan, push up the Hudson River, cross over to the Great Lakes, steam five hundred miles west, and never unload until Chicago, the front door of the western territories. The Erie Canal meant that every week a new flood of people, money, machines, factory goods, and crops piled up in New York and then washed through, leaving sediments of gold and filth, a residue that was stately and wretched in equal parts.

Ted Muggeridge would have been familiar with some of this, the rhythm of a metropolis. He had grown up outside of London, a sprawl five times the size of New York, and he seems to have lived there before emigrating. His London was a capital of empire, the place New York wanted to become. The rush of business in Manhattan, the preening of the rich on the streets, might have looked about the same as they had in England. Yet many things must have been new to Ted: the accents, the curses, the food. The slums in the neighborhood of Five Points, for instance, which differed in their poverty and desperation from London's East End. And the way Americans talked about their country, their attitude of national self-love, the idea that God had picked out their republic for a special destiny.

He had arrived with a job, salesman with the London Printing & Publishing Company, offices at 55 Dey Street, in the oldest and densest part of town.[2] To find it, start at City Hall, go south along Broadway for five blocks, then turn right; 55 Dey stood half a block down. London Printing & Publishing sold upmarket books and prints, respectable things, encyclopedias for the parlor, lithographs you could frame. The firm hired artists to make engravings and etchings, the kind to hang on the wall above the settee. A company inventory gives an idea of the prints Ted had to unload: a portrait of Shylock from the *Merchant of Venice*, *The Cartoons of Raphael*, *History of the Indian Mutiny*, *Picturesque Rambles in the English Lake District*. The immigrant came to America to spread the emoluments of English history and taste. In addition to art, the company published reference books, dignified volumes for proper libraries. The flagship product was its *Royal Dictionary-Cyclopaedia for Universal Reference* ("literary, classical, historical, biographical, geographical, scientific, and technological")—at fifteen volumes, almost a ship's ballast. Other titles included *A History of England* (in eight volumes), *Dictionary of the Science and Practice of Architecture*, and *The Heroines of Shakespeare*.

Ted's job was to sell the better part of Europe (rich in thought) to the better part of America (in need of refinement).

There is no evidence about how he lived, but it's likely he rented a room in a boardinghouse, of which there were thousands, the normal habitat for young people with little money. These three- or four-story townhouses held eight or ten young men (salesmen, office clerks), plus a handful of single women (servants, teachers), each tenant living in a single room (maximum, two) with a door that faced the stairs. It was a group of strangers who sat down together for breakfast and dinner—the board of "room and board"—shared the toilet on the stairs or in the backyard, went out to work in the morning, and came back to sleep at night. Polite greetings were expected on the landing.

The book-and-print trade used salesmen, and Ted would have spent much of his time making a pitch. To move books, he would have carried samples of the company's merchandise and his list of upcoming titles, visiting libraries and stationers and the occasional book dealer. New York in 1850 had about five hundred libraries, ranging from the largest one, the Astor Public Library (120,000 volumes), to myriad little collections like that of the Leake and Watts Orphan House (540 books).[3] Most libraries made good prospects for Ted's reference material. To sell prints, he would have visited photography studios and art galleries, tried to persuade them to take a few prints and to put one in the window facing the street. The location of the company office helped these rounds, because the blocks around Dey Street made up the culture district of New York. The American Museum stood on Broadway and Ann Streets, two minutes from the salesman's desk, and on either side of Broadway were music stores, dealers in art, stationers, and photographers.

It might have helped that he had an English manner and speech. In the mid-1800s, American literature and art looked like weak plants next to the British varieties, and the United States still leaned on England for its intellectual life. A few years earlier, Charles Dickens had come on his first American lecture tour, crisscrossing the country to perform excerpts from his fiction. Audiences had kept vigil for hours, and theater seats creaked from overload. New York art and book buyers thought Englishness of any kind to be nourishment, maybe even the accent of a small-town, twenty-year-old salesman.

In a typical day, Ted would have come to the office in the morning, talked up his sales calls, gathered his sample books and proof prints, and gone out. He packed his duffle, hit the pavement, and hoped for commissions. It is possible to imagine a solitary man who delivered bursts of promotional talk in the afternoon and retreated to his single room at night.

The bread and butter of the upscale publishing market was the book subscription. Like its later cousin, magazine subscriptions, the book subscription worked like a commodity future. Buyers put down cash to pay for books that would be published in six months or a year.

In this way, publishers raised money to offset the risk of expensive print runs. In later years, when he became a photographer, Ted would use subscriptions to finance his own art, showing examples of his work to art buyers and soliciting deposits for series of photographs he had yet to shoot and print. As a bookseller for London Print & Publishing, Ted sold subscriptions that included plenty of detail. The customer chose a binding (cloth, half leather, or "full Morocco," the showiest, all-leather volume) and arranged terms for paying the balance. Would there be any artwork to go with the order? Perhaps our lithograph of a Shanghai opium den, which our artist has depicted in full color?

Ted Muggeridge remembered, years later, that when he was new to America he used to travel for business. He remembered that he had gone to New Orleans and other places in the South. Travel might have taken him also to Boston, or to Philadelphia, or to Washington, D.C.—anyplace where he might find people with education and money, potential book buyers. His job was to find genteel people (and those trying to be genteel), people who might need prints on the wall and leather spines where friends sitting on the sofa might see them.

———

Brady's Gallery of Daguerreotypes stood on Broadway near Fulton Street two blocks from Ted's office in a building with a saloon on the ground floor and a model of a camera hanging on the front. Because photographer Mathew Brady did not practice shy marketing, over several years the camera mock-up grew until eventually it was eight feet high.

When Ted Muggeridge came to New York, a man called Silas Selleck worked as a camera operator at the Brady studio. Years later, Selleck testified that he had met Ted when they were in their early twenties. It's possible that Ted picked up his first interest in photography from Selleck, who worked a five-minute walk from Ted's desk.

Mathew Brady, Selleck's boss and the owner of the studio, was a busy exponent of the daguerreotype. An artist in Paris named Louis Daguerre had devised the daguerreotype—the first photographic process to find commercial success and the one that launched machine-made imagery—and announced it in 1839. Five years later Mathew Brady, age twenty-three, opened his photography shop on Broadway. Daguerreotypes made good money, and Mathew Brady shot thousands of the flinty, palm-sized portraits. Early and eager with photography, he found prominent clients. The year before Ted arrived in New York,

At Mathew Brady's studio on lower Broadway in New York, a camera operator named Silas Selleck befriended Ted Muggeridge when both were in their early twenties.

Brady persuaded Henry Clay, Daniel Webster, and John C. Calhoun to sit for his camera, and in 1850 he published a book of lithographs made from his pictures, the *Gallery of Illustrious Americans*.[4] When Ted came to America, Mathew Brady had a big presence in the book and art business, and his gallery would have been an obvious prospect for sales calls.

The volume of business at the Brady operation was such that the studio employed several camera operators, including twenty-three-year-old Silas Selleck. Selleck had been raised in Cold Spring, New York, a town on the Hudson River fifty miles north of Manhattan. He belonged to the photographers' guild as well as the New York Daguerreian Association, and his social streak extended to politics. Selleck would join the Republican Party and remain active in it for decades. As a cameraman at Brady's, Selleck would place a customer in a chair in the studio, a room with drawing room furniture and painted backdrops that depicted curtains or landscapes, fix the sitter's head into a bracket

that held it immobile, and make an exposure that averaged one minute, depending on sun from the skylight. Thanks and good-bye to that
subject, hello to the next. Selleck's job was one part artistry, two parts
customer relations.

Photographers sold printed art as a sideline. Ted Muggeridge, looking for stores to carry his company's lithographs, would have stopped at
the Brady place. Perhaps Selleck sympathized with the slightly younger
man—he was green, not an artist, and not American. Perhaps Selleck
persuaded Mathew Brady to take some of Ted's inventory. However it
happened, the two became friends, and their friendship lasted for thirty
years. To judge from their later relationship, which was documented,
whereas these years are not, it might be expected that Selleck took Ted
into the studio once or twice, or maybe many times. It might be that
Selleck gave Ted a demonstration of the newfangled medium of photography, and that he put an idea in his head that you could make a
living doing this. That you didn't have to be a salesman, and you could
make money instead as an artist who used chemicals and machines.

————

Ted Muggeridge made his sales calls, he spent time with Silas
Selleck. They talked photography, books, and art. Maybe they talked
money, women, and home. There is a good chance, from two clues, that
they talked about California. From the moment Ted got off his immigrant ship, the *Liverpool*, and planted himself in a rented room, a mania
for California, the newest state, twitched in New York City. And, as it
happened, Silas Selleck was getting ready to move there.

As a bookseller, Ted had reason to read *The Knickerbocker*, a
monthly journal of comment and the bellwether magazine of literary New York. The *Knickerbocker*'s editors in this period offered droll
remarks on New York's obsession with California. In a piece from
1850, the magazine complained that one of its readers in the far West
was not sending back gold. ("Living in California, could he not have
sent us some of the dust? A mere handful? What would it have been
to him?")[5] The summer of the same year, editors remarked on the
glut of books about the West ("Works on California are thickening
upon the public") and listed some titles. The publisher G. P. Putnam
had just brought out *El Dorado: Or, Adventures in the Path of Empire*,
Lea & Blanchard was selling *Six Months in the Gold Mines*, and a third

publisher had an advice book, *Notes on California: How to Get There and What to Do Afterwards.*[6]

As Ted settled in New York, a lot of its residents had California on the mind as a place of easy money. Between the years 1851 and 1855, the *New York Times* ran 960 items that brought together the words "California" and "gold," while the other three New York dailies, the *Herald*, the *Tribune*, and the *Sun*, filled their pages with much the same. America's new land on the West Coast sprang a river of fantasy that washed over people east of the Mississippi.

If California had not happened, Ted might have stayed in New York, shouldering dictionaries. If Ted had not met the photographer Silas Selleck, he would not have imitated him. Selleck went west in 1852. He tried digging for gold in California in the Sierra slopes, in Placer County. He came up with nothing and went to San Francisco to do what he knew, to take photographs. His first storefront went up in a graveyard. In October 1853, the *San Francisco Call* reported that one Silas Selleck had "erected a small building at Yerba Buena Cemetery to take daguerreotypes." Selleck ran an outdoor operation, taking photographs of the dead in their caskets before loved ones lowered them into the dirt.[7]

When Silas Selleck left New York for California, Ted Muggeridge followed; no one can say how, or when, but fall 1855 is likely. By way of the usual trip through Central America, San Francisco stood twice as far from New York as New York was from London: the move to California felt like Muggeridge's second emigration in five years. If he traveled like most (including Leland Stanford), he probably went over the isthmus at Nicaragua, a five-week haul: from New York, a steamship down to the eastern shore of Nicaragua, a second steamer up the western coast to San Francisco.

In 1855, California had precious little civilization on the ground. From a century of Spanish occupation, a few dozen haciendas and missions hugged the coastline, the thin inheritance of the sword and cross. Except for Sacramento, San Francisco, and the mining districts, the interior and north belonged to native people. When Muggeridge arrived, raids on Indian villages were escalating into deportation and a necklace of open jails, the reservations.

San Francisco, six years old, counted thirty-five thousand people, 75 percent of them men. (The masculine tide had receded a bit from three years earlier, when men comprised 85 percent of the population.) The Gold Rush was ending, but the frontier remained. Earlier that year the city's largest saloon and brothel, the Eldorado, shut its doors, perhaps to the frustration of the politicians at City Hall, which stood directly next door to it.

He reached San Francisco as one of thousands of new and always-being-replaced migrants, and made his first identity change. He became "E. J. Muggridge," softening the guttural of his surname. He was twenty-five years old.[8]

San Francisco had a footprint of two square miles, and it faced east, away from the Pacific Ocean and toward the Bay. A panoramic photograph of the peninsula made in 1851 shows a mishmash of two-room cottages that look to be sliding into crannies, and hillsides with rutted and zigzagging streets. Newspapers recorded four earthquakes in 1855. The streets guttered with a drunk here, a gunman there, lost and precarious men that gave the city its main seasoning.

It was a strange choice of habitat for a bookseller. The literary culture of New York turned on its hundreds of libraries and lecture halls, whereas San Francisco had a single library. Its most popular press consisted of bulletins with the weekly gold figures, printed next to advertisements placed by Chinese madams. The city had no paved streets, and sidewalks consisted of six-foot planks laid on the dirt. For drinking water, houses took delivery from horse-drawn tanks that filled barrels

San Francisco in 1856

kept in the kitchen. Whale oil or camphene lamps gave light at night. (Natural gas, new and fancy, was for the people back east.)

The main business strip, Montgomery Street, ran parallel to the waterfront, two blocks from the Bay. Muggridge took his first rental in a corner building at 113 Montgomery and in April 1856 put an ad in one of the newspapers, the *Daily Evening Bulletin*: "E. J. Muggridge has many fine books and works of art to sell." He was looking for a few readers who wanted to rise above the general cultural neglect.[9]

Muggridge had grown up in an old town with a childhood slowed to the hydraulic rhythms of a thousand-year-old river settlement. For some reason he had decided to fling himself to the unmade edge of America, the most accelerated place in the hemisphere. Why would he live in this half-made society? Most came to California for the money: mining had launched a hot economy that turned into real estate speculation and fast trade. But selling encyclopedias and lithographs? Maybe it was the adventure. He had made the first leap to America, here was the second. Maybe it was alienation. He went as far from home as possible without sailing to Asia, landing in a place where no one knew him and where he could invent himself—beginning with a new name.

When Ted Muggeridge became E. J. Muggridge, he coined a self, which was a common thing in California. People went west to disappear, to throw off families, to escape criminal records. Switching identities turns out to have been easy in the West—a name change was the least of it—because California was a churning river of people passing through. No one seemed actually to live there. Only 5 percent of the

names that appear in the state census of 1852 also appear in the one made in 1860. Nineteenth-century America already looked like a country of unstable regions, with people continually moving from one section to another, but California's retention rate of one in twenty in less than a decade took the national prize.[10]

In such a place, Muggridge's trunks full of sober reference books looked as useful as a silver tea set. And what was less promising for a bookseller than the reality that a third of the population did not use English? Twenty thousand Anglo-Americans shared the city with two thousand Mexicans, plus a big group of Europeans who spoke French or German, plus the biggest Asian settlement in North America, perhaps nine thousand Chinese immigrants (estimates vary). The phrase "China Town" appears for the first time in an 1853 newspaper item. (The neighborhood began at the intersection of Kearny and Sacramento Streets, two blocks from Muggridge's rooms.) Another twenty thousand Chinese worked in the mineral mines of the Sierra foothills.

Few Chinese immigrants—who accounted for 30 percent of Californians—had chosen to come in the get-rich-quick way that others did. In southeast China, the Taiping Rebellion against the Qing Dynasty had pushed thousands of peasants off their land and launched an exodus from Guangdong province that ended in South America and California. Most Chinese in the United States were bond labor, debt slaves who had taken passage and housing and who worked off their peonage in three-year contracts, saving some money before going home. Five Chinese-run labor procurers, so-called district companies, controlled Asian California, and the indentured men worked at their bidding, as did the women, at least half of them enchained to brothels.

There was old-fashioned American slavery, too, in the gold country. Southerners had brought enslaved black people to dig for riches—no shame in that, in the 1850s—and the slaveholders climbed accordingly. California state senator Thomas J. Green, from Texas, made his slaves pan for ore on the Yuba River, took the profit, and went into politics.[11]

The ornaments of power made California look like a white man's destination. The state constitution gave the vote to white men, and in 1855 the California Supreme Court held that Chinese, blacks, and Indians not only could not vote, they also could not testify in court, because "the law must, by every sound rule of construction, exclude everyone who is not of white blood."

Muggridge put down roots. He accepted the hierarchy in a lopsided

society, which had a weak legitimate elite on the one hand and a criminal gentry on the other. The state's economy, the legitimate domain,
teetered on a sandhill of greed and speculation. The year Muggridge
arrived, five of San Francisco's banks failed, taking with them the
resources of perhaps half the population. Levels of theft and violence,
meanwhile, approached a state of nature imagined by Thomas Hobbes.
In mid-November 1855, five minutes from Muggridge's rooms, a gang-
ster called Charles Cora killed a U.S. marshal, one William H. Rich-
ardson, in daylight and on the street. There was nothing unusual about
this. The *Alta California* newspaper reported that there had been 560
killings in California in 1854. With a state population of 100,000, this
amounts to about one hundred times the homicide rate of California
during the early 2000s.[12]

With the regular bloodshed from fights and occasional duels for
"honor," Muggridge might have looked out of sync with local norms,
especially when he placed his advertisements for books:

*Large Assortment of Baxter's Exquisite Oil Prints [and] a stock of
Illustrated, Fine Art and Standard Books . . . such as Halliwell's
Shakespeare; Hogarth's Works . . . Flowers of Loveliness; Switzerland
Illustrated; &c, &c, &c, all illustrated with highly finished steel
engravings.*[13]

This kind of effete inventory did not fly out the door. A year went
by, until, looking for better business, Muggridge improvised, putting
to work a printmaking scheme that might take advantage of the city's
violence and scandals.

In October 1855, a man who called himself "James King of William," a former banker put out of work by the financial failures, began
editing a newspaper, the *San Francisco Bulletin*. Charismatic and angry,
James King of William explained his strange name as follows: too
many men named James, too many named King, and his hometown
was called "William." Muggridge was drawn to the showy editor and
placed ads in his paper. The *San Francisco Bulletin* baited corrupt politicians, and in six months it became the city's biggest daily, with a circulation of ten thousand. Among his targets, King of William criticized
one James Casey, a member of the city's governing council, the Board
of Supervisors. The paper accused Casey of stuffing ballot boxes to
get elected in San Francisco and, for good measure, of being a former

inmate at New York's Sing Sing prison. On May 14, 1856, the exposé being too much truth to tolerate, Casey encountered King of William in the street, and shot him. A crowd gathered at the site, turned into a posse, and within a day several hundred men had come together at a meeting. The men, half of them "respectable," half of them less so, called themselves defenders of civilization and declared that they were tired of crime and corruption and random violence. They formed a gang, the Vigilance Committee.

James King of William lingered for a week and then died, becoming a martyr to law and order.

With news of his death, the vigilantes grew to 2,500 men, who occupied a warehouse and turned it into an armory—called "Fort Gunnybags" for the stacks of sandbags piled outside—built an arsenal of guns, and planned reprisals in behalf of middle-class virtue. They stormed the city jail and extracted two prisoners—Charles Cora, who had killed a U.S. marshal, and James Casey, killer of the newspaperman—and lynched both in front of an enormous crowd.

In the chaos, Muggridge saw an opportunity. James King of William in his death was transformed into a symbol of middle-class normalcy in lawless and backward California. In August, Muggridge advertised that he had hired "Mr. Chas. Fenderich, the well-known artist of this city, formerly of Washington, D.C.," to make an engraving of King of William, "a faithful likeness of the people's champion, who 'fell at his post doing duty.'" He promised that this piece of art, "published by E. J. Muggridge" and available for purchase, "shall be an ornament fit for the walls of the drawing-room."

The engraving sold, sold, sold. Muggridge placed ads for it eight times in four months, raking in money, until the fire went out of the uprising.[14]

For many weeks the Vigilance Committee put the legitimate government out of business and policed San Francisco with a private militia. The vigilantes hanged four men and drove thirty-two out of the city with death threats. Having faced down some criminals, the uprising looked elsewhere for enemies and found them among immigrants, especially Chinese. Hundreds of Chinese endured random attacks on the street—beatings, the cutting of the long braid, or queue, worn by men, and night raids that smashed storefronts in the Asian ghetto. Even though Muggridge had made money from the vigilante wave, as a recent immigrant the bookseller felt vulnerable to the nationalistic rage.

The redoubt in San Francisco known as Fort Gunnybags, from which vigilantes ruled the city using mob actions and lynching in 1856, the summer after E. J. Muggridge arrived.

Muggridge had been in San Francisco for just a year when, in November 1856, he filed an application for U.S. citizenship. Perhaps it was insurance—better to be naturalized than a crummy non-American, like the others—or maybe he liked what he had seen.[15]

―――

He was E. J. Muggridge to his customers, but in May 1856 came another name change: "Muygridge."[16] He put the new name in his advertisements (and probably pronounced it "*My*-gridge"). The bookseller had thrown off the grunting sound of his birth name and replaced it with a little melody.

E. J. Muygridge had a brother six years younger, named Thomas, who was fourteen when Muygridge left for America. At sixteen Thomas had moved from the brothers' hometown in England to a port city in Wales, where he apprenticed as a seaman. At the end of his contract, in 1856, when he was twenty, Thomas joined the merchant marine, and six months after he took his first bunk on a cargo ship, he decided to follow his older brother to America. Muygridge had possibly written home to Thomas, but letters or not, the magnet of get-rich stories pulled people out of Europe, and seamen notoriously deserted ships that made it to California. When the new sailor's clipper turned up in San Francisco, Thomas walked off the ship and didn't turn back.

The last of Muygridge's brothers back home was named George. Records are slim, but around this time George also fetched up in California. He was twenty-three, and he probably came the well-traveled route—Liverpool to New York, New York to the isthmus, a ship to San Francisco. George and Thomas must have looked up to their older brother, because when each of them reached town, each started using their brother's invented last name, Muygridge.[17]

The Golden State played on the fantasies of young men. Its stories had caused three brothers to come eight thousand miles from England to a place none of them had ever seen. George, Thomas, and Edward had this much in common with Leland Stanford and his family, although none of them knew it. Just as all the Muygridge brothers had gone to California, Stanford and all of *his* brothers, five of them, had done the same.

Thomas and George Muygridge went up from San Francisco into the Sierras, where they dug for gold or shoveled for copper, another mineral that had turned up. (On the way to the mountains, the Muygridge brothers probably provisioned in Sacramento, at one of the Stanford brothers' stores.) The mines never aroused Edward Muygridge, the oldest brother, who stayed in San Francisco with his books. Thomas and George left few traces, and in these years their brother Edward also appears only in scattered records. In October 1857, Muygridge published another moneymaker, a pamphlet about an enormous steamship that had showed up in the harbor, the *Great Eastern*. A new British vessel, the goliath *Great Eastern* could carry four thousand passengers—although half of them had to be crammed into steerage—and was designed to sail ten thousand miles without having to take on fresh coal for its boilers. Muygridge had a personal link to this giant machine. The *Great Eastern* was the improbable creation of an engineer named Isambard Brunel, a celebrity of industry in England and France. In England, Brunel had become famous for having built one of the earliest railroads, the Great Western line, which ran southwest from London through Kingston—the same train Muygridge had seen as a child, the one that blasted through his hometown. Muygridge made a pocketful of money publicizing Brunel's latest feat, a huge steamship riding out in San Francisco Bay.[18]

He must have sold inventory enough to stay afloat, enough pictures and engravings and prints, because he kept placing ads and more ads. In December 1856 Muygridge listed "Christmas & New Year's presents" for sale, pushing his "magnificent illustrated books" and pointing out that anyone could come around and look without having to buy. He said his little showroom ("upstairs" at 113 Montgomery) kept its door open until 10:00 p.m. (He probably lived and sold at the same address.) Like many in the city, he was transient, shifting around between rented rooms. In summer 1858 Muygridge moved two blocks north to 163 Clay Street, a few doors west of Montgomery.[19]

Despite the book dealer's efforts to prop up the standard of discourse, San Francisco's mental climate remained low and grainy. Next to Muygridge's ads in the paper were pitches in the vein of "Madam Sweit," a psychic entrepreneur. ("The renowned Clairvoyant, Madam Sweit, has returned for a short time to San Francisco, and can be consulted in the TRANCE STATE, on matters of business. She guarantees to her clients a more accurate delineation of character, capabilities, etc. than can be obtained from any phrenologist living.") Where Muygridge advertised books at five dollars or more, Madam Sweit had easier terms: "Ladies $2, and Gentlemen $3."

Good citizens in the Western frontier like Muygridge who felt they represented a wave of middle-class stability pushed for moral uplift. In 1856 a group of wage workers founded the Mechanics Institute, an effort to resist debt slavery and indentured labor. The flood of Chinese migrants, whose bosses pushed down wages for all workers, put at risk skilled labor—carpenters and metal workers, bricklayers and contractors, smiths and machinists. The Mechanics Institute opened in a pair of rooms, where its members held meetings and talks, and then put on a trade fair where its members could get out their message. Workers with a trade wanted California to know, in effect, that they were better than "slaves and coolies"—blacks and Chinese. The Mechanics fair was held in September 1857 in a makeshift building on Montgomery Street, and Muygridge pitched in by renting space for his books and prints. He also sold photographs, probably those of his friend Silas Selleck, as well as others he had bought to flip for a profit. In this quick-turnover group he advertised pictures by Carleton Watkins, who would later be his rival in the photography of Yosemite Valley.[20]

To judge from the newspapers, Muygridge was now running one of the few high-culture businesses in the city. Next to his one-inch-square

A commercial photograph by E. J. Muybridge, taken in 1872, depicts a stationer and bookstore in San Francisco, LeCount Bros. and Mansur's, the kind of good-citizen outlet where the bookseller marketed his encyclopedias and art prints.

announcements about art books appear several columns of ads for gin, cutlery, ale, cigars, furniture, Scotch whiskey, clocks, cognac, paper, and wine. One "teacher of the guitar, M.V. Ferrer," offers services, as do two daguerreotype artists, whose notices peek through the liquor-heavy consumer glut. One of these photographers is Muygridge's New York comrade, Silas Selleck.

In May 1858, Muygridge started publishing another money-maker, a patriotic serial. The *Alta California* ran an item on "a new work now being issued in numbers by the San Francisco publisher, E. J. Muygridge," called *The History of the United States*. This time, Muygridge took delivery of a manuscript from a writer in New York called Jesse Ames Spencer and published the result in pamphlet install-ments ("copies from one to four have been laid on our table," said the paper). As he had done back east, Muygridge sold this history serial by subscription, one piece at a time, until a full book could be put into a binding.

The English immigrant thought he would stay in San Francisco, so he pushed and tried to climb the social ladder. He got involved with the city's only book collection, the Mercantile Library, which had opened in 1853 with a collection of 2,500 books, shelved in two rooms, with fees required for access. Members of the Mercantile were merchants, men more polished than the carpenters of the Mechanics Institute, men who said they liked to read and to talk. Muygridge sold books to this kind of person. (The insecurity of such men, however, appeared in a disclaimer that the library included in its own printed catalogue: "If this publication is inferior in style to those issued from Eastern presses, its place of publication [San Francisco] is pleaded as an apol-ogy.") Muygridge advised on what materials the library should acquire and followed through by selling them just that, until the collection grew to eleven thousand books. The Mercantile Library soon named Muygridge to its board of directors, his first social promotion. In 1859, the library moved into a new space, with one room of books, a reading room hung with history paintings (*Arrival of the Immigrant Family* and *Landing of Columbus*), and a "chess room" furnished with sixteen inlaid game tables. In San Francisco, this was the most refined you could get, orderly and sedate, cigars and newspapers, with dues paid quarterly by a select 1,400 people. The affiliation helped Muygridge wear a little crown of respectability.[21]

———

The bookseller had pulled his brothers Thomas and George into the California gamble, but they decided to ignore books and went instead to the mines. Muygridge probably heard the news by word of mouth: in December 1858, George Muygridge died in the Sierras, age twenty-five. As often, the cause of death did not make it into the announce-ment, which itself appeared in the Sacramento paper four months late, suggesting that George Muygridge had been in a remote mining camp. George had followed his older brother to the edge of America and ended with nothing.[22]

Edward was twenty-eight. A few months after his brother's death,

Muygridge decided to get out of California and go home to England. The timing looks surprising: he was making money and fitting himself into the small bourgeois elite. But his mother, widowed and alone, was back in Britain, and she had seen all of her children go off to California. And Muygridge had been in America for nine years. Perhaps he felt something of his mother's loss, or maybe he just missed home.

He began by placing an ad in the paper, saying he was "selling off, to close business." The ad had no results, and in the fall he placed another, this time looking for assistants—"two salesmen," maybe in hopes that one might take the business off his hands. For the rest of 1859 Muygridge issued a string of must-sell notices. "Illustrated books, engravings, oil prints . . . the entire stock must be closed out by the Fifteenth Day of August," one said. These also drew a thin response. Finally he advertised that he was auctioning his inventory to get rid of everything. "Come and see!—Intends quitting business immediately after New Year's." Muygridge ran seven announcements about closing down shop in a period of six months. No one wanted to buy his business, and readers in the city failed to clean out his storage rooms. And so Muygridge decided to give what was left of the operation to his one living brother—Thomas Muygridge, age twenty-four—who was back in town from the mines and at loose ends.

In his notices, Muygridge left it unsaid whether he was leaving America for good. He mentioned he would take orders for European finery—the art books, architecture folios, and engravings—and ship them to clients in California from London. He gave rates (10 percent on small orders, scaling down to 2.5 percent for orders over $1,000). He would be happy to take deposits, he said, before June 5, when he planned to sail on the steamship *Golden Age*.[23]

————

The people on the stagecoach knew the crash was coming, because it took some time. E. J. Muygridge seems to have known he might die in the wreck. A report said he tried to save himself, but since he could not remember anything, someone told him what had happened—nine days later, when he woke up.

The steamship *Golden Age* had gone from San Francisco without him. Maybe the paltry income of recent months put the ticket out of reach—but fortunately a cheaper ride could be had. On July 2, Muygridge got on the Butterfield stage. The Butterfield Overland Mail

Company had a contract with the Post Office to carry letters going east of the Mississippi. Twice a week at 1:00 p.m. a stagecoach went out from San Francisco on a meandering, 2,800-mile, twenty-five-day trip. Sacks of mail made the money, while passengers, up to eight, meant cream on top. The stage turned into the poor man's American crossing. It replaced the covered wagon routes across the unbuilt midlands, adding new comforts, like dingy hotels and beer stops. To take the Butterfield meant six hundred hours inside a shaking cab, seventy-five food breaks, fifty stops to change horses, occasional overnights with no hotel, and uncountable roadside piss breaks—a dirty, boring, migraine-making trip, racketing down the straights, dribbling across streams, rivers of dust through open windows, three days descending the Sierras, saloons, lunches bought from kitchens at daybreak, up the rises, down the hollows, a different bed (and sometimes no bed) every night—from San Francisco to Los Angeles, across New Mexico, through the desert into Arizona, across Texas, through Arkansas, and into Missouri. Anyone who could stand it deserved to pay as little as possible. At the last stop, in St. Louis, the men who had endured a month on the road washed their clothes and got on a train, ending in New York or Washington, or Charleston or Atlanta. And it was usually men—when a woman took the Butterfield, it made the newspapers.

Muygridge might have thought the Butterfield would not be too bad. Wagons had flattened the route from California to St. Louis, the path was worn, a lot of hotels had gone in. But it does not appear that Muygridge had browsed the reports. If he had, he might have taken the boat, because news of killings on the Butterfield came every few days. Two weeks before his trip, at one of the line's horse depots, on the Concho River in northwest Texas, "Camanches" raided the stage, killing a station keeper and taking ten horses. The week Muygridge left, a Butterfield passenger called Schellenberger, in the middle of a cross-country slog, shot his wife in the stomach. "She is alive but not expected to survive," the stringer said. Was it an accident, or did the trip cause the man to lose it?[24]

Muygridge took the stage on a Monday. The eight seats were sold out, with four men taking the whole trip, four planning to stop along the way.

He had spent four years in California soaking up the strange pageant of the West, from the miners and speculators to Chinese bosses, gangsters, vigilantes, all sorts taking the main chance. He might go

The style of stagecoach that Muygridge took across the country in the summer of 1860. The Butterfield Overland Mail Company used a so-called Concord carriage, made in Concord, New Hampshire, with six or four horses, a duffle in the rear for the mail, and eight long-haul travelers in the cab.

home for good, or he might come back. He wasn't sure, but either way there was something about the Americans, their craziness and fantasies, that must have been hard to forget.

One more piece of public madness had lately exploded. In 1858, at a place called Virginia City, in a section of Utah Territory that was later wrapped into Nevada, miners found some "blue stuff," lead ore with lines of silver in it. Word went to the miners in California, many of

When his stagecoach crashed in eastern Texas and threw him from the cab, Muygridge was near the end of a four-week, 2,800-mile trip from California to Missouri.

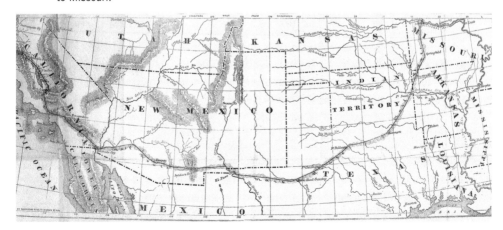

them working the sputtering gold fields. A stampede ensued almost as fierce as the Gold Rush ten years before. In six months, four thousand men went to Nevada from California as the ore strike known as the Comstock Lode turned into a river of silver. Between January and July 1860, another twenty thousand men went over the Sierra mountains and into the new mining hills. In the months before he left California, Muygridge would have watched San Francisco emptying out. He would have seen the silver lust in the eyes of plenty of men, a new tide washing his old turf.

His response to it was slow, but a reaction did eventually materialize. As Muygridge bumped and rattled east on the Butterfield, he seems to have thought about it. He had come to the United States to sell Europe to the Americans, hustling heavy books to a mainly indifferent public. Maybe he could do the reverse and sell America to the Europeans. He was now half American and half British. Maybe the craziness of California could be packaged and sold to his people back home. In England, as it turned out, Muygridge would eventually try to sell some of the fantasy of America, the silver rush, to his own countrymen, to English investors. He seems not to have told anyone about this plan, and it would be several years before it came into focus. But when the time came in London, he would try his hand raising money on the dream of the Nevada mines. Maybe with this, he could become one of the rich, half-mad Americans himself.

The Butterfield crept across the Southwest. Three weeks on the road passed without incident, until the stagecoach reached Texas. The stage rattled through the pinelands of eastern Texas, where the dry plains rolled like a fluttering sheet. It was the middle of a heat wave, with a week of hundred-degree temperatures reported in the papers. The passengers sweated and pulled up the canvas windows to admit only hot blasts. On July 22, 1860, sometime during the night—just beyond a place called Mountain Station, near what is now Fort Worth (according to the report telegraphed back to California)—the driver cracked his whip. The six horses, fresh from the last depot, started on a run, and the driver couldn't stop them. At a gallop, with the coach banging along behind, the stage came to an escarpment where the road began a long downhill stretch. Years later, Muygridge described what happened.[25]

"I recollect taking supper at a stagehouse on the road. We then got on board the stage, which was drawn by six wild mustang horses. After leaving that station we had traveled probably for half an hour—we were then just entering the Texas Cross Timbers. The mustangs ran and the driver was unable to control them." The Cross Timbers were a length of woods between Texas and southern Kansas. The coach started down the hill, swerving, the horses running for perhaps half a mile. "The brakes were applied, but were found to be useless," Muygridge remembered.

"Just as we were getting to the Timbers," Muygridge said, "I remarked that the best plan would be for us to get out of the back of the stage, because I saw that an accident would take place. I took out my knife to cut the canvas back, and was preparing to leave when the stage ran against a rock or a stump and threw me out. I landed against my head." He did not remember the next part. When the coach flew off the road, it threw him from the cab and headfirst into a tree, or a rock. (Another passenger, less badly hurt, had told him these things, and Muygridge repeated that man's story as his own.)

He was taken from the scene unconscious, perhaps in a coma. The next day another stagecoach arrived, and he was put on a stretcher and taken 150 miles to the first semblance of a city.

"I awakened nine days after the accident, in Fort Smith, Arkansas. I had a wound in my head, and double vision. I had no taste, and my sense of smell was impaired." He was also very deaf, he said.

Medical care on the frontier, less than ideal, delivered him to the care of a particularly meager doctor. Muygridge said that a Dr. Bowie, the physician at Fort Smith, "cupped me several times." Cupping involved a blade to cut the skin and a heated cup placed over the wound. The heat lowered the air pressure under the cup, and as it cooled, the skin was sucked upwards, creating blisters and forcing a spray of blood. A medieval method used by modern people.

Muygridge convalesced in Arkansas. Weeks passed. When he could get out of bed, he took a train to St. Louis, another to New York. His eyes and ears felt unreliable. He found a new doctor in New York, Willard Parker, a surgeon at Columbia College and associate at Bellevue Hospital. Despite his credentials, Parker seems not to have known what to do. He gave Muygridge one piece of advice, both sophisticated and useless: do not eat meat, and you will get better.[26]

Still seeing double, Muygridge listened to his American side, the litigious voice. He sued Butterfield Overland Mail, filing in district court and asking $10,000 in damages. Then he sailed to London.

Chapter 15

THE TRIAL

The Muybridge murder trial exhibited familiar parts—sex, betrayal, revenge—but a new element put them on everyone's lips, the speed of the information. Daily reports from the courtroom went down the wires by telegraph, the story ricocheting around America not unlike the trains. Writers for the California papers, scribbling in the courtroom gallery, took their notes to the telegraph depot at the Napa railroad station and dictated long features to the "brass pounders," the men who tapped out the sentences and sent them over the wire. The network resembled nothing so much as clotheslines strung alongside all the train tracks. Stories appeared the next morning in San Francisco and Sacramento in three-column spreads, and they flickered back across the country to surface in papers from Illinois to Georgia to Massachusetts, where editors had bought the material from news aggregators like the Associated Press and United Press, which packaged copy and sent it around by telegraph. Stories were blazoned of the wild seducer, Harry Larkyns, the beautiful and credulous wife, Flora Downs Muybridge, and the too-serious artist, Edward Muybridge. The admitted killer was sketched to be the saddest figure in the cast, a husband who paid the price for neglect.

The news network had gotten faster—it had added bandwidth, if you like—since the Western Union Company, which dominated national communication, put online a new invention, the "telegraph printer." Rather than tap out a message, dash by dot, a telegraph opera-

Napa, California, population three thousand, as seen from the roof
of the courthouse . . .

. . . became the unlikely focus, during the Muybridge murder trial,
of an early media sensation with a national audience.

tor sat at a machine like a little piano with lettered keys and typed in the text. At the other end of the line a separate machine printed the message, letter by letter, on a thin strip of paper at the rate of fifty words a minute. The new machines came in handy during the Muybridge trial because every day reporters on the murder in Napa, one hundred miles from their editors in San Francisco, filed 2,500-word features about the case. (A twenty-seven-year-old tinkerer in New Jersey, Thomas Edison, had lately made some changes to telegraph printers, patenting several improvements that started him in business as an inventor. Edward Muybridge, in the dock, had no reason to know about Edison or his role in speeding up the news of the trial, but eventually the two would meet and get to know each other, when Edison, years later, put himself in touch with Muybridge because he had heard about the photographer's moving pictures and thought he could make improvements to them.)

In early 1875, at the same time as the Muybridge case, another adultery trial filled newspapers everywhere in America, although this one didn't involve murder. On the East Coast, the preacher Henry Ward Beecher, the famous and righteous pastor of Plymouth Congregational Church in Brooklyn, tried to defend himself in a lawsuit brought by one of his male parishioners who said Beecher had been sleeping with his wife. Beecher the preacher was the brother of Harriet Beecher Stowe, author of *Uncle Tom's Cabin*, the novel about slavery that outsold the Bible for many years and helped to start the Civil War. The Beecher trial ran from January to July 1875, and its salacious testimony about the pulpit seducing the pew shot across the telegraph into newspaper stories everywhere. It was bigger still than the Muybridge case, but the two sex scandals, one in California, the other in New York, had the effect of pulling together, for a short time, the whole country.

It was in this climate of coast-to-coast chatter about two broken marriages that Edward Muybridge sat to defend himself. On the second day of the trial, February 4, the little courthouse in Napa filled up to the back, and would-be spectators spilled into the hall and out onto the lawn. The first of a procession of witnesses stood to be sworn. George Wolf, the young driver who had taken Muybridge to the Yellow Jacket Mine (and who had apparently recovered from the measles), described the hourlong buggy ride up the dark road to the mine. Wolf also said that Muybridge had made a strange remark on the way up the mountain. Wolf remembered that Muybridge had leaned forward and said, "I want to give Harry Larkyns a surprise."[1]

Another witness, Benjamin Pricket, who lived at the Yellow Jacket, testified that he had answered the door when Muybridge had knocked. Pricket said he went into the sitting room to get Larkyns, and when Larkyns went to the door, he looked outside. "And I heard him say, 'What is it? It is so dark I cannot see you.'"

The witness who came next, M. C. Murray, said he too was in the room during the shooting. Murray's memory was the most specific. After Larkyns went to the door, Murray heard these words: "It's Edward Muybridge. I have brought you a message about my wife." He said the photographer fired at the word *wife*. After the shooting, with Larkyns lying on the ground outside the back door, Murray remembered that someone wanted to send for a doctor, and that Muybridge himself spoke up. His buggy and driver were still outside, and he wouldn't mind lending them.

There was disagreement about what Muybridge said when he pulled the trigger. The photographer remembered that he had said, "My name is Muybridge, and I have received a message about my wife——." Others quoted more ironic words. James McArthur, the prosecution's lead witness, who had been sick when the trial began, now testified that he was playing cards with the others in the cabin when he heard at the door, "I have brought you a message *from* my wife," and the gunshot.

The pistol Muybridge had used, his Smith & Wesson #2, was produced and shown to McArthur, who said it was the one he had taken from Muybridge. McArthur added that he had noticed two of the six chambers were empty—one of them from the shot Muybridge had fired to test the gun on the buggy ride up. As McArthur handled the pistol in the witness box, Wirt Pendegast, the photographer's lawyer, realized that this little scene was not the best thing for his case. "We would rather admit that this is the pistol than to have it slung around here," said Pendegast. The gun was put away.

McArthur said that an hour passed after the shooting, during which "a desultory conversation was carried on." McArthur said, "He told us that this man Larkyns had 'destroyed his happiness,' or something like that, and that men of family would appreciate his position." In cross-examination, Wirt Pendegast asked McArthur, "Did he say, as one of his excuses, 'This man has seduced my wife?'" The prosecutor, the confusingly nicknamed Judge Stoney, objected—"That is not relevant, we cannot ask him anything about that"—but the question was upheld.

"He did not use the words 'seduce my wife,'" said McArthur, "but I understood that's what he meant from what he said about 'destroying my happiness.'"

McArthur added that after he put Muybridge in the cab for the ride to Calistoga, the two sat together in the backseat. He asked Muybridge why he had come at night, frightening everybody, instead of during the day, and Muybridge answered that he did not want to give Larkyns an easy chance to shoot him.

"I didn't question him further," said McArthur. "He volunteered all of this information. He said he went to Yellow Jacket to kill the man."

The Muybridge trial became an early media sensation. Stories reached a dozen newspapers—from Indiana's *Indianapolis Sentinel* to the *Arizona Miner* in Prescott, Arizona, from the *New York Herald* to the *Chicago Times*. The trial crowded pages in the *Baltimore Sun*, the *Philadelphia North American*, the Washington, D.C., *Daily Critic*, the *Daily Nebraska Press* of Nebraska City, Nebraska, and the *Owyhee Avalanche* of Silver City, Idaho.[2]

Muybridge was an artist already known around the country. His art had first caught the attention of editors—now his crime jittered across the telegraph.

———

When he started as a photographer, in 1868, Muybridge had bought a blank scrapbook, twelve by fifteen inches, maybe two hundred pages. He began collecting news items about himself and pasting them in the book, beginning with stories about his photographs of Yosemite, the ones he took in 1867.[3] Many more clippings appear that cover his doings for the next seven years, until 1874. After this they stop. In October 1874, Muybridge killed Harry Larkyns, and for the next seven months, his name appeared in the press only in connection with the crime. Muybridge's scrapbook, now in the archives of his hometown, contains nothing for the period October 1874–May 1875. The gap is an omission of both pride and shame. When he started to paste in news items again, they were the ones that called him an artist, a photographer making pictures, and not a killer hoping to be redeemed.

———

A glimpse of the national fascination with the Muybridge case (and one of the clippings he declined to save) can be seen in one story that came out of the Midwest. In the town of Arlington, in northeast Iowa, a spiritual medium leading a séance claimed to have contacted the ghost of Harry Larkyns. An Iowa paper called the *Weekly Hawk-Eye* told the story.

> *Mrs C. M. Sawyer, a spiritualistic medium, living at 1144 Mission St., on Thursday evening last, gave a special séance [in Arlington]. At eight o'clock a party, consisting of Sen. S. P. Jones, of Nevada, Capt. Lees, of the police, J. P. Goodman, formerly editor of the Virginia Enterprise, Judge Southard, D. F. Verdena, and several others . . . met at the house designated. The medium was introduced and requested that the committee of two gentlemen be appointed to examine the cabinet from which the materialized spirit of Harry Larkyns was to issue forth. . . . perfect precautions against trickery were taken. The room underwent a thorough search. . . . the committee tied the medium, and after ten minutes of silence she was compelled to ask that the cords might be taken off. Then followed a series of raps, voices, "materialized" hands, etc., but the whole affair was so shallow as only to excite ridicule. After waiting until after 11 o'clock to see something extraordinary, the visitors departed in disgust.[4]*

The skeptics at the Iowa séance may not have seen Harry Larkyns, but they knew his name, and to look for him.

———

Muybridge sat at the table with his lawyers, watching in silence. "A reserved looking man," one paper said.

Wirt Pendegast, the defense attorney, set out to establish that Harry Larkyns's seduction of Flora Muybridge—or rather, Muybridge's discovery of it—had driven the photographer to madness, and that he had tracked down his sexual competitor and shot his victim in an "uncontrollable" or "insane" impulse.[5] The insanity defense depended on two witnesses—Susan Smith, the midwife who told Muybridge about Flora and Larkyns, and William Rulofson, the art dealer who saw Muybridge the day of the shooting. Pendegast hoped both would depict his client as unhinged.

Susan Smith went first. "More than medium height, plainly dressed, she wore a flower-trimmed straw hat," said one paper. "A woman advanced in years" and "quite theatrical in manner, rising from her seat and gesticulating," said another. Judge Stoney, the prosecutor, worried the story of Flora's affair would come from Smith and that this would hurt his case. "There should be no testimony designed to show provocation," said Stoney, "or attempt to justify the killing." Pendegast answered that he wished to hear Smith's account in order to show insanity. Judge Wallace, from the bench, let Smith answer questions, and she went on to describe, minute by minute, her encounter with Muybridge in his state of shock and fear.

"I told him I could convince him of the guilt of his wife," Smith said. She went over the story of the afternoon Larkyns had visited Muybridge's house while Flora was in bed and had gone into her room and sat on the bed, where Flora was lying naked from the waist up.* On hearing this, "Muybridge was very much excited," said Smith.

Smith described how Muybridge had picked up a picture of Florado and seen the words "Little Harry" on the back, in his wife's handwriting. Smith remembered that Muybridge entered a howling fugue. "His appearance was that of a madman, his eyes glassy, his lower jaw hanging down, showing his teeth. He trembled from head to foot, and gasped for breath—he was terrible to look at. He fell on the floor as in a fit." If she could help him prove he was insane, Muybridge might avoid the gallows. Although the papers commented on Smith's change of loyalty from Flora and Larkyns to Muybridge, neither she nor Pendegast made an attempt to explain it. Smith said of Muybridge, "I was afraid he would die. When he walked to the door to leave, I spoke to him, and he muttered to himself, as if he did not hear me, and then I spoke to him again. He turned as though he had awakened from a trance. I thought as he left that he was insane."

At this point, Pendegast called as a witness William Rulofson, proprietor of Bradley & Rulofson, the gallery where Muybridge sold his photographs. More than Susan Smith, who gestured and jumped in the chair, Rulofson made a good witness. If Muybridge was rumpled, Rulofson was polished. The art dealer wore suits, and, except for muttonchop whiskers, he was clean-shaven, unusual during this era of bearded men. Where Muybridge was quixotic and uncomfortable, Rulofson was smooth.

Muybridge's defense required that he be sketched in a pitiful light.

---

* A reporter for the *San Francisco Chronicle* added, after referring to Flora's breasts, "Much more of this kind of testimony is omitted as unfit for publication."

It meant his friends and supporters had to make him look unstable, while Pendegast cultivated sympathy for his crime. From the moment William Rulofson took the oath, he described his friend and client Muybridge as a weird and unbalanced mess.

"I know all the parties in this case," said Rulofson, "and I knew the deceased lightly. About Mr. Muybridge, I have often noticed peculiarities in him, which led me to believe he was eccentric." Rulofson dropped into and out of the past tense, as though the defendant was not present in the room. "Mr. Muybridge used to take violent dislikes to people in my employment," Rulofson said, "and he possessed an utterly causeless aversion to some of them. He also could not keep a deal, although he was strictly honest. Muybridge and I would make a business arrangement, to sell one of his series of photographs, for instance, to which we would both agree, and we would write it out. And yet the very next day he would want an entirely new bargain made, as though nothing had been agreed. This happened thirty or forty times."

Pendegast did not have to coach Rulofson, who seemed to know his assignment: to make Muybridge look as difficult and changeable as possible.

"Another eccentricity about Muybridge was that in his work he would not take a picture unless the image suited him. He would go to the place he had in mind to photograph, or to a scene requested by a client, and if he thought the view would not be artistic, he would re-pack his camera and gear and come back to the studio, no matter what price was being offered. I found this truly strange."

To save Muybridge, Rulofson exaggerated the photographer's behavior. He apparently did not know, or did not mind, that the more he talked, the more he alienated Muybridge, the most successful artist in his gallery. Later on, Rulofson would have to pay for the insults he had heaped from the witness chair onto the head of his most profitable client.

"I saw Muybridge two or three days after the homicide, in the Napa jail," Rulofson went on. "He wept bitterly for a time, and then, recovering himself, he would declare indignantly that he was perfectly calm. These back-and-forth transitions continued throughout our meeting."

Under cross-examination by the prosecution, Rulofson stuck to his story that Muybridge was "mad," and not merely unusual. "I could relate a hundred instances of his peculiarities," he said, "a hundred reasons other than those I have stated for believing that Muybridge was insane."

Wirt Pendegast picked up a photograph from the defense table. The picture was the one Muybridge had taken of himself in Yosemite Valley, perched on a rock, his legs dangling over a precipice, a giant drop below him. Pendegast introduced the picture as evidence of the photographer's pathology.

"This is one of the strange, freak behaviors that Muybridge committed. He sat on a cliff at Yosemite, where a biscuit, if slightly tilted, would have dropped 2000 feet to the floor of the valley," said Pendegast. And although the lawyer had only recently met his client, he said, "In my opinion, for years he has been subject to fits of insanity."

On the third day of the trial, February 5, at 9:30 a.m., the defense put Muybridge in the witness chair.[6] Pendegast asked Muybridge nothing about the crime, or about his wife, Flora. Instead, the lawyer had the photographer tell the story of his stagecoach accident, fifteen years earlier. He hoped the story of the concussion could help prove the fragility of his mind.

"I remember taking supper at a stagehouse on the road," Muybridge began. The photographer told the whole long tale—about the "six wild mustang horses," about his being thrown from the cab and waking up, nine days later, in a small-town hospital 150 miles away. "When I recovered I found that each eye had its own vision, that in looking at a man I would distinctly see two men. I found that I had neither taste nor smell. This state of things continued acutely for three months and to a lesser extent for a year," Muybridge finished.

It was the only time Muybridge spoke during the case. "His demeanor on the stand was quiet, cool and reserved," one paper said. "He gave his testimony in a straightforward manner, and betrayed none of the nervousness which has marked his presence during the trial."

Pendegast ended his questions. Judge Stoney of the prosecution decided not to cross-examine. Too much sympathy already existed for the defendant—as a wronged husband, as a "madman," and now as the survivor of a near-fatal accident. To shore up this last story, Pendegast called witnesses to testify that the accident had changed the photographer.

Silas Selleck, the daguerreotype artist who had known Muybridge since they both were in their early twenties, living in New York, said that before Muybridge took the Butterfield stagecoach, "he was active, energetic, and strict in all his dealings, as well as open and candid." Selleck claimed that when Muybridge came back to California several years after the accident, "He was eccentric, peculiar, and had the queerest of odd notions, so much so that he seemed like a different man."

Another witness, one J. D. Eastland, said that he had known Muybridge for sixteen years, "and pretty intimately, but after the stagecoach accident the change was marked, and he became strange in manner and speech." A man called Matthias Gray said that prior to the accident Muybridge was genial and affable, but after it "there was a marked change in him"—not least in his hair, which had been dark but had fast turned gray.

Stoney tried to rebut the madness claims. The prosecutor called back as a witness James McArthur, who had taken Muybridge's gun after the shooting. McArthur said, "I observed nothing unusual in the way he carried himself. When I took his pistol from him at the time of the shooting I noticed that his hand was unusually steady." Stoney called as another rebuttal witness George Cramwell, the sheriff at Calistoga, where Muybridge was brought from the scene of the shooting. "I had him in my immediate custody most of the time from 1 o'clock Sunday morning until the train came down to pick him up and bring him to Napa," Cramwell said. "During that time, he was very cool—much cooler than I should be if I had just killed a man. He showed no excitement whatever."

Mental health, in 1875 on the California frontier, appeared on no one's list of advanced branches of medicine. Nevertheless, to answer the madness argument, the prosecution called the state expert, Dr. George Shurtleff, the most prominent specialist in mental illness in the West (also one of the only ones). Shurtleff, fifty-six, had helped establish the first state mental hospital, the Stockton Asylum for the Insane, and had run that place for ten years. A replacement for that institution was being built outside Napa, designed to house five hundred inmates, and Shurtleff would be appointed to run it, too. He was a professor at the University of California, Berkeley, and president of the Medical Society of California. Shurtleff had a wide, scowling face, a swirl of white hair combed straight back, and a long white goatee.[7]

"In forming an opinion of a man's sanity, great excitement would be an element in determining the question," Shurtleff said. "If he was calm just afterward"—as Muybridge had been—"that fact would weigh against him." Judge Wallace, who had been silent most of the trial, questioned Shurtleff himself.

"Supposing the defendant killed a man on the night of the 17th of October," Wallace asked. "Would his conduct the following day form a constituent circumstance in determining his sanity at the time? Suppose he were calm after the commission of such an act. Would that fact aid you in forming an opinion?"

Shurtleff: "If it was testified by the common observer that he was calm, I would have to take that as so much evidence going to show he was not insane."

Dr. George Shurtleff—who had, coincidentally, lately written a paper called "Medical Jurisprudence of Insanity"—was skeptical of the defense's claims.

"I have heard nothing to convince me that he was of unsound mind. The prisoner exercised his reasoning faculties in fulfilling his purpose. I think he thoroughly understood the nature and consequences of his act and knew it was unlawful. The evidence shows passion, not insanity." Shurtleff went on, dismissively. "If he were insane he would not recognize his own responsibility. Insane people regret the act and consider themselves innocent. If a man avows and justifies the act afterward, as the defendant has done, then it was a voluntary act on his part."

If that was not enough to put away Muybridge's "insanity," Shurtleff then turned to the story of the stagecoach accident. "The accident does not account for the defendant's eccentricities," he said. "The changes in his manner can be accounted for irrespective of the accident."

Cross-examined by the defense, Shurtleff didn't budge. Pendegast's partner, the lawyer Cameron King, read aloud from several case histories, but Shurtleff said none resembled the Muybridge case.

"In each of these examples, the patients were delirious—Mr. Muybridge was not. Yes, severe blows on the head can produce insanity. However, premeditation and design of the kind the defendant carried out are proof not of insanity, but self-possession and reason. Further evidence of Mr. Muybridge's state of mind can be found in at least one aspect of his behavior with regard to his wife's infidelity. When people take punishment into their own hands they seek publicity, because the publicity is a part of the satisfaction. If disgraced publicly, they seek public vindication—whereas an insane person feels disregard for the opinion of the public." Muybridge, while in jail awaiting trial, had taken pains to tell his story to the newspapers.

The prosecution called George W. Smith, the reporter who had interviewed Muybridge in jail for the *San Francisco Chronicle*. After the story ran, Smith had received a letter from Muybridge, and Judge Stoney had subpoenaed both Smith and the letter. The interview with Muybridge was read aloud in court. In it, the photographer said that he disagreed with his lawyers' plan to plead his insanity because he knew what he was doing at the time. Muybridge's letter was also read out—it included a polite thank-you to the reporter for being fair and a single minor correction. These things were evidence of Muybridge's clear mind, said Stoney.

The rebuttals sounded good, so by the end of the day, the sense in the media gallery was that the insanity defense would collapse.

"On the street corners knots of men were gathered," one reporter put it, "excitedly discussing the merits of the case. There seems to be a general impression that the attempt to prove insanity has utterly failed and that the jury must acquit the prisoner by justifying his deed or not at all."

———

Summary arguments, starting with Judge Stoney for the prosecution, came on the trial's fourth day. Despite his apparent victory in the quarrel over Muybridge's state of mind, Stoney knew sympathy flowed to the photographer. People in the West, or at least men, perhaps more than elsewhere, took the view that a husband could dispose of his sexual rival, if necessary, by killing the man, and that he could be excused for it. The prosecutor knew this, so Stoney began by feigning compassion for the defendant, claiming how unfortunate it was that he had to convict the poor man.

"I represent the people of California," he said, "and I have sympathy for the prisoner—however guilty he might be, or however much he might have violated the laws of God or man. But duty to country, to ourselves, to conscience, compels me to show the act of the prisoner in its true legal light."

In cases of adultery plus murder, the tendency of Western juries was to acquit. Stoney said that the jury had an obligation to see the laws enforced, but that he knew of the "unfavorable precedents," the tendency of courts to let a husband get away with killing his wife's lover. Nevertheless, said Stoney, he thought too highly of the jurors to believe that they would forget their duty to law. Stoney nodded to the tradition of husbands who got away with it. "It is customary for men to kill seducers, because juries are in a habit of acquitting them. But, gentlemen, juries can't make laws. Many cases of this kind have been decided incorrectly, in defiance of the law." The prosecutor brought up an infamous case. "This prisoner is ambitious of standing with Daniel Sickles and wants to compare with him in history."

In 1859, in Washington, D.C., a forty-one-year-old congressman from New York, Daniel Sickles, discovered that his wife, Teresa, age twenty-two, was having an affair with the city's district attorney, Philip Barton Key, the quietly sexy son of poet Francis Scott Key, who wrote "The Star-Spangled Banner." On a day in February, Sickles saw Key outside his window, waving to get the attention of Teresa, who was upstairs. Sickles left the house with two pistols and shot his rival in the groin and chest, killing him.

Sickles had the sympathy of Washington society, and in a three-week trial, his lawyers pushed the argument that his wife's infidelity had caused him "temporary insanity." The jury agreed—the first time such a defense prevailed in a murder case. In the aftermath, to the astonishment of many, Sickles reconciled with Teresa, and the two resumed married life. The congressman went on to become a Union general in the Civil War and lost a leg at Gettysburg.

"It is the view of this office," said Stoney, "that the enormity of the defendant's act in taking the law into his own hands has only been equaled by the enormity of the acts of juries in saying that certain defendants are justified in homicide, when they are not. You have sworn not to decide in that way, but to decide according to the law and the evidence."

He turned to the insanity question.

"The defendant is a man of culture and intelligence, I admit," Stoney went on. "Muybridge's intelligence even rises to genius. He knows what he is doing. But this allowance of eccentricity for insanity is a dangerous principle, because the law requires a man to control his passions.

"Here are the facts. The proof of the defendant's determination to take life is incontrovertible. It is unnecessary to go over the testimony on this point. No one disputes it. The defendant even justifies the act, and he glories in it. He has made a statement, published in a newspaper, in which he says he went to kill a man, and claims that it was justifiable. His was a voluntary, deliberate act. He is guilty of deliberate murder, unless he can show that he was insane at the time. Yet there is no form of insanity that strikes a man like a flash of lightning, compelling him to commit an awful crime, and then passes away as in a dream, leaving no trace behind. If the defense fails to satisfy you of this man's insanity, there is only one verdict you can render."

Stoney then threw a gamble at the jury. "This case is one of murder or nothing! I ask no compromise verdict. If he is not guilty, do not find him guilty of anything!

"The defendant has received a wrong. It was a great wrong, and I have no word of extenuation for it. But the victim is dead. He has paid the penalty of his misdeeds! Larkyns's character is not before the jury. An adulterer does not forfeit his life, even to the husband whose wife he may have debauched. The defendant here has counsel, court, jury, and the protections of law. Larkyns had no opportunity to show palliation or extenuation, or even the falsity of the charges against him. The defendant assumed to himself the rights of the judge, the jury, and the executioner. It is for this that he is on trial here."

Stoney's oration continued for an hour—uneasily, because he was arguing against the mood of the crowd—and when finally he sat down, he shook his head left to right, because he knew that most if not all the men of the jury could put themselves in the shoes of the killer.

———

It was a Friday night. The trial had become the entertainment of the townspeople of Napa for that weekend. At 7:00 p.m., Wirt Pendegast stood to begin final arguments for his client.

Pendegast was tall and strongly built, with a large, handsome head. He had a mesmerizing effect on a room. "Few could resist the fascination of his presence," said one lawyer who had opposed him. A reporter described Pendegast's face as "chaste and terse" but said his manners, "easy and pleasing," warmed up his aloof appearance. His summation stunned the courtroom.

"I ask, at the request of the defendant, that the jury agree with the counsel for the prosecution, and either acquit my client of any crime whatever or send him to the gallows," he began, throwing away the chance of a jail sentence for a lesser charge. "The killing is admitted, as are all, or nearly all, the attendant circumstances testified to. But who was Harry Larkyns? He was just one of a class of men—and that class of man, in seducing a man's wife, makes a dreadful gamble. He was one of a class who stake their lives on moments of sensual gratification. Larkyns played that game and lost, and he was compelled to pay the penalty.

"Edward Muybridge recognized the difference in tastes and temperaments between himself and his wife. The difference in their ages accounted for those, and he indulged his wife in all those innocent amusements that she loved—in clothing and in the theater, in a hundred small diversions—while he cared nothing for them. My client permitted his wife to go where she liked and to enjoy herself in ways that had no attraction for him. During their marriage he loved her deeply, madly, with all the strong love of a strong, self-constrained man. And all at once, like a clap of thunder from a clear sky, came upon him the revelation that his whole life had been blasted. The whole miserable, sickening, damning story was revealed to him by Mrs. Susan Smith, the nurse, when she set before him the picture in all its horrible blackness. Mr. Muybridge learned that his wife had been false in every way, false even to the extent of palming off upon him as his own the child of her libertine seducer.

"Gentlemen, there is no statute in such cases that permits a man to slay his torturer. But, law or no law, every fiber of a man's frame impels him to instant vengeance, and he will have it, even if hell yawns before him afterward. My client was driven—the prosecutor himself has showed that the prisoner did not halt from the time he left San Francisco until his object was accomplished. It is a shame of our law that there is no adequate punishment for such crime as that perpetrated by Harry Larkyns. The letters before you show that after the poor woman had escaped him, he was still plotting to get her back to California, or to join her in Oregon, there to renew these unholy relations. Muybridge was not only revenging his wrongs when he shot Larkyns dead, he was protecting his wife against him in the future! Because Larkyns was still pursuing his victim.

"And the defendant—this poor, wronged, and maddened man—is asked by the prosecution to keep perfectly cool? He is asked perhaps to bring a lawsuit against Larkyns for criminal conduct? Under the law, if Larkyns, after being warned away from the defendant's property—as Muybridge warned him away from his wife—had wrenched just one shingle from the roof of the defendant's house, my client would have been justified in shooting him dead. But when this defiler takes the wife of a man's bosom, writes the word 'prostitute' upon her brow, blackens the name of his child, and dishonors and ruins the happiness of his home, what is that husband to do? He is to ask the law merely to protect him from the repetition of such conduct? As if it could be repeated! This debaucher, this libertine, holds a man's wife in his arms on the night of the birth of the child, kisses her lips, calls her his baby, intrudes himself into the sacred precincts of the birth-chamber, and afterward exchanges with her ribald jokes at the expense of the man whom they had wronged!

"You, gentlemen of the jury—you who have wives whom you love, daughters whom you cherish, and mothers whom you reverence, will not condone Larkyns's crime. I cannot ask you to send this man back to his happy home. The destroyer has been there, and has written all over it, from foundation-stone to roof-top, the words, 'Desolation, desolation!' His wife's name has been smirched, his child bastardized, and his earthly happiness so utterly destroyed that no hope exists of its reconstruction. But let him go forth from here again—let him go once more among the wild and grand beauties of nature, in the pursuit of his loved profession. Let him go where he may perhaps pick up again a few of the broken threads of his life and attain such comparative peace as may be attained by one so cruelly stricken through the very excess of his love for his wife."

Pendegast spoke for two hours, and when he sat down the courtroom shook with applause. The yelling and whistling annoyed the judge, William Wallace, who told the sheriff to arrest the loudest cheerers. The sheriff seized one man, a Napa landlord called Dan McCarthy, but when McCarthy protested that he had only done the same as everyone else, Wallace relented. He scolded McCarthy for shouting, told the bailiff to release him, and announced that he would clear the courtroom if any more demonstrations of sympathy were made.

Judge Wallace gave his instructions to the jury. He told the men that they could render one of four different verdicts: guilty in the first degree, and death; guilty and imprisonment for life; not guilty; or not guilty by reason of insanity. (Wallace left off another option, not guilty with justifiable homicide. He banned that verdict outright.) Insanity, he said, "must be proved affirmatively and conclusively." If Muybridge believed he was justified in shooting Larkyns, it didn't matter, "unless his belief arose from his insanity." Further, if the victim of the murder seduced the defendant's wife, "that was no justification for the homicide, because the defendant was not warranted in taking the law into his own hands." The judge gave the jury foreman a written description of each verdict he would accept, and at 9:30 p.m., after the jury left to deliberate, Judge Wallace adjourned the court.[8]

————

The feeling in the crowd was that the jury would come back quickly with an acquittal—even Stoney, the prosecutor, thought he had lost the case. The courtroom stayed full until midnight. Muybridge drifted here and there; he felt gregarious, a social reflex he rarely had, although his bonhomie had a manic tinge. He had acquired an entourage, and as friends and sympathizers crowded around him, everyone's talk rose high and loud. One reporter said that Muybridge "joined in jokes, raillery and laughter," talking about his travels and adventures.

Muybridge and his group moved their drama into the office of the defense lawyer. Wirt Pendegast worked at the center of the tiny Napa legal world: his law firm rented rooms in the courthouse, on the same hallway as the courtroom, only two doors down. He and his partner, Cameron King, felt none of the elation around them and sat grimly in the office. One reporter said they "chafed with anxiety," whereas Muybridge, flanked with admirers, seemed "perfectly cool and collected."

At 12:00 a.m., Sheriff Corwin approached Muybridge to return him to jail for the night. The photographer said good-bye to the crowd, and the two climbed the stairs. As he walked into his cell, his home for the previous three months, Muybridge stopped at the iron door.

"This is too bad, I thought last night was my last in prison," he said.

The crowds milled in the courtroom until 1:00 a.m., when some realized a verdict might not come. There was a dwindling in twos and threes, but at 3:00 a.m. many remained.

Chapter 16

THE SPECULATOR

He used to be vigorous, now he felt disabled, at age thirty. Muygridge could not taste anything, couldn't smell, and he saw double. "If I looked at you," he said, "there were two of you."

He left New York for London around the time of the presidential election—whether by coincidence or design, a good time to get out of America. The victory of Abraham Lincoln in November 1860 would lead to the secession of the South and the War of Rebellion. By leaving, Muygridge escaped the draft in the North that would soon snare most men under forty, both immigrant and native born. It may not have been an accident that Muygridge got out just as the Civil War began and stayed away until a bit after it ended, in 1865. His writings say nothing about politics, but the timing has the fingerprints of self-preservation.

In London, Muygridge found a Dr. William Gull in a clinic on Harley Street, a prestige medical address. Gull's clients included Queen Victoria and the Prince of Wales, a fact he was loath to let people forget, and likely the reason Muygridge came around. Gull has a deathless place in medical history: he published the original study of anorexia nervosa (and named the eating disorder) in a paper that presented three women patients, the misses "A," "B," and "K," whom he also claimed to have cured. That was after Muygridge saw him, however. (William Gull's name also survives because he would eventually be attached to the case of Jack the Ripper, the unknown mass murderer who mutilated five women in East London in 1888. Gull was not the clinician in the case, but suspected as the possible killer, along with the artist Walter Sickert. He was implicated by Sickert's son, who spun the tale after his father, and everyone else concerned, was long gone.) The famous and infamous Dr. Gull could not do much for head injuries, however, and told Muygridge his concussion had to mend itself.

Having been out of England for ten years, Muygridge seems to have moved in with his mother, who was then living in London at St. John's Wood, three miles northwest of Charing Cross. Susannah Muggeridge, fifty-four and widowed, her three remaining sons having gone to America, looks to have been quite alone. Muygridge had no doubt written her about his brother George, whose sudden death in California had left Susannah with two sons—Thomas, still in San Francisco, and Edward himself, recovering from a gruesome accident.

His case against the stagecoach company would not come up in the American court for several months, so Muygridge set up house with his mother. He had been working on a pair of inventions, and he brought with him two sets of drawings. The date on one suggests he had made it while recovering from his accident in New York, where apparently his double vision didn't affect his mind or hand. In March 1861 Muygridge would pay a visit with his inventor's papers to the British patent office; six months later he would visit again, with a second folder, and the second invention. He had come back to England to remake himself.

Sometime in 1861 Muygridge returned to New York to push his lawsuit. The Butterfield Overland Mail Company could outspend and outwait a plaintiff, and it had good connections in Washington. Muygridge seems to have realized this and decided to negotiate. In lieu of the $10,000 he had demanded, he took a $2,500 payout and went back to London with the cash in hand. It was the equivalent of the salary for one year of an upper-middle-class manager.

With money to live on, Muygridge moved out of his mother's place to new rooms in Covent Garden, at 16 Southampton Street, off the Strand, an address in a neighborhood given over to market halls and the trading of commodities—also a kind of inventors' district that happened to be near the patent offices. The move says something about his motives, and about the man he hoped to become. Muygridge seems to have gone home to make money, to attempt a run up the social and class ladder. The bookseller had spent a decade as a salesman, lifting boxes of books and pushing someone else's art and merchandise. Now he was looking for a way to climb. His sight and hearing having finally stabilized, the man with double vision focused his attention.

He had two inventions. If he could get a pair of patents for them, if he could sell his own intellectual property, he might break from the salesman's treadmill. Muygridge was aroused enough by what he had done with his drawings to brag about them. He sent the plans to an uncle who was living in Australia, Henry Selfe, and offered to give him a franchise on one of his machines. "These papers would enable any carpenter and machinist, upon reference, to construct such a device without difficulty," he said. Muygridge urged his uncle to take out a patent on the device in Australia, but warned Selfe that if the thing took off, he might come around to collect money from him.

———

On August 1, 1861, Muygridge walked into the Great Seal Patent Office in London, at 25 Southampton Buildings, Chancery Lane. The name of the agency referred to the fat wax seal that dangled by a ribbon from the patent letters the office handed out. The seal represented the sovereign, Queen Victoria, and meant the head of state had indulged the patent holder with the right to exploit his intellectual property, which she would protect. As Muygridge made his way through the Great Seal building, he might have glanced in at two other agencies that shared a floor with the patent office, the offices of the Secretary of Bankrupts and the Secretary for Lunatics. Those two agencies ran prisons for debtors, on the one hand, and lockups for mental patients, on the other. Muygridge edged past Bankrupts and went by the door of Lunatics before arriving with his packet of materials at a large room dotted with desks—the patent bureaucracy.

It was the start of Muygridge's career in ingenuity, the end of his salesman's life. From 1861 forward, he would make his living as an inventor, a photographer, and a lecturer. Eventually he would patent several things—a clock, a shutter for a high-speed camera, and an apparatus to generate stop-motion photography, which involved equipment that filled a barn. But on this visit, one of his first to the Great Seal office, he brought something more modest. The envelope of papers in his hands contained drawings for a machine Muygridge thought could turn him a quick profit—a tabletop, hand-crank clothes washer.[1]

Muygridge exchanged words with the clerks, handed over his dossier, and left. Afterward, someone made a note on his file: the application had come from "Edward James Muygridge, of San Francisco." A strange label. He was a native of metropolitan London, but a clerk had pigeonholed him as an American.

By the mid-1800s, the "English inventor" was very much a type. Thousands of tinkerers and amateur chemists lived in and around London, and many of them shuffled to and from Chancery Lane, their papers and drawings falling out of folders. Inventors did not typically come from the gentry, nor were they professional scientists. They were usually lower-middle-class men who cobbled up gadgets in workshops set out in the backyard garden. Inventors had an acquaintance with chemistry, sometimes with metals. They were strivers, not necessarily educated, and not at all rich. But if they came up with the right patent for a process or a piece of equipment, and if they could get some capitalist who owned a factory to pay for it, they could get rich in a hurry. Two big "if"s, but Muygridge, at least for a while, put his faith in them.

The hand-crank washing machine was a mechanical substitute for a servant. He had apparently built a model of it, and in any case he had paid an artist to make an engraving of the thing and hired Eyre and Spottiswoode, a fancy publisher, to print it. The washing machine was an oblong metal box, three feet long and a little less wide, and eighteen inches deep—big enough to stand on a table, but not so big that it took over the room. You put the clothes inside it, and soap and water, and closed the lid. The metal walls were corrugated on the inside "like a washboard," Muygridge said, and the box made a big trough for sloshing. Instead of human arms to scrub, there were two upright metal poles, and at the end of each pole a metal "pounder," like a hand, which beat the clothes against the washboard walls. "The pounders vibrate to and fro alternately, by means of rods connected to their arms, and to cranks upon a shaft, which is caused to revolve by the turning of a hand wheel," said the description. Muygridge thought he could sell the machine to commercial laundries and maybe also make a smaller, domestic model. (He made another drawing for this kitchen version.)

The Muygridge washer was about speed. It reduced the drudgery of cleaning clothes, a serial process. Speed and acceleration were themes he would come back to.

The clothes washer was actually Muygridge's second try at a patent—his first attempt had come the previous year. In September 1860, while convalescing in New York, recovering from the crash, he had come up with an invention that would change the technology for printing works of art, specifically, intaglios, a medium using engraved metal plates. (A washing machine and art prints—something low for the servants, something high for the salon.) Recumbent in bed, Muygridge had sent this design from New York to the office of a solicitor, one Augustus Frederick Sheppard, who did business from 38 Moorgate Street, off Finsbury Circus in London. Sheppard worked a mile and a half from the Great Seal patent office, a little far, but he still knew its ins and outs.[2]

When he hired Sheppard, Muygridge revived his long-abandoned birth name, "E. Muggeridge," to sign the patent application for his printing process. Attorney Sheppard, for his part, wrote a description of Muygridge's scheme and brought it to the patent bureaucracy on his client's behalf.

Perhaps Muygridge had hired a patent solicitor because he knew the kind of gauntlet that awaited anyone trying to make it in London as an inventor. In America, a patent application cost fifteen dollars, a month's worth of unskilled wages, and a single visit or even a mailing to the relevant office in Washington, D.C., sufficed. In England, however, inventors had to petition upward of seven government offices in person, and fees amounted to £100, about four times the average person's annual income.[3] In 1860, the U.S. Patent Office granted 4,819 patents, compared with 2,047 granted in Britain, with its richer and more mature economy.[4]

Charles Dickens had satirized the cumbersome intellectual property laws of Britain in a short story, "A Poor Man's Tale of a Patent," published in the magazine *Household Words*. In Dickens's piece, written in the first person, a befuddled blacksmith named John tries to patent an invention he calls "the Model." John takes his device through a labyrinth of government offices, paying fees at each station, encouraged by every clerk to go further into the government beast, up to the next office and down to more fees. "No man in England could get a Patent for an Indian-rubber band, or an iron-hoop, without fee-ing all of them," says Dickens's discouraged protagonist.

The solicitor hired by Muygridge, Augustus Sheppard, ran the papers through the long labyrinth for his client, and sometime in 1861 succeeded in retrieving patent 2352, "an improved method of, and apparatus for, plate-printing"—Muygridge's process for the intaglios.

By the mid-1800s, lithographs and intaglios dominated the market for mass-produced art, and Muygridge had handled a lot of both as a bookseller. Color prints that depicted farm life, theater celebrities, or military exploits could hardly be kept off the walls of modest people, especially those who would have rather been born into the middle class. In California, Muygridge had stepped out of merely selling prints and into making them. He had used intaglio to print his portrait of James King of William, the editor of the *San Francisco Bulletin* who became a hero to vigilantes when he was shot in the street, and he had made good money from it. Art prints, the readymade decor in Victorian rooms, as common on the wall as lace on a table, looked to Muygridge as though they might become even more profitable, if only they could be made more quickly. With patent 2352, Muygridge thought he could accelerate the printing process.

An intaglio was a print made using an etched copper or zinc plate that had been soaked with ink so that it penetrated into the grooves of the etching, wiped with a cloth to clean ink from the ridges, or relief, and pressed on paper. The trouble was that you had to ink the plate and wipe it clean for each impression. Muygridge guessed that he could speed up the process by cutting out the re-inking step. He added a reservoir of ink to the printing press that automatically fed onto the plate from below through perforations, thus dispensing with the step of re-inking by hand from above. Like the clothes washer, this invention, too, was about velocity, and about quickening a serial process.

In early 1862, the Great Seal office approved the clothes washer, and on January 27, Muygridge went to 25 Southampton Buildings to retrieve his patent for "Improvements in Machinery or Apparatus for Washing Clothes and other Textile Articles," a heavy sheet of cotton paper with a red wax seal dangling from the bottom of the page.[5]

———

He now had two pieces of intellectual property in hand. Marketing came next.

During the late 1800s, inventors hustled their goods face to face at trade shows, and the biggest shows were the new "world's fairs." It had been ten years since the first one, the Great Exhibition of 1851, in London, which had risen up in a vast iron and glass hall, dreamily remembered as the Crystal Palace. The template for a dozen trade shows that succeeded it, the Great Exhibition brought together thousands of exhibitors, millions of ticket buyers, and a fascinated press. It showed off both the machines of industry and the industrial state of mind, in which science pointed to mechanization, and inventions looked like the path to the future. (Muygridge had immigrated to America in 1850, so he had missed the event, but he no doubt studied it in the New York newspapers.) The Great Exhibition produced imitators, and throughout the 1850s similar trade shows went up in New York, Munich, and Paris, each pulling in enormous crowds and making pots of money for its sponsors.

In 1862, a new world's fair came together in London, the so-called International Exhibition, housed, like the previous one, in an enormous trade hall. Invitations to exhibitors went out (rent for space supplemented ticket sales), and a site was cleared on land in the neighborhood of South Kensington. Muygridge put in an application; he would rent the smallest possible exhibition space to show off his two inventions.

The monstrous Exhibition Palace, covering sixteen acres, opened to visitors in May 1862, an H-shaped big box in tan stucco. It had fifty arched windows running like two-story piano keys along the four-hundred-yard facade, two long wings set at right angles on each end of the main structure, and two giant glass domes for a roofline. Inside, upward of twenty-eight thousand exhibitors from thirty-six countries, many of them small-change inventors like Muygridge, competed for the attention of a swarming public. Here was an ocean of apparatus—cameras, textiles, scientific instruments, steel, nonbreakable pottery, steam engines, conveyors, pumps, fans, shuttlecocks, sluices, stamp-

In London, a wing of the main building in the International Exhibition of 1862, where Muybridge showed his patents

ing tools. The tide of industry flooded in and washed the eyes with an unintelligible spectacle.

According to the catalog, the inventions of "E. J. Muygridge" occupied two marvelously obscure corners. His Exhibit 5310a lay somewhere in the rooms devoted to publishing, in an annex on the north face of the building. There on a shelf, below and above other shelves, a handful of intaglios struck from Muygridge's patented process ("specimens of the inventor's plate-printing") were framed amid a clutter of other paper. To their left stood a display of ornamental bookbinding, and to the right, the exhibit of the British and Foreign Bible Society, "191 versions of the Holy Scriptures in various languages."

Muygridge's washing machine, Exhibit 2037, appeared at the west end of the vast hall in the gallery labeled "Machinery in General." It sat high above the floor on a shelf, flanked on one side by a display of drainpipe and wire netting and on the other by a pile of leather hoses and belts.

It would have been an easy matter for the six million visitors to the 1862 world's fair to walk past the two tiny Muygridge exhibits and see nothing of them, which is what they did.[6] Meanwhile, throughout the summer of 1862, Muygridge waited, sitting around in his apartment at 16 Southampton Street, off the Strand. The first-time inventor hoped some manufacturer might step forward with an offer on one or the other patent. But the rich buyers who might have paid for his ingenuity and given him a leg up into the bourgeoisie stayed away.

The big trade show plan failed him, but France beckoned. After London, Paris comprised the other big market where inventors might find buyers, so Muygridge paid a fee to the French government to extend his English patents to France (receiving *brevet d'invention* no. 1198). He wrote his uncle, Henry Selfe, in Australia: "I will shortly leave for Europe on business that may detain me for some months," and sometime in 1862 crossed the English Channel, fitted out with hope, to transplant himself and his sales pitches to Paris.[7]

At this point in the story, we have to make room for unintended consequences. In Paris, a new character appears like an eruption, as intaglios and washing machines fade into the background, and Muygridge discovers a fresh obsession—photography.

First, however, a newspaperman takes notice. Although Muygridge had left America two years before, a San Francisco reporter who was in France thought his appearance in Paris was important enough to send word of a sighting. "There has been a great influx of Californians [to Paris] within the past few weeks," the *Alta California* said in a bulletin dated October 24. "E. J. Muygridge was here a few days since."[8]

Initially, Muygridge's trip to France took the shape of a sales call, but the Paris junket turned into the occasion for his leap into photography, the art that would occupy him for the rest of his life. The evidence accumulates that Muygridge got involved with cameras in the fall of 1862. In the letter to his Australian uncle, the inventor said that he was taking up offices at 9 rue Cadet, Paris, in the 9th arrondissement, and that people should send correspondence to him there. The address, it turns out, was that of the photography studio Maison Hélios operated by the Berthaud brothers. Muygridge used the Berthauds' studio as his business address, while he probably slept at a hotel.

Paris, at this time, had an obsession for photography. In a book published the year Muygridge turned up in France, a pair of art critics surveyed the young art, waxing excitedly about the French fixation on the camera. "Words cannot describe the almost giddy infatuation that has taken hold of the Parisian public," wrote Léopold Ernest Mayer and Pierre-Louis Pierson, in *Photography Considered as an Art and an Industry*. "The sun rises each day only to find innumerable instruments leveled at the horizon in anticipation—everyone, from the scholar to the respectable bourgeois, having become experimenters under the camera's influence."[9] Photographers in Paris were public figures, thanks to Félix Nadar, a master of publicity stunts. The photographer Nadar drew headlines when, as a deft showman, he went up in balloons to photograph Paris from above—no one had ever before photographed a city from the sky—and used the flare of gas jets to make pictures underground, in the sewers and catacombs. When Muygridge arrived, Nadar was ballooning over Paris, a caper that resulted in a caricature by Honoré Daumier, published in the newspaper *Le Boulevard*, which showed the photographer looking down at rooftops through his camera.[10] To an English inventor, Nadar must have seemed a romantic and superb figure.

Circumstantial evidence implies that Muygridge learned about cameras, photo chemicals, and lenses at Maison Hélios, his contact address in Paris. As I mentioned earlier, the evidence consists of a name, on the one hand, and a logo, on the other. The Berthaud brothers named their business after Helios, the Greek god of the sun, and ran a photographers' guild, Société Hélios. Muygridge appropriated both the name of the Berthauds' studio and its logo—the word "Helios" with rays of light emanating from the center—when he established himself in San Francisco as a photographer four years later.

In Paris, Muygridge got nowhere with his inventions. He sold nothing, and he returned to London. One trouble was a glut in the washing machine market. Some twenty-six designs for similar devices had already received patents in France during the five years before Muygridge entered the clothes-cleaning trade.[11] As a result, Muygridge had time on his hands, which he seems to have spent at the photography studio, Maison Hélios.

———

Edward Muygridge seems to have had a distant cousin, an influential figure in London politics, Sir Henry Muggeridge. Sir Henry was both an alderman in London and a former sheriff of the city. He must have been a formidable presence in a room. In a photograph, he is stout like a good Victorian, has a wraparound "chin curtain" beard, and looks like a walrus in costume, wearing the regalia of a Freemason, a getup of skirts, jacket with braids, and epaulettes. (He belonged to the city's Lion and Lamb lodge.) As sheriff during the 1850s, Sir Henry had been knighted after running security during the state visit from France of Emperor Louis Napoleon. But his job in the constabulary took up just part of his time—the sheriff also served as an alderman on the Court of Common Council, London's governing assembly.

Between his two political posts, Sir Henry felt at home with both preening businessmen and gin-racked criminals. In 1859, at age forty-five, Edward Muygridge's cousin acquired another line of power when he helped to found a new finance company, the Bank of London. Within three years, the Bank of London, with Sir Henry as one of ten directors, had a branch on Threadneedle Street and another near Charing Cross, reported £300,000 on deposit, and posted a superb profit for investors.[12]

Henry Muggeridge and Edward Muygridge were two leaves on the same family tree, with Sir Henry fifteen years older than Edward.[13] Both came from Muggeridge families in Banstead, a village ten miles southwest of London. Sir Henry had been born and raised there, while Edward Muygridge's father, John Muggeridge, also had been born in Banstead, before his family had moved to the town of Kingston, a bit to the north. To possess a well-placed cousin when he was angling to change careers and looking for the main chance was a circumstance not

to be ignored, and Muygridge had already turned to his London relatives, the more successful ones in his father's family, when he needed a
job as a teenager. This much is conjecture, but to judge from the strange
veering in Muygridge's life in the year 1863, it appears Sir Henry helped
to guide our protagonist's next move.

When he returned to London from France, Muygridge would have
seen occasional items in the papers about deals made by the Bank of
London and Sir Henry. He might have merely read the notices, or, more
likely, he heard from his own family that Henry's new bank (Remember your father's cousin?) was piling up opportunities, and tracked
the man down. The banking success of Henry Muggeridge begins to
explain why and how that year Edward Muygridge suddenly decided to
try his hand in another area, namely finance, and to fit himself into the
unlikely role of an investor and capitalist.

Edward Muygridge was living as a changeling, adopting positions
and putting on masks: inventor . . . would-be photographer. . . . He
had seen how precarious the life of an inventor could be, how industry
threw only occasional scraps to the actual innovators of machines and
processes. And although the photography tryout in Paris might have
gone well, he remained an amateur at that. Banking? Muygridge had
no experience with money, but it didn't seem to matter.

The 1860s in London were high times for bankers and financiers,
a relatively fresh class of economic masters in the capital of capitalism.
During the early nineteenth century, much of England's wealth had
come from the new, dirty industries—coal, textile mills, and iron. The
factory became the hinge of the economy, and the cult of the machine
combined with masses of workers to make England into the workshop
of Europe. That was in the period of Muygridge's childhood. But for the
ten years that Muygridge was away in America, England had started a
second kind of capitalist revolution. New money flowed into banking,
joint-stock companies, and insurance, and finance replaced industry
as the prime mover of economic life. By 1860, the owners of financial
houses in London—Barings, Lloyds, the new Bank of London—
overtook factory owners as the richest class of businessmen.[14]

Sir Henry Muggeridge, the sheriff-turned-capitalist, was himself
a first-time operator in finance, but it is not impossible that he showed
his cousin Edward Muygridge how he had done it. Muygridge as a
striver stood outside gentlemen's circles, and if he wanted to set up his

own bank—which for some reason, he did want to do—he had to follow some mentor. Sir Henry, the heavyset Mason in his father's circle,
would have been the obvious beacon.

The background for this weird turn, Muygridge's chase after
money, involved a new law in finance on the one hand, and an old war
on the other. During the late 1850s, Parliament had changed the laws
around partnerships, allowing for joint-stock companies while simultaneously limiting the liability of shareholders. The result, after 1860,
was a speculation bubble in finance. Dubious investment schemes and
stock offerings spread like weeds, along with stories of quick fortunes.
In this climate Muygridge came to think that he, too, might make some
easy money, and, improbably, the event that drew him into finance was
England's war in the Crimea. The Crimean War, a fight for influence
over the decaying Ottoman Empire, seated in Istanbul, was waged
around the Black Sea between Russia on one side and France and
Britain on the other. It ended in 1856 with a treaty that left Istanbul
a colonial dependent of Western Europe. Acquiescing to London, the
Ottoman premier, Sultan Abdülmecid, opened the financial markets
of Istanbul to English investment companies, and some speculators in
London thought new fortunes might be had from the Ottoman spoils.

Edward Muygridge, donning the financier's uniform of spats and
top hat, formed two companies to raise money. Both existed on paper,
but neither had visible staff. As a vehicle to raise money, he set up the
Ottoman Company, a brokerage firm, with eight other directors. "This
company is formed at the express solicitation of merchants and others
engaged in trading and monetary operations in the Ottoman Empire,"
said the prospectus, probably a lie.[15] As a former dealer in art prints,
Muygridge approved the design of the Ottoman Company's printed
shares. The picture engraved on the stock offering showed a man wearing a turban and seated on a camel. (At this time no camels existed
in the Ottoman Empire, but no matter—the Oriental fantasy played
well.)

In November 1865, Muygridge and seven other directors formed
a second entity, which they called the Bank of Turkey.[16] Despite its
name, it was neither a firm in Istanbul (it was in London) nor a bank
with branches (it had a post box), but a paper company intended to loan
money (once it was raised). These two firms, the Ottoman Company
and the Bank of Turkey, were interlocking schemes: the idea was to

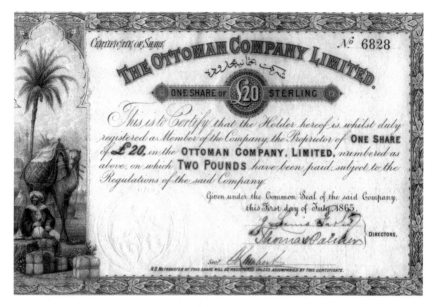

A stock certificate for the Ottoman Company, Muygridge's investment firm
in London, ca. 1865

use the first to fund the second. The Ottoman Company sold itself in
shares in order to finance the Bank of Turkey, which possessed a limited franchise to operate in Istanbul but as yet had no clients, the shares
guaranteeing a right to the bank's profits, if they appeared. It was a
shaky plan, a glimmer on the Oriental bubble then swelling through
the London money markets.

Muygridge took out new rooms, moving from his Covent Garden
apartment to a better address, 4 Brompton Square, in Knightsbridge.
The Covent Garden rooms had been in the inventors' district, the
Knightsbridge place sat squarely in the financial center. It was the second time he had positioned himself in the London geography of the
business he wanted to join. In Knightsbridge, it would be easier to look
like a financier. And, as he had done with his inventions, Muygridge
in his Brompton Square rooms waited for the money to present itself.
Unfortunately, as had happened with the washing machine, the
expected swarm of investors stayed away.

He walked central London, the same streets he had traipsed as a
boy twenty years before. But on these new promenades he dressed in
striped vest and trousers with silk piping, clothes to imitate as best he
could the appearance of a man of means. At age thirty-five, Muygridge
thought he could turn himself into a dealmaker.

Once he was in, he couldn't stop, and in 1865 Muygridge added a third start-up, this time with an American slant, an investing scheme he called Austin Consolidated Silver Mines. Six other directors joined him on that paper board, convinced it might work and pay everyone a fortune. Austin Silver was Muygridge's attempt to cash in on the money rush around the Comstock Lode, the big ore strike in Nevada that had turned into a fever just as he had left America, in 1860. He hoped that to London investors, Nevada silver might look like the new California gold, and that his years in the American West would turn him into an expert on mining. He had seen Nevada, the faraway place with its strange frontier society and casual murders between miners fighting over claims. The prospectus for Austin Silver said that Muygridge, the lead director, was "well acquainted with the silver mines," which was not at all true. It also said that the company planned to buy four mines on the Reese River, near the Nevada town of Austin, "and set up quartz mills at each mine." (Quartz mills were the most advanced mining technology at the time, involving machines that used quartz-tipped teeth to crush ore.) The chairman of Austin Silver was the U.S. consul in London, one Freeman H. Morse, and the company put itself on sale at £5 per share. It looked like a genuine venture.

He placed the newspaper advertisements, an attempt to raise £100,000, putting twenty thousand shares of Austin Silver on sale. Muygridge and company asked for a leveraged investment of ten shillings per share, or one half of face value, with the balance on possession. The terms were reasonable, and they were also doomed.[17]

It is possible to imagine Edward Muygridge presenting one, two, or all three of his companies in pitch meetings, pushing his schemes to businessmen in heavy mustaches, cigars in their hands. Most of his prospects would have been superior to him in education, in experience, and maybe in emotional stability. (Muygridge was single and itinerant, while many investors were married, stay-in-England types.) It is possible to imagine Muygridge gesturing with his arms in the air, his chin rising, voice falling on the word "Nevada," spraying a little fantasy about a gush of money.[18]

The investment bubble burst in the second half of 1865, and Muygridge's money dreams popped with it. After an important railroad company sold a large stock offering at a discount and then went bankrupt, the money markets shook. Interest rates rose from 3 percent to 7 percent, to 10 percent. In May 1866, the big investment firm Overend,

Gurney & Co. failed, carrying down debts of £19,000,000, emptying thousands of wallets, and triggering a run on joint-stock firms. Bust followed boom in a panic that continued into the summer. Muygridge's three speculations—the bank, the brokerage, and the silver mine—all fell apart. He looked to his calling card tray on Brompton Square for envelopes with investors' notes and found nothing. The money rush to the Ottoman dream and the Nevada promise both came to an end, and buyers beat at the doors to get their money out.

A shareholder in the Bank of Turkey sued the board, alleging a corrupt deal with its partner, the Ottoman Company. The suit pointed at "a secret arrangement made between some of the defendants who were directors of both companies." So much was plausible. The judge in the shareholder's suit scolded Muygridge. "Professional gentlemen," the judge said, "mix themselves up in these schemes for the concoction of companies . . . many of which [have] turned out to be illusory."

The other directors made themselves scarce, leaving Muygridge to clean up the bankruptcy. His cousin who had gotten him into this business, Sir Henry Muggeridge, could not help him. Sir Henry's Bank of London had also failed, and Muggeridge, out of money, became a defendant in his own lawsuit. In April and May 1866, Muygridge chaired two shareholders meetings that dissolved the Bank of Turkey. At these events, pelted by the derision of men who had invested in a fantasy, in rooms full of cigar smoke and heckling, Muygridge took insult after insult. He took apart the Bank of Turkey, and he threw away the Ottoman Company. What liability he personally assumed is unclear—the law protected investors from individual responsibility. But chances are good he lost his own money, and it is telling that he soon left London again for America.

It's interesting that when he faced the scorn of his stockholders, Muygridge (the bookseller, inventor, photographer, and banker) did so with a fresh name. The *London Gazette* named the chair of these meetings as "E. I. Muybridge." The middle initial was a typo, an *I* instead of a *J*, but the surname was real, the first appearance of a new name, "Muybridge." On this occasion, the name wouldn't stick, but it would come back later.

Things went just as badly with the mining scheme. A year after Austin Silver went on sale, the directors of the company saw they had nothing to pay out from the Nevada dig and shut down the company. It was June 1865, and the *Times* of London said that shares of Austin

Silver would be settled in mid-November. But the company delayed, apparently with no money for even a token few shillings on the pound. The following year, in June 1866, Muygridge placed an advertisement that asked creditors to bring their claims to the board's final meeting, on July 5. There is no account of that desultory event, but Muygridge again sat in the chair, and angry investors probably did not let things go quietly. A weird concatenation of events in the end produced our photographer. Edward Muygridge was shaped by the humiliation of his failed inventions, his lost contracts, and broken rungs on the ladder that he thought might take him up into the cloud of the business class. Sometime in late summer 1866, he traded the fantasy of the entrepreneur, the one in which greed might solve his problems, for a different fantasy, the one around art. Muygridge, molting again, discarded his chase after money and chose art and independence in its place. He gave up the identity of the banker in spats and went back to California. He became a photographer, with a new name. He was now Helios, like the god of the sun.

Chapter 17

VERDICTS

The twelve men in the Muybridge jury picked a foreman, a man called Sterling. On the first ballot, five voted to convict (the jurors Pratt, Garfield, Hallet, Greenwood, and Klam), seven to acquit (Sterling, Chapson, Newcomer, Connery, Smith, Forester, and Kruze). One of the jurors for acquittal made a show of taking off his coat and bunching it into a pillow on the floor, then lying down to close his eyes. When those who would hang Muybridge came over to his side, he said, the other jurors should wake him up, because he wasn't going to change his mind.

According to a reporter who talked to them, the jurymen at first avoided arguing altogether and talked about money instead. They talked about paper currency (a novelty at the time and controversial in the West) and the exchange rates for gold. They talked about taxes and the paltry amount they were being paid for the trial. Unused to an overnight case, the Napa court did not book hotel rooms, so the jury chambers had to double as a barracks. It was 11:00 p.m . . . midnight . . . one by one they fell asleep, until Sheriff Corwin was the only one awake.

At 9:30 a.m. on Saturday, February 6, the jury went to breakfast, where one of them said, while eating, that if necessary, he would stay in the jury room for three days—the case was important enough. At 10:00 a.m. the men returned to their conference room, unwashed, and took the second ballot, with the same result: five to convict, seven to acquit. Finally they started the argument, and their differences turned on the question of insanity. No one believed Muybridge was insane. Some said the testimony of the midwife, Susan Smith, who had several times called Muybridge "mad," had no credibility. The jurors ridiculed Smith as a witness—she was a go-between in a sexual arrangement, and she had deceived everyone involved. William Rulofson, Muybridge's art dealer, had said the photographer was "eccentric" and "disturbed," but those things were a long throw from madness. George Shurtleff, the insanity expert, had said straight out that he doubted Muybridge was insane—he had been too calculated in the commission of the crime, and too composed after it. The quarrel went on. The problem for acquittal was that Judge Wallace had said Muybridge's verdict depended on his sanity. The only basis for an "innocent killing"—the only justification for murder—was self-defense, and the shooting of Larkyns, whatever else it was, involved nothing like that. If Muybridge was to be justified, said Judge Wallace, it had to be as an insane person, and nobody believed he was mad.

The men talked for an hour, 11:00 a.m. came and went. To most of the jurors, the justice of the murder did not require the cover of insanity. Even the five who wanted to convict said they did not care whether Muybridge was insane. All thought Muybridge was "justified" in killing Larkyns for having seduced his wife. The men tossed the question around the room—if you found yourself in similar circumstances, what would you do? Nearly all said they would have done as Muybridge did, or would have tried. A room full of men in bloody California in 1875 would say that to each other—it would be part of their masculine pose. Everyone agreed it was a righteous killing, that the murder was defensible, if not in self-defense.

Those who wanted to convict now swung around to "not guilty." What would seem to have been the main fight, Muybridge's guilt or innocence, moved offstage, replaced by a fresh, narrower quarrel about the form the verdict should take—whether simply "not guilty," or "not guilty by reason of insanity." On this the jury had its most bitter dispute, and the argument went on for an hour, during which the majority insisted that Muybridge was not insane. The ones who said he was mad were the same who had wanted to convict—they clung to insanity as a way of explaining and ameliorating the killing. Of these, the juror named Pratt was the first to waver. When Pratt let go of the idea of Muybridge's madness, a third ballot was taken. A few minutes earlier, the jury had had no expectation of agreeing on the insanity argument, but to everyone's surprise, all voted for the plainest verdict, "not guilty." It was 12:00 noon.

The courtroom had been full for four hours, and Muybridge and his lawyers stood in a sea of spectators, but the photographer kept up an uncanny calm. "As the morning went on," said a reporter, "Muybridge's friends lost confidence, but the defendant showed no sign of wavering, doubt or fear." He appeared to be in good spirits and talked to anyone who approached him.

The announcement was made that the jury was to be brought in. Judge Wallace entered and sat at the bench. Muybridge sat between two of his lawyers. A reporter said that Wirt Pendegast leaned over to coach his client, saying, "Now, Muybridge, you have acted the man all through this. When the verdict comes, restrain your feelings." Muybridge gave a telling answer—"I am prepared to meet anything, except that which we most desire."

The clerk called the names of the jurymen and asked whether they had reached a verdict. Sterling, the foreman, rose and said, "We have," handing up a slip of paper. The clerk read it, then passed the paper to Judge Wallace, who read it and returned it to the clerk.

The judge nodded, "Record the verdict, Mr. Clerk."

"Gentlemen of the jury, listen to your verdict as it stands recorded. In the People vs. Muybridge—we, the jury, find the defendant not guilty."

One writer described the scene at length. When Muybridge heard the verdict, he gasped and sank forward in his chair. He then seemed to lose control of his muscles; Wirt Pendegast caught the photographer in his arms and in this way kept him from falling to the floor. Muybridge's body appeared limp, but then he began to tremble, and within a minute he went into convulsions. "His jaws set and his face was livid," said a reporter, and "the veins of his hands and forehead swelled out like shipcord." A seizure took possession of him, and Muybridge moaned and wept in waves, but he could say nothing. He sat up in his chair and began rocking back and forth, his face a field of contortions, then his convulsions returned.

Judge Wallace dismissed the jury and, apparently unable to watch Muybridge's reaction, got up to leave the courtroom. The clerk who had read the verdict covered his face with a handkerchief. Judge Stoney, the prosecutor, left the room next, as did several of the jurors, the sight being too much for them. Some of Muybridge's friends surrounded him. They tried to console him, and several began to weep themselves.

Wirt Pendegast, at first gently, then harshly, begged Muybridge to get possession of himself. He asked his client to stand up and give the customary thanks to the jury for their verdict. Muybridge stood and tried to speak, but he could say nothing, and he fell back in his chair in an apparent delirium. He was carried out of the room by Pendegast and another man and laid on a sofa in Pendegast's office, a couple of doors away. A physician was sent for, who appeared at Muybridge's side, but he could do nothing but watch. Finally, one of Pendegast's partners spoke up with a scolding voice. "Muybridge, I sympathize with you, but this exhibition of emotion is extremely painful to me, and for my sake alone I wish you to desist!" At this, the photographer straightened himself. Fifteen minutes had passed. He said, "Yes, I will. I will be calm, now. I am calm now." The fugue state lifted, and Muybridge walked back to the courtroom, teetering, sitting down again at the defense table.

Judge Wallace was brought back from his chambers to the bench, Pendegast made a motion to free his client, and Wallace discharged Muybridge from custody. When the photographer reached the street, a large crowd in front of the courtroom erupted in cheers and applause, and he was mobbed, unable to move along the sidewalk.

"The satisfaction with the verdict was very nearly unanimous," said a reporter, and those who felt otherwise "were in an insignificant minority."

———

Six weeks before the trial, Flora Muybridge had filed for divorce.[1] In the late 1800s, to end a marriage, even on the frontier, where social ties changed as often as flies alighting on food, required disastrous circumstances and heavy court involvement. By killing his wife's lover, Muybridge had provided drama enough for a case, but a judge was not inclined to look benignly on Flora, who was a "fallen woman." In her divorce plea, Flora said that in early 1874, when she was pregnant with her son, Muybridge had accused her of adultery and of carrying another man's child—falsely, she said—and had threatened to kill her. She said Muybridge was "fitful, violent, and jealous," and she claimed "extreme cruelty" as grounds to break the marriage.

Flora's plea went on to say that one night Muybridge had come to their bedroom, watched her while she slept, and when she woke up, gone into the hall to hide from her. When she pretended to sleep again, he had come back in the room, and the scene had been repeated. "These acts of cruelty affected her in such a manner that she has ever since been miserable," said the brief. It was a meager catalog of abuse, because Flora could not tell it straight: her husband had killed the man she loved.

Muybridge now despised his wife (although he told the newspapers he loved her), while Flora needed money and had no one to lean on. She said that she alone cared for and supported her baby son (true, since her husband stopped giving her money) and that she had no means to earn a living (less true). She pointed out that Muybridge had money and that the Bradley & Rulofson gallery owed him $5,000 or even $10,000. She asked the court for alimony in addition to a divorce.

On Tuesday, January 5, a month before the murder trial, while Muybridge sat in jail, a judge ordered that the photographer show cause why he should not pay fifty dollars a month alimony and child support. Three days later, after Muybridge's lawyer Wirt Pendegast contested the judgment with a flourish of argument that no one wrote down, the same judge dismissed his order and postponed the case.

After Muybridge was acquitted in Napa, Flora went back to court to try again.[2] It was March 1875, and this time she escalated her language. She said she had lived with Muybridge "in fear of her life," and went on to tell the story of how they had first come together as a couple. Flora said that Muybridge had hired a lawyer to help her get a divorce from her first husband, Lucius Stone, the heir to a saddle-making company in San Francisco. She said that the day after her divorce Muybridge had given her money to buy clothes, but that when she did not spend it the way he expected, he had verbally abused her and demanded the money back. She had returned the money and then broken off their relationship, her complaint said, but Muybridge had "renewed his attentions" and threatened that if she did not marry him, he would take revenge. She worked as a photo retoucher for the Nahl brothers' gallery, but had also been doing work on Muybridge's pictures. As a sometime employee, as well as his girlfriend, she said she depended on Muybridge for a living and agreed to marry him.

The complaint went on. Flora said that Muybridge had slept with another woman in the summer of 1874, when their baby boy, Florado, was just three months old (she did not name the woman). She said she believed Muybridge would have killed her over Harry Larkyns if he could do it and go unpunished, and that it was still his intention to kill her. She mentioned that Muybridge "is capable of earning $500 a month" with his camera, that she wanted a divorce, a division of property, and permanent alimony.

This filing made a stronger impression than the first, and a Judge Wheeler of the Nineteenth District Court in San Francisco issued an order compelling Muybridge to show cause why he should not pay alimony. On May 1, 1875, Wheeler gave Flora a victory when he ordered Muybridge to pay her fifty dollars in monthly alimony, pending the outcome of her divorce filing. "It was only fair," the judge said, and "the circumstances that gave rise to the divorce suit cannot be taken into consideration."[3] Flora's court victory came three months too late, however, because when the decision came, the photographer was out of the country.

Before he killed Larkyns, Muybridge had cut a deal with a steamship firm, the Pacific Mail Company, to go to Central America and take publicity photographs. He started the job right after his acquittal—he wanted to get out of town and escape his notoriety. Two weeks after the trial, on the night of February 19, 1875, Muybridge hired a rowboat to take him out to a Pacific Mail steamship, which he boarded. He had already sent his cameras and other equipment out to the ship, conniving against Flora, who he knew was in court lobbying for money from him, and to attach his property to her alimony case. He made a stealthy escape from the divorce judgment. Where once he had told a reporter that Flora "would not go without" his money and support, Muybridge now decided not to give her a dollar without a fight.

Leland Stanford's railroad had ties to Central America, and it may have been Muybridge's friend, again, who got him the assignment, a job that let him get out of California after the trial. For twenty-five years there had been a road across the isthmus (and, after 1870, a railroad) to take people and freight to and from the East and California. After Stanford's transcontinental line linked New York with San Francisco, the train depleted travel across Central America, but it was still cheaper to go through Panama or Nicaragua than it was to take a train through the Midwest.[4] Rather than let themselves be undercut by lower fares, Stanford and his associates made a deal with Pacific Mail to subsidize its revenue: the Central Pacific, in effect, bribed the competition to keep its rates up. The steamship line, with the subsidy, got cash flow with-

Muybridge, *Weeding and Protecting the Young Coffee Plant from the Sun. Antigua*—Guatemala, 1875

A group of Native American *alcaldes*, or mayors, at Santa María, Guatemala

Muybridge, *A Roadside Scene, San Isidro*. Maya women bathing

Muybridge, *Reception of the Artist,* Panama, 1875. Muybridge was regarded as an important visitor to the isthmus and treated to military receptions. In the central square of Panama City, he stands at left, wearing a straw hat, his back to the camera, facing a rifle company.

out having to carry freight and charged artificially inflated ticket prices that pushed traffic back to Stanford's railroad. In the weird economy of transport, Muybridge was hired, for this trip, to make handsome photographs of Central America that might encourage passengers to put down money in the isthmus, to invest there rather than just pass through.

To start, the photographer brought out an old routine—he changed his name. He printed a brochure in Spanish that announced him as Señor Eduardo Santiago Muybridge, or "Edward the Saint." Eduardo Santiago stopped at several Mexican ports and arrived in Panama in March 1875. He stayed for two months in Panama City and then sailed for Guatemala, where he stayed another six months. The previous February, he had escaped the gallows. Now, in town after town, he was received as an important visitor.

Muybridge shot coffee plantations and their workers: the manor houses, plus half-clothed Maya Indians bent over plants in the field. He shot military drills on big town squares: two hundred militia in formation, showing off their rifles. He photographed mountains, Baroque churches in ruins, extinct volcanoes. He framed the moon, and the sunset, and the rivers. As was always the case in Muybridge's photographs, the people within them looked like appendages to their setting. Muybridge took a greater interest in what was around people, in the frame, than in the people themselves.

———

Flora Muybridge appears to have been living with her baby, Florado, in a San Francisco boardinghouse belonging to a Mrs. Mary Goss. She fell ill, and, quickly and cruelly, life closed in around her. In early July 1875, Flora suffered what a reporter called "a stroke of paralysis," and she landed in St. Mary's Hospital. The paralysis turned out to be an invention of an excited press, which still despised her as an errant wife: she actually had some kind of influenza. After two weeks ("She never rallied from her illness"), Flora died at 5:00 p.m. on July 18, 1875.[5] One newspaper, dancing somewhat over her body, ran the headline DEATH RELIEVES MRS. FLORA MUYBRIDGE FROM A LIFE OF SIN AND SHAME and added, "Her sad fate was in keeping with her checkered career." She was twenty-four.

A French family living on Mission Street took in Florado Muy-

Life around the master's house at the Hacienda Serigiers, a coffee plantation
in central Guatemala, with the señor's family in promenade

bridge, fifteen months old. The family cared for the baby when his
mother fell sick, and, according to one paper, it was believed that they
would adopt him. Flora was buried on July 20 in a cemetery just west of
the city.

Muybridge, *Planting the Seed at Las Nubes,* Guatemala, 1875.
Muybridge photographed people only in clusters, including workers
clearing a tract to plant more coffee.

Muybridge, *Plaza of Antigua*, 1875. Maya Indians trading on market day at the center of the city of Antigua

Muybridge photographed St. Vincent's Orphanage in the town of San Rafael, north of San Francisco. The picture of boys in the yard—in military formation, with a band playing—suggests something of the setting in which the photographer left Florado to be raised.

———

In November 1875, Muybridge came back from Central America with 250 new photographs.[6] He had been gone nine months—the fever around the murder had cooled, but he would be followed by it.

The photographer put his life back together, renting new rooms at 163 Clay Street and hiring a new art dealer, Morse's Gallery. Muybridge resented his former art dealer, William Rulofson, for the insult of testifying that the photographer was insane. Muybridge fired him, and the two men became enemies, with Rulofson afterward sniping at Muybridge in the newspapers.

When he arrived back in San Francisco, Muybridge learned that Flora had died and that his son, Florado, was in the hands of a family from France. He visited the boy's caregivers and was told that they had just placed the child in an orphanage run by the Catholic Church. Muybridge evidently didn't want his son. He thought Florado wasn't his to care for, because he wasn't his son in the first place. Some months later, Muybridge retrieved Florado and put him in San Francisco's Protestant Orphan House. Florado was three years old when his father put him on the shelf.[7] Muybridge visited the boy at the orphanage, but did not make an effort to raise him. For years he paid the bills sent by the orphanage for expenses to take care of Florado, but he couldn't face the child. When Florado was about age nine, the two saw each other for the last time. On that occasion, the photographer gave his son a gold watch and a framed portrait of himself, and said good-bye. Florado Muybridge grew up to become a ranch hand and a gardener in towns around central California. It was said by people who knew him that Florado took pride in his father, whom he didn't really know, and that he told anyone who would listen that he was the son of the famous photographer.

A murder victim, a dead wife, an abandoned son. He purchased a little freedom at high cost. And now the way forward, as far as Muybridge could see, looked clear.

PART THREE

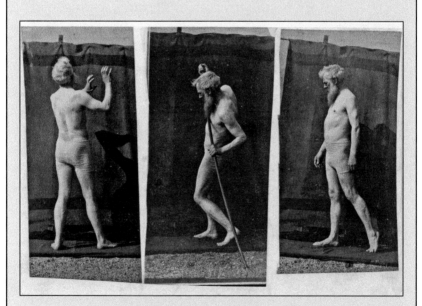

Muybridge, *Self-portrait*, ca. 1885

Chapter 18

THE HORSE LOVERS

The house took up much of the block, and when the huge new mansion was done, Governor Stanford brought in his old friend Muybridge to take pictures of it. Did the richest man in the West think twice before employing a killer? The Octopus might have, had he lived somewhere else in America, but in California Muybridge's social capital went *up*, not down, after the trial. By the code of Western justice, the verdict of the individual and the law of the gun, Muybridge had avenged himself and gotten away with it, and an atmosphere of dark supremacy hung around him. In summer 1876, Stanford hired the photographer again, with no regrets.

Leland and Jenny Stanford had been living in a rented house on California Street, a few numbers down the slope from the tract at the top of the hill where their fifty-thousand-square-foot crib was ready to be occupied. Twenty-plus years in the state made them old-timers, but this was the first time they'd lived in the real city. The Central Pacific had moved its headquarters from Sacramento to San Francisco, getting out of a town with cows in the street to the little metropolis on the Pacific. The Stanford family followed the company and decided to build a house to match their self-regard: they moved into the rental to watch their fifty-room place come together. (The newspapers vied for superlatives: "the Stanfords' palace," "the great villa," "a mansion with no equal.") The house was finished in summer 1876, a brown cube the scale of a public building, all wood, but covered with stucco etched to look like stone. It stood at the top of the highest hill, with views of the city and Bay to the south, east, and north.

One morning, as a crew skittered like ants over the building, Stanford invited a reporter to talk, gestured up at the men on scaffolding, and extemporized about what it all might mean. He pointed to a corner of the mansion and said, "When it is finished, I shall hope to sit upon yonder balcony and look down upon the city embracing in itself and its suburbs one million people. I shall look out through the Golden Gate and I shall see fleets of ocean steamers bearing the trade of India, the commerce of Asia, the traffic of the islands of the ocean."[1] Stanford did not separate his personal comfort from the public good. The master's view from his bedroom on the one hand, a churning port economy on the other.

In July they moved in. The Stanford family, at this point, comprised Leland and his mother, his wife, Jenny, and *her* mother (the two older women, widowed and in their seventies, had both been brought west from Albany), Jenny's sister, Anna Lathrop, and six-year-old Leland Stanford Jr. Seven or eight servants moved in, the on-site half of the

Entrance hall of the Stanford mansion, San Francisco, photographed by Muybridge in 1877

The library on the first floor of the house

staff, while another seven or eight came from their dank rented rooms elsewhere to clean and do the Stanfords' bidding during the day.

Three years had passed since Muybridge had made the stop-motion photographs of Occident. Returning from Guatemala, Muybridge threw off the name "Eduardo Santiago" and returned to Stanford's orbit. In 1877 the photographer took a wagon up California Street to make the first pictures. He photographed the new house from the out-side, shooting upward from a low point to make it loom like a pyramid at Giza, and then room by room, touring it with the lens.

He took his camera through the front door into the big center hall, onto which all the main-floor rooms opened with sliding double doors.[2] The first room on the left was the India Room, upholstered in black satin, with Indian embroideries adorning the walls. Everything smelled new, with paint and varnish and clean rugs. Next on the left came the library, its paneled walls flanked with books. If he was at home dur-ing the day, Leland spent his time here. Following that was the billiard room, in which most furnishings and the walls were fitted out in brown leather. Then came a sitting room, the busiest in the house, because the family gathered there at night. Upholstered in purple and gold velvet, it had a south-facing bay window overlooking the city, a piano, rocking chairs, reading tables, a flower stand, and a sofa. The servants brought in birds from the second-floor aviary to serenade the Stanfords here in nightly roundelays. Muybridge photographed everything.

At the end of the hall was the conservatory, which connected the rooms at the back of the house. It had windows with big views and a fountain in the middle. From it a door led into the dining room, at the right rear of the house, where the table could seat thirty-six. From the dining room you walked into the music and art gallery, which had three walls hung with pictures, and statuary on plinths. The fourth wall of the gallery was taken up by an orchestrion, the sound system of the day, an automatic music-making machine, six feet wide, that reached twelve feet up, floor to ceiling. Stuffed with organ pipes and percussion devices, the orchestrion ran on electricity, the new power source that only a few houses in the city had installed. When switched on, it imitated the sounds of a wind orchestra, playing selections from operas and symphonies that had been programmed into a set of changeable, revolving cylinders. Stanford had a love for gadgets, especially ones that seemed to be alive—his automatons, and now his orchestrion. Elsewhere in the gallery stood several leafy plants, and on their branches sat brightly colored birds, mechanical animals that came to life and sang at the flick of a switch.

Next to the music and art gallery, entered through double doors, was the Pompeian Room, which the Stanfords used to receive guests (and where Muybridge, four years later, would introduce his projection device). In the center of the room stood a round table whose top consisted of a slab of onyx, which had been cut from a pillar at St. Peter's, in Vatican City. Unlike the rest of the room and the rest of the house, this table was not an imitation of something far away, not ersatz, but an authentic object. Jenny Stanford liked to impress visitors with its story. A pillar at St. Peter's had been discovered to have a fault, she said, and it had to be replaced. Removed from the cathedral, the column was cut into slabs, and one of them came into the hands of the Stanfords for a fee transferred to Vatican coffers—they made it into a card table.

Muybridge's pictures are empty of people—the dwelling seems to have no inhabitants. The house and the family were all about display and excess, and the photographer knew that mere people could not compete with the prodigious interiors, the rooms like tombs full of money.

———

According to one of Stanford's secretaries, Frank Shay, Muybridge and Stanford could not stay away from one another. "They would sit together sometimes for several hours, talking and discussing," Shay said.[3] It wasn't that the photographer and the capitalist had much in common. In temperament and behavior, the two men were divided as by a river. Muybridge was a man who had rebounded from his crime into a new bohemian style. He was an *artistique au possible*, a London paper said, with a loosely tied neck ribbon, a velvet coat, and gray felt sombrero. These "might be called Californian, were they not the true artistic style of the London and Paris ateliers."[4] As for Stanford, he was painfully well groomed, vested in wool, with a silk hat at the ready and an ivory-headed, gold-inlaid cane.

Still, they became friends—again. The rail man largely ran the economy of the West, and his time was not a currency Stanford liked to give away. Nevertheless, when Muybridge felt like it, he would stop by the Central Pacific offices and see Stanford "at any time," according to Frank Shay, who saw it happen day after day.

As a thank-you gift to Jenny and Leland for taking him back into their circle, Muybridge chose sixty-three of his photographs of the mansion and bound them in two identical volumes, inscribed with the title "Leland Stanford's Residence Album." Jenny added notes to her copy, describing the colors of the rooms, which could not be told from the black and white images. After the earthquake of 1906 destroyed the house, it was this album that people curious about the mansion would refer to, because it was the only thing left of it.

———

Wirt Pendegast, the man who had gotten Muybridge off on the murder charge, died in March 1876, at age thirty-four. (Despite his youth, the papers ignored the custom of stating the cause of death. Had it been a suicide? It's impossible to say.) Judge Thomas Stoney, who had prosecuted Muybridge, gave the eulogy. "His mind was of the very brightest order," Stoney said from the pulpit. "His oratory was splendid. His person was handsome, and his manners were charming."[5] His eulogist lathered on the praise, even about the time Pendegast had opposed him. "In the courtroom, during the trial of Edward Muybridge, with the evidence overwhelmingly establishing the guilt of his client, and with the law confronting him on every side, relying solely on his own resources, Pendegast extorted from the jury a verdict of 'Not guilty!'

Not by perverting the facts, nor by distorting the law, but by raising the minds of the twelve men whom he addressed above the influence of the law and the facts."

Muybridge sent condolences to the widow of the lawyer who had kept him from the gallows, enclosing for Pendegast's wife an album of photographs. She had written to thank him, and Muybridge replied:

> *My Dear Madam,*
>   *It is I who should and do thank you for permitting me to offer you so slight an acknowledgment of my lasting appreciation of the noble and disinterested generosity shown me by your late husband, when I, bowed down by grief and crushed with broken pride, so sadly needed the support and friendship I received from him. He was the best and dearest friend I ever had.*[6]

If Muybridge felt cool toward his son, whom he had put in an orphanage, it sounds as though he wept when he heard of the death of Pendegast.

———

The Stanfords funneled their money into land, houses, and horses. After moving into the new house, Leland and Jenny looked for a second place outside San Francisco, because they weren't happy unless they were acquiring something. Stanford wanted a big tract for his horses, half of which were still in Sacramento, the other half in San Francisco at the Bay District track. They first bought a ranch at the southern end of the Bay, near the San Jose Mission, in 1874, but a year later told each other the place was too hot. They signed it over to Leland's brother Josiah as a gift.[7]

The most important purchase the couple made—and the reason people remember the name "Stanford"—came in 1876, when they bought a 650-acre farm known as Mayfield Grange, thirty-five miles south of San Francisco, in an empty township called Menlo Park. The farm stood next to Central Pacific track, which meant an easy hourlong ride to and from the city.

The name of the summer home bothered Stanford. "Mayfield Grange" reminded him of the Grangers, the farmers' movement that hated him. So he and Jenny looked around for something else. Two tall sequoias stood next to the railroad track as you came in, looking like a single tree with two trunks. Stanford thought "tall tree" suited the place, so he gave it the Spanish name "Palo Alto."[8]

The Stanfords bought Palo Alto from the estate of George Gordon, a San Francisco developer who among various projects had built the English-style townhouses around South Park, one of which had housed Edward Muybridge. The new place had a huge clapboard house with turrets, bay windows, and a porch, but Stanford was keen on enlargement and would eventually double the size of it. Within two years, thirteen more land deals had multiplied the tract tenfold, and Palo Alto counted 6,967 acres. In most places this would have made a giant ranch, but by California standards it was merely large.

Mayfield Grange became the Palo Alto Stock Farm, "stock" pointing to the horses to which the place was devoted. Stanford thought his new ranch could be the showiest horse operation in the West, and he poured money into it, hiring a trainer named Charles Marvin to oversee operations.[9] A giant stable went up, eight oval tracks went down, houses for dozens of workers with families appeared, plus dormitories for single men. From the Central Pacific rail yards, Stanford ordered a new train car built that would move his horses around. "Stanford's equine palace car," a paper called the animal parlor on wheels. Within a short time, Palo Alto had thirty employees, including drivers and jockeys, trainers, grooms, teamsters to haul feed, a horseshoe maker, wheelwrights, hostlers (with two different teams of handlers, for brood mares and for stallions), and a timekeeper. There was a designated man for "halter breaking and care of weanlings."[10] There were shops for harnesses, blacksmith furnaces, a dining hall, and a school for children of staff.

Collis Huntington, the financial hinge of the Central Pacific, mocked his partner's strong feeling for horses, which he saw not as love, or even obsession, but merely as vain. Huntington worked ten-hour days in New York to keep loans flowing to the company, and he regarded Stanford as an idler. "Stanford will go to work for the railroad company as soon as the horse races are over," Huntington wrote in a letter to Mark Hopkins. "Of course, I do not expect anything from him until then."[11] Stanford moved his horses down to Palo Alto and kept adding more.

He sent his trainer, Charles Marvin, to Kentucky to buy twenty brood mares from racing stock there, and on trips to the East Coast the rail president shopped for horses on his own. In fall 1876, on Long

Paddocks at the Palo Alto Stock Farm, in the foreground, and the huge main barn, to the rear, photographed by Muybridge in 1881

Island, he bought a trotter called Electioneer. Turf writers of the day said the horse was a bad purchase because he had gone lame at age three, but Stanford thought Electioneer looked like a good source of more trotters. The horse traveled by train across the country to Palo Alto, where he was turned loose among dozens of mares as a stud. Stanford eventually made Electioneer the most promiscuous of studs, and the stallion sired a hundred racers in five years.[12]

Leland liked to go into his paddocks, pet the young colts, stroke their necks, and gaze at their feet and legs. On one visit, his silk hat fell to the ground, and a colt stamped it and kicked it up over the fence. The hat was destroyed and couldn't be fixed, but Stanford laughed loud and long, because he loved his animals.

Charles Marvin and Stanford worked up a training protocol that became famous as the "Palo Alto system," one principle of which was to exercise horses at a slower gait and to use speed only in sprints.[13] Stanford acquired a reputation for supreme gentleness with his horses. For young colts, he had his men build a "kindergarten track," an oval the size of a tennis court, with banked turns. Word went out that he fed his animals warm meals cooked from recipes (it was true). Trainers and

Thomas Hill, *Palo Alto Spring*, 1878. Oil on canvas, 87 x 138 inches. Stanford hired artist Thomas Hill to depict his family and friends on the lawn of the house at Palo Alto, and the result gives the impression of a lord and his court at leisure. Jane Stanford sits far left. Leland eyes the viewer, holding a picture on his lap, and Leland Jr. sits in striped stockings, holding a hat. When he painted this picture, Hill was trying to finish an even larger canvas, *The Last Spike*, that glorified Stanford for completing the transcontinental railroad.

handlers used soft, whispering voices because their boss banned harsh talk to a horse. Stanford was unembarrassed about caring what the animals felt. "It seems to me that if you would write a treatise on horses' feet," he said in a letter to one trainer, "it would be an act of kindness and charity to the horses themselves."[14] The animals never went back to the stable tired, and no beating would be tolerated (although use of the whip in a race still suited). One day at the stable, Stanford saw a filly rush into its stall—one of the grooms had apparently hit the horse. "Fire the man," the rail president told Marvin.

Palo Alto became a playground for Stanford and also for his son, Leland Stanford Jr., eight years old. The boy got a pony named Cheetem and his own miniature train. Little Leland's train wasn't a tabletop toy but a real locomotive and cars, built by company engineers to quarter scale. Young Stanford's train ran a half-mile circuit from the house out to the stable and back, so the boy could be like his dad, and ride Cheetem when he felt like it.

Mark Hopkins, one of Stanford's rail partners, built a house next door to him in San Francisco. Hopkins's place looked like an experiment in towers and bulges, a turreted behemoth in the jigsaw Victorian style, elbowed with wavy extensions and random bay windows, unexplained curves and parapets. Edward Muybridge, on his visits to Stanford, saw the turrets going up—they had suddenly become the highest outlooks in the city—and thought they might flatter his camera. Muybridge got Hopkins's permission to climb up into an unfinished piece of the house, the framed shell of a tower, and use that turret to make a picture series, a 360-degree view of San Francisco.

Muybridge had already made, in 1868, a half-circuit panorama, a 180-degree view of San Francisco. In June or July 1877, he climbed onto the narrow tower of the Hopkins house with his cumbersome gear to make a full circle. Over five hours, cranking the camera across the city, he made eleven pictures.[15] These he printed and attached side by side to a single long sheet of linen. The Muybridge panorama was bound like an accordion into a folio that resembled a book. Unfolded, with its simultaneous views in all directions, it showed San Francisco from a perspective impossible to the human eye.

Muybridge's San Francisco panorama made a commercial splash and became, after the murder, his reentry into the art market. He printed several versions, some with clouds, some a blank sky. He made a list of landmarks and attached it like a wordy caption, naming fifty-three of the city's buildings and sites. There was a foldout version, and there was a piecemeal stack of pictures sold in a box. All varieties made money, and all inflated his name.

Sometime in 1876 Stanford, the horse connoisseur, stumbled on the writings of a French scientist, Étienne-Jules Marey, a professor of

(Following pages) Muybridge, *Panoramic San Francisco from California Street Hill*, 1877. Muybridge occupied an unfinished tower in the Nob Hill mansion of railroad associate Mark Hopkins to produce a panorama of San Francisco, generating the impossible perspective of a 360-degree inspection of the city.

MUYBRIDGE. Photo.   Morse's Gallery.

PANORAMA OF SAN FRANCISCO,

FROM CALIFORNIA-ST. HILL.

natural history at the Collège de France. Marey was trying to map the movements of horses using quirky new equipment he had built. He especially wanted to know how the animals' legs rose and fell. Marey's investigations had made their way six thousand miles around the world to the desk of Stanford, whom they quickly obsessed. Years later, looking back, Muybridge tried to explain Stanford's intensity on this subject, writing blandly that Marey "inspired in Stanford the desire to solve the problem of locomotion."[16] There is no evidence that Stanford browsed the original scientific literature in French, and he probably did not read Marey's book *La Machine Animale*, published in France in 1873 and in translation in London in 1874. What Stanford likely saw was a feature in the monthly magazine *Popular Science*. On December 4, 1874, the New York–based serial ran an article about Marey under the headline "The Paces of the Horse," describing Marey's design for studying the gait of animals.[17]

Étienne-Jules Marey, a portly, urbane man with a liking for wool suits and mustache wax, thought to measure the steps of horses by attaching rubber tubes to their legs and hooves. With each tread, air pressure pushed through the tubes, registering the footfall by moving a stylus that scratched a squiggle on a piece of paper wrapped around a rotating cylinder. Mapping these marks, Marey showed in what order the animal's feet hit the ground, answering a thousand-year-old mystery. What especially excited Stanford was Marey's hypothesis that all four hooves of the animal did, in fact, leave the ground during a gallop. It was a question the horse collector regarded as second only, perhaps, to the enigma of conception.

Stanford wanted to know the position of the legs (bent? straight?) and the sequence of the animal's steps. (Was it left front, right rear, right front, left rear, or some other order?) He wanted to incorporate this knowledge into his training. When do horses' hooves leave the ground during a trot, and when at a gallop? With a copy of *Popular Science* in hand, the rail president summoned Muybridge and put the question to him. Would he try, again, to stop motion?

Photographers using wet-plate negatives, Muybridge's technique, had been trying to freeze movement for decades. The idea of making a split-second image mesmerized so many people that a professional subset of "instantaneous photographers" appeared. During the 1850s, Gustave Le Gray, in France, had photographed the sea in a way that seemed to freeze waves in mid-swirl, clouds in the sky, and boats in full sail. In Britain, photographer John Herschel coined a word when he called these fast pictures "snapshots." Charles Darwin became fond of quick photographs, collecting examples of speedy images and hiring a cameraman to photograph facial expressions. In 1872, just as Muybridge was starting his first round of horse pictures, Darwin, in London, published a book, *The Expression of the Emotions in Man and Animals*, illustrated with pictures of crying children caught in sobs, their faces contorted.

In the late 1870s, photography journals were still talking about what might be instantaneous and what was not, and spreading advice about taking faster exposures. Speed as ever added value. Studios advertised that they could make portraits with an "instantaneous process." With less available light indoors, this meant more than five seconds but fewer than sixty. A businessman presenting himself to be photographed for a *carte de visite* did not have to sit rigidly, but with a shorter exposure time could appear more at ease.

This was the context in which Muybridge went back to Stanford's horses, knowing plenty about instantaneous photography but also knowing that few cameras actually had stopped motion.

A receipt shows that on November 23, 1876, Muybridge bought "a lot of lenses and other photographic material" from a man called J. Mansur; it might have been the big order for the new horse pictures. There's also a letter from Muybridge to Stanford's assistant, Alfred Poett: "I saw Gov. Stanford a few days ago," Muybridge wrote on May 21, 1877, "and he told me you could arrange all about photographing the horses."[18]

In July 1877, four years after he had last photographed Occident and come up with a blurry image, Muybridge took his gear out to Sacramento's Union Race Track to make another attempt. As before, he tried to photograph Occident trotting with a sulky in a two-and-a-half-minute mile. And as before, he caught the horse but again thought the picture wasn't good enough to print and circulate. Stanford, however, wanted some version of it to hang on the wall. With Stanford paying, Muybridge had the image copied by a painter named John Koch, who, like the photographer, worked out of Morse's Gallery.[19] Koch made a replica on canvas of the best photograph, calling his two-by-three-foot picture in watercolor and gouache *Occident Trotting*. The painting kept the position of the horse but cleaned up the photograph's blur. Muybridge asked Stanford if he could take that image and sell copies of it, and Stanford nodded. The photographer wanted to add at least one original element from the photograph to Koch's painting, the head of the driver, James Tenant, which he cut out of a photographic print and glued to the painting like a patch; he then photographed the painting with the patched-on head.

It sounds dubious. Nevertheless, this was a time when photographs were retouched, when people were not yet attached to the idea of the camera as the single "realistic" medium. Muybridge sold his photo of the Koch painting as evidence that he had stopped motion, and it was taken that way. The picture printed well in color engravings; it looked like a soft-focus photo with a clear head. Muybridge then printed it on five-by-seven-inch cardstock; the cards sold and sold, turning into a money faucet.

At the beginning of August, Muybridge took the photo of the painting and the original negative around to the newspapers. The *San Francisco Bulletin* ran an item on August 3, calling the two "a triumph of photographic art." A reporter asked how Muybridge had done his magic, the act of stopping time, and the photographer told a story. He had been returning from Central America on a steamship, he said, when he decided to try some instantaneous photography, aiming his camera at the waves from the moving ship deck. The experiment led him to "test chemical formulas" that would stop motion.[20] After the

Muybridge, *"Occident," Owned by Leland Stanford; Trotting at a 2:30 Gait over the Sacramento Track, in July, 1877.* The first stop-motion photograph sold by Muybridge, a photograph of a painting, itself copied from a photograph

Bulletin story, papers around the country ran items about the picture, and it started appearing in magazines and journals as an engraving. (A technique for publishing photographs had not yet been developed, and all pictures in the press were engravings.) The published engravings and the Koch painting were pieces of art, but they looked like neutral data, and people accepted that behind the pictures was a photo, clean and true.

Muybridge copyrighted his photograph of the John Koch painting with the Library of Congress. "The details have been retouched by Koch," he wrote, but "in every other respect, even to the whips of the driver, and the dust flying from the foot of the horse, the photograph is precisely as it was made in the camera."

———

During the same weeks that Muybridge was pushing his stop-motion picture of Stanford's horse out into the world, Stanford himself became distracted. His interest in the horse farm flagged for a time because a popular revolt threatened to put him out of business. On July 23, 1877, eight thousand people, 5 percent of the population of San Francisco, went into the streets to support a railroad strike that had launched in the East. The action against rail companies had begun in mid-month in eastern states, and the Workingmen's Party, a leftist group with ties to Karl Marx's International Workingmen's Association in Britain, had organized a rally in California to try to move the strike to the West Coast.[21]

What would later be called the Great Strike of 1877 started when one thousand track workers in Maryland walked out from the rail yards of the Baltimore and Ohio Company. Their complaints were about their pay and the dangers of the equipment, which killed dozens of workers every year. One by one, rail operators east of the Mississippi watched similar walkouts from their yards, until eighty thousand track workers in ten states were on strike, according to the *New York World*. The rail action mushroomed into a general uprising, and to everyone's astonishment, hundreds of thousands of other workers in unrelated jobs walked out on their jobs in solidarity with the rail men.[22] The railroads, and for that matter most industries, were almost entirely without unions. During the summer of 1877, for one of the rare times in American history, masses of working people spoke in a single voice, spontaneously and without leadership. More than one hundred people would die in riots during the strikes, most of them at rail yards in the East, most of them shot by law enforcement.

Stanford made no mention of these events in his personal papers, at least not in the ones he left behind, but letters written by other rail owners, his comrades, show that during this time Stanford trembled for his future.

In San Francisco, the year 1877 turned dangerous for the train magnates when a gravelly-voiced man named Denis Kearney started leading anti-railroad marchers through the streets. One part socialist, one part racist (he hated Chinese immigrants), Kearney, an Irish immigrant, proved very good at mobilizing rallies and goading a crowd. For a while, at least, Stanford had much to fear from him. Kearney led demonstrations in support of the rail strikes until fall 1877, when he brought the uprising to Stanford's doorstep. On the night of October 29, Kearney led a mob up California Hill to Stanford's house, where Leland sat bunkered in his mansion. (By that time, people were calling it Nob Hill.) In front of a crowd of three thousand, torches aloft, Kearney yelled, "The Central Pacific Railroad men are thieves, and will soon feel the power of the working man! We will march through the city and compel the thieves to give up their plunder!"[23]

As Stanford looked out the window, horses and Muybridge were nowhere on his mind. He wrote a message to the city's chief of police, Henry Ellis, and sent one of his servants to deliver it. "I know the mob have considered the question of burning my house and also the house [next door] of Mr. Hopkins," the note said, with artificial calm. "Their threats may be serious. I would be glad to have you detail a proper guard. Yours truly, Leland Stanford."[24]

A posse was dispatched, Kearney was arrested, and he was, for a time, taken out of action.

Muybridge took no photographs of the workers' eruption: aside from the notable exception of killing Harry Larkyns, he didn't take many chances with authority. Stanford was his patron and protector, and Muybridge submitted in silence to his interests. If the photographer felt at all ambivalent about the railroad's domination of California, he kept it to himself.

In Washington, D.C., about this time, President Rutherford Hayes wrote in his diary, "The strikers have been put down, by force." The national strike of 1877 came to a bloody end in a hundred places, but street agitation continued over the winter and into the spring. A police

On the night of October 29, 1877, labor leader Denis Kearney marched a mass rally up the hill to the door of Stanford's house and threatened to burn the one-year-old mansion.

guard continued to patrol the Stanford mansion, but Denis Kearney, the white man's populist whom Stanford had put into jail, had been brought to heel.

———

With threats from the street fading, Stanford and Muybridge resumed their conversations. Sometimes the horse collector seemed to believe in photography more than the photographer: Stanford now wanted a series of pictures that would show the full cycle of the animal's gait, every muscle, twitch, and footfall.

Muybridge thought he could get better results without the bother of the curious crowd that seemed always to appear when he set up his camera at the very public Sacramento track. He told Stanford's assistant Alfred Poett that pestering onlookers bothered him there, making it hard to work. "I wish I was assured that I would not be interfered with by people exercising horses, and others of the public," he wrote Poett. Muybridge wanted to move the horse pictures to the stock farm, where the vast private property ensured he would be left alone. He told Poett, "I have asked the Governor, suggesting that we make the series of photos . . . at Palo Alto." Stanford acquiesced.[25]

The photographer ramped up his ambition. Why one camera, producing a single image? Why not a dozen, making twelve pictures at almost the same time? With many lenses, he would have a better chance of freezing a horse's gait. From the Scovill Company in New York, Muybridge ordered twelve cameras. From J. H. Dallmeyer, an English optics company, he ordered twelve lenses. The bills ran into the thousands, but Muybridge and Stanford were just beginning to spend.

To make a dozen cameras work, Muybridge knew he had to do two things: increase the light and cut the exposure time. He could boost the light and arrange the apparatus, but he needed an engineer to build a fast shutter that would shrink exposures to a split second. Some photographers, not all, used shutters, cards or pieces of tin slid by hand in front of the lens, but for precision, Muybridge wanted something automatic.

Stanford told engineers in the Oakland office of the Central Pacific to help the photographer however they could. Muybridge took what he called a "crude model" of the multi-camera scheme to the chief engineer of the railroad, Steven Montague. Montague brought in a superintendent called Arthur Brown, and Brown handed Muybridge over to a young engineer named John Isaacs. Isaacs designed a shutter that resembled a miniature guillotine, consisting of two slats of wood, each four by six inches, which would slide in front of the camera at high speed, allowing light to hit the lens for the tiniest moment. Each camera had its own external shutter, and each of the twelve shutters was strung with heavy rubber bands and cocked shut. Isaacs and Muybridge came up with various ways that the running horse might snap the shutters open and closed, "by levers or some means," as Isaacs remembered in a deposition.

While Isaacs worked on the shutters, Muybridge had Stanford's

The camera shutter operated by electricity, devised for Muybridge by John Isaacs, an engineer at the Central Pacific

groundskeepers build him a studio and experimental track. The studio consisted of a long, narrow shed, fifty by twelve feet, a single open window with no glass running the length of the wall. Twelve cameras (later twenty-four) went inside the shed in a long row, the cameras twenty-one inches apart, each on a stand and aimed out the window. The lenses pointed at a horse track twenty feet away, whose surface dirt had been covered with sheets of rubber, and, on top of that, a heavy dusting of white lime. Beyond the white track stood a ten-foot-high wooden fence that had been painted white and tilted back at an angle. Muybridge wanted the fence at an angle to catch the sun and throw light on the running horses.

The first method of "shooting" the twelve cameras in sequence involved twelve silk threads strung across the track. As the breast of the horse broke each thin thread, the camera shutter to which it was attached took a picture. This approach was unreliable: horses balked at the string, and because each thread broke at a different tension, the pictures fired off at changing intervals. John Isaacs, the engineer, suggested to Muybridge that he use electricity to trigger the rapid-shutter action and made some drawings.[26] Isaacs designed a different triggering mechanism that involved wiring linked to electromagnets next to the shutters, which slapped them down when burst with current.

Speed was the object, and the key was the electrical trigger. Muybridge recruited the San Francisco Telegraph Supply Company, which made hardware for telegraph operators, to provide wiring and electromagnets. John Isaacs, the engineer, had attached twelve strips of wood to the ground, covered with dirt, across which the horses ran in front of the cameras. On top of each strip was placed a wire that reached from the horse track to the camera shed. The wires were exposed to one wheel of the sulky, and as the wheel crossed each wire, it completed a circuit that caused an electromagnet to pull on a spring, which snapped the shutter of each camera. "The horse takes its own picture," Muybridge said.

What happened next required a technician, a hustler, and a showman. Muybridge was all three. "I would like to see you," the photographer wrote to Stanford, "and show you the apparatus and electrical machines I am having constructed, and which are nearly finished." The studio was up and running by May 1878, and that month Muybridge made the first multiple-camera sequences. He had the horses at his disposal, five or six assistants, a trainer, and a jockey. Muybridge shot a

The "studio" at Palo Alto, a camera shed and experimental track, where in 1878 and 1879 Muybridge made the multiple-camera motion studies of horses that became moving pictures. Initially the animals ran in front of the camera shed, tripping each shutter by breaking a thread stretched across the track.

few test series of trotters, and they worked. On June 11, he took the first complete, twelve-camera sequence of a trotter.

Because Muybridge wanted to photograph galloping horses without a sulky, as well as trotters, John Isaacs designed another trigger scheme that didn't require a carriage wheel. It involved a clocklike mechanism, "a machine constructed on the principle of a music box," as Muybridge put it, "containing a cylinder with a row of twelve pins on it, arranged in a spiral." As the cylinder turned, each pin in succession completed a circuit and threw the electromagnets, snapping the shutters. A careful turning of a crank in sync with the horse's progress could approximate the split-second sequence required, and the cameras would sound off in a percussive clatter.

The photographer invited reporters to see the whole business, and a train car full of newspaper writers came to Palo Alto on June 15 for a demonstration. It's not too much to say that this erstwhile press conference represents a kind of early birthday for motion pictures, one to add to the several others that film historians bunch together fifteen years later, during the 1890s.

For the press demonstration, Muybridge set up a developing room on site, next to the camera shed. The first horse photographed for the press contingent was Abe Edgington, a favorite of Stanford's. After he ran the gauntlet, Muybridge immediately developed the plates and within twenty minutes had showed them to reporters. The next day the *San Francisco Morning Call* said, "There is a feeling of awe in the mind of the beholder, as he looks at the glass plate . . . and he sees the miniature of the neighing horse so perfect that it startles him. . . . This is a new era in photography."[27]

In the next two months, Muybridge moved as fast as any entrepreneur racing to a market. On June 17, 1878, just after the press event, the photographer laid claim to his invention with an application for a U.S. patent on a "Method and Apparatus for Photographing Objects in Motion." (The days of patenting washing machines were long behind him.) Patents 212864 and 212865 arrived by mail from Washington, D.C., the following spring.[28]

He had images he could print straight, with no need for a scene painter, so by July 1878, Muybridge published a series of six cabinet cards he called "The Horse in Motion." Each five-by-seven-inch card showed twelve (or sometimes six) pictures, side by side, of a different horse in various stages of gallop: "The stride of the trotting horse, 'Abe

Muybridge, *"Occident" Trotting at a 2:20 Gait*, 1878. Another early stop-motion series of the horse Occident, which Muybridge sold as a so-called cabinet card

Edgington,'" "'Occident' trotting at a 2:20 gait," "'Mahomet' canter-ing," "'Sallie Gardner' running at a 1:40 gait," and two others. The card sets sold madly around America. Reprinted in Europe, they sold throughout Britain, France ("Les Allures du Cheval"), and Germany ("Das Pferd in Bewegung"). It's obvious to anyone who looks at them: Muybridge's camera was the first to capture time, and these are the pho-tographs that launched moving pictures.

Three weeks after the demonstration for reporters, Muybridge showed his material to a paying audience. The first talks, with pictures, took place on July 8 and 9 at the San Francisco Art Association, on Pine Street near Market. He used glass slides, two-and-a-half-inch-square copies of the negatives, projected one at a time with a magic lantern, the slide show of the day. The next year Muybridge would build his projector, or zoopraxiscope, that put them in motion. By 1878 various kinds of projectors that used lenses and a light source had been around for two hundred years. During the seventeenth century in the Neth-erlands (it is said), the astronomer Christiaan Huygens built a device that brought together a lens and a light source to throw pictures on a wall. The descendants of Huygens's projector spread through Europe as "magic lanterns," a name embedded with the mystery and deception of the images it generates, which seem to float on air. Magic lanterns initially relied on candles or oil lamps, but by the middle of the nine-teenth century, a flaming gas jet that blended oxygen and hydrogen made for bright slide shows. The magic lantern became commonplace entertainment, with traveling lanternists who made their money by showing funny or louche scenes, as well as lecturers whose uplifting talks used respectable pictures to guide the mind.

Muybridge owned a projector, perhaps made of brass and wood, that he used to show his photographs to big groups. At his first "screen-ings" of the horse pictures at the Art Association, most viewers were women. "The auditorium," one paper said, "was crowded with an intelligent and fashionable audience, which was feminine by a pleasant majority."[29] He gave four or five nights of talks and slide shows, and public interest ran high.

The horse pictures took most of his time, but Muybridge during the summer of 1878 acted like a person obsessed with grabbing all the images he could: he picked this heavily booked moment to make a sec-ond, technically difficult panorama of San Francisco. Again he went up to the tower of the Mark Hopkins house, this time with the biggest gear on the market, a mammoth plate camera. Muybridge had used it before, to photograph at Yosemite. Whereas the first panorama shot from Hop-kins's house consisted of images wider than they were tall, in landscape view, if you like, for this second version, Muybridge turned the big camera on its side, so that each of the thirteen images came out taller than it was wide, in portrait view. The result gave the series a vertical space so high that the eye seemed to be freed from the horizon. The photographer bound the giant prints, each one nearly seventeen inches wide by twenty-three inches tall, into accordion albums. Unfolded, the length of the thing ran to seventeen feet. Muybridge's two panoramas took the city apart, analyzed it, and reassembled it into a stop-motion series, not unlike a strip of film.

The pictures he made in 1877 and 1878 point toward the visual media that engulfed the twentieth century, in film and television, and the beginning of the twenty-first, with the ubiquity of moving pictures on screens. If Muybridge had not photographed Stanford's horses in 1877, visual media as we know them might not have fallen into place—or, at least, they would be very different.

To read the press on Muybridge from these months, you get the feeling that wonder and delirium swirled around him and what he did. His photographs were "enough to turn your brain," wrote the editor of the *Philadelphia Photographer*. "We stretch our imagination to the maximum and are forced to cry 'stop.'"

While Muybridge occupied center stage, Stanford stood in the wings, taking his own credit in separate interviews with reporters. "It was the intention of Mr. Stanford to have a series of views taken," said the *Alta California*, "so as to settle the controversy among horsemen about the question whether a fast trotter ever has all its feet in the air at once."[30] In London, the *Photographic News* said, "It is difficult to say to whom we should award the greatest praise: to Governor Stanford, for the inception of an idea so original, and for the liberality with which he supplied the funds for such a costly experiment, or to Muybridge for the energy, genius and devotion with which he has pursued his experiments, and so successfully overcome all the scientific, chemical, and mechanical difficulties."[31]

Before the summer of 1878, Muybridge had been a working artist, represented by a gallery; now science began to claim him. After the "Horse in Motion" pictures, he gave up his stake in the art world and started to reposition himself as a scientist. Some of this was his own doing, some was projected onto him, but in any event, it happened quickly. In October 1878, the magazine *Scientific American* published engravings made from the Palo Alto photos, along with heavy praise. (The editor of the magazine added a note in which he suggested that readers might want to cut out the pictures and mount them on strips for use inside their personal zoetropes. In other words, they might want to make Muybridge's still images into moving pictures.)[32] In December, in Paris, the French science journal *La Nature* published five sequences of the photographs. *La Nature* was the kind of periodical pored over by chemists and engineers and physicians, not artists. The French scientist Étienne-Jules Marey happened to be one reader who saw the pictures. Marey was the man whose studies of horses in motion had gotten Stanford to revive the photo experiments in the first place. Marey wrote the editor of *La Nature* after seeing Muybridge's images. To photograph other animals in motion would be "an easy experiment for Mr. Muybridge," Marey said, "and what beautiful zoetropes he would be able to give us: in them we would be able to see all imaginable animals in their true paces. It would be animated zoology." Then Marey got in touch with Muybridge directly, writing him in December 1878 to say that he loved the new material coming out of California and asking for help in photographing birds in flight.[33] Marey told Muybridge that he should "animate" his photos—put them in motion on screens—because this "would create a revolution." This was the second time someone suggested that Muybridge try moving pictures.

The photographer wrote Stanford to boast that the scientist Marey had contacted him and sent him a copy of *La Nature*, "in which I am designated *l'eminent savant Americain*"—the American scientist.[34]

———

At the end of 1878, Stanford gave Muybridge the go-ahead to install twelve more cameras, bringing the total to twenty-four, and to do more motion studies. Stanford and Muybridge decided to photograph not only horses but whatever other animals they could get their hands on, in addition to people. The doubling of the scale to twenty-four images meant Muybridge could capture some one and a half seconds of movement, instead of, as before, something less than one second.[35]

In March 1879 the *Philadelphia Photographer* asked Muybridge what chemicals he had used to get fast exposures. What was his magic? The photographer considered the answer a trade secret, and he dodged the question, writing back that he had done nothing in particular. "I have not, nor do not claim any credit for these photographs; whatever praise others may have felt proper . . . Leland Stanford is entitled much more than I. He originally suggested the idea."[36]

About the process that Muybridge used, no one really knows, although some photography historians have speculated.[37] Insensitive chemicals had remained the standard in collodion photography, with outdoor exposures of a second or more common. Muybridge used reflective surfaces, both on the ground and on a background fence, to amplify this advantage. Because longer focal lengths ate up light, Muybridge used medium distances in his pictures: the horses ran twenty-five feet from the camera. In the same vein, he used a wide-aperture lens (lenses were sold with fixed apertures, not adjustable openings, as later) to throw more light on the surface of the plate. Although this shrank the depth of field—the range of focus, from nearest to deepest, in a photo—Muybridge kept the movement along a predictable plane. He never described the mix of chemicals he used to process his negatives, but he claimed to make photographs with short exposure times, citing a figure to reporters of one one-thousandth of a second.

The blasting light of California, specifically of Palo Alto, gave him an advantage over photographers, say, in England, where sunlight never rose to the intensity of the Pacific West. But as for some breakthrough formula, it remains an enigma.

Beginning in spring 1879, and using the twenty-four-camera arrangement, Muybridge photographed twenty-five horses: Sallie, Nelson, Clyde, Dandie, Sharon, Gypsy, Albany, Nimrod, Oakland Maid, Eros, Mohawk, Elaine, Clay, Hattie H., Florence, Phryne L., Gilberta, Vaquero, Riata, Frankie, Lancaster, Abe Edgington, Mahomet, Sallie Gardner, and Occident (the last four for the second time). He photo-

graphed a greyhound, an ox, a bull, a cow, a deer, a goat, and a boar, all brought to heel, running past the battery of cameras. The animals walked, paced, cantered, trotted, ambled, ran, leaped, hauled, and stood for the camera, building a pile of raw data to describe the movements of mammal bodies.[38]

In August 1879, a group of male athletes from the Olympic Club in San Francisco came to Palo Alto, and Muybridge photographed them fencing, tumbling, jumping, and boxing. He directed the men in standing leaps, running leaps, high jumps, back somersaults, twisting somersaults, javelin throws, club and pick swinging, wrestling, and standing

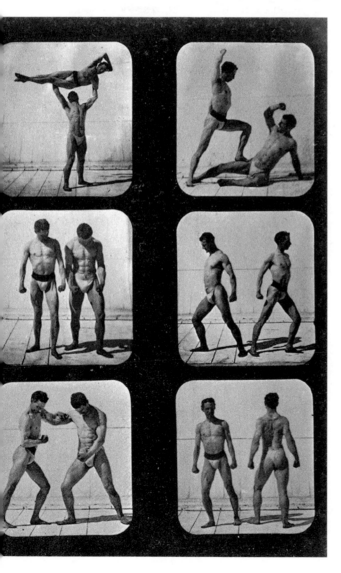

Athletes from the Olympic Club in San Francisco showing off their bodies and greeting Muybridge (holding his hat, and shaking hands) at the Palo Alto Stock Farm, 1879

around, posturing and flexing their muscles. The *San Francisco Chronicle* said it was marvelous how "all of their intricate movements were instantaneously and exactly pictured."

The obsessive streak that Stanford and Muybridge both shared appeared in late summer. It was at this point that Muybridge took off his clothes for the first time in front of the cameras. He photographed himself naked, swinging a pickax: a forty-nine-year-old man, trim and sagging only slightly, a twenty-pound hammer arcing overhead. In these pictures, the braggadocio of the photographer is palpable. He seems to know what he is doing will change ways of seeing.

A second stroke of obsession came from Stanford's side. The governor had become so fixed on demonstrating the movement of limbs that he bought the skeleton of a horse. He acquired one on the East Coast, from a taxidermist or a natural history museum, and had it sent by train to California. There Muybridge carefully arranged the bones of the beast in various positions—standing, trotting, running, and leaping a hurdle—and photographed them as though they were alive.

Muybridge, *Leland Stanford, Jr., on his Pony "Gypsy"—Phases of a Stride by a Pony While Cantering,* 1879

When projected on a screen, the skeleton looked like one of Stanford's stallions executing a perfect canter, in death.

For the rest of the year, the press explosion around Muybridge continued. His name became a commonplace in American papers, while in Europe, news editors found him fascinating. Reports about the photographer appeared in the *Illustrated London News* and the *Times* (Britain), *L'Illustration, Journal Amusant, Le Temps, Figaro,* and *Le Globe* (France), *Berliner Fremdenblatt* (Germany), and *Wiener Landwirtschaftliche Zeitung* (Austria).

In June 1879, a writer for the London-based magazine *The Field* said, "It is obvious that if the figures in the stages in the stride of the racer could be . . . seen in rapid succession, the appearance of the horse in action should . . . be reproduced." Another call for projected movement.[39]

The costs mounted. Stanford told his office to give Muybridge whatever money, men, and material he needed. The photographer sent his invoices, and Stanford's accountants kept their own figures. By the end of 1879, Frank Shay, one of the accounts keepers, estimated that Stanford had spent some $42,000 for all the experiments, or about $950,000 in 2010 dollars.[40]

Chapter 19

PRESTIDIGITATOR

ometime after the last horse tripped the cameras, after the last acrobat somersaulted and the skeleton ran, Muybridge went home to his studio on Montgomery Street and took out his magic lantern. He owned a fancy one, a projector of the kind used by the lantern showmen who made a living in theaters and lecture halls. He owned a decent projector because he wanted to show his awfully impressive pictures. He wasn't a "lanternist," an impresario who screened little dramas made from slide shows. He didn't carry stacks of painted glass slides and doctored photographs, slides to turn into ghost stories and slapstick, pictures that jiggled when you pushed them in and out of the projector to make them more watchable, as such people did. He knew that type. He had seen plenty of lantern shows ever since he was a boy in London, where the most famous screen tricksters did shows in theaters around Leicester Square. And he probably saw more of the same after moving to New York. Then in San Francisco he had gotten together a lantern show of his own, as a kind of brand extension. People would pay to see his Yosemite pictures, which looked shockingly good on a screen, blown up to eight by twelve feet (so did everything else look good—lighthouses, Alaska, the panoramas). When he gave his first shows of the horse pictures, he threw in some from Guatemala for variety.

He brought out the projector this time to try something nobody had done. He would take his weird new invention—two seconds of stop-motion photography—and bring it back to life. He had stopped time, and now he would restart it.

Muybridge cut a piece of glass into the shape of a disk about sixteen inches in diameter and put it on a spindle so it could turn. The idea was to take a magic lantern, which everyone used to project one image at a time, and make it throw twelve or twenty-four pictures up in succession on a screen. To make a kind of zoetrope, but to toss the movement out to an audience.

At Stanford University, in the vault of the art museum, there is a set of seventeen glass slides, each a centimeter square, each depicting a step in the stride of a horse photographed at Palo Alto. The glass chips look to be one of Muybridge's first moving picture experiments: they fit perfectly, with a few missing, around the edges of a disk the size of the ones Muybridge tinkered with on his modified lantern in the fall of 1879.

Muybridge altered his slide projector, putting the disk with pictures around the edge on a wheel in front of the light and lens, and now the lantern behaved differently. He gave the projector a name: the zoo-gyroscope (combining zoetrope and gyroscope). A few months later, he changed the label to zoopraxiscope (zoetrope plus praxinoscope, the

Muybridge, *Nimrod Pacing*, ca. 1879. Maquette for a zoopraxiscope disk. This set of tiny slides arranged around a disk to fit his invention, the zoopraxiscope, appears to have been an early attempt by Muybridge to project movement.

unlovely name of another device, made in France by a lanternist called Émile Reynaud). Muybridge was good at naming things as confusingly as possible.[1] Whatever the label, it was the "Muybridge projector," because it made pictures move.

Here and there a lanternist had hammered together a tabletop machine to make an image jiggle, but as far as anyone can tell, Muybridge built the first moving picture projector. During the years before cinema, several "science toys" available in Europe and in the eastern cities of America could fake a moving image. They had tongue-twisting names: the phasmatrope, the phenakistoscope, the choreutoscope, the praxinoscope. Some of these tools point in the direction of Muybridge's device, but none used photography as its basis, and none involved a light source and screen. These are what give the Muybridge invention its originality and its place as first in line, if you like, of the media.

The zoopraxiscope threw pictures on a wall, but they ran together and blurred. What it needed was a shutter to separate the individual frames—a glimpse of one, a black screen, a glimpse of the next, a black screen, and so on. Muybridge cut a disk the size of a dinner plate out of a piece of tin and then cut twelve slots into it, radiating from the center. He mounted the disk on an axle, so that it could spin like a wheel, and placed it in front of the light source of the projector. The light would be released through a slot as the disk turned, then blacked out, then released through the next slot, giving a fraction of a second of time for the pictures to move ahead without blurring. A last problem with the half-rigged lantern was the compression of the image. As pictures wheeled past the light, they seemed by optical illusion to narrow—a horse with a leg stretched out ahead seemed foreshortened.

Muybridge wanted the glory of motion, so he hired a painter named Erwin Faber, who worked with magic lantern slides, to paint facsimiles of the photographs on the glass disks. He told Faber to give the horses elongated legs and torsos, counteracting the optical distortion. Faber painted, in color, around the edges of the disks, replicas of the photos of Occident, Sallie Gardner, and the rest. When projected, the pictures looked like the horses themselves, running, cantering, and trotting.

He believed he had left art behind and become a scientist, but what he really became was a kind of prestidigitator. At the start of this book we witnessed the night in January 1880 that Stanford asked Muybridge to give a demonstration, a show for ten tuxedoed moneymen and politicians and their wives, at the California Street mansion. With this the

In fall 1879 Muybridge modified a magic lantern, which threw still images on a screen, into a moving picture projector.

photographer satisfied his patron by rolling out the Muybridge projector for its debut appearance. Afterward, he set up its public debut, renting the lecture hall at the San Francisco Art Association, downtown on Clay Street, for several nights of talks and shows. No one scribbled box office numbers, but it was a Tuesday night when pictures moved for a paying audience for the first time, the night a roomful of viewers felt transfixed by life on a screen.

The *San Francisco Chronicle* ran a news item headlined "Moving Shadows," but the writer said the images were more than dim shade. "The effect was precisely that of an animal running," the reporter wrote.[2]

The Art Association stood next door to the Bohemian Club, a clique of writers and artists, very much in an artist's, and not a scientist's, part of town. It was here that Muybridge chose to do what an artist does, to make the world strange, to make it new. In three nights of shows, moving pictures ceased to be a private trick paid up by a rich patron, and they became a public commodity on the market for anyone.

The verisimilitude of Muybridge's moving pictures turned into news on the light-quick telegraph, and items about the photographer appeared in papers and journals. "The simulation was admirable, even to the motion of the tail as the animal gathered for the jump, the raising of the head—all were there," said the *New York Times*.[3] A piece reporting on the projection ran in *Scientific American*. Newspapers picked up the story around the country, and Muybridge again became a famous person. This time his crime went unmentioned. He was treated as a magician with a camera, not a killer with an obsession.

The only way the photographer had to share his invention was to carry it from audience to audience. In 1880, Muybridge acquired a new renown as well as a kind of rebirth: he made himself into a showman with a fresh performance, a lantern operator with a moving picture act. Show followed show, and news stories came in clusters. Stanford had in hand the motion studies, the proof of his ideas about the gait of the animal, and he had another spurt of fame, vicarious this time, through his hired camera hand. But how strange, the railroad man might have thought, that the photographer drew more attention than his boss.

In May 1881, Muybridge put together the results of the Palo Alto experiments into a handmade book that he called *The Attitudes of Animals in Motion*. The album contained series photos of most of the animals, along with some of the people he'd photographed. He made five copies, giving one to Stanford, keeping the rest. Muybridge didn't know it at the time, but before long he would need to sell the other copies, like exotic consumables, merely to have an income.

Stanford and Muybridge had started the horse pictures in 1872, but in eight years, the patron had never paid his photographer. The artist quit the project from 1874 through 1876 (the years of the murder and trial), but he came back and spent much of the years 1877–80 at Stanford's beck and call. Yes, Stanford had paid for the gear—cameras, lenses, buildings, a supporting cast of horse handlers and camera assistants, and of course the animals. Altogether it was a giant investment, but no money was forthcoming for Muybridge. (Stanford later claimed the photographer told him he would work without pay, just for expenses.) I suspect Muybridge played a ruse, expecting Stanford would pay him a big chunk out of gratitude if he succeeded and if the giant scheme ever wound down.

After Stanford picked up his album, *The Attitudes of Animals in Motion*, the Octopus had one of his assistants write a check to the photographer for $2,000 (in 2010 money, about $40,000). Muybridge did not record what he thought about this, but under the circumstances (obsessive work, the invention of a new way of seeing), the sum felt small. He took the check as a sign of Stanford's condescension, and wrote him a polite thank-you note.[4]

————

Stanford might have been distracted, because about this time he was reminded that many people wanted him dead. One week after the public showing of the zoopraxiscope, Leland again had to leave behind the fun of moving pictures to respond to an uprising. This time the fight did not come to his door by torchlight with mobs shouting for him to hang; it came from among people out on the fringe of the railroad empire. The episode, in the central San Joaquin Valley, two hundred miles southeast of San Francisco, picked up a name—the Mussel Slough Massacre, a shooting spree named after a ditch called Mussel Slough near the town of Hanford, California, where state marshals, doing the bidding of the Octopus, killed a clutch of people who dared to defy the railroad.

Since the mid-1870s, the Central Pacific had surrendered its glory as transcontinental hero to become a subsidiary of one of the associates' acquisitions, the Southern Pacific Railroad, a smaller California track. (The Central Pacific owed the federal government upward of $50 million for construction loans; the associates had the idea of subordinating the firm to another company and starving the Central of capital, so as to enable it to go bankrupt when the notes came due.) After 1875, the Southern Pacific, with Stanford as president, claimed the Central as one of its failing branches.

By the land grant deal with Washington, the railroad picked up mile-square tracts of land on alternating sides of the track that it built into the San Joaquin Valley, a 250-mile stretch in central California. The rich farmland had little agriculture as yet, but when the rail went down, ranchers and farmers moved onto it, expecting easy delivery to markets by grain cars and rising land values. Some squatted on land owned by the train, some leased at low rates, hoping to buy their way cheaply into tracts by making them productive and building settlements. The Southern Pacific first signaled that it would sell this homestead land at $2.50 an acre, but when sale contracts came out of the company's legal department, they carried prices of $17 to $40 an acre.

Ranchers at Hanford had built houses, barns, and schools, which they would have to surrender if they couldn't meet the railroad's terms, and most could not. Some tenants were former Confederate soldiers who had immigrated to California and who did not mind settling disagreements with guns. The squatters' colony formed a militia led by a former Confederate Army major, Thomas Jefferson McQuiddy, and hundreds met in Hanford to plan their resistance to Stanford.

In March 1880, Leland took his private rail car to Hanford to meet with McQuiddy and other ranchers. There is no account of the meeting, but Stanford's phlegmatic ways—his speechlessness and habit of bearing no opposition—suggest things went badly. In April, Stanford sent an agent to Hanford to start selling the land at the higher price.

About the same time as all this, Muybridge was showing off his projector at the Art Association in San Francisco. Stanford didn't attend. The situation at Hanford had been heating up, and anyway, too many common people turned out at the auditorium on Clay Street. On May 11, one week after the Muybridge screening, Stanford sent a U.S. marshal to Hanford with eviction notices, and with an armed escort of four, the marshal went from house to house to kick families off the land. Some of McQuiddy's militia appeared, and a gunfight ensued. Seven men were killed, six of them settlers, after which the marshals for the railroad fled for their lives.

The dead from the gunfight became martyrs to the railroad, and Stanford, blood on his hands, faced a public relations crisis. Newspapers called it a massacre and blamed the shootout on the greed of the Western oligarchs. A dozen land squatters were put on trial for manslaughter (they had been present but had not killed anyone), and when five received jail sentences, they, too, became heroes of a populist, anticorporate cause.

The legend of the Octopus, the venal and avaricious corporate beast, grew from this point. The *San Francisco Wasp* newspaper ran a cartoon depicting Stanford and his partner Charles Crocker as grave robbers pilfering the cemetery at Mussel Slough, with the following lines appended to that image:

These mounds are green where lie the brave
Who fought and fell at Hanford;
O point me out I pray,
The grave of Leland Stanford.

After Mussel Slough, little could soften Stanford's image, and California turned hard against the man. The story of the people the railroad evicted and killed launched at least three novels. In 1882, the novelist William Morrow, an Alabama native who had moved west, published *Blood Money*, a story of Stanford and his partners as an evil cabal. Josiah Royce, a philosopher who taught at Harvard, but was California born, wrote *The Feud at Oakfield Creek*, which portrayed the railroad men as a corrupt clique whose greed ran bottomless. And in 1901, writer Frank Norris published the most popular rendering of Mussel Slough, nicely exaggerated, in his novel *The Octopus*. The railroads "had been hated long and hard," Norris wrote, because they operated like "a splash of blood and destruction, a monster." Most had no trouble with the broadbrush hyperbole.

In 1881, a year after Mussel Slough, the Stanford family, their lives turned sour by the people's distaste, decided to get away from the chorus of slander and take a long trip. Sometime that spring Leland and Jenny, plus twelve-year-old Leland Jr., fled California on a private train to New York, joined by two servants and a cook, a man called Homer Bishop. From there they sailed to Europe, the first trip to the Continent for all three in the family. They planned a buying expedi-

After the Mussel Slough shooting in May 1880, the *San Francisco Wasp* ran this cartoon showing Leland Stanford (locomotive in hand) and his partner Charles Crocker robbing the graves of those killed by railroad marshals, with a comet of retribution descending.

tion through the art districts of Italy and France—in search of jewelry, antiques, and paintings, things not plentiful in California, but which the Stanfords required to maintain their perch atop the class pyramid. Leland Jr., on this trip, would also be allowed to make acquisitions. A lifetime of private teachers and nannies had made the boy precocious, perhaps a little fey. Somehow he had developed a taste for antiquities, little statuary and oddments from Egypt, Rome, Mesopotamia. Fortunately, his parents had the buying power to satisfy it. Fortunately also, streams of relics flowed from looted sites in the ancient world into galleries in Europe—plaques, friezes, cuneiform tablets, bas-reliefs, stone figurines. As they set off from New York, the family had a shared agenda: visit a few Old World monuments and then hit the auction houses.

The Stanfords, on this trip, also wanted to collect portraits of themselves. With their many previous commissions, they had nearly exhausted the pool of California painters, and a month in Paris, capital of the art world, could solve the problem. Bona fide French artists might provide a harvest of new pictures for the Palo Alto house. For her portrait, Jenny Stanford had in mind the painter Léon Bonnat, a forty-eight-year-old artist known for his severe realism and restrained palette. Leland Jr. had been assigned to a different master. Leland Sr. wanted to sit for the most famous painter of the decade, a grandiose, long-haired maestro named Jean-Louis-Ernest Meissonier. The choice might have touched a bit on horses, because Meissonier's reputation for portraits was equaled by his fame for equestrian scenes. He painted, many times, the campaigns of Napoleon, crowding dozens of horses into the frame. Society figures went to Meissonier for his frosty realistic style, which made everyone look stately and pensive. Stanford wanted that appearance for his own picture, which he intended to hang in his study.

The trouble was that Meissonier did not paint just anybody, and he took pleasure in turning down supplicants who came for the glamorous touch of his brush. Stanford knew of Meissonier's testiness, and his high fees, so as an insurance policy of sorts he packed for the trip his copy of Muybridge's handmade album, *Attitudes of Animals in Motion*. The book had become his chief conversation piece—whenever it came out, guests browsed it with awe and envy. Stanford hoped the album would appeal to the horse connoisseur in Meissonier and raise the likelihood the artist would take on a new client.

May was spent in Italy, and in mid-June family and servants

Jean-Louis-Ernest Meissonier,
Leland Stanford, 1881.
Oil on canvas

arrived in Paris. Sightseeing and shopping ensued, followed by one-on-one meetings with their chosen portrait artists. Meissonier received Stanford, who showed him the Muybridge book, which had the desired effect. The artist gave his fee at $10,000, five times what Stanford had paid Muybridge for his eight years on the horse photographs. The client agreed, and a dozen or more sittings followed.

The small painting that emerged, just twelve by seventeen inches, shows a corpulent Stanford, seated in a U-shaped Empire chair, dressed in his habitual three-piece suit, a gold watch on the vest, leaning on an armrest and inspecting the viewer. On the man's face Meissonier painted the blankness of affect that everyone who met Stanford commented upon (but a dignified blankness).[5] Under his left arm in the picture is the copy of Muybridge's album, open to a page showing a horse in mid-trot. It almost looked as though Muybridge's fame had elbowed out that of the railroad man.

Time was made for more spending. Jenny wanted diamonds, so she and Leland went to a jeweler, Debut & Coulon, where among other trinkets they bought a thirty-carat diamond broach, for 62,000 francs, or about $270,000 in 2010 dollars.[6]

In July 1881, by telegraph from France, Stanford told his lawyers to transfer patent interest in Muybridge's photographs and equipment to the photographer. The two had agreed on a price: one dollar, and the deal was done.[7]

———

From San Francisco, Muybridge wrote his admiring friend Étienne-Jules Marey in Paris, sending Marey a plan for a new kind of camera, a kind of photo-gun. Marey wanted to photograph birds in flight, and in March 1881 Muybridge drew a design for a camera that looked like a rifle with a disk embedded in the barrel, enclosing drawings and an explanation. The idea was to photograph the birds by following them, as though with a gun. (The same year, Marey would build a gun-camera close to Muybridge's designs, and it would become one of his lasting creations.)[8] Marey encouraged Muybridge to come to France so he could widen his audience.

In August Muybridge set off for France—a week by train from San Francisco to New York (no private car), a steamship across the Atlantic (second class). His trip would not be a buying tour, but something closer to a victory lap. He had been getting favorable press in France and Germany, and his name had become known in both art and science circles. He brought his projector and a desire to spread the astonishment the machine created. One thing made Muybridge's new European fame a pleasure for him: the murder didn't distort his story. In France, if anyone knew about the crime, it was a sentence or two, and the strangeness of it might even have imparted a mystique. Muybridge could play, at least in France, the part of a brilliant experimenter, a man with an interestingly deviant past.

Whereas Stanford was received like a walking dollar sign in Paris, Muybridge met with the welcome given an intellectual star. His dealings with Marey probably helped. Marey belonged to the science establishment; he admired Muybridge and wanted to bring him on board. A party seemed the natural thing, so on September 26, Marey gave a reception for the inventor at his house on Boulevard Delessert. Several eminences turned up, including the physicists Hermann von Helmholtz of Germany and Carl Bjerknes of Norway. The photographer and showman Félix Nadar came. As the guest of honor, Muybridge was asked to perform for the crowd of 150. He brought out the zoopraxiscope and gave the party a glimpse of the world he had conjured. Newspapers reported a general astonishment. *Le Globe* said, "We see pass before our eyes long rows of horses galloping, coming together, moving apart, with the most surprising suppleness. It is a diabolical parade, an infernal chase. We cannot say enough about it: the gallery of Muybridge is limitless."[9]

Although he was just across town, Stanford kept his distance from all this. The more Muybridge's name got around, the more Stanford seemed to cool toward his friend. Although their time in Paris overlapped for at least a month, the two never saw each other during that time.

It could not have helped that Muybridge pulled in attention from people Stanford considered his own to influence, including the portraitist Meissonier. Stanford's hired flatterer admired Muybridge more than he did the railroad builder, and Meissonier's own influence stretched far and wide. As Marey was to the cadres of science, Meissonier was to the cliques of Parisian art. The month after Marey's party for Muybridge, Meissonier threw not one, but two parties for the photographer, with guest lists drawn from the high ateliers. On Friday, November 3, Muybridge accepted toasts from a few dozen members of the art establishment gathered in Meissonier's house at 131 Boulevard Malesherbes. Apparently the event stirred gossip, because the painter threw a much bigger party three weeks later. On November 26, according to the paper *Le Figaro*, two hundred came to Meissonier's house to pay homage and witness the marvel of the zoopraxiscope. (This time Muybridge hired a projectionist so that he could talk without standing next to the machine.)[10] Well-known artists filled seats in the screening room: the writer Alexandre Dumas (fils), Léon Bonnat (who had just finished a portrait of Jane Stanford), history painter Jean-Léon Gérôme, sculptor Aimé Millet, and the academic painters Alexandre Cabanel, Jules Lefebvre, Édouard Detaille, and Alphonse de Neuville. Whereas at Marey's, Muybridge the chameleon took the part of a scientist, at Meissonier's he was the consummate artist.

Members of the artistic elite were fascinated, perhaps, because they saw the outlines of a new medium. Painting had already withstood an assault on its terrain from photography, as the camera effortlessly took over the role of representing the experience of the glimpse. In moving pictures, the art world recognized an even stronger claim on the eye— and where would it lead?

"Happily I have strong nerves," Muybridge wrote home to California after his round of parties, "or I should have blushed with the lavishness of the praise."[11]

Stanford remained absent. He could have been preoccupied with finding just the right gold watch. It's more likely he wondered why no one threw plaudits at him. It cannot have been a coincidence that Stanford and family left Paris a few hours before Muybridge's big social triumph, at the second Meissonier party. Muybridge saw the Stanfords off at the train station, the only time they crossed paths, in a chilly bon voyage. "The governor did not look well today," he wrote home before heading over to the Boulevard Malesherbes.

Back in San Francisco, Stanford got in touch with his physician and friend Jacob Stillman. The two had known each other for twenty-five years, since the pioneer days. Jacob Stillman, age sixty-two, was no provincial. He had published a memoir, *Seeking the Golden Fleece*, about his years during the Gold Rush, and he had written two other manuscripts about traveling the continent (though these hadn't found their way into print). Stanford and Stillman thought, separately and together, that if Muybridge could make a name for himself with the sensational horse pictures, they could do the same. At Stanford's encouragement, Stillman had been working up a book based on Muybridge's photographs. He planned to reprint dozens of them by adapting them as lithographs and adding a text of his own. The book had a working title, "The Horse in Motion," the name of a photo series Muybridge had made four years before. Stanford, when he got back to San Francisco, still stinging from Muybridge's French celebrity, immediately hired a publisher, Osgood & Company, out of Boston. The company agreed to print the picture book, lavishly, for Stanford's cash in hand.

Still in Paris, Muybridge thought things were all right, if a little rocky, between Stanford and himself. In fact, the photographer sent a stream of letters to the railroad president about a new project he was trying to get off the ground. Muybridge, hoping to recruit him again to the patronage that had worked so well, wanted Stanford to bankroll a bigger round of motion studies, one that would include people, animals, and dozens more cameras. Stanford ignored the mail.

In February 1882, in Boston, Osgood & Company published *The Horse in Motion*, with Muybridge's pictures. It contained five reproductions of the horse photographs, as well as ninety-one photolithographs based on Muybridge's prints. These words appeared on the title page: "The Horse in Motion, as shown by instantaneous photography—by J. D. B. Stillman." And: "Executed and published under the auspices of Leland Stanford." Muybridge's name did not show up. Stanford wrote a preface to the book in which he remembered, somewhat vaguely, that he had found a photographer to take pictures of his animals, like a hired hand. He mentioned Muybridge's name once.[12]

———

It was in Paris, apparently, that Muybridge had learned to use a camera and had borrowed his first nom de plume, Helios. In 1882, he decided that France was, once again, the place to change his name. With this visit, he stopped calling himself Edward Muybridge and became instead *Eadweard* Muybridge. The name appears initially in his letters from this time, as well as some announcements, printed up for his talks. A weird name, difficult to spell. It would be the last occasion when he changed his name. He was fifty-two.

In February, after six months in France, Muybridge left Paris for London, hoping to extend his victory lap from Europe into his home country. He had not returned to England in sixteen years. He had not been home since he started as a photographer, since the murder, and all the rest of it. Back in London, he took a train out to his hometown, Kingston, to pay visits. (His parents were dead, but he had cousins, aunts, and uncles there.) Then he rented rooms in London, because this was to be a stay of several months.

Muybridge wrote home to California and the presumed author of the "Muybridge" book, Jacob Stillman. He had given Stanford's friend a few photographs and thought the book, which he had heard about, would have the name "Muybridge" all over it. He asked Stillman the name of the publisher and when the book might be available, not knowing that *The Horse in Motion* was already in print.

His first appearances in London, his first shows, came in March, at the Royal Institution. With its posh address, on Albemarle Street in London's Mayfair, its decent age (eighty years), and its charter from the queen, the Royal Institution promised a grand entry into public life. The Royal Institution tilted toward hard science, usually inviting physicists or chemists to talk to its members. A lecture slot for Muybridge meant that science was allowing an artist-cum-scientist, and a curious man, through the door.

The date of the talk came, March 13. The Prince of Wales, Albert Edward, age forty-one, heir to the throne of his mother, Queen Victoria, sat in the chair to call the event to order. In the rows of stiff oak seats sat other prime movers—Alfred, the Duke of Edinburgh ("a distinguished photographer, it may be remembered," said a newspaper); Alfred Lord Tennyson, poet laureate at the time; William Gladstone, the future prime minister; the scientist Thomas Huxley; and a cast of hangers-on. It was as though Muybridge, the bargeman's boy from the village, was applying for membership in a very restricted club. At least some in the room must have seen it this way.

At one point Prince Albert spoke up. "I should like to see your boxing pictures," he said. "I shall be very happy to show them, Your Royal Highness," Muybridge answered, and then loaded a disk to show two athletes punching away at each other. The audience laughed in delight—more important, the prince laughed. "I don't know that these pictures teach us anything useful," Muybridge said, acting the professor, "but they are generally found amusing." Waves of applause.

The papers had a good time of it. The *Illustrated London News* said, "It would have been difficult to add to the *éclat* of such a first appearance," and called Muybridge's equipment "an astonishing apparatus." Another writer gave a genuine welcome kiss to a new way of seeing. "Mr. Muybridge's pleasing display was the essence of life and reality," said the *Photographic News*. "A new world of sights and wonders was, indeed, opened by photography, which was not less astounding because it was truth itself."[13]

A dozen other shows in London followed. The Savage Club, in Covent Garden (four hundred comfortable members) . . . the Royal Society of Arts (by the Strand, central London) . . . the South Kensington Museum (which became the Victoria and Albert Museum) . . . the Royal Academy of Arts (the art school of choice, in Piccadilly) . . . He basked in the praise, and reporters put him under a magnifying glass. "With grey hair carelessly tossed back from an intellectual forehead, bright flashing eyes and a pleasant mouth," one wrote, "Mr. Muybridge must himself make an interesting subject for a photograph, whether in motion or repose."[14]

Muybridge spent a couple of weeks writing a paper for the Royal Society, another science hub. Where the Royal Institution was more clubby, the Royal Society was more serious. Charles Darwin sat on its board, as did another eminence of the day, Francis Galton. The Royal Society accepted Muybridge's paper, "On the Attitudes of Animals in Motion," and scheduled it for publication. High prestige and high stakes were involved. The acceptance of the paper signaled that he had arrived at the heart of the science world.

Muybridge looked like a phenomenon, until April. That month, a London publisher by the name of Trübner issued a British edition of the Stillman book, *The Horse in Motion* (Stanford spent a lot of money to get it out in two countries). Trübner sent the book to reviewers, and one copy came to the Royal Society, where it was handed around. Members of the board saw the book and failed to find Muybridge's name all over the pictures. They became suspicious, turned against him, and speculated that he had plagiarized the work of others. "There is some dispute about the scientific proprietorship of the photographs," Francis Galton complained, as he canceled the offer to publish Muybridge's paper. The photographer's would-be patrons now recoiled from him. Gossip followed Muybridge around town, and some saw him as an impostor.[15]

Muybridge remembered the shock of it. "Altogether a brilliant and profitable career seemed opened to me in London," he later wrote, describing his initial success. "This was then brought to a disastrous close."[16]

The lecture dates dried up, dinner invitations stopped. Within a few weeks, Muybridge ran low on money. He had brought with him four copies of *Attitudes of Animals in Motion*, the handmade books. He had to sell them for money to live on. (Buyers took him at his word that he was the inventor he claimed to be.) The books brought enough money for a steamship ticket back to America, and on June 13, feeling humiliated, he sailed from Liverpool to New York aboard the *Republic*.

In the United States, Muybridge fell back on the customs of his adopted country: he sued, hiring the New York law firm of Allen, Hemenway, and Savage and accusing the publisher Osgood & Company of Boston of copyright infringement (he had, after all, bought the rights to the pictures from Stanford for a dollar), demanding $50,000 in damages. Because the publisher had offices in Boston, Muybridge brought suit in a federal circuit court in Massachusetts. A Boston paper threw sympathy his way. "The case will be interesting as casting some light on the question whether a poor scientific investigator has any rights that our plutocracy is bound to respect," said the *Evening Transcript*.[17]

The lawsuit meant a dead stop to all dealings between the tycoon and the inventor. "Muybridge wants damages and claims that the idea of taking photographs of horses in motion originated with him, and not with me, and that I set up that claim in the book," Stanford told Stillman, his hired author. "When I first spoke to Muybridge about the matter, he said it could not be done." Meaning, no one could take stop-motion pictures of horses at gallop. "I insisted, and he made his trials," Stanford said. "I think there will be no difficulty in defeating his suit, and showing that his merit such as it is, was in carrying out my suggestions. I think the fame we have given him has turned his head."[18] Stanford disliked having handed away renown.

The good doctor Stillman turned out to be a nasty man. "I believe Muybridge to be very unsafe and unscrupulous," he wrote in a letter. "If he does not wear hay on his horn he does carry a pistol in his pocket and he did shoot a friend in the back and plead insanity."[19] (Muybridge shot a man, not quite his friend, in the chest.)

The lawsuit soaked money from the impecunious photographer. His lawyers wanted fees, and the depositions seemed endless—Stillman, Stanford himself, plus several engineers from the Central Pacific. But the inventor had discovered a new revenue stream, showing off his projector.

He took the zoopraxiscope around, hauling it on the train where invitations took him—to little theaters, to lecture halls, collecting fees for the novel bursts of life he could blast on screens. He hired a lecture agent—Kelley's Musical and Literary Bureau, in Boston—and soon the talks came, which were really shows featuring his moving picture machine. Harvard College and the Massachusetts Institute of Technology, in Cambridge. The National Academy of Design and the Union League Club, in New York. "Mr. Muybridge gives lectures illustrated with his unique instrument, the zoopraxiscope," said one paper, "by means of which horses, deer, oxen and anything you please are put through their paces, life-size and quite natural on the screen, before the astonished gaze of an audience."[20]

On one trip, he made a stop in Philadelphia, where he drew a crowd that included a well-known artist, Thomas Eakins. A realist painter with a sometimes flamboyant, sometimes erotic brush, Eakins taught at Philadelphia's Academy of the Fine Arts. He had traded letters with Muybridge and counted himself among the photographer's fans. And it seems to have been from Thomas Eakins, on this lecture tour, that Muybridge took the idea for a new project. He needed something to pull him out of the mess into which he'd fallen.

It was early in 1883. The Stillman book with Muybridge's pictures had cost Stanford a pile, and it wasn't selling, but the paymaster did not mind terribly. "Don't allow matters to worry you," Stanford wrote Stillman. "If the people don't buy the book it is their misfortune as well as ours." What interested Stanford was not the book, but his vanity. "The Muybridge suit interests me," he wrote. "I want to prove up the whole history. The actual facts are from beginning to the end he was an instrument to carry out my ideas."[21] Stanford wanted to lay claim to whatever he could.

Muybridge lost the lawsuit when the judge dismissed the case. Copyright law, a weak legal plant, could not withstand the sucking strength of the Octopus.

"Stanford is a man of contemptible tricks," Muybridge wrote, feeling his old venom. "I thought he was a generous friend, but his liberality turns out to have been an instrument for his glorification."[22] The two men now detested each other.

Chapter 20

MOTION, STUDY

He signed his name in loopy handwriting with extra lines, the kind of thing people sometimes do who have a taste of renown. You could find artists and scientists among his fans, and plenty of ordinary people who liked his play with screens. You could also find schools. Colleges shined up their reputations by having the photographer come in for a show. Muybridge had been looking for a new patron who could pay for his expensive camera work, and he realized that a school with a thick wallet might suffice. He found one, the University of Pennsylvania, a 125-year-old eminence in Philadelphia.

They called themselves the Muybridge Commission, a tableful of men—some rich people, some academics—with links to the university they called Penn, which stood just across the Schuylkill River from the city of Philadelphia. The Muybridge Commission included an art collector, Fairman Rogers, and the school's provost, William Pepper, plus a bona fide artist, Thomas Eakins. Eakins and Rogers had both seen the Muybridge show. The group put out an invitation to their hero: if he would only do it here, with them, the photographer could produce images by the thousand that dwarfed the Palo Alto pictures in scale and style.[1]

Muybridge wanted, among other things, to upstage Stanford, and he hoped for a big sequel to what had gone before. He took the Penn deal in early 1883 ("your offer is entirely reasonable," he wrote, blandly, feigning indifference). He deposited the check with his advance money and moved to Philadelphia in spring 1884. The prospectus he wrote

said that Penn, by hiring him, could sweep the terrain of motion studies, pulling together human and animal movement into an immortal
archive. Penn had its reasons for reeling him in: the school wanted to
burnish its credentials, and trustees thought Muybridge would impart a
glow to the campus.

Once again the photographer split the difference between science
and art. Penn set up a committee to supervise Muybridge, naming an
engineer and a physicist on one hand, a painter and a sculptor on the
other. The veterinary program turned one of its buildings into a studio
for the "scientist," while Thomas Eakins's Academy of the Fine Arts
sent assistants and models.[2]

The idea that Muybridge might enhance Penn's reputation did not
move him to groom himself, or dress better. One of his helpers at the
time, Thomas Grier, saw the photographer as a dingy presence around
campus. "Muybridge was a peculiar man who did not give a hang for
clothes, and we had to keep an eye on him in the studio," Grier remembered. "I would see him with pants so decrepit that it was not safe for
him to go outside."[3] The provost, William Pepper, told a story about
the photographer's response to complaints about his clothes. "What's
the matter with my way of dress?" Muybridge said to Pepper. "Take
for example your hat," the provost answered. "It has a hole in it through
which your hair is protruding." The photographer took off his hat and
looked at Pepper. "Well, it *does* have a hole in it," he said.[4]

In a few months others got to know Muybridge. Edward T.
Reichert, a doctor at Penn, called him "the most eccentric man I ever
knew." Reichert said, "He was very much of a recluse, so that very few
got to know the man, and likely no one ever learned hidden secrets that
must have radically influenced his life." (Some secrets might have been
whispered.) Reichert remembered that Muybridge had an appetite for
cheese flies, sometimes called "skippers," little insects about one-fifth
of an inch long, that hop around old cheese. "Muybridge's fondness for
skippers (cheese maggots) was amazing and insatiable," Reichert said
in a letter. "He frequently lunched with me in my laboratory, bringing
a small package containing his tid-bit, and after he had started to consume this delicacy it was not uncommon for one or more of my guests
to find excuses to finish their lunch elsewhere."[5] Reichert did not talk
about the photographer's other eating habits.

At age fifteen, slender and tall, with a flop of straight brown hair, the beautiful boy Leland Stanford Jr. seemed to desire more from Europe than little statues from Mesopotamia. His parents, who wanted to deepen their only child by bathing him in Continental ways, indulged him. And in any case California remained an unpleasant address for anyone named Stanford, so the family planned a return trip to Europe—Leland, Jenny, and Leland Jr. In May 1883 the three Stanfords again sailed from New York, this time intending to stay a year.

They right away split into groups. Jenny's eyes were bothering her, so she went with her son to Le Havre, on France's northern coast, to see an ophthalmologist and to take in some of the sharp light over the English Channel. Leland felt weary, so he peeled off from his wife and son for the resort remedy that fit his station: the Bad Kissingen spa in Bavaria. The medicinal springs at the town of Kissingen, in southern Germany, where well-paying clients soaked themselves in hot mineral water for days on end, had become a chic destination to rejuvenate. Czar Alexander II of Russia, Empress Elisabeth of Austria, and Chancellor Otto von Bismarck had all visited. (He didn't say it, but Stanford probably saw himself as their American equivalent.) After a month in the mineral tubs, Leland felt better.

The family reunited in Paris, Leland and Jenny telling each other

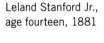

Leland Stanford Jr.,
age fourteen, 1881

they were restored. In November, the Stanfords went to southern France, after that to Italy (Genoa, Venice), and finally to Austria for Christmas in Vienna. Not only did the family fit the emerging template of the rich, grasping Americans with no obligations but to look, eat, and buy, they showed Europe one of the first examples of that stereotype. The weekly uprooting and travel ran the risk of exhausting them, but the Stanfords' cash, which purchased velvet-lined train cars and circles of attendants and guides, softened the effects of all their shuttling around.

On January 1, 1884, in severely cold weather, the family left Vienna, making their way into Turkey and to Istanbul, where there would be good collecting of antiquities for young Leland. In Istanbul, they hired a steam launch, which Leland Jr. told his parents he wanted to captain. The couple acquiesced, ordered the rudder man aside, and the boy piloted the boat from the Golden Horn to the Black Sea, "all day long, with a sharp wind blowing in his face and spray dashing over the deck," his mother said. The next day Leland Jr. was pale and sick. He recovered somewhat, the requisite shopping was done, and the family reached Athens in mid-January. In Greece, several rare snowstorms threatened to slow the trip, but (as Jenny remembered) Leland Jr. visited a number of temples and oracle sites knee deep in snowdrifts. Then it was on to Naples in mid-February.

Young Leland arrived sick and faint, and his mother described it in the detached way that clings to fear. "He was well enough to leave Naples for Rome, but his health did not improve, and it was deemed advisable to take him to a more bracing climate." On February 20, the family went north to Florence, "and there the fever which had been smoldering within him broke out in all its malignity," Jenny remembered. The boy lay burning in the most luxurious suite of the Bristol Hotel. His parents retained a roomful of nuns from a nearby convent to nurse him. Doctors applied the medicine they knew: they wrapped Leland Jr. in ice-cold wet sheets, which he pleaded to have taken away. The clatter of carriages outside came through the window, so the Stanfords paid the hotel manager to spread straw on the street to stifle the noise.

Jenny watched her son suffer. "For three weeks, alternate hope and fear reigned in the darkened room, while the silver cord was loosening day by day," his mother said. "His mind was lucid at times and at times wandering, but even in his delirium he was always the pure-hearted youth that he had been in health."[6] He died on March 13, age fifteen years, ten months.

His father, the monopolist and master of his world, "broke down completely." Leland, according to one biographer, "threw himself on a couch in the room adjoining that in which lay the earthly remains of young Leland" and writhed and wept, day in and day out. Jenny said she feared for her husband's reason and for his life. While in that state, as he remembered it, Stanford said to himself, like an incantation, "I now have nothing to live for."

———

Muybridge, at this moment, had little idea what the Stanfords were doing; he did not know or care what had happened with his ex-friends. Muybridge had known Leland Jr., whom he had photographed, but when the photographer eventually heard about the teenager's death, how did he take it? Did he write a letter of condolence? Probably not. Did he feel sadistic pleasure, schadenfreude, that the Octopus was suffering? Did he just fix his eyes on the new job at Penn and shrug?

The building the school had loaned him stood on Thirty-sixth Street at the corner of Pine Street, and Muybridge set up his studio in a courtyard behind it. The outdoor space formed an isosceles triangle about the area of a tennis court, hidden from the street, with two brick walls for borders and the third side blocked from view by a high fence. Everyone understood the reason. For these pictures, Muybridge wanted to put a lot of naked women and men in front of his cameras. The photographer ordered forty lenses from England for the purpose, and the school paid. But even before he began, some administrators in their ribbon ties and trimmed beards were wondering whether Muybridge's plans for copious nudity would offset the benefit to Penn's reputation.

Just as he had in Palo Alto, Muybridge built a long shed in the private yard, the "camera house," a bank of twenty-four cameras standing side-by-side inside and peering out of a twenty-four-foot-wide opening, like a long window. In front of each camera, he put electric shutters to be set off at intervals by a timing device, similar to what he had used before. But there were improvements. He built a new apparatus—twelve cameras, rammed together in a four-foot-wide cluster and mounted on legs—which could be moved around and aimed at the subject at any angle. (The cameras in the cluster used smaller negatives, less than two inches square.) Another upgrade came in the nega-

At the University of Pennsylvania, Muybridge built a camera shed similar to the one at Palo Alto and added a cluster of cameras on a stand (at left, with a man bent over it), which could be moved around to change points of view.

tives themselves. Whereas Muybridge had used wet plates in California (the old collodion technique, the plates hand prepared one at a time), at Penn he used a new emulsion on glass, so-called dry plates, manufactured negatives you could buy in packs of a hundred. Dry plates gulped more light, took faster pictures than collodion, and froze motion easily.[7] The extra cameras and new plates meant a huge increase in volume and sharper, brighter freeze-frames.

For his first subjects (he started in June 1884), Muybridge turned the cameras on everyday life. Consistently, sometimes for a week straight, he photographed naked women. "The female models were chosen from all classes of society," he said in his notebook. "Number 1, is a widow, aged thirty-five, somewhat slender and above the medium height; 3 is married, and heavily built; 4 to 13 inclusive are unmarried, of ages varying from seventeen to twenty-four." And so on. These were to be motion studies and moving pictures that looked at ordinary people, unclothed, but also at extraordinary ones. "Model number 20 is unmarried, and weighs 340 pounds," he said of one woman.[8]

"Professor Muybridge," one newspaper said, "protected from the sun by an old straw hat, walks about the field like a Western stock farmer." (The photographer referred to himself as, and insisted that others call him, "professor," although he had no diplomas above high school, and never taught a class.) "He fixes the slides, gives out orders, like the mate of a schooner in a gale, and when everything is ready the professor sits on a small beer keg, holding an electric key in his hand."[9] The image of Muybridge sitting to one side with a device in hand and a fierce eye trained on actors without clothes may, to a later generation, look like the classic pose of a filmmaker.

He photographed women and men performing a hundred tasks, each movement two or three seconds in duration. Half the scripts involved athletes, half ordinary folk. Muybridge photographed his models naked more than half the time: a blacksmith with a hammer on an anvil; a woman pouring water from a pitcher; two male wrestlers trying to throw one another; a woman picking up a baby; a man executing a high jump; a woman greeting a dog; two male boxers punching one another; a woman putting on a gown; a man hitting a baseball; two women kissing one another on the lips; a man shoveling dirt; a woman

The majority of the 781 separate series of photographs that Muybridge made at the University of Pennsylvania depicted not animals but people, including *Two Women Shaking Hands and Kissing Each Other* . . . Most photographs were nudes, and many told a story, often sexual.

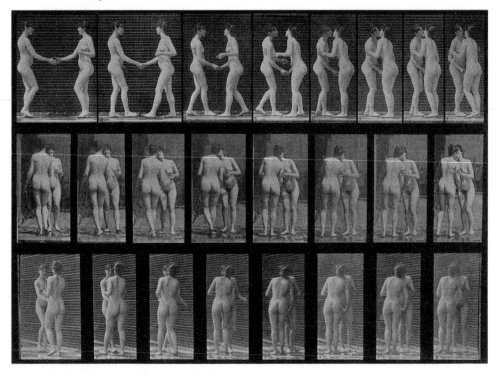

. . . Walking, Saddle; Female Rider, Nude . . .

bathing in a tub; a male acrobat doing a backflip; a woman rolling a stone along the ground; a woman doing a knee-high jump; a woman smoking; Muybridge himself, naked, throwing a discus.

The penises of the men flopped (especially the acrobats), and their testicles flew for the cameras. The breasts of women heaved up and around.

The photographer kept good records of everything.

PHOTO SERIES

July 16, 1885
900. Miss Aimer, nude, getting into bed.
904. Miss Aimer, nude, walking, with hat and high heel shoes on

July 18, 1885
938. Miss Aimer, nude, jumping a string, 2 ft. high
939. Miss Aimer, nude, bathing, pouring water over head
948. Miss Aimer & Mrs. Cooper, nude, waltzing
949. Miss Cooper, nude, giving Miss Aimer drink from water jar
954. Miss Aimer & Mrs. Cooper, nude, meeting and kissing

The model "Miss Aimer" seemed most compliant as the "scientific" investigation gave free rein to voyeuristic pleasure. One day Muybridge

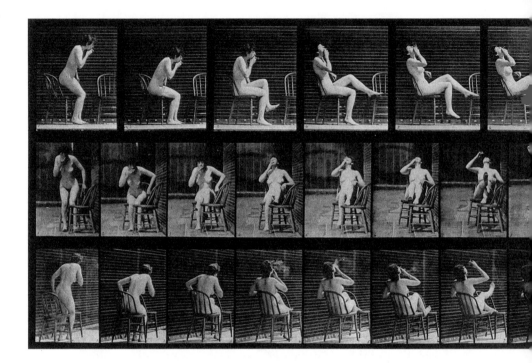

asked Miss Aimer to crawl naked on her hands and knees, anticipating a porn movie trope from a hundred years later. Muybridge took only slightly less interest in "Miss Edmundson," who in photograph #692 walked naked up and down a set of stairs. "Miss Edmundson is age 23 yrs," Muybridge wrote in his notebook. "Wt 111 lbs, ht 5 ft 2½ in., shoe 2½, hips (max) 37½ in., waist 26 in., around shoulders 37½ in., bust, 33½ in."[10] He had a naked Miss Edmundson bend over a lot (to pick up a handkerchief and other things), as well as splash around in water with another nude model.

Inside men at the university worried about the nudes. Anyone could see that what the hired star wanted to photograph was strange, prurient, and taboo. Edward Coates, a member of the Muybridge Committee, wrote Penn's provost about censoring some of the pictures. "There are probably some lines to be drawn with regard to some of the plates," Coates said. But it was somebody else's problem, Coates said, displacing his anxiety onto others. "That there will be objections in some quarters to the publication would seem to be most likely if not inevitable."

Coates was president of Philadelphia's Academy of the Fine Arts, and when he couldn't censor Muybridge, he came down hard on some-

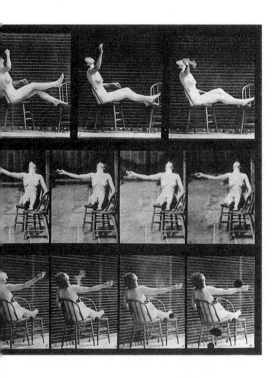

Muybridge, *Woman, Sitting and Smoking*, 1887

Muybridge, *Stages of Men Wrestling*, 1887

Muybridge, self-portrait, *Walking, Ascending Step, Using Shovel, Using Pick*, 1887

one else, Muybridge's friend Thomas Eakins, the artist who had helped bring the photographer to Penn. Eakins, who taught classes in painting, also broke the rules with nudes. The painter had a reputation for close relationships with his students at the art academy, men as well as women. In 1883, Eakins, age forty, painted a landscape, *The Swimming Hole*, depicting himself swimming in a pond toward six nude men. Eakins, inspired by Muybridge, had been photographing his students, and himself, in the nude, ostensibly to improve instruction in drawing. One photo he took showed Eakins and one of his women students, both naked, facing the camera—it caused enough trouble and gossip that Edward Coates fired the artist from the school. Eakins became collateral damage from the Muybridge project.[11]

In May 1885, Muybridge turned again to animals, taking his portable apparatus, the cluster of cameras on a stand, to the Philadelphia zoo. On the first grueling day amid the cages in near-hundred-degree heat, he photographed pigeons. Bird number one saw its cage open, but with the heat, it did not fly out, spoiling the photos. When an animal wrangler opened the cage of bird number two, it flew too fast, and Muybridge missed the picture. With bird number three, the cage opened and the bird flew straight across the target background, a twelve-foot expanse. The shutters went off, according to one newspaper, "like a miniature Gatling gun," grabbing the flight. Afterward, Muybridge went around the zoo to photograph a Bengal tiger, a lion, and a rhino, each of them moving around in its cage. He also took one photo series apiece of a kangaroo, baboon, sloth, raccoon, camel, jaguar, elephant, buffalo, giraffe, elk, deer, and hog. He had trouble with the lions (named George and Princess); the photographer had put a screen in their cage to reflect more light, and Princess ripped it down because it covered the door to her lair.

Returning to Penn, Muybridge seemed to feel he had little "natural" movement left to photograph, so he looked to "unnatural" motion. His starting point would be people with disabilities. He persuaded a physician, Dr. Francis Dercum, to bring him patients from the Blockley Hospital for the Poor, across the street from Penn. And just as he had taken a voyeuristic interest in women, Muybridge now shot "interesting cases"—mentally ill patients, people with amputations, others with "spastic gait" or "locomotor ataxia."[12] In one case, he asked Dercum to apply electric shocks to a patient in order to provoke convulsions, and then photographed those. The interest of science covered many things.

Muybridge took pictures by the bargeload. I looked at one notebook from the fall of 1885, after he had been shooting for a year. During a period of twenty-four days, from September 15 to October 28, the photographer and his helpers shot 218 subjects, producing 5,837 negatives. A man called Henry Bell developed most of the Penn material, and he remembered later that he had processed about 21,600 photographs over a two-year span. (If one minute of film, at twenty-four frames per second, amounts to 1,440 frames, this added up to fifteen minutes of projected "footage.") It is hard to imagine that anyone, before this, had exposed so much to the camera. The mass of images might be seen as the first media flood: Muybridge generated an initial stream of pictures that anticipated the river of images in which later generations would bathe.

He still smoked a pipe (although he had given up the corncob as too rustic). He was aging, but his face kept the glow of desire. "Mr. Muybridge looks and talks like a philosopher," said a writer who met him about this time. "He is a genial gentleman in the prime of life, and, although his beard is long and white, and hair and eyebrows shaggy, his countenance is ruddy, clean-cut, and intellectual." Where one reporter called him "intensely enthusiastic," a later generation might call him obsessed.[13] One of his workers, Erwin Faber, said Muybridge had a manic appetite for work, but he lived like an ascetic. "While working with him I had occasion to go to his room in the second floor of a house on 33rd Street," Faber remembered. "He lived modestly, cooking most of his very simple meals. He had one curious idea, that lemons were good for him, and he consumed them by the dozen."[14]

He sorted and edited his photographs, selecting 781 plates, each plate having from twelve to twenty-four photos. The 781 included some 561 with photos of people, 100 with horses, and 120 with other animals. He planned to sell them in several forms—a complete edition in eleven big volumes, in selections of one hundred, or in folios of twenty. Penn produced a book, *Animal Locomotion, the Muybridge Work at the University of Pennsylvania*, with essays that spun the business as both science-for-art and the reverse. A catalog that listed the plates appeared, and Penn sent it around.

————

The Stanfords took a train from Italy to France, hauling a casket with the body of their son. In Paris, they met with a Reverend Augustus Beard, a minister from New York who ran the American Church on the Rue de Berri. Leland Jr.'s body went into the chapel, and every day the parents visited the bier. Beard wrote down what Stanford said to him, or something close to it. "This bereavement has so entirely changed my thoughts and plans of life that I do not see the way in front of me," Stanford told the cleric, whom he barely knew. As always, Stanford spoke slowly. "I have been successful in the accumulation of property, and all of my thoughts of the future were associated with my son. I was living for him and his future—this was the reason for our travel abroad, for his education."

Grasping after their loss, Jenny and Leland tried to communicate with their son. Spiritual mediums occupied a high berth in the cultural firmament of the late nineteenth century, and in Paris the Stanfords took part in the first of many séances directed at the boy's ghost. Divines promised to lead them to the speaking soul of Leland Jr., and saw in the parents two clients who could really pay. The hocus-pocus, which began in Paris, continued for years, long pursued by Jenny Stanford.[15]

With the blandishments of mediums still in their ears, Leland and Jenny talked about starting a school. "Since I can do no more for my boy, I might do something for other people's boys, in Leland's name," Stanford told Reverend Beard. The rich man, who had no diplomas of his own, translated his grief into the idea of educating people. Beard, who took the Stanfords to mean what they said, suggested they talk to a man he knew back in America, Andrew Dickson White, the president of Cornell University. A few days later Beard went to the Stanfords' hotel to act as witness to a new will the couple had written. An earlier will, organized around their son, was moot, and in its place they had sketched a bequest for a college of some kind to be set up on the horse farm. The unnamed school was to be a "technological institution," the will said, that stressed science and engineering.[16]

In late April, Leland, Jenny, servants, and the casket sailed from France, arriving in America on May 4. The couple stayed on the East Coast until November. In New York, Leland and Collis Huntington, Stanford's partner in the Octopus, worked on a design for the legal entity of the Southern Pacific Railroad, the company that held most of the monopoly's assets. That was during the day. At night, Leland and Jenny met for séances with Maud Lord Drake, a famed spiritualist to rich clients, who attempted to contact the dead boy in the afterlife. Years later, Maud Lord Drake, the medium, took credit for the launch of Stanford University—she told newspapers that she guided Leland and Jenny, telling them how best to memorialize their son: with an engineering school.

From New York the Stanfords went up to Boston to see Charles Eliot, president of Harvard University. In that meeting, Leland asked Eliot how much they should spend to start things going with their school. Eliot deflected the question, whereupon Leland asked the dollar value attached to Harvard—the physical plant, assets, and endowment. "About five million dollars" was the reply. Eliot remembered Stanford's answer. "Well, Jenny, we can manage that, can't we?"

Stanford University was born in the library of the mansion at 901 California Street, in a ceremony that must have felt like a wake, in November 1885. The couple had set up a trust, granting the would-be school big tracts of land and naming a board of trustees. (Money would come later, they promised.) Leland walked up and down the rug, talking about his son, explaining the land grant—in effect, the school was the horse farm, plus some thousands of acres more. Lawyers and trustees sat around, listening gravely. In the same house where Muybridge invented moving pictures, Stanford created a university.

Few schools admitted women, but Leland and Jenny wanted theirs to differ. Leland had gone to school with women in the liberal academies he attended in upstate New York, and now he took a progressive view, not to say a radical one. "We deem it of the first importance that the education of both sexes shall be equally full and complete," Stanford told the room, the politician in him coming out. "The rights of one sex, political and otherwise, are the same as those of the other sex, and this equality of rights ought to be fully recognized." Stanford then ritually handed over the grant of endowment, including deeds for the land and the stipulation that the school should carry his son's name— Leland Stanford Junior University.

The land was worth about $5 million, and the Stanfords promised an endowment when they died. The total for the school (at least, the number that went around in the press) came to $20 million. Newspapers from coast to coast and overseas mentioned the figure in hushed tones, with amazement.

———

Back in Philadelphia, Muybridge's nudes stayed in the inventory. (They made up more than half the pictures, and the trustees couldn't figure out how to remove them.) The photographer chose the Photogravure Company, in New York, to make the reproductions. At some point in 1886 he moved to New York, renting rooms at 42 East Fourteenth Street, in order to monitor the project of turning his glass negatives into prints. Photogravure, the main technique at the time for publishing photographs in quantity, involved a painstaking process of transferring an image from its glass original to an etched copper plate, inking the plate, and turning out paper reproductions on a hand-operated press. Once the photogravures were done, Muybridge took them back to Philadelphia and turned them over to his publisher, J. B. Lippincott Company. Lippincott would bind the pictures in a portfolio or deliver them loose, as the customer preferred. "We have ready, awaiting your orders, 1200 copies in cloth; 250 half-morocco; and 50 in seal," Joshua Lippincott wrote Muybridge after the job went through.[17] The leather (so-called morocco) and sealskin jackets meant the photographer aimed at collectors with deep pockets. Showing again his pleasure in awkward names, he chose a title for the extravaganza: *Animal Locomotion: An Electro-Photographic Investigation of Consecutive Phases of Animal Movements, 1872–1885.* Although he photographed mostly people, he used the word "animal" in the broad, Darwinian sense.

Muybridge had to sell a lot of books and folios to have any hope of recouping money for Penn. He told a reporter that he needed five hundred subscriptions at $100 apiece to make things pay—or $50,000 (the same amount Stanford had spent on him in Palo Alto).[18] Only a handful of libraries could afford the eleven-volume encyclopedia version, and midsized orders were slow in coming. Most people wanted just a few of his unusual plates, a little dollop of his sexy photos.

———

The Stanfords entombed Leland Jr. in a marble mausoleum a short walk from the front door of the Palo Alto house: they could not come or go without seeing it. Jenny continued to float on despair and conduct the occasional séances, while her husband drifted back down to the secular. The boy's death had one immediate effect: it detached Leland from the railroad and reattached him to politics. Twenty years had passed since he served as governor of California, but he remembered the time nostalgically. (He compelled everyone else to remember it, too. Just as the photographer was Professor Muybridge, the railroad man insisted people call him Governor Stanford.) But now he wouldn't mind a stint in Washington, perhaps as a senator.

At this time, before the idea of one man, one vote, state legislatures, and not a popular ballot, chose men to send to the U.S. Senate. Under such a system, would-be senators who possessed resources sometimes thought that a benign distribution of funds might influence the deliberations of the assembly. The term of one California senator was about to expire, and Leland put his name in the "race." No one can say what

When Stanford became a U.S. senator in 1885, he and his wife, Jenny, mixed their entertaining with politics. On the lawn of their house at Palo Alto, Stanford (holding a top hat) welcomed a coterie from Washington that included former president Rutherford Hayes (right hand jammed in his coat) and former Union general William T. Sherman (fifth from left).

precisely transpired, but within two months, without facing the public or having to address a single audience, he was picked by the California legislature. Despite an outcry in the papers (the Octopus!), Leland became Senator Stanford in January 1885.

Jenny and Leland moved to Washington, D.C., and into a superb house at 1701 K Street, on Farragut Square. Stanford, a Republican, fitted himself into life on Capitol Hill, where Republicans dominated the Senate. (A Democrat, Grover Cleveland, occupied the White House.) But the couple continued their mourning; they wore black every day and did not make the rounds of political dinners. By the following year, 1886, the Stanfords lifted their show of grief and started to entertain, putting on extravagant parties and dinners like the ones they used to stage in California. The guests lists may have differed— rooms full of congressmen, drawn at least half by curiosity about the show of money—but the scenes looked familiar: truckloads of silver service, rivers of silk and gilt, French menus that few could read. President Grover Cleveland became a Stanford guest, and when Cleveland's successor moved into the White House—Benjamin Harrison, a Republican—he turned into a good friend.[19]

One ceremony pulled Leland and Jenny out of Washington. In spring 1887, the couple took a train home to Palo Alto when the cornerstone of Stanford University's first building was laid on May 14, Leland Jr.'s birthday.

———

Muybridge's *Animal Locomotion* appeared that summer, to a mixed reception. The *New York Times* said the photographer showed the "wonders of the camera," but the paper threw in a qualification, because of the naked skin. "Care is taken that the nude series cannot be bought by those who do not intend to use such work for serious study. None but known and responsible persons are permitted to subscribe."[20] The paper did not define the elusive class of people who might be "known and responsible."

The photographer sold some subscriptions and covered some expenses, but the bulk of the material did not move. Almost no one bought the complete set, few wanted the hundred-picture folios, and Lippincott was lucky to make sales of twenty-image packs. Muybridge's patrons at Penn, seeing the underwhelming response, grew tired of him. He had cost them too much, and his pictures did not generate the sensation that the earlier motion studies did. In reaction, Muybridge pulled an old identity from his bag, that of traveling salesman. He went from city to city, taking the zoopraxiscope, putting on shows, talking to audiences, trying to drum up orders. Through charm from the lectern and dazzlement on the screen, he sold ten or twenty prints at a time. (If he could have sold them the way he showed them—moving pictures rather than prints—the inventory might have flown out the door.) From Pittsburgh, he wrote William Pepper, the Penn provost, to say that he had eaten a good dinner the previous night at the house of the governor of Pennsylvania, James Beaver, but that he'd sold only two small batches of pictures after his talk.[21] In New York, after speaking at Cooper Union, he wrote that his hosts wanted to make sure he used the zoopraxiscope for another event, at the city's Union League Club—it would bring more buyers.[22] From Boston he wrote that "business has not been very lively," and he was leaving Massachusetts for shows in Rhode Island.[23]

No one quite understood how to project moving pictures, so Muybridge sent word ahead telling them what to prepare. "I write to ask you if you will be kind enough to attend to the following particulars, necessary for the successful exhibition of the Zoopraxiscope," said a standard letter.[24] "Have delivered . . . 2 pairs of Cylinders (2 oxygen, 2 Hydrogen) each pair capable of running full headway for 3 hours; furnish 2 capable and handy men to attend to the lanterns [and] receive instructions; and have a table constructed." The custom-built table measured six feet by four feet. It was to stand on a platform three feet high, placed forty-five feet from the screen—the projection booth. The screen had to measure sixteen feet square, hang two feet from the wall and "not less than four feet from the ground." From his specifications, it could be said that Muybridge established some of the basic viewing conditions for the movies.

Still touring, he wrote to Penn, chagrined, "It may surprise you that in Boston I met people who had no idea who 'Muybridge' was [or] even that there was a University of Pennsylvania." The situation felt grim. He took a train to Wisconsin to speak in Milwaukee and Madison, then went to Illinois, where he wrote, relieved, "I did pretty well in Chicago, bringing on fourteen $100 subscribers, and two complete series at $600 each." He took trains to St. Paul, Denver, and Cincinnati.[25] All the way, he polished his act—half sales pitch for the pictures, half screen entertainment. Muybridge crisscrossed the country, by his count doing two hundred appearances, but it wasn't enough: audiences liked the show but thought the pictures too expensive. The publisher, J. B. Lippincott Company, sent him caustic letters about thirty thousand unsold prints. The press kept paying him homage, but the Philadelphia project looked like an albatross.

Then, something strange happened (something promising—or at least, so he thought). In January 1888, the weekly *Nation* magazine ran a story. The unsigned item speculated about a new invention, "one that could join Muybridge's photographs to Edison's phonograph."[26] It might have been that the photographer talked to the *Nation*'s editors on one of his stops in New York, planting the item; or it might have been that Thomas Edison, well known for his work on electricity, not to say his invention of the phonograph, had whispered the idea to some journalist. However it came about, the *Nation* story kicked a chain of events into motion.

Thomas Alva Edison, as an inventor and businessman, stood head and shoulders above Muybridge. At age forty-one, he already possessed more than four hundred patents. He or his employees had designed things from lightbulbs to telephones, and the Edison Company operated little power stations that delivered the newfangled juice of electricity to tens of thousands of customers. Where Muybridge lived small, Edison lived large. Edison worked out of a complex of labs and offices in central New Jersey, occupied a mansion, and vacationed at a winter retreat in Fort Myers, Florida.

One month after the *Nation* item ran, Muybridge gave a talk and screening in the town of Orange, New Jersey, five miles from Edison's lab. It was a Saturday night, February 25, at the Orange Music Hall, when he showed off the projector for the umpteenth time to an audience pulled together by a local club. Edison might have attended, or he might have sent someone to report on things.

Unfortunately, Muybridge didn't seem to know about the reputation Edison had among engineers. He did not know that the American inventor had a habit of borrowing the work of others and not returning it. And so perhaps what happened next could have been avoided. At the minimum, the story of who would get credit for the invention of visual media might have turned out differently.

Chapter 21

CELLULOID

Thomas Edison didn't mind that they thought of him as a sorcerer, the "Wizard of Menlo Park." Like a magician, he had conjured up an electricity network, a better telegraph, and an uncanny device that recorded sound, the phonograph—all of it in Menlo Park, New Jersey. His inventions gave him riches and made his name one of the most familiar in America before he turned forty. But the Edison Company outgrew its first home, and in 1887, Edison moved his operation to a new plant in the town of West Orange, New Jersey, twenty miles west of New York City. That year the new Edison laboratory rose like a village in a field. Its main building, red brick, 150 by 50 feet, four stories, had a skirt of smaller structures around it, plus two hundred employees. By putting his plant in West Orange, Edison instantly became that town's leading citizen. He housed his family in an enormous house near the plant—the kind with a name, in this case, Glenmont. (Jigsaw-Victorian in style, it had twenty-five rooms, half the size of the Stanford place, but still impressive.)[1]

In late February 1888, Eadweard Muybridge gave a talk and show at the Orange Music Hall, a theater that sometimes sold uplift in the form of lectures but was not averse to comedians and singers wearing blackface. Muybridge brought the zoopraxiscope, the same brass and wood machine he'd built eight years earlier for his friend Stanford, the same two canisters of oxygen and hydrogen. As usual, Muybridge screened scenes of naked people jumping and running, including himself. The local paper complained about the "propriety of exhibiting nude human figures to a promiscuous assembly," meaning men seated next to women in the audience.[2] He drew a crowd, people fascinated by his pictures, and if Thomas Edison sat in the audience that Saturday night, the Wizard might have exercised his prerogative as an eminence and introduced himself. This would explain why, two days later, Muybridge went to visit Edison at his laboratory. The photographer took that meeting without flinching: he had experience handling a big man in industry. On Monday, February 27, Muybridge, at age fifty-eight an older man and the worse for wear, sat in Edison's office to answer a stream of questions from the youngish tycoon.

And in a gambling stroke, the inventor Muybridge made a proposal: he and Edison should collaborate. Why not combine Edison's phonograph, a sound recording device, and the zoopraxiscope, a motion projector? They could make moving pictures with sound. Years later, Muybridge remembered, "We talked about the practicability of using the Zoopraxiscope in association with the phonograph, so as to combine, and reproduce simultaneously, in the presence of an audience, visible actions and audible words." They talked about, in other words, a recipe for sound movies.[3]

Muybridge knew he lacked the money to develop his own machines beyond what he had already done. (He might have known he also lacked the business skills.) He did not know that in throwing his idea on the table, he had handed a notion to someone who would, in a few years, turn it into an industry.

A writer for the *New York World* got Edison's take on the meeting, which matched Muybridge's own. "Mr. Edison said that Prof. Eadweard Muybridge, the instantaneous photographer, had visited him and had proposed to him a scheme which, if carried to completion, will afford an almost endless field of instruction and amusement," he wrote. "The photographer said that he . . . had almost perfected a photographic appliance by which he would be able to accurately reproduce the gestures and the facial expression of [an actor] making a speech. And he proposed to Mr. Edison that the phonograph should be used in connection with this invention." In this little scene I see the hazy but recognizable foundations of a media-made world. Especially in the reporter's last line: "This scheme met with the approval of Mr. Edison, and he intended to perfect it at his leisure."[4] Curiously Muybridge had never patented the zoopraxiscope. He had taken out patents on his apparatus for photographing motion and on several other devices, but not on the projector.

Edison, a businessman not shy about taking ideas from others and writing his name on them, saw in Muybridge a new vein of gold. He had what he wanted, and he sent the photographer on his way. And although the two corresponded, they never saw each other again.

Within a short time, Edison assigned staff to start work on something like a movie device, a machine that would exceed the zoopraxiscope. He had little incentive to add Muybridge to the project, and every reason to leave him out. (The photographer, who was not an employee, could not be chained to Edison patents.) Three months after their brainstorm session, in May 1888, Thomas Edison opened his mail and found a fat pamphlet from Muybridge, the catalog he had asked the photographer to send, which listed the series from *Animal Locomotion*. Edison was not really interested in individual photos, but in how to throw numbers of them on a screen. He sent a note to his assistant, "Tell him to make the selection for me," meaning, tell Muybridge to pick out fifty plates.[5] When those pictures arrived, big sheets with twenty-four images of people sweeping this or jumping that, they were placed conspicuously in the company library, a room on the second floor of the main building. Every week, all of Edison's technicians came through the library to look at patent filings and to do their correspondence—

Thomas A. Edison in a lab at his West Orange, New Jersey, compound, ca. 1890

Edison wanted everyone to see the pictures and figure out how to copy them.

In October, Edison wrote a two-page statement called a "caveat," an announcement of research plans, and submitted it to the U.S. Patent Office. A caveat was like a flag planted on new ground, a claim by an inventor that he or she had come *very close* to some discovery or apparatus. A patent, on the other hand, like a title to a piece of land, affirmed the thing was done. The Patent Office had a policy of informing the writer of a caveat when another company made a claim that might interfere with it. By filing one, Edison marked out turf and made it difficult for others to operate without his knowing.

"I am experimenting upon an instrument which does for the Eye what the phonograph does for the Ear, which is the recording and reproduction of things in motion, and in such a form as to be both Cheap, practical, and convenient," said the moving picture caveat of October 8, 1888.[6] At the time, Edison possessed no such "instrument." The description of the device ("which does for the eye what the phonograph does for the ear") covered what Muybridge had already created but linked Edison's nonexistent version of the technology with the phonograph, one of his big publicity coups.

Edison assigned to the project a twenty-eight-year-old engineer, William L. Dickson, an immigrant from Scotland. A slender man with wavy dark hair and a handlebar mustache, Dickson recruited as helpers two other tinkerers from the technical pool (one the superbly named Fred Ott), and the team went to work. They looked first at in-house options. The Edison phonograph, now ten years old, worked by means of cylinders. A sound recording consisted of a little scroll, twelve inches long, two inches thick, with the sound etched on a metal sheet wrapped around the cylinder and a needle following the groove as the thing turned. Dickson thought that instead of sound modulations, he might put rows of pictures on a similar scroll. Dickson had his team paint photography emulsion directly on phonograph cylinders and devised a way to expose tiny pictures, each a quarter of an inch square, as the tubes turned. To play back the scene, the viewer looked through a microscope at the pictures on the spinning tube. One of the few cylinders that survives from this period shows an Edison employee dressed in white and making faces. Dickson called it *Monkeyshines*.[7]

In summer 1889, Edison went to France for the Paris Exposition, a world's fair where hundreds of engineers showed off their inven-

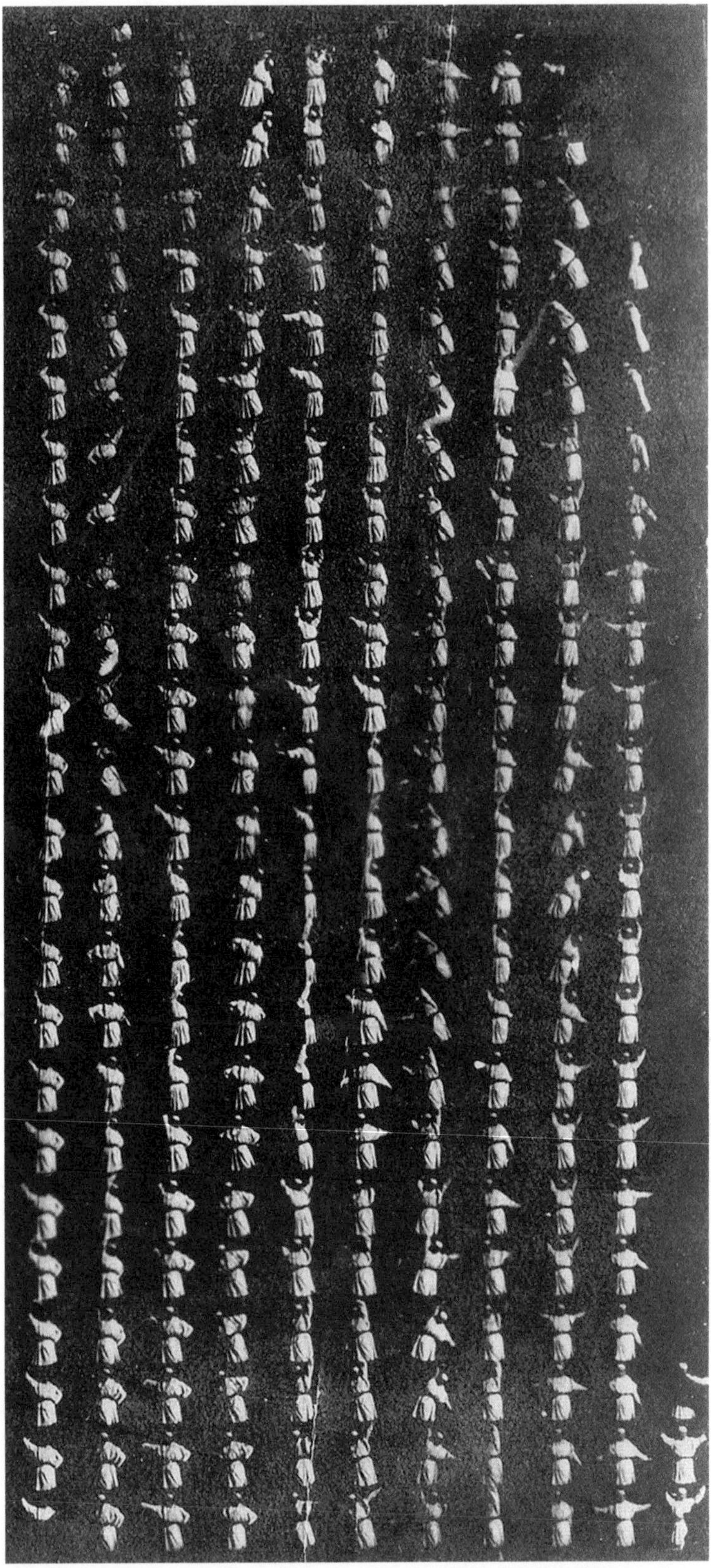

tions and tried to sell ideas. (Among the strange structures that went up at the fair was the Eiffel Tower, which drew hordes.) Edison's own company display covered nearly an acre inside the main glass-covered pavilion. In Paris, Edison looked up Muybridge's admirer Étienne-Jules Marey, who showed the American inventor some of his own stop-motion pictures. The rendezvous with Marey hastened the Wizard's competitive sprint, and, returning to New Jersey in the fall, Edison wrote another caveat that made a broad claim on motion pictures as his invention and his alone. He sent this, too, to the Patent Office.

The cylinder idea didn't work, in part because squinting through a microscope lens made viewers feel as though they were viewing a biological specimen. Disappointed, Edison took Dickson and his team off the project and assigned them to something different for a year. Then, in fall 1890, Dickson and his assistants went back to the "movie" scheme. A new material had turned up that promised to change everything—a substance known as celluloid.

———

Muybridge took his show to Europe, hoping to sell pictures from *Animal Locomotion* and placate his printers, the Photogravure Company, who threatened a lawsuit for nonpayment. In February 1889 he arrived in London to begin a year of meandering about his home country, screening and hustling. After the dustup over the Stillman book, *Horse in Motion*, seven years before, the science coterie in England had shunned Muybridge, but by now his claim had been vindicated. On this trip he found all scores evened and every auditorium with an open door. He hired a projectionist to run the equipment, a man called Ernest Webster, so he could walk and talk around the screen. The pair started with a screening at the Royal Institution in London, where he had appeared once before. This time, according to one paper, "Mr. Muybridge, when the animals were thrown on the screen in actual motion, brought down the house."[8] Muybridge and Webster did all of the "royals": the Royal Institution, the Royal Academy of Arts, the Royal Society. Praise flowed in the press, but sales of the photos could have been better.

(Facing page) In 1889, Edison engineer William Dickson and team photographed one of their earliest short subjects, a man dressed in white, goofing around, which they called *Monkeyshines*.

An influential photographer of the day, C. H. Bothamley, heard Muybridge talk in Leeds, in north England, and published his reaction. When the projector showed the flight of a bird, "a cockatoo, I believe," Bothamley wrote, "a murmur of astonishment and pleasure went through the whole audience, and the persistent demands for the repetition of what was as beautiful a picture as I have ever seen on a screen."[9]

The projectionist Ernest Webster remembered these days. "I operated the Zoopraxiscope for him," Webster wrote, years later. "Muybridge was extremely vain and intolerant of contradiction, very impatient if everything was not exactly to his previous instructions by post, and he was very dictatorial to porters and caretakers. Muybridge during the show walked about the stage with a little steel 'clicker' in his hand, and this he used as a signal when he wanted a change in the picture. He was a very voluble speaker and he told me that he never suffered from nervousness. He was always announced as 'Professor Eadweard Muybridge,' and woe betide anyone who spelled his Christian name 'Edward.'" Eadweard was never "Edward" again, apparently, except by mistake.

Webster had this to say about his employer's criminal past. "The secretary of one of the societies we visited told me that Muybridge had killed a man. Although we sat side by side on our long railway journeys, and also at meals at hotels, Muybridge never told me anything of his private affairs. I never heard any details or any other reference to the murder."[10] The photographer must have been relieved to travel and bow to applause as an artist and technician, and not a killer who had made good.

Muybridge did shows in England, Scotland, and Ireland, and in 1891 he crossed the Channel to the Continent to keep touring. March found him in Berlin, putting on screenings at the Kunstgenossenschaft (Art Association) and at the Urania Theater, to an audience of five hundred. From there he took his show to Bavaria for screenings in Munich. The *Neueste Nachrichten* newspaper, uncharacteristically excited, said, "The room was filled to the last corner, and nearly all the royal family and the ministers were present."[11] He went on to Italy, where he wrote to a friend at Penn from Rome ("to my surprise I found but few painters of any great distinction in this city"). The photographer gave shows at two theaters in the capital before going to Naples for more screenings and pitches. Taking a day off, Muybridge looked at the ruins of Pompeii, walking up and down Mt. Vesuvius and around the first-century town ("I wandered through the once animated streets of Pompeii, but my experiences were probably the same as those of most visitors"). He zigzagged Europe—Germany, Switzerland, Austria, Italy, France. (After two months, he wrote, "I now speak Italian, German, and French with equal fluency," happily exaggerating.) In a jumbled list, he wrote down the places where he gave his talks and showed his spinning images: "Berlin, Paris, Munich, Naples, Leipzig, Rome, Bologna, Turin, Bern, Tübingen, Wurzburg, Geneva, Freiburg, Basel, Halle, Jena, Göttingen, Bonn, Strasbourg, Vienna, Heidelberg, Prague, Genoa, Zurich, Pisa, Innsbruck, Budapest, Florence, and Padua." On another list he named "the royal and other academies" that had given him a stage and a screen.[12]

Then it was back to England for more shows. All the touring gave Muybridge a strong drink of fame: everywhere, audiences gasped and laughed, and their praise washed over him. But in August 1891, when he was in Britain, Muybridge might have seen an item in the London magazine *The Leisure Hour* about some doings back in the States.

"Mr. Thomas A. Edison, the famous American inventor, has just launched upon the world a description of the highly sensational feat he believes he has accomplished in reproducing sights," a reporter wrote. The magazine quoted Edison, "'My idea was to take a series of instantaneous photographs of motions so rapidly that in the reproduction photographic representations would become dissolved in pure motion.'" But the editors were skeptical. "So far we are told nothing new," the feature said. "By the visits of Mr. Muybridge to England, large audiences in all our great towns have been familiarized with the same kind of phenomena. His pictures are perfectly successful and give absolutely correct representations. Edison's machine adds nothing to our knowledge of the production of moving pictures, next to the system familiarized to us by Muybridge."[13] At least in London, Muybridge kept his reputation as the inventor.

He sailed back to America on November 25, on the steamship *Ohio*, from Liverpool.

———

They called them "begging letters." For many years Leland and Jenny had gotten streams of them. Everyone knew about the Stanford money, and hundreds wrote to ask for cash. Only the simplest address

An aging Leland Stanford,
about 1890

was necessary—"Leland Stanford, San Francisco"—and the letters always arrived.[14]

Rowena Geer, of Little River, Kansas, wrote, "It has been some years since I picked up a paper for the first time with the name Stanford (I do not remember the first name) as having an immense fortune. I have been wondering if you could be any relation to my Mother, her Maiden name was Stanford. If we are any relation I am glad you have the good fortune to have plenty of money whereby you can help the rest of us who is not so fortunate."

Lena Bailey, a student in New Hampshire, said, "I am a young girl of eighteen who has been for three years in the Stevens High School here in this town. I need about $100 dollars to complete my course, including graduation expenses. One hundred dollars would be to me what a million is to you. I shall anxiously await your reply, as it will decide my future."

S. J. Cox in Johnston, South Carolina, wrote:

"I have two little children, one a boy and one a girl, who are motherless. I need help to patent and perfect a horseless vehicle. Can you help me?"

A man in Iowa called A. D. Corbin sent this plea:

"We, the Negro Business League of Davenport, Iowa beg leave to put before you for your consideration our struggle to secure for ourselves one large public building, which will cost about $10,000."

Leland and Jenny ignored most of this (although Leland sometimes had a secretary send a brief "I-can't-spare-a-dollar" reply). Jenny, however, occasionally gave money to sick people. After sending a check to a young woman with tuberculosis, she told a secretary, "I received a thank-you letter from the mother. It was the most illiterate scrawl! She could not cross her T's or dot the I's. She used no paragraphs. But I suppose she wrote the letter many times before she mailed it. The poor, ignorant Irish woman." For Jenny to loosen her grip on money seemed to ease the grip money had on her.

In March 1889, the Stanfords went to the White House to attend the inaugural ball of President Benjamin Harrison. The incoming president was a Republican, like the Stanfords, and they struck up a friendship. Leland and Jenny sometimes found themselves at the White House for dinner with Harrison, and the president came to eat at the Stanfords' house on Farragut Square. Although Senator Stanford played the part of a backbencher in Congress, his friendliness with Harrison, noticed by the press, lifted him to a prominent spot on the Washington stage.

In May 1890 the Stanfords left for Europe to take the waters again at the Bad Kissingen spa in southern Germany. The railroad tycoon was falling into bad health. Leland, in his mid-sixties, struggled to get up from a chair and leaned on his showy gold-tipped cane when he walked. After several weeks in the mineral tubs, he and Jenny decamped to Vienna and after that to St. Petersburg, returning to California in October.

At the minimum, the trip must have helped Leland's appearance, because in January 1891, the California legislature voted him into another six-year term as senator.

The friendship with President Benjamin Harrison deepened. That summer, Harrison took a train from Washington to California to visit the Stanfords at their mansion in San Francisco. Receptions were arranged, dinners staged. The friendship had a public side—it helped Stanford more than Harrison—and in the eyes of railroad skeptics there was something opportune to it. As it happened, a fight had been brewing in Washington around the figure of Stanford. The railroad bonds issued by the federal government thirty years earlier, the money that built the transcontinental tracks, would come due in two years. Neither Stanford nor his old partner, Collis Huntington, felt inclined to repay the big loans—to do so would clean out their fortunes. (The other two of the "Big Four," Mark Hopkins and Charles Crocker, had died in the 1880s.) Litigation and an inquest by Congress looked likely. With a political squall gathering, Stanford knew it would be good to have the president around eating his food, riding his horses.

But to distract him from anxiety, there was now something good on the Palo Alto farm, just a stone's throw from the porch. Stanford University, a new quadrangle of buildings, looked like a medieval cloister in the crackling sun. The rusticated beige compound, Romanesque and stone, stood between the house and the horse tracks. On October 1, 1891, Leland and Jenny stepped off the porch and walked across the lawn to the opening day ceremony. Classes were to begin the following morning. A sizable audience—the first 555 students, a knot of well-wishers, a faculty of fifteen, the trustees—sat on the lawn in folding chairs for speeches and music. Senator Stanford, with the pride of ownership, leaned on his cane and gave the curtain-raiser.

———

Muybridge's life in show business crested at a world's fair. In 1893 in Chicago, on the shore of Lake Michigan, a cluster of mostly white buildings went up, gorgeous and ephemeral. The stage set had an official name, the World's Columbian Exposition, but everyone knew it as the Chicago World's Fair, or just "the White City." Science and art went on display in a six-month exhibit, and before it was done twenty-seven million had toured the grounds. Among the pavilions stood a theater devoted to one artist, Eadweard Muybridge, the motion studies man. His was not a name like Edison, but it had resonance nevertheless.

One writer called the Muybridge auditorium in Chicago "the world's first commercial motion picture theater," and I don't think this is overstatement.[15]

The Muybridge pavilion was brown and columned, its plaster facade etched with grooves to make it look like stone. Pamphlets said the photographer's show "may not be unworthy of the attention of the Philosopher," but will also "entertain popular and juvenile audiences." Between March and October, ticket buyers paid for a seat to watch "Professor Muybridge," age sixty-three, white-haired and tweedy, flickering his scenes on a big screen. From a gift stand at the entrance, a clerk sold photos and other Muybridgiana, as well as a short book with

Muybridge's pavilion, which he called Zoopraxographical Hall, at the World's Columbian Exposition in 1893

a choking title, *Descriptive Zoopraxography*, which the photographer had written for the fair.

He called his theater Zoopraxographical Hall, which did not siphon in many strollers walking by on the boulevard. The name said, in effect, "this is high science," especially to crowds that walked the Midway.

The typical layout of world's fairs, well honed by this time, forty years after the Crystal Palace exhibition in London, divided grounds into a "serious" section, with a dignified cluster of pavilions, and an amusement park, where impresarios put up attractions. At Chicago the Muybridge building went up with the amusements, on the so-called Midway, a walking strip three hundred feet wide and a mile long, lined with follies. Muybridge had polished his act at universities and lecture halls, and it didn't quite lock into place at a theme park. Two doors down from the Zoopraxographical Hall stood a scale model of the Eiffel Tower, and next to that a Ferris wheel. Just behind the Muybridge show, a huckster had built an alley modeled on old Cairo ("reproducing the street Bein el Kasrein in the city of the Khalifs, with mosques and bazaars, donkeys and camels," according to a printed guide). Across the road stood the Moorish Palace and the "Turkish Village, with a street of Constantinople." In other words, the inventor found himself in an Orientalist playground, where people paid to see belly dancers, jugglers, and acrobats.[16] In the middle of the kitsch, Muybridge put on a different kind of show, one that had played well in Europe, a high-minded talk broken up with bursts of pictures.

The show flopped, according to the Chicago *Daily Tribune*. "Attendance was not large," and Muybridge often "talked to empty seats." Ticket prices might have been high, but there were other reasons why few wanted to pay for the inventor's stand-up. One might have been sexual: boxed in by the fair's standards, he showed no naked pictures. For the family-keyed White City, all of his dancing and jumping models wore loincloths or gowns and covered their nipples. Another problem was that Muybridge seemed too familiar. Since the last motion studies in Philadelphia, now seven years back, the appetite for the inventor's brand of entertainment had faded, and he was selling a dimming novelty. When he photographed Occident at Palo Alto for the first time (and that was fifteen years before), Muybridge had stood in the vanguard. The Chicago World's Fair told him his influence had dribbled away.

Leland and Jenny Stanford paid a visit to Chicago for a few days in April. Age sixty-nine and weak, Leland rolled around in a wheelchair pushed by a minder. He and Jenny stayed with the main attractions, avoiding the Midway and making no attempt to see their old friend Muybridge. Stanford's every move made headlines, which means the photographer in his empty pavilion must have heard about the visit. The snub added a poisoned flower to his memory of the days when they were close.

———

In May 1893, Stanford went home to Palo Alto from Chicago, wheelchair bound, his breathing heavy. Dr. Jacob Stillman, Muybridge's enemy and Stanford's friend, put him up to convalesce. On the night of June 20, Leland's gasping woke Jenny, who sent one of the servants for a doctor in the town of Menlo Park. Stanford was dead by the time the doctor reached the house. In the aftermath, Jenny, whose son had also died and left her, could not relinquish her husband to an undertaker, and for the next three days Leland's body stayed in the bed where he died.

The funeral took place Saturday, June 24, in one of the quadrangles of the new school. "The casket was opened for all to look upon the man's face," one account said.[17] A giant floral arrangement formed the shape of a locomotive in roses and lilies, with yellow pansies to represent brass bits around the engine. Some two hundred workers from the Palo Alto Stock Farm lined the path of the dirge walk, and the pallbearers were the eight engineers who had worked at the railroad for the longest time.

Stanford's will gave sums to his three surviving brothers (Thomas, Josiah, and Philip), as well as to the children of the three brothers who had already died. It also set aside money for the children of Jenny's brothers, but none of the bequests cut deeply into the fortune. The will gave the biggest cache to the school, including stock in the railroad (32,873 shares Central Pacific, 24,468 shares Southern Pacific) and $2.5 million, or about $150 million in 2010 dollars.[18]

――――――

The development of celluloid, the original plastic material, made possible the first movies, which everyone knew, even at the time, came directly from Eadweard Muybridge. The word *celluloid* derived from cellulose: the initial technique for making the tough synthetic involved soaking wood chips and plant fibers in nitric acid, along with solvent.[19] Celluloid appeared during the 1880s as a cheap substitute for bone and rubber. It caught on quickly in all sorts of places—buttons, electrical insulation, billiard balls, shirt collars, false teeth, hair brushes—because everywhere people used it, celluloid cut costs to a fraction.

Photography began to substitute stiff celluloid backings for the accustomed glass plate negatives about 1885 (just as Muybridge was taking his last pictures, on glass, in Philadelphia). George Eastman, a plate maker in Rochester, New York, used hard celluloid for his early negative products before he founded the Eastman Kodak Company near the end of the decade. The first Kodak camera—the people's equipment, an amateur thing, not for professionals—which Eastman put to market in 1888, initially used paper as a backing for emulsion. It was wrapped around rolls mounted inside the boxy camera body. But the paper tore, so Eastman found a thin variety of celluloid that could be rolled like paper but was more flexible, firm, and transparent, and used it as a substitute. In September 1889, Eastman Kodak started selling celluloid roll film to be loaded in its patented cameras.

The Edison team in New Jersey, working on a moving picture camera, copied the scheme almost immediately. Engineer William Dickson ordered flexible sheets of celluloid from the Keystone Dry Plate Company in Philadelphia and put aside the idea of painting emulsion onto phonograph cylinders. Dickson wondered how celluloid might work in a fast-moving roll: the challenge was to build a machine to expose hundreds of photographs in sequence rather than just twenty-four, the upper limit that Muybridge reached. In late 1889, Dickson made a prototype for a camera that would use celluloid film on a rapid-turning spool, in imitation of the Kodak camera. He widened the roll to a width of thirty-five millimeters, creating a larger picture surface, and introduced sprocket holes, perforations along the edge, where metal teeth could grab the film and yank it along. He also thickened the film, making it tough enough to run through a camera at high speed. Dickson began buying rolls of celluloid directly from Eastman Kodak, and when that company's supply ran low, from another roll film maker, the Blair Camera Company in Boston.[20]

In the backyard of the Edison plant, using a camera the size of a desk, and rolls of film that careened through it at a rate of forty pictures per second, Dickson made his initial "movies." He pointed the lens at boxers and gymnasts, and also at men smoking pipes. If his initial subjects were close to the ones picked by Muybridge years earlier, this was because Dickson had paged through *Animal Locomotion* in order to figure out what to photograph. Edison called the camera the kinetograph, a coinage from Greek meaning "movement writing."[21]

The playback machine went by a different name: the kinetoscope. A wooden box, it stood four feet tall and eighteen by twenty-eight inches at the base. Inside, celluloid strips were threaded into a loop around a batch of spools. To look at things, you bent your eyes to a pair of goggles on the top and turned a crank on the side to advance the film. The machine could fit a sixty-second scene before running out of room.

The kinetoscope provided a private, voyeuristic experience, whereas the Muybridge scenes involved shared public viewing—a big screen and a room of people. In spring 1893, Edison's two machines, the kinetograph movie camera and the kinetoscope peep-show box, were almost finished. Edison wanted to introduce them at the Chicago World's Fair and had arranged exhibition space, but Dickson and his team fell behind schedule, and when the fair opened, they possessed only prototypes of the devices. With more tinkering necessary before production—Edison tools always went to market—Dickson would not let the prototypes leave the West Orange plant. This meant, among other things, that the kinetoscope did not face off against the Zoopraxographical Hall in Chicago.

Nevertheless, Muybridge knew something was going on. Edison was good at publicity, and the photographer would have seen an item or two. In the five years since they'd met, he'd never heard from Edison, and this grated on him. When, sometime later, he commented on this period, Muybridge took credit for giving Edison the idea to make pictures move. "The zoopraxiscope was the first instrument, and for many years it was the *only* apparatus," he wrote. "It was not until 1893, or more than thirteen years after it was first used, that any improvement in its construction or in its effects on the screen were made—improvements due to the invention of celluloid."[22] Muybridge knew that plastic, and the Wizard, had made possible what he could not.

William Dickson wanted a place to shoot his film. Just as Muybridge had once turned a shed in California into a camera house, Dickson, in early 1893, put up a little wooden structure in the yard of the plant. It functioned as a kind of movie studio, before such a thing existed. The building measured forty-eight by twelve feet, was taller at one end than the other, and was wrapped entirely in black tar paper. Edison workers gave it a name, the "Black Maria" (pronounced Mar-*eye*-uh, a Black Maria was a police van used for an arrest roundup, which looked like a black box on four wheels). The name pleased Dickson, because with his kinetograph camera, he thought he had made something very cool and strange.

The roof on the Black Maria had a big, hinged panel that opened to the sky, letting sun fall directly onto a stage, built inside, where scenes could be "filmed." Huge numbers in lumens, measurements of the quantity of light, were needed to get pictures on the fast-moving film. If you looked at the building from the side you could see that it stood a foot off the ground. Underneath, in the middle, it sat on a pivot, which made it into a kind of spinning platter. By pushing at its ends, a pair of men could rotate the building like a propeller, making the skylight face the light as the sun moved across the afternoon sky. The Black Maria functioned as the main location for Thomas Edison's moviemaking, with some two hundred short subjects shot there over a period of seven years.

Dickson shot a twenty-second short, *Blacksmith Scene*, which showed three men hammering at an anvil (another Muybridge subject, with two differences: the men wore clothes in the Dickson scene, and

An early "film studio," the so-called Black Maria, in the yard of the Edison plant in New Jersey, where, between 1893 and 1900, William Dickson and his crew shot some two hundred short subjects for distribution to kinetoscope parlors, music halls, and vaudeville theaters

there was a coda, which showed the men drinking beer). The filmstrip was loaded into the kinetoscope, where it became one of the first "movies." A month later, Edison okayed the final design for the kinetoscope, the viewer that would be the company's main product. Contracts were signed and exhibitors brought on board. (Edison could do a dozen things Muybridge could not, most notably, improve and perfect his equipment, develop merchandise, and bring it to market.) In January 1894, Dickson shot another of the founding reels in film history, *Kineto-scopic Record of a Sneeze*, a filmstrip showing a blast into a handkerchief by the engineer Fred Ott. Publicity for the sneeze went national: a few frames appeared in the magazine *Harper's Weekly* as a stop-motion series.

Edison knew Muybridge would see the *Harper's* story. Perhaps he wanted to explain himself to the photographer for having forgotten their handshake agreement to do something together. Having ignored him for years, Edison wrote Muybridge on February 14 to describe what he had been up to. "I have constructed a little instrument which I call a Kinetoscope," Edison told Muybridge. "It has a nickel and slot attachment," meaning a place to feed the money, "but I am very doubtful if there is any commercial feature in it and fear that the machines will not

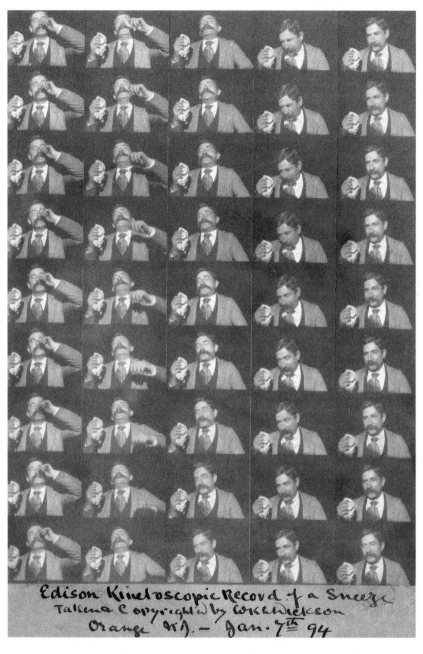

William K. Dickson, *Edison's Kinetoscopic Record of a Sneeze (Fred Ott's Sneeze)*, 1894. A stop-motion sequence published in *Harper's Weekly*

earn their cost." Edison dissimulated, pretending to have dreamed up a dumb failure. "These devices are of too sentimental character to get the public interested," he wrote, not telling the truth about his expectations, while also apprising Muybridge to keep away from his turf.[23] Muybridge wrote back on February 26, suggesting another plan to work together. Edison didn't answer this time, because he had nothing to gain.

Later that year Edison went into business as a "filmmaker," a new job description he had just created. He hired a manager named William Gilmore, who would help integrate production (sixty-second reels shot in the Black Maria) and distribution (viewing parlors full of kinetoscopes). The Edison Company opened its first kinetoscope parlor in April 1894, installing ten kinetoscopes in a big storefront in New York, in the Holland Brothers emporium at 1155 Broadway, near Twenty-seventh Street. The machines stood like iceboxes lined against the walls, with ushers in suits to show you how to use them. It cost a nickel to see a one-minute "show," twenty-five cents for five. (No volume discount—the movies were bite-sized, and customers ate a lot of them.) The company delivered novelty scenes, removed by a good distance from both science and art. One kinetoscope might crank up roosters fighting. Another, trained bears leaping. There was no sound, just pictures. (Although Muybridge had wanted Edison to link sound to the movies, Dickson and his team had trouble synchronizing the phonograph to the picture. Sound would not come into wide use in film until 1927, more than thirty years later.)

Edison took credit for everything, but he tipped his hat to Muybridge at least once. "I believe that in coming years by my own work and that of Muybridge," he said, talking to a writer for *Century* magazine in June 1894, "that a show can be given at the Metropolitan at New York without any material change from the original and with artists long since dead."

When the Wizard formed the Kinetoscope Company to distribute his machines, dozens of theater producers opened coin-operated parlors, and from the compound in New Jersey, Edison produced content to feed his hardware. Among the talent brought to the Black Maria to shoot reels for the chain: a strongman called Eugene Sandow (who flexed his muscles), a dancer named Annabelle Whitford (who undulated), and a tightrope walker named Juan Caicedo (who teetered on his cable). Buffalo Bill did a few seconds of his Wild West Show, and

A kinetoscope parlor in San Francisco in 1894, where men in suits showed customers how to use the viewing apparatus that imitated moving picture effects devised by Muybridge

Annie Oakley, the sharpshooter, fired her gun. Nickels and quarters dropped, until Edison was making a good sum—$89,000 profit for the year 1894, or about $2.5 million in 2010 dollars.

Jenny Stanford, still sifting through her late husband's papers, was compelled to think about Edison and Muybridge when she opened a letter from William Berry, in upstate New York. "I am a married man, forty years old," said the begging letter. "A few years ago I lost my left hand while working at my trade as a machinist, and it deprives me a great deal in finding employment. I have come to the conclusion that one of Edison's Kinetoscopes, with its first-class moving pictures, would bring in enough money to take care of my family. I wish to hire from you money to buy one, on two years time, with interest. Please consider this."

Two impresarios, Frank Maguire and Joseph Baucus, bought the rights to sell the Kinetoscope abroad and took the device to Paris in October 1894. They arranged a demonstration at a shop on the Boulevard Poissonnière, where among the many curious spectators were two brothers, Louis and Auguste Lumière. The Lumière brothers, ages thirty and thirty-two, came from the city of Lyon, in the south, where they ran a factory, the largest manufacturer of photographic plates in

France. Their father, Antoine Lumière, had started the business—the brothers were his princely heirs—and the Lumière family employed some one hundred workers. Not incidentally, their factory relied heavily on celluloid. Rich and comfortable from the photography trade, the Lumières wanted to diversify. They found themselves fascinated by what Edison's equipment did but disappointed that you had to squint into a box to see it. Would it be possible to put the minute-long pictures on a screen instead of peering into a box? The Lumières knew the answer because they were familiar with Muybridge and his French counterpart, Étienne-Jules Marey, who had done exactly that.

Louis and Auguste Lumière returned to Lyon and began work on a camera the size of a shoebox, with a crank, which could shoot film of what it saw. They wanted to be able to use the same machine, after the pictures were developed, as a projector in the Muybridge fashion. On February 13, 1895, the brothers took out a patent on the device, which they called the *cinématographe*, a name copied from the Edison machine, the kinetograph.[24]

A near-cube of wood that measured only twelve inches in length, the *cinématographe* shot film more slowly than the Edison machine, sixteen pictures per second instead of forty, but it weighed ten pounds, rather than 150. A month after taking out the patent, the Lumières brought their device to the Société d'Encouragement pour l'Industrie Nationale in Paris, where they used it to show on a screen a thirty-second movie, *La Sortie des usines Lumière à Lyon* (Workers leaving the Lumière factory at Lyon), in which the family's assembly-line crew, most of them women, streamed out of a barnlike factory door. Nine months later, on December 28, the brothers gave their first public show of the *cinématographe* to a paying audience, screening ten strips of film in a big room in a restaurant in Paris, the Grand Café, at 14 Boulevard des Capucines. Among the subjects: a man spraying a garden hose, a woman feeding a baby, and (what since Muybridge had become a staple) a pair of blacksmiths hammering at an anvil.

The show at the Grand Café, a block from the Paris Opéra and on a Saturday night, is usually singled out by historians of media as a kind of official birthday for moving pictures. Other birthdays can be found, of course, including one nearly sixteen years earlier: the night at the Stanford house in San Francisco, on January 16, 1880, when Muybridge, for an audience of Stanford's friends, put his horses in motion on a screen.

Back in America, Edison's kinetoscope turned out to be a fad—after two years, the machine lost its appeal, and traffic at the parlors thinned. The problem seemed to be both physical and psychological. The Edison arrangement for looking at movies involved one viewer bent over a tall box and squinting into two eyeholes. It seemed people preferred something closer to the Muybridge experience—a room full of spectators, everyone seated, and a communal gaze.

Edison learned about the Lumières and moved to outflank them. In late 1895, two engineers from Washington, D.C., Thomas Armat and Francis Jenkins, brought their design for a compact projector, which they called a "phantascope," to Edison. The machine used an intermediate step, stopping and fixing the film for an instant on each image before pushing it to the next frame. The change eliminated much of the flickering light that viewers complained about in moving pictures. In January 1896, Edison committed to building the phantascope and claimed it as his own device, renaming it the "vitascope."

By spring that year, three months after the Lumières made their machine public in Paris, Edison had a marketable projector. Screenings started in New York in Herald Square, at Koster & Bial's Music Hall, Broadway and Thirty-fourth Street, on April 23. In one feature, a woman did an "Umbrella Dance," and in another, waves crashed on a beach. By this time Edison's engineers had also built a portable camera that resembled the Lumières' *cinématographe*. In May, that camera went out for a test, filming crowds that streamed along Broadway. And in a technique the Lumière brothers had used in France, which astonished audiences, the Broadway shots were shown the same night at Koster & Bial's.

In June, the *cinématographe* came to New York for its first American screenings. Soon, in big eastern cities, a dozen *cinématographe* cameramen were shooting during the day and giving shows at night. Things moved quickly. By this time Edison engineer William Dickson had quit in disgust over receiving so little money and credit for his work. Dickson founded another company, American Mutoscope, which showed moving pictures in vaudeville theaters. It was with Dickson, and at this point, that movies broke through from storefronts to the mainstay of American popular culture, vaudeville. Variety theaters and music halls around the country now showed film shorts as warm-ups for live acts. Another pair of Edison employees left to form a third competing outfit, the International Film Company. All the while, projectors of different design came into the market from other American engineers, and from Europe.[25]

———

Muybridge was sixty-five. He knew he had missed the last turn. He knew his product, two seconds of animals jogging, no longer held anyone's attention. Between Edison and the Lumières, it looked clear that the future belonged to movies on celluloid.

In 1895—a year or so after he shut down the Zoopraxographical Hall at the Chicago World's Fair and a few months after Edison opened the first kinetoscope parlors—Muybridge left America and moved home to England, permanently. He landed in his hometown, Kingston, southwest of London, as an elder adrift. He had not lived in England for an extended length of time in forty-five years. A few in his family, proud of what he'd done in America, put him up, and after a period of borrowing rooms he moved into a handsome house on Kingston's Liverpool Road. The single-family had four bedrooms, Gothic detail, and a garden in the back. To share expenses, Muybridge had two cousins move in with him, and because after a solitary life, he wanted company. His roommates were George Lawrence, a fortyish cousin by marriage, and Catherine Plow Smith, a twenty-year-old grandniece of his mother. The three hired a live-in servant, a woman named Florence Gibbs, to round out the house at four.[26]

Muybridge did more talks and screenings here and there in England, but the zoopraxiscope looked to audiences like old shtick. He gave his last show at the Artists' Society, in the town of St. Ives, in Cornwall, in summer 1896.

A period of summing up followed. In 1897 Muybridge made a deal with a London publisher, Chapman and Hall, to write two books that pulled together what he had done. The first, *Animals in Motion*, came out in 1899. At 264 pages it was a relatively short thing (compared to his previous output), but it had half-tone photographs, a technical advance over photogravure, the older image standard. In an essay with the pictures, Muybridge claimed (gently, no bitterness) to have been the originator of movie technology. Although no film industry yet existed, by this time hundreds of theaters ran shows of short subjects based on Muybridge-like excerpts, and talk in the press promised a world of bigger things to come. "My zoopraxiscope," Muybridge wrote, "was the prototype of all the various instruments which, under a variety of names, accomplish a similar purpose at the present day." He was right. In 1901 Muybridge published *The Human Figure in Motion*, another short book with a few dozen photographs, plus an essay that said his inventions should rank first in the story of movies, because they made movies possible.[27]

Chapter 22

THE FLOOD

The question of who launched moving pictures and with them the visual media that hold us captive is not an idle enigma. Media are the addiction no one goes without, and we live by creation myths. What wove the fabric of invented dreams? Who stands at the headwaters of the image flood?

Historians of media look for ancestors of cinema and find a dozen. Magic lantern, zoetrope, camera obscura. Impresarios did part of the job, like Louis Le Prince and William Friese-Greene (in England), Muybridge's friend and rival Étienne-Jules Marey (France), and Ottomar Anschütz (Germany). But it was Muybridge who carried out the assignment, throwing a bridge from photography to projection, turning himself into a showman with a river of pictures on five hundred screens. After Muybridge, the quantity of images overwhelms and sweeps away the dams of memory.

The photographs he made possess "the trauma, strangeness, the uncanniness of the impossible instant," in the phrase of film writer Mary Ann Doane. You feel the unease in the runner immobilized at half step and the horse stopped in a freak pose. But Muybridge put his frozen instants back into the natural clothing of real-time vision. When the images were replayed on screen, the zoopraxiscope made his weird hijacking of time appear as normal as the drift of seconds and minutes.

When he projected his running animals, Muybridge stunned people with the little screen dramas. (So much pleasure! Show it again!) But twenty years passed before his kind of exquisite shock became wide-spread, thanks to celluloid, and another ten years before millions of people rose up from their living rooms, found seats in the new cinemas, and locked their eyes onto the big screen, giving themselves up to Muybridge's creation.

Thomas Edison knew that recorded movement would fix the eye on it, and audiences would rush to pay—thus the endless dancers and acrobats in the Black Maria. After the *cinématographe*, the Lumière brothers employed a team of cameramen who traveled Europe and America, shooting during the day and screening reels at night. They made "actualities," in the jargon, street scenes with trolleys, movies of zeppelins landing, ships launching, water crashing. The opening moment in a Lumière show was a trick the brothers learned from Muybridge: project a motionless frame on the screen, and then kick it into action. Muybridge set it all up for followers to exploit—he was the advance man for the businesspeople, who turned his little spectacle into real revenue.

By the year 1900, three machines in three countries did, with celluloid, what our hero, the murderer, did with glass plates: the *cinématographe*, in France; the vitascope, in the United States; and, in Germany, a projector called the Bioscope, built by engineer Max Skladanowsky. In 1901 Edison opened a production office at 41 East Twenty-first Street in New York and hired a movie exhibitor named Edwin Porter to staff it. A glassed-in stage was built on the roof, and that became the studio (like the Muybridge camera house), with lab work for the film sent to West Orange. Edison ramped up output. He wanted to become the dominant maker of movies and refiled patents claiming most of the technology as his personal creation. Beginning in 1902, he sued every movie producer in sight for patent infringement.

Edwin Porter liked the reels made by Georges Meliès, a former magician in Paris, which included shots that would enter film vocabulary—close-ups, cutaways, and special effects. Actualities faded and storytelling seeped in to occupy the place vacated by the real. Edwin Porter copied Melies's methods and in 1903 made *Life of an American Fireman*, a twelve-minute reel in which a fireman rescues a mother and child. (Edison raised Porter's salary to thirty-five dollars a week, hoping he wouldn't follow Dickson and quit.) In November, Porter started a bigger project, *The Great Train Robbery*. Shot in New Jersey, the movie told the story of a train holdup in the Old West, plus

At the Edison film studio in the Bronx, New York, Edwin S. Porter directs
A Country Girl's Seminary Life and Experiences, 1908.

a shootout that kills the robbers. (It would have appealed to Stanford, had he lived.) The reel went into every vaudeville house to become the most popular show of the day.

———

He was seventy-four years old in spring 1904, and Muybridge's stake in the visual culture had shrunk to nothing. He hadn't shot a photograph since 1886. Occasionally he sent letters to magazine editors about a museum show or a scientific discovery. He tended his reputation in an old-fashioned, reference-book way, making sure the word *zoopraxiscope* appeared in dictionaries. He lived with his cousins, went to hometown events, and befriended the local librarians, who helped him put his papers in order. And he gardened.

In March he seems to have been sick, because in the middle of that month Muybridge wrote a will. It left his cousin Catherine Smith his books and the income from a savings account (a tiny amount, not enough to live on); to his other housemate, George Lawrence, he left his cameras and equipment (they were out of date and might be sold for a small chunk). Two bequests went to his hometown: about £1,000 to the Kingston library to buy "artistic and scientific" books, and "my

Eadweard Muybridge,
ca. 1900

Zoopraxiscope, and negatives, and plates concerned with the investigation of animal locomotion" to a group planning a local museum.

The will made no mention of his son in California. Florado Helios
Muybridge, the boy born to Flora, trigger for the crime that nearly sent
Muybridge to the gallows, was now a thirty-year-old man. He hadn't
heard from his father since he was nine years old, since the photographer paid a last visit to him in 1883. Florado's father had an unmatched
record for burning bridges.

On May 8, 1904, Muybridge was digging the ground behind his
house, trying to cut out a model of the Great Lakes. A strange design
for a den, except when you remember that the photographer once ran
a building in Chicago, on the shore of Lake Michigan, dedicated to
himself. The world's fair, the lakes, the ocean-sized freshwater sea:
the scale must have made an impression, and he wanted to remember
them. He must have been stunned also by the scale of his own fifty-year
detour in America, and he wanted to remember that. While shoveling
in the backyard, carving out the shape of one of the lakes, Muybridge
collapsed and died. The papers made no mention of the cause. He was
cremated and buried in the town of Woking, twenty miles from Kingston, a fifteen-inch square slab of brown marble over his grave. The register of the crematorium called him "Eudweard Muybridge": a clerk got
the last name right but messed up the first. The gravestone reads EAD-

WEARD MAYBRIDGE: the stonecutter got the first name right but messed up the last. All this continued a pattern set in motion by the deceased himself, who, whenever he changed his name, raised the bar in spelling.

————

If you take the long view, you can think of media as a collision of railroads and photography, the accident that brought together Stanford and Muybridge. You can see media as the fusion of wealth with the arts, the first represented by a man who coined himself once, as a money maven, and the second by the strange, marginal man who coined himself repeatedly. The invention of media required two things: a pile of capital and a parallax view of art. Media and their make-believe worlds still work by that arrangement.

One year after Muybridge died, the first movie house went up in America. Until that time, movies ran in vaudeville theaters and in music halls, as teasers before the live entertainment. But in 1905, the Nickelodeon Theater opened on Smithfield Street in Pittsburgh, Pennsylvania, the original film theater, an auditorium where, from 8:00 a.m. to midnight, movies made the only attraction. The name of the theater came from the five cents charged for a reel, and "nickelodeon" turned into the generic label for all movie houses for years, until ticket prices rose.[1]

The code Muybridge cracked, the crime he committed for which

The Nickelodeon Theater, Pittsburgh, Pennsylvania, ca. 1905

no one charged him, was the kidnapping of time. Before his camera, three media—writing, theater, and music—acted as vessels of time. Writing housed experience (reading let you relive life), and music and theater made two temporal arts, places where duration might be stored and retrieved. Muybridge added moving pictures to the list, another place to archive time. Movies hold the world in a perpetual present, bringing dead time (and the dead themselves) back to life. When he animated the running horse, Muybridge entered time into a retrievable file, made it a dataset, and on the foundation of that stolen second crafted the mechanism that led to the visual media and their vast sensorium of images. André Bazin, the French writer on film, said that moving pictures "embalm time."[2] Where photography makes possible the rescue of an instant, Muybridge made possible the rescue of any length of past, restoring it to the here and now.

He uncovered the miraculous in moving pictures, whose marvelousness is linked with death. By restoring motion, some visual media bring dead events back to life. (An early name for the movies was "animated pictures.") "The ghost will walk," said a French reporter who had seen a Muybridge show in 1881, "and science will succeed in abolishing death, its sole obstacle and only enemy."

I don't want to say that Muybridge is the point of origin for the frenzy of looking that characterizes our own screen behavior in the twenty-first century. He is more like a railroad switch in the development of vision. After his camera, the media become possible, because all media came to rely on the template he designed. And more media to come, I would think, will grow from the same model.

Leland Stanford, despite the turbulence of time, would recognize Stanford University as his latter-day offspring. The school whose leaders turned it into a driver of innovation in technology remains faithful to its founder as a huge formation of capital and a safe redoubt for the grooming of managers. Stanford the man was above much else an executive, and the university that carries his name carries also his love for engineering, for organizations, the promise that lies in money and an unquesting belief in machines.

Following in the steps of Stanford and the railroads, Thomas Edison began a long reign as the monopolist of early film. For more than a decade his Motion Picture Patents Company and its licensed producers controlled over 75 percent of the market for filmmaking and distribution—that is, until the year 1915, when a federal court, enforcing the Sherman Antitrust Act, took the company apart. Disappointed, Edison sold his movie interests and got out of the media business. He died in 1931.

A camera was not on hand to record his death, or for that matter the death of Florado Muybridge. On January 28, 1944, in Sacramento, at the corner of Twenty-fifth and I Streets, Florado Helios, age sixty-nine and a part-time gardener, was hit by a car. He died in a hospital four days later. Florado's father came to time too early. The driver of the car that killed his son, a man called Ernest Tulgham, age forty-two, said he was driving eastbound and did not see the man in the intersection until the time was too late.[3]

ACKNOWLEDGMENTS

Thank you to my editor at Doubleday, Gerry Howard, and agent at International Creative Management, Kris Dahl. I thank Stephen Herbert, of Hastings, England, for his scholarship on pre-cinema and Edward Muybridge, which lighted my road. Gratitude to an exceptional researcher, Christine Delucia, who visited archives of Muybridge and Stanford material and excavated some of the best bits from them. People who look after the old papers and photographs do not receive enough credit, and I'm grateful to all staff with keys to the vaults of primary materials. Some who helped include the folks at the Archives of American Art at the Smithsonian Institution; Bancroft Library at the University of California, Berkeley; California Historical Society; California State Library; California State Railroad Museum; Cantor Center for Visual Arts at Stanford; George Eastman House International Museum of Film and Photography, in Rochester; Kingston Local History Room and Archives, in Kingston, UK; Stanford University Library and Archives, in Palo Alto; and the University of Pennsylvania Archives and Records Center, in Philadelphia. Many film scholars have written about Muybridge and early cinema, and I am a guest in their house. An incomplete list: Richard Abel, Brian Coe, Jean-Louis Comolli, Mary Anne Doane, Anne Friedberg, Tom Gunning, Hermann Hecht, Stephen Herbert, Laurent Mannoni, Jean Mitry, Charles Musser, Steve Neale, and Deac Rossell. Other writers who brought this story into focus include Marta Braun, Philip Brookman, Robert B. Haas, Gordon Hendricks, Oscar Lewis, Anita Ventura Mozley, Phillip

Prodger, Rebecca Solnit, and Richard White. As I spun out the manuscript, three friends read it—historians Beverly Gage, Claire Potter, and Paul Sabin—and I'm grateful to them for commentary. Thanks to a Yale graduate student, Christopher Kramaric, for collecting photography permissions. When I felt history fatigue, the person who helped was Candace Skorupa, who cannot have escaped collateral numbness from this tale, four years in making, plus a year off for illness; loving thanks to her. If there are factual or chronological errors in the story, they are mine, because book writing, let's face it, is something you do alone.

NOTES

ABBREVIATIONS

LSP: Leland Stanford Papers, Special Collections, Stanford University

MC: Muybridge Collection, Kingston Museum and Heritage Service, Kingston, England

PREFACE

1. Many writers on media have excavated the visual equipment of the nineteenth century. For the prehistory of moving images, see, among others, Hermann Hecht, *Pre-Cinema History: An Encyclopaedia and Annotated Bibliography of the Moving Image before 1896* (London: Bowker, Saur, 1993); Stephen Herbert, *A History of Pre-Cinema*, 3 vols. (London: Routledge, 2000); Franz Paul Liesegang and Hermann Hecht, *Dates and Sources: A Contribution to the History of the Art of Projection and to Cinematography* (London: Magic Lantern Society of Great Britain, 1986); Laurent Mannoni, *The Great Art of Light and Shadow: Archaeology of the Cinema*, trans. Richard Crangle (Exeter, UK: University of Exeter Press, 2000); Charles Musser, *The Emergence of Cinema: The American Screen to 1907* (New York: Scribner, 1990); and Deac Rossell, *Living Picture: The Origins of the Movies* (Albany: State University of New York Press, 1998).

CHAPTER 1: THE STANFORD ENTERTAINMENT

1. There are other versions of the appearance or "birth" of moving pictures in France, Germany, and America. I have put together this one from newspapers, Eadweard Muybridge's writings, and these sources: "The Stanford Entertainment," *San Francisco Daily Call*, Jan. 20, 1880; "The Zoogyroscope," *San Francisco Daily Call*, May 5, 1880 (reprinted in the *New York Times*, May 19, 1880); Diana Strazdes, "The Millionaire's Palace: Leland Stanford's Commission for Pottier & Stymus in San Francisco," *Winterthur Portfolio* 36, no. 4 (2001): 213–43; "Stan-

ford and the Earthquake," *Stanford Alumnus* 7 (May 1906): 5; George Thomas Clark, *Leland Stanford, War Governor of California, Railroad Builder and Founder of Stanford University* (Palo Alto, CA: Stanford University Press, 1931), 367–68; Eadweard Muybridge, preface to *Animals in Motion: An Electro-Photographic Investigation of Consecutive Phases of Muscular Action* (London: Chapman & Hall, 1925); Eadweard Muybridge, "The Attitudes of Animals in Motion, Illustrated with the Zoopraxiscope," March 13, 1882, lecture at the Royal Institution of Great Britain, pamphlet (London: Clowes & Sons, 1882).

CHAPTER 2: THE YELLOW JACKET MURDER

1. "Financial Genius," *San Francisco Chronicle*, Mar. 14, 1873.
2. This account draws on and condenses several newspaper reports, including "Harry Larkyns—the Life and Death of an Adventurer," *San Francisco Daily Examiner*, Oct. 19, 1874; "A Startling Tragedy," *San Francisco Chronicle*, Oct. 19, 1874; "Major Larkyns' Fate," *San Francisco Chronicle*, Oct. 20, 1874; "The Calistoga Tragedy," *San Francisco Chronicle*, Oct. 21, 1874; "The Fatal Amour," *San Francisco Chronicle*, Dec. 21, 1874; "A Startling Tragedy: Chevalier Harry Larkyns Shot Dead by Edward J. Maybridge, the Photographer," *San Francisco Bulletin*, Oct. 19, 1874; and "Muybridge in Jail," *San Francisco Bulletin*, Oct. 21, 1874.

CHAPTER 3: GOD OF THE SUN

1. Muybridge and Maison Hélios: *Alta California*, Dec. 3, 1862. A letter from Edward Muybridge, in London, to his uncle, Henry Selfe, in Australia, dated August 17, 1861, says that Muybridge will "shortly leave for the continent . . . on business that may detain me for some months," in Robert Haas, *Muybridge: Man in Motion* (Berkeley: University of California Press, 1976), 10. He says that he can be reached at 9 rue Cadet, Paris, in the 9th arrondissement. A researcher in French photography, Yves Lebrec, outlined the history of Maison Hélios and the Berthaud brothers at http://www.blogg.org/blog-93964.html, accessed July 9, 2012; additional information is available at http://laphotoduxix.canalblog.com/archives /berthaud/index.html, accessed Aug. 18, 2011.
2. Art dealer William Rulofson, quoted in the *San Francisco Bulletin*, Feb. 5, 1875; *Daily Morning Call*, Feb. 4, 1875, p. 3.
3. The word *photography* appears in London talks by John F. W. Herschel: "On the Chemical Action of the Rays of the Solar Spectrum on Preparations of Silver and Other Substances, Both Metallic and Non-Metallic" and "On Some Photographic Processes," published in *Philosophical Transactions of the Royal Society of London* 130 (1840): 1–59.
4. The legacy of Nicéphore Niépce is guarded by a state-run museum in France, Maison Nicéphore Niépce, in the village of Saint-Loup-de-Varennes, Burgundy (http://www.niepce.com/).
5. John Hittell, *Yosemite—Its Wonders and Its Beauties* (San Francisco: H. H. Bancroft, 1868), 36.

6. "A.M. Maybridge" at Yosemite in November 1867, *Mariposa Gazette*, cited in Rebecca Solnit, *River of Shadows: Eadweard Muybridge and the Technological Wild West* (New York: Viking, 2003), 262.

7. Helmut Gernsheim, *The Rise of Photography, 1850–1880: The Age of Collodion* (London: Thames and Hudson, 1988), 66.

8. Theodore H. Hittell, *History of California*, vol. 4 (San Francisco: N. J. Stone, 1898), 465.

CHAPTER 4: HARNESSING THE ELEPHANT

1. George Thomas Clark, *Leland Stanford, War Governor of California, Railroad Builder and Founder of Stanford University* (Palo Alto, CA: Stanford University Press, 1931), 189–206; Stuart Daggett, *Chapters on the History of the Southern Pacific* (New York: Ronald Press, 1922), 1–26; Theodore H. Hittell, *History of California*, vol. 4 (San Francisco: N. J. Stone, 1898); Richard Rayner, *The Associates: Four Capitalists Who Created California* (New York: Norton, 2008), 35–55; Norman E. Tutorow, *Leland Stanford: Man of Many Careers* (Menlo Park, CA: Pacific Coast Publishers, 1971), 70–80; Norman E. Tutorow, *The Governor: The Life and Legacy of Leland Stanford, a California Colossus*, vol. 1 (Spokane, WA: Arthur H. Clark, 2004), 190–226.

2. Clark, *Leland Stanford*, 185.

3. Leland Stanford to Abraham Lincoln, Sept. 29, 1862, Special Collections, Stanford University.

4. Leland Stanford to Mrs. [Elizabeth] Stanford, Dec. 13, 1862, and Dec. 24, 1863, Special Collections, Stanford University.

5. Hittell, *History of California*, vol. 4, 465.

6. Tutorow, *The Governor*, 208–89; Clark, *Leland Stanford*, 207–73; California State Railroad Museum, Sacramento, Records of the Central Pacific Railroad, Newton Cope Collection, 1868–1922.

7. Tutorow, *The Governor*, 128–35.

8. Estimate by a Chinese American historian who canvassed payroll sheets, in William F. Chew, *Nameless Builders of the Transcontinental Railroad* (Bloomington, IN: Trafford Publishing, 2004), 36–49.

9. Quoted in Gunther Barth, *Bitter Strength: A History of the Chinese in the United States, 1850–1870* (Cambridge, MA: Harvard University Press, 1964), 119.

10. Payroll sheets, Central Pacific Railroad collection, 1864–69, MS 79, box 22, California State Railroad Museum, Sacramento.

11. Quoted in Tutorow, *The Governor*, 248.

12. *Sacramento Reporter*, June 30, 1870.

13. "C.P. Railroad Co., Abstract of Earnings, March 1864 to Dec. 1869," Gilbert Harold Kneiss Collection, 1864–92, California State Railroad Museum, Sacramento.

14. John Robinson, *The Octopus: A History of the Construction, Conspiracies, Extortions, Robberies, and Villainous Acts of the Central Pacific, South Pacific of Kentucky,*

Union Pacific, and Other Subsidized Railroads (New York: Arno Press, 1981), 1–44 (original published 1894); for the burned ledgers, see Rayner, *The Associates*, 109–10.

15. Tutorow, *The Governor*, 311ff.

16. Richard White, *Railroaded: The Transcontinentals and the Making of Modern America* (New York: Norton, 2011), 50.

CHAPTER 5: THE PHOTOGRAPHER

1. Philip Brookman et al., Corcoran Gallery of Art, *Helios: Eadweard Muybridge in a Time of Change* (Göttingen, Germany: Steidl / Washington, DC: Corcoran Gallery of Art, 2010), 46–47.

2. "Destruction of Property in Various Parts of the City," *San Francisco Morning Call*, Oct. 22, 1868; stereographs: *Alta California*, Oct. 28, 1868.

3. Muybridge uses native names in his *Catalogue of Photographic Views Illustrating the Yosemite, Mammoth Trees, Geyser Springs, and Other Remarkable and Interesting Scenery of the Far West* (San Francisco: Bradley & Rulofson, 1873), Bancroft Library, University of California, Berkeley.

4. *The Philadelphia Photographer*, vol. 5 (November 1868), cited in Robert Haas, *Muybridge: Man in Motion* (Berkeley: University of California Press, 1976), 19.

5. *Daily Morning Call*, Feb. 17, 1868.

6. Helen Hunt Jackson, *Bits of Travel at Home* (Boston: Roberts Brothers, 1878), 87.

7. Marta Braun, *Eadweard Muybridge* (London: Reaktion Books, 2010), 50–53.

8. Jackson, *Bits of Travel at Home*, 86.

9. Gordon Hendricks, *Eadweard Muybridge: The Father of the Motion Picture* (New York: Grossman Publishers, 1975), 27.

10. Mead B. Kibbey and Peter E. Palmquist, *The Railroad Photographs of Alfred A. Hart, Artist* (Sacramento: California State Library Foundation, 1996).

11. Peter E. Palmquist and Thomas R. Kailbourn, *Pioneer Photographers of the Far West: A Biographical Dictionary, 1840–1865* (Palo Alto, CA: Stanford University Press, 2000), 415–17.

CHAPTER 6: FLORA DOWNS

1. Gordon Hendricks, *Eadweard Muybridge: The Father of the Motion Picture* (New York: Grossman Publishers, 1975), 30; *San Francisco Chronicle*, Oct. 19, 1874, Oct. 20, 1874; 1870 United States Federal Census, San Francisco, Ward 10.

2. *San Francisco Chronicle*, Oct. 20, 1874.

3. Bertha Berner, *Mrs. Leland Stanford: An Intimate Account* (Palo Alto, CA: Stanford University Press, 1935), 15.

4. Listing for Thomas and Flora Stump, 1870 Federal Census, West Dalles Precinct, Wasco, Oregon; "Awful Calamity," *Alta California*, Feb. 20, 1856 (Thomas Stump in a steamboat accident); 1860 Federal Census, Sacramento, CA, Ward 2; U.S. IRS Tax Assessment Lists, District 4, Sacramento, CA, Annual and Special

Lists (1863); Norman E. Tutorow, *The Governor: The Life and Legacy of Leland Stanford, a California Colossus*, vol. 1 (Spokane, WA: Arthur H. Clark, 2004), 468–69; detail on Lucius Stone saddlery from "Among the Convicts," *San Francisco Chronicle*, June 22, 1873.

5. Schulz & Fischer, invoice, for "Finishing 2 Gold Spikes," May 4, 1869, LSP.

6. George Thomas Clark, *Leland Stanford, War Governor of California, Railroad Builder and Founder of Stanford University* (Palo Alto, CA: Stanford University Press, 1931); Theodore H. Hittell, *History of California*, vol. 4 (San Francisco: N. J. Stone, 1898); Richard Rayner, *The Associates: Four Capitalists Who Created California* (New York: Norton, 2008); Tutorow, *The Governor*; Central Pacific Railroad Company and Gerrit L. Lansing, *Relations Between the Central Pacific Railroad Company and the United States Government: Summary of Facts*, pamphlet (San Francisco: H. S. Crocker, 1889); Robert S. Graham, *Central Pacific Railroad Company: Facts Regarding Its Past and Present Management, by a Stockholder and Former Employee*, pamphlet (San Francisco, 1889).

7. "Mystery of the 'Last Spike' Finally Solved," *New York Times*, Nov. 27, 1910.

8. Hendricks, *Eadweard Muybridge*, 28.

9. Philip Brookman et al., *Helios: Eadweard Muybridge in a Time of Change* (Göttingen, Germany: Steidl / Washington, DC: Corcoran Gallery of Art, 2010), 52–53; Marta Braun, *Eadweard Muybridge* (London: Reaktion Books, 2010), 58–60.

10. San Francisco *Morning Call*, July 18, 1871. Rev. H. A. Sawtelle: San Francisco *Daily Evening Bulletin*, Nov. 10, 1866, May 25, 1867.

11. Hendricks, *Eadweard Muybridge*, 29–30.

CHAPTER 7: OCCIDENT

1. "Stanford the Railroad King's Party, Event of the Season," *San Francisco Call*, Feb. 7, 1872.

2. Leland Stanford to A. P. Stanford, Oct. 11, 1844, Special Collections, Stanford University Libraries.

3. "Notable equine purchase": George Thomas Clark, *Leland Stanford, War Governor of California, Railroad Builder and Founder of Stanford University* (Palo Alto, CA: Stanford University Press, 1931), 342–43; and Norman E. Tutorow, *The Governor: The Life and Legacy of Leland Stanford, a California Colossus*, vol. 1 (Spokane, WA: Arthur H. Clark, 2004), 438 ff.; "I bought a little horse": Stanford in an interview, cited in Anita Mozley, introduction to *Eadweard Muybridge: The Stanford Years, 1872-1882* (Palo Alto, CA: Stanford University Press, 1973), 8.

4. "Occident's Pedigree," *San Francisco Chronicle*, Oct. 18, 1872; and Joseph Cairn Simpson, "Horses of California," *Sunset* magazine, Nov. 1900, 86–97.

5. Peter E. Palmquist and Thomas R. Kailbourn, *Pioneer Photographers of the Far West: A Biographical Dictionary, 1840–1865* (Palo Alto, CA: Stanford University Press, 2000), 415–17.

6. "Muybridge vs. Stanford," *New York Sun*, Jan. 29, 1883.

7. Accounts of these first photographs of Stanford's horses by Edward Muybridge include "Photograph Studies: Quick Work," *Alta California*, April 7, 1873. Muybridge wrote a four-thousand-word account of his horse pictures—headlined, "Leland Stanford's Gift to Art and to Science, Mr. Muybridge's Inventions of Instant Photography," it was unsigned—and published it in the *San Francisco Examiner* on Feb. 6, 1881. (In 1972, art historian Anita Mozley identified the essay as Muybridge's own and reprinted it in Mozley, *Eadweard Muybridge: The Stanford Years, 1872–1882*, 199–223. Muybridge wrote another account twenty-five years after the events, published in the introduction to his 1899 book *Animals in Motion* (repr., London: Chapman & Hall, 1925).

8. Newspapers ran stories about the scene ten months later, probably after Muybridge brought his pictures to editors to show them off. The first item appeared in the *Alta California*, April 7, 1873.

9. Cited in Phillip Prodger and Tom Gunning, *Time Stands Still: Muybridge and the Instantaneous Photography Movement* (New York: Oxford University Press, 2003), 140–42.

10. *New York Times*, May 2, 1873; *Atlanta Constitution*, May 8, 1873; Philip Brookman et al., *Helios: Eadweard Muybridge in a Time of Change*, 106 (fn 134).

11. John Cameron, "Occident, the California Wonder," lithograph (Currier & Ives, 1873); Thomas Kirby van Zandt, *Abe Edgington with Sulky and Driver Budd Doble*, painting (1876), Iris & B. Gerald Cantor Center for Visual Arts, Stanford University.

CHAPTER 8: HARRY LARKYNS

1. "Financial Genius," *San Francisco Chronicle*, Mar. 14, 1873.

2. Passenger Lists of Vessels Arriving at New York, New York, 1820–97, Records of the U.S. Customs Service, Record Group 36; National Archives, Washington, DC.

3. Robert Haas, *Muybridge: Man in Motion* (Berkeley: University of California Press, 1976), 43; Muybridge, *Catalogue of Photographic Views Illustrating the Yosemite, Mammoth Trees, Geyser Springs, and Other Remarkable and Interesting Scenery of the Far West* (San Francisco: Bradley & Rulofson, 1873).

4. Helen Hunt Jackson, "Bits of Travel," *The Independent* (New York), Aug. 29, 1872.

5. "Photograph Studies: Eight Hundred Views of Yosemite Valley and the Big Trees," *Alta California*, April 7, 1873.

6. "The Fatal Amour," *San Francisco Chronicle*, Dec. 21, 1874.

7. "Brief Mention," *San Francisco Evening Bulletin*, May 11, 1874, June 4, 1874.

8. Rebecca Solnit, *River of Shadows: Eadweard Muybridge and the Technological Wild West* (New York: Viking, 2003), 103–20; Gordon Hendricks, *Eadweard Muybridge: The Father of the Motion Picture* (New York: Grossman Publishers, 1975), 47–49; Peter Palmquist, "Imagemakers of the Modoc War: Louis Heller and Eadweard Muybridge," *Journal of California Anthropology* 4, no 2 (1977): 206–41.

9. *Harper's Weekly*, June 21, 1873.

10. *Yreka Journal*, June 11, 1873, quoted by Palmquist, 208.

11. "The Fatal Amour," *San Francisco Chronicle*, Dec. 21, 1874.

CHAPTER 9: THE OCTOPUS

1. *Crofutt's Western World* (November 1871), clipping, Stanford Scrapbooks, vol. 1, Special Collections, Stanford University.

2. *Annual Report of the Board of Directors of the Central Pacific Railroad Co.* [1873] (San Francisco: H. S. Crocker, 1874), 21.

3. Quoted in George Thomas Clark, *Leland Stanford, War Governor of California, Railroad Builder and Founder of Stanford University* (Palo Alto, CA: Stanford University Press, 1931), 310.

4. Richard White, "Information, Markets, and Corruption: Transcontinental Railroads in the Gilded Age," *Journal of American History* 90, no. 1 (June 2003): 19–43.

5. Richard White, *Railroaded: The Transcontinentals and the Making of Modern America* (New York: Norton, 2011), 64–67, 83–90.

6. Leland Stanford to Charles Crocker, Jan. 15, 1869, Stanford papers, Special Collections, Stanford University Libraries.

7. Collis Huntington to Mark Hopkins, Dec. 23, 1872, Hopkins correspondence, Timothy Hopkins Transportation Collection, 1816–1942, Special Collections, Stanford University Libraries.

8. Richard Rayner, *The Associates: Four Capitalists Who Created California* (New York: Norton, 2008), 160–62.

9. *The California King: His Conquests, Crimes, Confederates, Counselors, Courtiers and Vassals: Stanford's Post-Prandial New-Year's Day Soliloquy*, pamphlet (San Francisco: San Francisco News Company, January 1876).

10. Alfred A. Cohen, *The Central Pacific Railroad Company vs. Alfred A. Cohen* and *The Central Pacific Railroad Company vs. Alfred A. Cohen: Argument of Defendant on Motion of Plaintiff to Strike Out Portions of Defendant's Answer*, pamphlets (San Francisco, 1876); "Cohen's Camera," *San Francisco Chronicle*, Oct. 11, 1876; White, *Railroaded*, 179–84.

11. Norman E. Tutorow, *The Governor: The Life and Legacy of Leland Stanford, a California Colossus*, vol. 1 (Spokane, WA: Arthur H. Clark, 2004), 361–68; Archibald Treat, "The Stanfords and Their Golden Key," typescript (1937), Stanford Family Collection, Special Collections, Stanford University.

12. Item on purchase of land at 901 California Street ("Brief Mention"), *San Francisco Daily Bulletin*, Jan. 8, 1874; Diana Strazdes, "The Millionaire's Palace: Leland Stanford's Commission for Pottier & Stymus in San Francisco," *Winterthur Portfolio* 36, no. 4 (2001): 213–43.

13. "Famous Spite Fence Has Outlived Its Purpose," *San Francisco Chronicle*, Nov. 1, 1902; "'Spite Fence' Now Useless," *New York Times*, Jan. 20, 1904.

14. The story of an unnamed businessman's dinner with Stanford appears in Oscar Lewis, *The Big Four: The Story of Huntington, Stanford, Hopkins, and Crocker, and of the Building of the Central Pacific* (New York: A. A. Knopf, 1938), 158–59.

CHAPTER 10: LITTLE HARRY

1. Flora Muybridge to Susan Smith, July 11, 1874, quoted in Robert Haas, *Muybridge: Man in Motion* (Berkeley: University of California Press, 1976), 66.

2. Harry Larkyns, death notices, *San Francisco Evening Bulletin*, Oct. 20, 1874; "Major Harry Larkyns," *San Francisco Examiner*, Oct. 19, 1874.

3. "John Wilson, 1829–85," biographical entry, http://www.circushistory.org /Clipper/Clipper1860s.htm, July 9, 2012.

4. Harry Larkyns to Susan Smith, n.d. [July 1874], in "The Muybridge Trial," *San Francisco Call*, Feb. 5, 1875.

5. Harry Larkyns to L——, Aug. 29, 1874: quoted in "A Startling Tragedy," *San Francisco Chronicle*, Oct. 19, 1874.

6. "Major Larkins' Fate," *San Francisco Chronicle*, Oct. 20, 1874; "The Fatal Amour," *San Francisco Chronicle*, Dec. 21, 1874; "The Trial of Muybridge," *San Francisco Evening Bulletin*, Feb. 5, 1875.

7. "The Trial of Muybridge," *San Francisco Chronicle*, Dec. 21, 1874.

8. "The Depth of Infamy," *San Francisco Examiner*, Oct. 20, 1874.

9. "Harry Larkyns," *San Francisco Chronicle*, Oct. 19, 1874.

10. "Examples of Infamy," *San Francisco Evening Bulletin*, Oct. 20, 1874.

11. "The Ellis-Darcy Troubles," *San Francisco Examiner*, Oct. 21, 1874.

12. "Contempt of the Dead," *San Francisco Evening Bulletin*, Oct. 22, 1874.

13. Henry Edwards, *A Mingled Yarn: Sketches on Various Subjects* (New York: G. P. Putnam's, 1883), 151–53; "Major Larkyns's Funeral," *San Francisco Examiner*, Oct. 20, 1874.

14. "Muybridge in Jail," *San Francisco Evening Bulletin*, Oct. 21, 1874; "The Fatal Amour," *San Francisco Chronicle*, Dec. 21, 1874.

15. *Alta California*, Nov. 1, 1874.

16. Janet Leigh to H. Cross, Oct. 8, 1931, MC.

17. Stanford solicited a pardon for railroad worker Timothy Lynch, serving time at San Quentin for assault: Leland Stanford to Governor George C. Perkins, Sacramento, CA, Sept. 27, 1882, Leland Stanford Correspondence & Papers, C-B 644, Bancroft Library, University of California, Berkeley.

CHAPTER 11: KING EADWEARD

1. Maybanke Anderson, *Maybanke, a Woman's Voice: The Collected Works of Maybanke Selfe-Wolstenholme-Anderson, 1845–1927*, ed. Beverley Kingston and Jan Roberts (Avalon, New South Wales, Australia: Ruskin Rowe Press, 2001), 15–31.

2. Census Returns of England and Wales, Kingston, Surrey, 1851 and 1861, National Archives.

3. Anderson, *Maybanke*, 17.

4. Charles Creighton, *A History of Epidemics in Britain*, vol. 2 (Cambridge, UK: Cambridge University Press, 1894), 203.

5. Deaths Registered in October–December 1847, Kingston District, Surrey, England and Wales Civil Registration Indexes, General Register Office; "Irish fever," see Creighton, *Epidemics in England*, 205–11.

6. Registrar-general of Shipping and Seamen, Cardiff, Wales, to Robert Haas, Los Angeles, Apr. 18, 1958, Robert Haas papers, Kingston Museum and Heritage Service. (Muybridge biographer Robert Haas found this evidence of Muggeridge apprentice work in the merchant marine.)

7. *Post-Office London Directory* for 1813, 1823, 1830, 1836, and 1848; *Perry's Bankrupt and Insolvent Gazette* (London, 1835) (lists Muggeridge stationers going out of business); *Hodson's Booksellers, Publishers and Stationers' Directory* (London: W. H. Hodson, 1855), 47, 90; *British Library General Catalogue of Printed Books to 1975*, 360 vols. (London: Clive Bingley, 1979–88); "The London Book Trades 1775–1800: A Topographical Guide," Exeter Working Papers in British Book Trade History website, Jan. 30, 2007, http://bookhistory.blogspot.com/.

8. Anderson, *Maybanke*, 25.

9. Passenger Lists of Vessels Arriving at New York, New York, 1820–97, Records of the U.S. Customs Service, Record Group 36, National Archives, Washington, DC.

CHAPTER 12: MARITAL RIGHTS

1. Oscar T. Shuck, *History of the Bench and Bar of California* (Los Angeles, 1901), 593–94; C. A. Menefee, *Historical and Descriptive Sketch Book of Napa, Sonoma, Lake and Mendocino* (Napa, CA: Reporter Publishing House, 1879), 349–50; Theodore R. Copeland, "Men of the Day," *Californian Illustrated Magazine*, Jan. 1894, xviii–xix.

2. "The Calistoga Tragedy," *San Francisco Chronicle*, Oct. 21, 1874.

3. "The Fatal Amour," *San Francisco Chronicle*, Dec. 21, 1874.

4. W. F. Wallace, *History of Napa County* (Oakland, CA: 1901), 84–87; *History of Napa and Lake Counties, California* (San Francisco: Slocum, Bowen, 1881), 80–84.

5. C. A. Menefee, *Historical and Descriptive Sketch Book of Napa, Sonoma, Lake and Mendocino Counties* (Napa City: Reporter Publishing House, 1879), 349–50.

6. Muybridge trial: "The Larkyns-Muybridge Tragedy," *San Francisco Evening Bulletin*, Feb. 3, 1875; "The Muybridge Trial," *San Francisco Chronicle*, Feb. 4, 1875; "Muybridge—Trial of the Man Who Shot Harry Larkyns," *Daily Morning Call*, Feb. 4, 1875; "The Muybridge Case," *Alta California*, Feb. 4, 1875.

CHAPTER 13: THE GROCER

1. Josiah Stanford, "Dictation of Josiah Stanford" (1889), Hubert Howe Bancroft Collection, Bancroft Library, University of California, Berkeley (in the late 1800s, some prominent Californians gave oral histories to publisher Hubert Bancroft); George Thomas Clark, *Leland Stanford, War Governor of California, Railroad Builder and Founder of Stanford University* (Palo Alto, CA: Stanford University Press, 1931), chap. 1; Norman E. Tutorow, *The Governor: The Life and Legacy of Leland Stanford, a California Colossus*, vol. 1 (Spokane, WA: Arthur H. Clark, 2004), chap. 1; "In the Matter of the Estate of Leland Stanford, deceased," No. 13,690, Dept. 9 [1899], Superior Court, San Francisco County, LSP.

2. Leland Stanford to Thomas Stanford, Jan. 5, 1850, LSP.

3. Leland Stanford to Josiah Stanford, May 21, 1841, LSP.

4. Richard Eddy, *Universalism in America: A History*, vol. 2 (Boston: Universalist Publishing House, 1886), 417ff.

5. Leland Stanford to Josiah Stanford, Jan. 7, 1842, LSP.

6. Leland Stanford to Charles Stanford, Jan. 25, 1844, and Leland Stanford to A. P. Stanford, Feb. 13, 1844, LSP.

7. W. S. Smyth, *First Fifty Years of Cazenovia Seminary, 1825–75* (New York: Nelson & Phillips, 1877), 13–26, 115–25, 134–39; John W. Barber and Henry Howe, *Historical Collections of the State of New York* (New York: S. Tuttle, 1842), 255–56; *A Gazetteer of the State of New-York* (Albany: J. Disturnell, 1842), 109.

8. Leland Stanford to Charles Stanford, Mar. 23, 1844, and Leland Stanford to A. P. Stanford, Feb. 13, 1844, LSP.

9. "Striving after something higher": Leland Stanford to Charles Stanford, Mar. 23, 1844, and Leland Stanford to Dewitt Stanford, Jan. 25, 1845, LSP.

10. Leland Stanford to A. P. Stanford, Oct. 11, 1844, LSP.

11. Leland Stanford to Josiah Stanford, May 31, 1844.

12. Clark, *Leland Stanford*, 39.

13. Clark, 35–43; Tutorow, *The Governor*, 9–15.

14. Leland Stanford to Mr. and Mrs. Stanford, Apr. 1, 1852, LSP.

15. Stanford, "Dictation of Josiah Stanford."

16. Tutorow, *The Governor*, 45–46.

17. *Alta California*, Mar. 16, 1853.

18. Tutorow, *The Governor*, 53ff.

19. Leland Stanford to Mr. and Mrs. Josiah Stanford, May 4, 1856, LSP.

20. Philip J. Ethington, *The Public City: The Political Construction of Urban Life in San Francisco, 1850–1900* (New York: Cambridge University Press, 1994), chaps. 1 and 2.

21. *Auburn [CA] Placer Herald*, July 30, 1859, cited in Tutorow, *The Governor*, 105.

22. Leland Stanford, quoted in Tutorow, *The Governor*, 98.

23. Leland Stanford in the *Sacramento Union*, June 8, 1859, cited in Tutorow, *The Governor*, 101–2.

CHAPTER 14: THE IMMIGRANT

1. Maybanke Anderson, *Maybanke, a Woman's Voice: The Collected Works of Maybanke Selfe-Wolstenholme-Anderson, 1845–1927*, ed. Beverley Kingston and Jan Roberts (Avalon, New South Wales, Australia: Ruskin Rowe Press, 2001), 25.

2. *Trow's New York City Directory*, comp. by H. Wilson (New York: John F. Trow, 1856), 497.

3. Database of American Libraries before 1876, the Davies Project at Princeton University, http://www.princeton.edu/~davpro/databases/index.html, accessed Nov. 25, 2011.

4. *Doggett's New-York City Directory 1848–49* (New York: John Doggett, 1849), 60; Beaumont Newhall, *The Daguerreotype in America*, 3rd rev. ed. (New York:

Dover Publications, 1976), 57; Mary Panzer et al., *Mathew Brady and the Image of History* (Washington, DC: Smithsonian Institution Press for the National Portrait Gallery, 1997), xvff.

5. *The Knickerbocker*, Aug. 1850, 175.

6. *The Knickerbocker*, June 1850, 546.

7. *Alta California*, Oct. 1, 1853, p. 1.

8. *Sacramento Union*, Feb. 5, 1875, quoted in Rebecca Solnit, *River of Shadows: Eadweard Muybridge and the Technological Wild West* (New York: Viking, 2003), 28; Robert Haas, *Muybridge: Man in Motion* (Berkeley: University of California Press, 1976), 7.

9. Advertisement, *San Francisco Daily Evening Bulletin*, Apr. 28, 1856.

10. Philip J. Ethington, *The Public City: The Political Construction of Urban Life in San Francisco, 1850–1900* (New York: Cambridge University Press, 1994), Introduction, Chapter 1.

11. Gunther Paul Barth, *Bitter Strength: A History of the Chinese in the United States, 1850–1870* (Cambridge, MA: Harvard University Press, 1964), Chapters 3–4.

12. "San Francisco Gold Rush Chronology 1855–56," *Virtual Museum of City of San Francisco*, http://www.sfmuseum.org/hist/chron4.html, accessed Mar. 26, 2010; according to the U.S. Census Bureau's 2011 *Statistical Abstract of the United States*, there were 5.8 homicides per 100,000 in California in 2008.

13. Advertisement, *Daily Evening Bulletin*, July 28, 1859.

14. *San Francisco Bulletin*, Aug. 25 and 26, Sept. 1 and 25, Oct. 6, 13, 14, and 30, 1856.

15. E. Muygridge, application for citizenship, Nov. 7, 1856, Index to Declarations of Intention for Citizenship, 1851–1906, Selected Indexes to Naturalization Records of the U.S. Circuit and District Courts, Northern District of California, 1852–1928, Series T1220, Record Group 21: Records of District Courts of the United States, 1685–2004, National Archives, Washington, DC.

16. Gordon Hendricks, *Eadweard Muybridge: The Father of the Motion Picture* (New York: Grossman Publishers, 1975), 8.

17. H. Cross and F. J. Owen, "Eadweard Muybridge: Information Abstracted from Muybridge Files," memorandum, 1972, MC. The brothers' name change: "List of Pony Express Letters," including one to "T.S. Muygridge," *San Francisco Bulletin*, June 26, 1861; death notice of "George Muygridge," *Sacramento Bee*, Apr. 23, 1859.

18. "Brunel's mammoth ship . . . the *Great Eastern*," pamphlet (San Francisco: E. J. Muygridge, 1857), Bancroft Library, University of California, Berkeley.

19. *San Francisco Bulletin*, Dec. 16, 18, and 22, 1857. 163 Clay Street: Handbill, "E. J. Muygridge . . . To Gentlemen Furnishing Libraries" (1858), Eadweard Muybridge materials, California Historical Society, San Francisco; Hendricks, *Eadweard Muybridge*, 8.

20. Advertisement, "a large case of splendid books," *San Francisco Bulletin*, Sept. 11, 1857; Watkins photos: *Alta California*, Dec. 13, 1858.

21. "First Report of the Mercantile Library Association of San Francisco" (1854),

Hunt's Merchants' Magazine and Commercial Review 33, no. 3 (Sept. 1855), 317–23; *Catalogue of the San Francisco Mercantile Library* (San Francisco: Daily Evening News, 1854); Solnit, *River of Shadows*, 261.

22. *Sacramento Bee*, Apr. 23, 1859 (he died Dec. 13, 1858, and the death notice appeared four months later).

23. Advertisements, *San Francisco Bulletin*, July 28, 1859, Dec. 30, 1859, May 15, 1860; Hendricks, *Eadweard Muybridge*, 8–10.

24. *San Francisco Bulletin*, July 2, 1860; for the Butterfield Mail murders, see *San Francisco Bulletin*, July 23, 1960.

25. *San Francisco Bulletin*, Aug. 7, 1860; for Muybridge's later account of the accident, see "The Muybridge Trial," *Napa Daily Register*, Feb. 5, 1875, and the *San Francisco Chronicle*, Feb. 6, 1875.

26. Hendricks, *Eadweard Muybridge*, 12–13.

CHAPTER 15: THE TRIAL

1. "The Larkyns-Muybridge Tragedy," *San Francisco Evening Bulletin*, Feb. 4, 1875; "The Muybridge Trial," *San Francisco Chronicle*, Feb. 5, 1875; "The Muybridge Trial," *Daily Morning Call*, Feb. 5, 1875.

2. *Arizona Miner*, Oct. 23, 1874; *Indianapolis Sentinel*, Oct. 28, 1874; *New York Herald*, Nov. 1, 1874; Sunday *Times* (Chicago), Nov. 1, 1874; *Baltimore Sun*, Nov. 7, 1874; *Philadelphia North American*, Dec. 10, 1874; *Daily Critic* (Washington, DC), Dec. 24, 1874; *Owyhee Avalanche* (Silver City, Idaho), Jan. 15, 1875.

3. Eadweard Muybridge Scrapbook, Kingston Museum and Heritage Service, Kingston, UK.

4. *Burlington Weekly Hawk-Eye* (Arlington, IA), Jan. 28, 1875.

5. "The Trial of Muybridge," *San Francisco Evening Bulletin*, Feb. 5, 1875 and Feb. 6, 1875; "The Muybridge Trial," *San Francisco Chronicle*, Feb. 6, 1875; "The Higher Law," *San Francisco Chronicle*, Feb. 7, 1875; "Muybridge Cleared," *San Francisco Call*, Feb. 7, 1875.

6. "Not Guilty," *Napa Daily Register*, Feb. 6, 1875.

7. *A Memorial and Biographical History of Northern California* (Chicago: Lewis Publishing Company, 1891), 290–91.

8. "The Higher Law," *San Francisco Chronicle*, Feb. 7, 1875; "Muybridge Cleared," *San Francisco Daily Morning Call*, Feb. 7, 1875; "The Trial of Muybridge," *San Francisco Evening Bulletin*, Feb. 6, 1875.

CHAPTER 16: THE SPECULATOR

1. "Improvements in Machinery or Apparatus for Washing Clothes and Other Textile Articles," patent no. 1914, Aug. 1, 1861, Muybridge papers, Kingston Museum and Heritage Service; *Chronological Index of Patents Applied for and Patents Granted for the Year 1861* (London: Eyre & Spottiswoode, 1862), 126.

2. "An improved method of an apparatus for plate printing" (Sept. 28, 1860), patent no. 2352, *Alphabetical Index of Patentees and Applications for Patents* (Lon-

don: Eyre & Spottiswoode, 1861), 130, cited by Stephen Herbert, *The Compleat Eadweard Muybridge*, http://www.stephenherbert.co.uk/MuybridgePatents.htm, accessed December 21, 2011.

3. B. Zorina Khan, "An Economic History of Patent Institutions," March 16, 2008, *EH.Net Encyclopedia*, Economic History Association website, http://eh.net /encyclopedia/article/khan.patents, accessed Dec. 21, 2011.

4. *Annual Report of the Commissioner of Patents for 1861*, 37th Congress, 2nd Session, U.S. House of Representatives.

5. Muygridge retrieved his patent on Jan. 27, 1862, and it was filed Jan. 31, 1862, per Stephen Herbert, webmaster, *The Compleat Eadweard Muybridge*, http://www .stephenherbert.co.uk/MuybridgePatents.htm, accessed Dec. 21, 2011.

6. *Official Catalogue of the Industrial Department* (London: Truscott, Son, & Simmons, 1862), 82 (plate printing), 33 (washing machine).

7. Muybridge to Henry Selfe, Aug. 17, 1861, in Robert Haas, *Muybridge: Man in Motion* (Berkeley: University of California Press, 1976), 10.

8. *Alta California*, Dec. 3, 1862.

9. Léopold Ernest Mayer and Pierre-Louis Pierson, *La photographie considérée comme art et comme industrie: histoire de sa découverte, ses progrès, ses applications, son avenir* (Paris: Hachette, 1862).

10. "Elevating Photography to the Condition of Art," caricature by Honoré Daumier, published in *Le Boulevard*, May 25, 1862.

11. Subject-matter index of patents for inventions (*brevets d'invention*) granted in France from 1791 to 1876 inclusive. Comp. & trans., U.S. Patent Office (Washington, DC: Government Printing Office, 1883), 889–90. Also, Loi du 5 Mai 1844, *Sur Les Brevets d'Invention*. Muygridge's French patent: *Table Décennale du Bulletin des Lois, 1854–1863* (Paris: Ministry of Justice and Culture, 1865), Appendix, 645.

12. Frederick Boas, *Modern English Biography*, vol. 2 (Truro, UK: Netherland and Worth, 1897), 1018; *Saturday Review*, Aug. 7, 1858, p. 143, and Dec. 15, 1855, p. 124 (about the Bank of London).

13. E. C. G. Muggeridge to Robert Haas, June 16, 1968, Robert Haas Papers, Kingston Museum and Heritage Service.

14. Among the richest estates in probate during the 1860s—those that left more than £500,000 to heirs—more than half belonged to bankers. W. D. Rubinstein, *Men of Property: The Very Wealthy in Britain Since the Industrial Revolution* (London: Croom Helm, 1981).

15. "What happened to the money?" blog posting, Dec. 1, 2007, Stephen Herbert website, *The Compleat Eadweard Muybridge*, http://www.stephenherbert.co.uk /muy%20blog.htm.

16. *The London Review*, Nov. 25, 1865, invitation to investors.

17. Stephen Herbert, *Muy Blog*, "Edwd. J. Muybridge—Venture Capitalist?" blog posting, Apr. 21, 2009, http://ejmuybridge.wordpress.com/.

18. *Manchester Guardian*, June 24, 1865; *London Gazette*, July 10, 1866.

CHAPTER 17: VERDICTS

1. "Mrs. Muybridge's Divorce Suit," *San Francisco Chronicle*, Jan. 10, 1875.

2. "Flora Muybridge Again," *San Francisco Chronicle*, Apr. 1, 1875.

3. *San Francisco Daily Examiner*, May 1, 1875.

4. Richard White, *Railroaded: The Transcontinentals and the Making of Modern America* (New York: Norton, 2011), 166.

5. *San Francisco Evening Bulletin*, July 19, 1875; *San Francisco Daily Examiner*, July 19, 1875.

6. Robert Haas, *Muybridge: Man in Motion* (Berkeley: University of California Press, 1976), 79–82.

7. Philip Brookman et al., *Helios: Eadweard Muybridge in a Time of Change* (Göttingen, Germany: Steidl / Washington, DC: Corcoran Gallery of Art, 2010), 70, fn.

CHAPTER 18: THE HORSE LOVERS

1. *San Francisco Chronicle*, May 19, 1875.

2. Bertha Berner, *Mrs. Leland Stanford: An Intimate Account* (Palo Alto, CA: Stanford University Press, 1935), 18–20.

3. Stanford's secretary Frank Shay, cited in Robert Haas, "Eadweard Muybridge, 1830–1904," in Anita Ventura Mozley, *Eadweard Muybridge: The Stanford Years, 1872–1882* (Palo Alto, CA: Stanford University Press, 1973), 29.

4. Reporter Olive Logan sent a dispatch to the *Philadephia Times* in 1882 after seeing Muybridge that year in London. Cited by Mozley in *Eadweard Muybridge: The Stanford Years*, 9.

5. "Judge Thomas Stoney's Remarks on the Life and Death of William Wirt Pendegast," Napa County Bar Association memorial service, ca. March 1876 (transcript, 5 pp.), in Janet Leigh to H. Cross, Oct. 8, 1931, Robert Haas papers, Kingston Museum and Heritage Service (enclosure in a personal letter).

6. Edward Muybridge to Mrs. W. W. Pendegast, May 23, 1876, Walter Miles Research Concerning Eadweard Muybridge, 1928–32, Special Collections, Stanford University Libraries.

7. Berner, *Mrs. Leland Stanford*, 20.

8. Gunther W. Nagel and Jane Lathrop Stanford, *Jane Stanford, Her Life and Letters* (Palo Alto: Stanford Alumni Association, 1975), 15; Norman E. Tutorow, *The Governor: The Life and Legacy of Leland Stanford, a California Colossus*, vol. 1 (Spokane, WA: Arthur H. Clark, 2004), 402–6.

9. Tutorow, *The Governor*, 427–50.

10. "List of employees of Palo Alto Department and supposed amount of salaries for same during the month of September," 1878, LSP.

11. Collis Huntington to Charles Crocker, 1871, quoted in Richard White, *Railroaded: The Transcontinentals and the Making of Modern America* (New York: Norton, 2011), 99.

12. Tutorow, *The Governor*, 442–44.

13. Archibald Treat, "The Stanfords and Their Golden Key," typescript, 1937, Stanford Family Collection, Special Collections, Stanford University, 7–8.

14. Leland Stanford to Robert Bonner, Feb. 1, 1890, LSP.

15. Philip Brookman et al., *Helios: Eadweard Muybridge in a Time of Change* (Göttingen, Germany: Steidl / Washington, DC: Corcoran Gallery of Art, 2010), 74–76.

16. Edward Muybridge, letter to the editor, *La Nature* (Paris), Feb. 17, 1879, cited in Laurent Mannoni, *The Great Art of Light and Shadow: Archaeology of the Cinema*, trans. Richard Crangle (Exeter, UK: University of Exeter Press, 2000), 305.

17. "The Paces of the Horse," *Popular Science*, Dec. 4, 1874.

18. Edward Muybridge to Alfred Poett, May 12, 1877, cited in Brookman et al., *Helios*, 78.

19. Phillip Prodger, *Time Stands Still: Muybridge and the Instantaneous Photography Movement* (New York: Oxford, 2003), 143–47.

20. *San Francisco Bulletin*, Aug. 3, 1877.

21. Kevin Starr, *California: A History* (New York: Modern Library, 2005), 124–29.

22. Philip Foner, *The Great Labor Uprising of 1877* (New York: Pathfinder Press, 1977), 189.

23. *San Francisco Evening Bulletin*, Nov. 5, 1877.

24. Leland Stanford to Chief H. H. Ellis, handwritten note, n.d. [prob. Nov. 1877], LSP.

25. Edward Muybridge to Alfred Poett, n.d. [Sept. 1877?], private collection, London, cited in Brookman et al., *Helios*, 81.

26. Depositions of Arthur Brown and John D. Isaacs (July 18, 1883) and Frank Shay (July 23, 1883) in *Stanford v. Muybridge*, court records, Collis P. Huntington Collection, George Arents Research Library, Syracuse University.

27. *San Francisco Morning Call*, June 16, 1878, Kingston Museum scrapbook, 21.

28. Haas, "Eadweard Muybridge," 23.

29. *San Francisco Examiner*, July 14, 1878, quoted in Gordon Hendricks, *Eadweard Muybridge: The Father of the Motion Picture* (New York: Grossman Publishers, 1975), 108–9.

30. *Alta California*, Aug. 11, 1877, quoted in Hendricks, *Eadweard Muybridge*, 101. "The right forefoot," Stanford told one writer, "which moves in unison with the left hindfoot, having already been raised nearly twelve inches from the ground, as is shown by the third horizontal line, which is twelve inches above the track." See *Resources of California*, August 1878, quoted in Hendricks, *Eadweard Muybridge*, 114.

31. *Photographic News* (London), July 26, 1878, quoted in Hendricks, *Eadweard Muybridge*, 110.

32. *Scientific American*, Oct. 8, 1878, cited in Robert Haas, *Muybridge: Man in Motion* (Berkeley: University of California Press, 1976), 116.

33. Haas, "Eadweard Muybridge," 24.

34. Muybridge to Poett, Jan. 13, 1879, quoted in Brookman et al., *Helios*, 85.

35. *Janesville Gazette* (Wisconsin), Dec. 6, 1878: "Mr. Stanford has become so deeply interested in the work, that he has instructed Mr. Muybridge to purchase 12 more cameras."

36. *Philadelphia Photographer*, March 1879, quoted in Hendricks, *Eadweard Muybridge*, 113.

37. Prodger, *Time Stands Still*, 65–72.

38. Muybridge, *Animal Locomotion*, Preface (signed, "Muybridge, Menlo Park, May 15, 1881").

39. W. B. Tegetmeier, "The paces of the horse," *The Field, the Country Gentleman's Newspaper*, June 28, 1879, Kingston Museum scrapbook, p. 62.

40. Tutorow, *The Governor*, 475.

CHAPTER 19: PRESTIDIGITATOR

1. A prolific market for visual "science toys" flourished in the cities. A concise description of them appears in Charles Musser, *Emergence of Cinema: The American Screen to 1907* (New York: Scribner, 1990), 48–54; and Deac Rossell, *Living Pictures: The Origins of the Movies* (Albany: State University of New York Press, 1998), 18–24. An encyclopedic treatment appears in Hermann Hecht, *Pre-Cinema History: An Encyclopaedia and Annotated Bibliography of the Moving Image before 1896*, ed. Ann Hecht (London: Bowker, Saur / British Film Institute, 1993).

2. *San Francisco Chronicle*, May 5, 1880.

3. "The Zoogyroscope," *New York Times*, May 19, 1880.

4. "Receipt for Two Thousand Dollars received from Ariel Lathrop, on a/c of Leland Stanford," May 30, 1881, Collis P. Huntington Papers 1856–1901, cited in Stephen Herbert, "Chronology, 1881–82," *Compleat Eadweard Muybridge*, http://www.stephenherbert.co.uk/muybCOMPLEAT.htm, accessed Mar. 6, 2012.

5. Jean-Louis-Ernest Meissonier, *Leland Stanford*, oil on canvas, 1881. Iris & B. Gerald Cantor Center for Visual Arts, Stanford University.

6. Receipt, Debut & Coulon, Jewelers, Paris, Nov. 1881, LSP.

7. Transfer of Patent, Leland Stanford to Eadweard Muybrige, July 7, 1881, Eadweard Muybridge papers, Bancroft Library, University of California.

8. Edward Muybridge to Professor Étienne-Jules Marey, July 17, 1882 (photocopy), MC.

9. *Globe* (Paris), Sept. 27, 1881; *Alta California*, Nov. 16, 1881.

10. *Figaro* (Paris), Nov. 27, 1881; *London Standard*, Nov. 28, 1881; *American Register* (Paris), Dec. 3, 1881; *Scientific American Supplement*, Jan. 28, 1882, 5058–59.

11. Eadweard Muybridge to Frank Shay, Nov. 28, 1881, quoted in Anita Ventura Mozley, *Eadweard Muybridge: The Stanford Years, 1872–1882* (Palo Alto, CA: Stanford University Press, 1973), 115–16.

12. J. D. B. Stillman, *The Horse in Motion, as Shown by Instantaneous Photography* (Boston: J. R. Osgood, 1882).

13. Muybridge's talk on March 13, 1882, revised as an essay, appears in *Notices of the Proceedings of the Meetings of the Members of the Royal Institution of Great Britain* 10 (1882–84): 44–56; *Illustrated London News*, Mar. 18, 1882; *Photographic News*, Mar. 17, 1882.

14. *Philadelphia Times*, Mar. 26, 1882.

15. On May 19, the geneticist Francis Galton wrote to the Royal Society that he

was "unable to advise the Society to order Mr Muybridge's paper to be presented." Stephen Herbert, "Chronology, 1881–82," *Compleat Eadweard Muybridge*, http: //www.stephenherbert.co.uk/muybCOMPLEAT.htm, accessed Mar. 6, 2012.

16. From a draft of a ten-page letter that Muybridge wrote, and perhaps did not send, ten years after the events. Eadweard Muybridge to Leland Stanford, May 2, 1892, Eadweard Muybridge papers, Bancroft Library, University of California, Berkeley.

17. *Boston Evening Transcript*, Oct. 21, 1882, quoted in Robert Haas, *Muybridge: Man in Motion* (Berkeley: University of California Press, 1976), 137.

18. Letters between Muybridge's opponents paint him as vain and deluded. See Osgood & Co. to J. D. B. Stillman, Mar. 18, 1882; Stillman to Osgood & Co., Apr. 10, 1882; Osgood & Co. to Stillman, Apr. 18, 1882; Leland Stanford to J. D. B. Stillman, Oct. 23, 1882; Stanford to Stillman, Jan. 5, 1883. All letters in Mark Hopkins papers, 1861–78, Stanford University Libraries, Division of Special Collections.

19. J. D. B. Stillman to Alfred Cohen, July 25, 1883, quoted in Mozley, *Eadweard Muybridge: The Stanford Years*, 30.

20. "Mr. Muybridge at Harvard," *Boston Daily Advertiser*, Nov. 10, 1882; *Boston Transcript*, Oct. 21, 1882; lecture agent: Haas, *Muybridge: Man in Motion*, 142.

21. Leland Stanford to J. D. B. Stillman, Jan. 5, 1883, Mark Hopkins papers, Stanford University Libraries, Division of Special Collections.

22. Muybridge to Professor Marey, July 17, 1882, typed transcript, MC.

CHAPTER 20: MOTION, STUDY

1. Gordon Hendricks, *Eadweard Muybridge: The Father of the Motion Picture* (New York: Grossman Publishers, 1975), 152–54; Robert Haas, *Muybridge: Man in Motion* (Berkeley: University of California Press, 1976), 143–46.

2. *Philadelphia Ledger and Transcript*, Sept. 6, 1884, quoted in Sarah Gordon, "Prestige, Professionalism, and the Paradox of Eadweard Muybridge's Animal Locomotion Nudes," *Pennsylvania Magazine of History and Biography* 130, no. 1 (Jan. 2006): 79–104.

3. Thomas G. Grier to George Nitzsche, Apr. 11, 1929, Eadweard Muybridge Collection, University Archives and Records Center, University of Pennsylvania.

4. Quoted in Hendricks, *Eadweard Muybridge*, 170.

5. Edward T. Reichert to Walter Miles, n.d. 1928, Walter Miles Papers, Special Collections and University Archives, Stanford University Library.

6. George Thomas Clark, *Leland Stanford, War Governor of California, Railroad Builder and Founder of Stanford University* (Palo Alto, CA: Stanford University Press, 1931), 380–85; Bertha Berner, *Mrs. Leland Stanford: An Intimate Account* (Palo Alto, CA: Stanford University Press, 1935), 30–35.

7. Description of the studio in Philadelphia: Beaumont Newhall, "Photography and the Development of Kinetic Visualization," *Journal of the Warburg and Courtauld Institutes* 7 (1944): 40–45; Robert Haas, *Muybridge: Man in Motion* (Berkeley: University of California Press, 1976), 146–53; Gordon Hendricks, *Eadweard Muy-*

bridge: The Father of the Motion Picture (New York: Grossman Publishers, 1975), 160–73.

8. *Animal Locomotion* prospectus (p. 12), Muybridge Collection, University Archives and Records Center, University of Pennsylvania, Philadelphia.

9. *Evening Telegraph* (Philadelphia), Aug. 13, 1885.

10. Eadweard Muybridge, Laboratory Notebook no. 2 (May 2 to Aug. 4, 1885), George Eastman House Library, Rochester, NY. Muybridge kept records amounting to some two hundred pages of who, what, when, where, and how he photographed.

11. Gordon, "Prestige, Professionalism."

12. Haas, *Muybridge: Man in Motion*, 153–62; Hendricks, *Eadweard Muybridge*, 162.

13. *The Pennsylvanian* (Philadelphia), Mar. 16, 1886.

14. Erwin Faber to George Nitzsch, n.d., Muybridge Collection, University Archives and Record Center, University of Pennsylvania, Philadelphia.

15. Four years after Leland Jr. died, his parents still dealt with mediums, including Meary Stanton, in New York, to whom they sent a photograph of the boy and a request for a "physiognomical delineation of his character." Meary O. Stanton to Leland Stanford, Dec. 28, 1888, LSP.

16. Clark, *Leland Stanford*, 383–403.

17. J. B. Lippincott to William Pepper, July 23, 1888, Muybridge Collection, University Archives and Records Center, University of Pennsylvania.

18. Haas, *Muybridge: Man in Motion*, 154.

19. Clark, *Leland Stanford*, 425–50.

20. "Wonders of the Camera," *New York Times*, Mar. 5, 1888, 3.

21. Eadweard Muybridge to William Pepper, Dec. 27, 1887, photocopy, in Robert Haas Collection, Kingston Museum and Heritage Service.

22. Eadweard Muybridge to Jesse Burk, Feb. 7, 1888, Eadweard Muybridge Collection, University Archives and Records Center, University of Pennsylvania.

23. Eadweard Muybridge to Jesse Burk, July 10, 1887, Eadweard Muybridge Papers, University Archives and Records Center, University of Pennsylvania.

24. Eadweard Muybridge to Pennsylvania Academy of the Fine Arts, Feb. 3, 1883, quoted in Hendricks, *Eadweard Muybridge*, 149.

25. Eadweard Muybridge to Jesse Burk, June 22, 1888, Eadweard Muybridge Papers, University Archives and Records Center, University of Pennsylvania; Hendricks, *Eadweard Muybridge*, 152.

26. *The Nation*, Jan. 19, 1888.

CHAPTER 21: CELLULOID

1. Charles Musser, *Thomas A. Edison and His Kinetographic Motion Pictures* (New Brunswick, NJ: Rutgers University Press, 1995), 5–8.

2. *Orange Journal* (New Jersey), Mar. 3, 1888, quoted in Musser, *Thomas A. Edison*, 53.

3. Eadweard Muybridge, *Animals in Motion* (London, 1899), 15; Musser, *Thomas A. Edison*, 3–7; Gordon Hendricks, *The Edison Motion Picture Myth* (Berkeley:

University of California Press, 1961), 6–12; Paul C. Spehr, "Edison, Dickson, and the Chronophotographers: Creating an Illusion," in François Albéra, Marta Braun, and André Gaudreault, eds., *Arrêt sur image, fragmentation du temps: aux sources de la culture visuelle moderne* (Lausanne, Switzerland: Éditions Payot, 2002), 189.

4. *New York World*, June 3, 1888.

5. Edison's dealings with Muybridge appear in Hendricks, *Edison Motion Picture Myth*, 27–35.

6. Thomas Edison, Motion Picture Caveat 1 (Oct. 8, 1888), reprinted in Hendricks, *Edison Motion Picture Myth*, 158.

7. Musser, *Thomas A. Edison*, 5–10.

8. Travels of Muybridge in the U.K. detailed in Herbert, Compleat Eadweard Muybridge Chronology, *The Compleat Eadweard Muybridge*, http://www.stephen herbert.co.uk/muychron04.htm, accessed July 9, 2012; *Notices of the Proceedings at the Meetings of the Members of the Royal Institution of Great Britain*, vol. 12 (London: William Clowes & Sons, 1887–89).

9. C. H. Bothamley, "Early Stages of Kinematography," in Raymond Fielding, ed., *A Technological History of Motion Pictures and Television* (Berkeley: U.S. Press, 1967), 7.

10. Ernest Webster to Janet Leigh, Nov. 18, 1931, photocopy, Robert Haas papers, Kingston Museum and Heritage Service.

11. Quoted in Stephen Herbert, "Chronology, 1891." *Compleat Eadweard Muybridge*, http://www.stephenherbert.co.uk/muybCOMPLEAT.htm, accessed Mar. 30, 2012.

12. Muybridge to Jesse Burk, July 15, 1891, Eadweard Muybridge Collection, University Archives and Records Center, University of Pennsylvania.

13. "Notes on Current Science, Invention, and Discovery," *Leisure Hour* (UK), Aug. 1891, 711–12.

14. Jane Stanford Papers, correspondence, Stanford University, Special Collections and University Archives.

15. Robert Haas, *Muybridge: Man in Motion* (Berkeley: University of California Press, 1976), 174.

16. *Handbook of the World's Columbian Exposition* (Chicago: Rand, McNally, 1893), 216; Haas, *Muybridge: Man in Motion*, 174–77; Hendricks, *Eadweard Muybridge: The Father of the Motion Picture* (New York: Grossman Publishers, 1975), 217–19.

17. Memorial Addresses on the Life and Character of Leland Stanford (Washington, DC: Government Printing Office, 1894), 19–26.

18. Settlement of the will, dated Nov. 29, 1886, occurred only in 1899, after a court fight over federal loans to the railroad. Estate papers, LSP.

19. Deac Rossell, "Celluloid," *Encyclopedia of Early Cinema*, Richard Abel, ed. (New York: Routledge, 2005), 106–07.

20. Hendricks, *Edison Motion Picture Myth*, 27–45.

21. Musser, *Thomas A. Edison*, 9–19; Thomas A. Edison (1891a), "Kinetographic Camera" (U.S. patent application no. 403,534) and "Apparatus for Exhibiting Pho-

tographs of Moving Objects" (U.S. patent application no. 403,536), both signed July 31, 1891, and filed August 24, 1891, in Mannoni et al., *Light and Shadow*, n.p.

22. Eadweard Muybridge, preface to *The Human Figure in Motion* (London: William Cloves and Sons, 1901).

23. Thomas Edison to Eadweard Muybridge, Feb. 14, 1894, quoted by Paul C. Spehr, "Edison, Dickson, and the Chronophotographers: Creating an Illusion," in François Albéra, Marta Braun, and André Gaudreault, *Arrêt sur image, fragmentation du temps: Aux sources de la culture visuelle moderne* (Lausanne, Switzerland: Editions Payot, 2002), 212.

24. "Entretien avec Auguste Lumière," *L'Illustration* (Paris) no. 4836, Nov. 9, 1935; Vincent Pinel, *Louis Lumière: Inventeur et cinéaste* (Paris: Éditions Nathan, 1994), 15–20; Stephen Neale, *Cinema and Technology: Image, Sound, Color* (Bloomington: Indiana University Press, 1985), 43–46.

25. Musser, *Thomas A. Edison*, 20–30.

26. Robert Haas, *Muybridge: Man in Motion* (Berkeley: University of California Press, 1976), 180–85; Hendricks, *Edison Motion Picture Myth*, 220–23.

27. Eadweard Muybridge, *Animals in Motion* (London: Chapman & Hall, 1899; reprt. New York: Dover, 1957), 15; Eadweard Muybridge, *The Human Figure in Motion* (London: Chapman & Hall, 1901; reprint New York: Dover, 1955).

CHAPTER 22: THE FLOOD

1. E. W. Lightner, "Pittsburg Gave Birth to the Movie Theater Idea," *Pittsburg Dispatch*, Nov. 16, 1919.

2. André Bazin, "The Ontology of the Photographic Image," in *What Is Cinema?* vol. 1, Hugh Gray, trans. and ed. (Berkeley: University of California Press, 1967).

3. *Sacramento Bee*, Feb. 3, 1944.

BIBLIOGRAPHY

Edward Muybridge's work appears in museum exhibitions, on websites, in artworks, videos, comics, and catalogs; his life is the subject of documentaries, plays, and an opera. I've omitted the art, film, theater, and other nonprint material about Muybridge and Stanford to foreground the texts on which they all depend—books, libraries, and archives—and that I used to tell this story.

BOOKS

Abel, Richard. *Encyclopedia of Early Cinema*. New York: Routledge, 2005.

Albéra, François, Marta Braun, and André Gaudreault. *Stop Motion, Fragmentation of Time: Exploring the Roots of Modern Visual Culture*. Lausanne, Switzerland: Éditions Payot, 2002.

Altick, Richard D. *The Shows of London*. Cambridge, MA: Harvard University Press, 1978.

Ambrose, Stephen E. *Nothing Like It in the World: The Men Who Built the Transcontinental Railroad, 1863–1869*. New York: Simon & Schuster, 2000.

Anderson, Maybanke. *Maybanke, a Woman's Voice: The Collected Works of Maybanke Selfe-Wolstenholme-Anderson, 1845–1927*. Edited by Beverley Kingston and Jan Roberts. Avalon, New South Wales, Australia: Ruskin Rowe Press, 2001.

Auerbach, Jonathan. *Body Shots: Early Cinema's Incarnations*. Berkeley: University of California Press, 2007.

Badger, Reid. *The Great American Fair: The World's Columbian Exposition and American Culture*. Chicago: Nelson-Hall, 1979.

Bancroft, Hubert Howe. *History of the Life of Leland Stanford: A Character Study.* Oakland, CA: Biobooks, 1952.

Barnouw, Erik. *The Magician and the Cinema.* New York: Oxford University Press, 1981.

Barth, Gunther Paul. *Bitter Strength: A History of the Chinese in the United States, 1850–1870.* Cambridge, MA: Harvard University Press, 1964.

Barthes, Roland. *Camera Lucida: Reflections on Photography.* Translated by Richard Howard. New York: Hill and Wang, 1981.

Beebe, Lucius Morris. *The Central Pacific & the Southern Pacific Railroads.* Berkeley, CA: Howell-North, 1963.

Berglund, Barbara. *Making San Francisco American: Cultural Frontiers in the Urban West, 1846–1906.* Lawrence: University Press of Kansas, 2007.

Berner, Bertha. *Mrs. Leland Stanford: An Intimate Account.* Palo Alto, CA: Stanford University Press, 1935.

Braudy, Leo, and Marshall Cohen. *Film Theory and Criticism: Introductory Readings.* 5th ed. New York: Oxford University Press, 1999.

Braun, Marta. *Eadweard Muybridge.* London: Reaktion Books, 2010.

———. *Picturing Time: The Work of Etienne-Jules Marey (1830–1904).* Chicago: University of Chicago Press, 1992.

Brookman, Philip, Marta Braun, Andy Grundberg, Corey Keller, and Rebecca Solnit. *Helios: Eadweard Muybridge in a Time of Change.* Göttingen, Germany; Seidl / Washington, DC: Corcoran Gallery of Art, 2010.

Buckland, Gail. *First Photographs: People, Places, and Phenomena as Captured for the First Time by the Camera.* New York: Macmillan, 1980.

Burch, Noël, and Ben Brewster. *Life to Those Shadows.* Berkeley: University of California Press, 1990.

Burns, E. Bradford. *Eadweard Muybridge in Guatemala, 1875: The Photographer as Social Recorder.* Berkeley: University of California Press, 1986.

Ceram, C. W. *Archaeology of the Cinema.* New York: Harcourt, 1965.

Chanan, Michael. *The Dream That Kicks: The Prehistory and Early Years of Cinema in Britain.* London: Routledge & Kegan Paul, 1980.

Chew, William F. *Nameless Builders of the Transcontinental Railroad.* Bloomington, IN: Trafford Publishing, 2004.

Clark, George Thomas. *Leland Stanford, War Governor of California, Railroad Builder and Founder of Stanford University.* Palo Alto, CA: Stanford University Press, 1931.

Clegg, Brian. *The Man Who Stopped Time: The Illuminating Story of Eadweard Muybridge: Pioneer Photographer, Father of the Motion Picture, Murderer.* Washington, DC: Joseph Henry Press, 2007.

Coe, Brian. *The History of Movie Photography*. London: Ash & Grant, 1981.

———. *Muybridge and the Chronophotographers*. London: British Film Institute, Museum of the Moving Image, 1992.

———, and Mark Haworth-Booth. *A Guide to Early Photographic Processes*. London: Victoria and Albert Museum, 1983.

Conkling, Roscoe Platt, and Margaret B. Conkling. *The Butterfield Overland Mail, 1857–1869: Its Organization and Operation over the Southern Route to 1861; Subsequently over the Central Route to 1866; and under Wells, Fargo and Company in 1869.* Glendale, CA: A. H. Clark, 1947.

Conningham, Frederic A. *Currier & Ives Prints: An Illustrated Check List*. New York: Crown Publishers, 1949.

Cook, Olive. *Movement in Two Dimensions*. London: Hutchinson, 1963.

Crary, Jonathan. *Suspensions of Perception: Attention, Spectacle, and Modern Culture*. Cambridge, MA: MIT Press, 1999.

Cresswell, Tim, and Deborah Dixon. *Engaging Film: Geographies of Mobility and Identity*. Lanham, MD: Rowman & Littlefield, 2002.

Daggett, Stuart. *Chapters on the History of the Southern Pacific*. New York: Ronald Press, 1922.

Dagognet, François. *Etienne-Jules Marey: A Passion for the Trace*. New York: Zone Books, 1992.

Danly, Susan, and Cheryl Leibold. *Eakins and the Photograph: Works by Thomas Eakins and His Circle in the Collection of the Pennsylvania Academy of the Fine Arts*. Washington, DC: Smithsonian Institution Press, 1994.

De Lauretis, Teresa, and Stephen Heath, eds. *The Cinematic Apparatus*. London: Macmillan Press, 1980.

Deleuze, Gilles. *The Movement-Image*. Minneapolis: University of Minnesota Press, 1986.

Doane, Mary Ann. *The Emergence of Cinematic Time: Modernity, Contingency, the Archive*. Cambridge, MA: Harvard University Press, 2002.

Eadweard Muybridge of Kingston Upon Thames: An Introduction and List of Exhibits to the Exhibition at Kingston Upon Thames Museum and Heritage Center, Opened May 1984. Kingston upon Thames, 1984.

Elsaesser, Thomas, and Adam Barker. *Early Cinema: Space-Frame-Narrative*. London: BFI Publishing, 1990.

Ethington, Philip J. *The Public City: The Political Construction of Urban Life in San Francisco, 1850–1900*. Cambridge, UK: Cambridge University Press, 1994.

Fardon, G. R. *San Francisco in the 1850's: 33 Photographic Views*. New York: Dover Publications, 1977.

Fels, Thomas Weston, Therese Thau Heyman, and David Travis. *Watkins to*

Weston: 101 Years of California Photography. Santa Barbara, CA: Santa Barbara Museum of Art, 1992.

Foner, Philip Sheldon. *The Great Labor Uprising of 1877.* New York: Monad Press, 1977.

Frampton, Hollis. *Circles of Confusion: Film, Photography, Video: Texts, 1968–1980.* Rochester, NY: Visual Studies Workshop Press, 1983.

Francaviglia, Richard V. *Over the Range: A History of the Promontory Summit Route of the Pacific Railroad.* Logan: Utah State University Press, 2008.

Friedberg, Anne. *The Virtual Window: From Alberti to Microsoft.* Cambridge, MA: MIT Press, 2006.

———. *Window Shopping: Cinema and the Postmodern.* Berkeley: University of California Press, 1993.

Galloway, John Debo. *The First Transcontinental Railroad: Central Pacific, Union Pacific.* New York: Simmons-Boardman, 1950.

Gernsheim, Helmut. *The Rise of Photography, 1850–1880: The Age of Collodion.* London: Thames and Hudson, 1988.

———, and Alison Gernsheim. *The History of Photography from the Camera Obscura to the Beginning of the Modern Era.* 2d ed. New York: McGraw-Hill, 1969.

Giedion, Siegfried. *Mechanization Takes Command: A Contribution to Anonymous History.* New York: Oxford University Press, 1948.

Gmelch, Sharon Bohn. *The Tlingit Encounter with Photography.* Philadelphia: University of Pennsylvania Museum of Archaeology and Anthropology, 2008.

Griswold, Wesley S. *A Work of Giants: Building the First Transcontinental Railroad.* New York: McGraw-Hill, 1962.

Haas, Robert Bartlett. *Muybridge: Man in Motion.* Berkeley: University of California Press, 1976.

Hannavy, John. *Encyclopedia of Nineteenth-Century Photography.* New York: Routledge/Taylor & Francis Group, 2007.

Harris, David, and Eric Sandweiss. *Eadweard Muybridge and the Photographic Panorama of San Francisco, 1850–1880.* Montréal: Canadian Centre for Architecture, and Cambridge, MA: MIT Press, 1993.

Hecht, Hermann. *Pre-Cinema History: An Encyclopaedia and Annotated Bibliography of the Moving Image before 1896.* Edited by Ann Hecht. London: Bowker, Saur / British Film Institute, 1993.

Hendricks, Gordon. *Eadweard Muybridge: The Father of the Motion Picture.* New York: Grossman Publishers, 1975.

———. *The Edison Motion Picture Myth.* Berkeley: University of California Press, 1961.

————. *The Life and Work of Thomas Eakins*. New York: Grossman Publishers, 1974.

Henisch, Heinz K., and Bridget Ann Henisch. *The Painted Photograph, 1839–1914: Origins, Techniques, Aspirations*. University Park: Pennsylvania State University Press, 1996.

Herbert, Stephen, ed. *Eadweard Muybridge: The Kingston Museum Bequest*. Hastings, UK: Projection Box, 2004.

————. *A History of Early Film*. 3 vols. London: Routledge, 2000.

————. *A History of Pre-Cinema*. 3 vols. London: Routledge, 2000.

————, and Luke McKernan. *Who's Who of Victorian Cinema: A Worldwide Survey*. London: British Film Institute, 1996.

Hinton, Marion. *Eadweard Muybridge of Kingston upon Thames*. Kingston, UK: Kingston Museum, 1984.

Hively, William. *Nine Classic California Photographers*. Berkeley: Friends of the Bancroft Library, University of California, 1980.

Howard, Robert West. *The Great Iron Trail: The Story of the First Transcontinental Railroad*. New York: Putnam, 1962.

Hoyt, Edwin Palmer. *Leland Stanford: A Biography of the Innkeeper's Son Who Became Governor of California, Builder of a Great Railroad, U S. Senator, and Founder of Stanford University*. New York: Abelard-Schuman, 1967.

Issel, William, and Robert W. Cherny. *San Francisco, 1865–1932: Politics, Power, and Urban Development*. Berkeley: University of California Press, 1986.

Jackson, Helen Maria Fiske Hunt, H. H. Oscar Lewis, and Mallette Dean. *Ah-Wah-Ne Days: A Visit to the Yosemite Valley in 1872*. San Francisco: Book Club of California, 1971.

Johnson, Edwin Ferry. *Railroad to the Pacific*. Fairfield, WA: Ye Galleon Press, 1981.

Josephson, Matthew. *The Robber Barons: The Great American Capitalists, 1861–1901*. New York: Harcourt, 1934.

Keller, Corey, ed. *Brought to Light: Photography and the Invisible, 1840–1900*. San Francisco: San Francisco Museum of Modern Art / Yale University Press, 2008.

Kibbey, Mead B., and Peter E. Palmquist. *The Railroad Photographs of Alfred A. Hart, Artist*. Sacramento: California State Library Foundation, 1996.

Kirby, Lynne. *Parallel Tracks: The Railroad and Silent Cinema*. Durham, NC: Duke University Press, 1997.

Klein, Henry Oscar. *Collodion Emulsion and Its Applications to Various Photographic and Photo-Mechanical Purposes with Special Reference to Trichromatic Process Work*. London: Penrose, 1905.

Kluger, Richard. *Seizing Destiny: How America Grew from Sea to Shining Sea*. New York: Knopf, 2007.

Kracauer, Siegfried, and Thomas Y. Levin. *The Mass Ornament: Weimar Essays*. Cambridge, MA: Harvard University Press, 1995.

Kraus, George. *High Road to Promontory: Building the Central Pacific (Now the Southern Pacific) across the High Sierra*. Palo Alto, CA: American West Publishing, 1969.

Lavender, David Sievert. *The Great Persuader*. Garden City, NY: Doubleday, 1970.

Lewis, Oscar. *The Big Four: The Story of Huntington, Stanford, Hopkins, and Crocker, and of the Building of the Central Pacific*. New York: Knopf, 1938.

Liesegang, Franz Paul, and Hermann Hecht. *Dates and Sources: A Contribution to the History of the Art of Projection and to Cinematography*. London: Magic Lantern Society of Great Britain, 1986.

Lothrop, Eaton S. *A Century of Cameras from the Collection of the International Museum of Photography at George Eastman House*. Dobbs Ferry, NY: Morgan & Morgan, 1973.

MacDonnell, Kevin. *Eadweard Muybridge, the Man Who Invented the Moving Picture*. Boston: Little, Brown, 1972.

Macgowan, Kenneth. *Behind the Screen: The History and Techniques of the Motion Picture*. New York: Delacorte Press, 1965.

Manes, Stephen. *Pictures of Motion and Pictures That Move: Eadweard Muybridge and the Photography of Motion*. New York: Coward, McCann & Geoghegan, 1982.

Mannoni, Laurent. *The Great Art of Light and Shadow: Archaeology of the Cinema*. Translated by Richard Crangle. Exeter, UK: University of Exeter Press, 2000.

Marks, William Dennis, Harrison Allen, and Francis X. Dercum. *Animal Locomotion: The Muybridge Work at the University of Pennsylvania—the Method and the Result*. Philadelphia: J. B. Lippincott, 1888.

Mathews, Nancy Mowll. *Moving Pictures: American Art and Early Film, 1880–1910*. Manchester, VT: Hudson Hills Press / Williams College Museum of Art, 2005.

Mozley, Anita Ventura, Robert B. Haas, and Françoise Forster-Hahn. *Eadweard Muybridge: The Stanford Years, 1872–1882*. Rev. ed. Palo Alto, CA: Stanford University, 1973.

Mumford, Lewis. *Technics and Civilization*. New York: Harcourt, 1934.

Murray, Keith A. *The Modocs and Their War*. Norman: University of Oklahoma Press, 1985.

Musser, Charles. *The Emergence of Cinema: The American Screen to 1907 (History of the American Cinema)*. New York: Scribner, 1990.

———. *Thomas A. Edison and His Kinetographic Motion Pictures*. New Brunswick, NJ: Rutgers University Press, 1995.

Muybridge, Eadweard. *Animal Locomotion: Images from the Philadelphia Years, 1885–1985: A Selection of Collotypes from the Series Animal Locomotion, an Electro-Photographic Investigation of Consecutive Phases of Animal Movements, 1872–1885, from the Collection of the Williams College Museum of Art.* Organized and with essays by Robert J. Phelan and Thomas Weston Fels. Albany: University Art Gallery, State University of New York at Albany, 1985.

————. *Muybridge's Complete Human and Animal Locomotion: All 781 Plates from the 1887 Animal Locomotion.* New York: Dover Publications, 1979.

————. *Syllabus of a Course of Two Lectures on the Science of Animal Locomotion in Its Relation to Design in Art.* London: Royal Institution, April 1882.

Naef, Weston J., and James N. Wood. *Era of Exploration: The Rise of Landscape Photography in the American West, 1860–1885.* Buffalo, NY: Albright-Knox Art Gallery, 1975.

Nagel, Gunther W. *Jane Stanford, Her Life and Letters.* Palo Alto, CA: Stanford Alumni Association, 1975.

Neale, Stephen. *Cinema and Technology: Image, Sound, Color.* Bloomington: Indiana University Press, 1985.

Newhall, Beaumont. *The Daguerreotype in America.* 3d rev. ed. New York: Dover Publications, 1976.

————. *The History of Photography from 1839 to the Present Day.* New York: Museum of Modern Art, 1949.

Norris, Frank. *The Octopus: A Story of California.* New York: Doubleday, Page & Company, 1901.

Nygren, Edward J., and Frances Fralin. *Eadweard Muybridge: Extraordinary Motion.* Washington, DC: Corcoran Gallery of Art, 1986.

Oettermann, Stephan. *The Panorama: History of a Mass Medium.* New York: Zone Books, 1997.

Osborne, Carol Margot, Paul Venable Turner, and Anita Ventura Mozley. *Museum Builders in the West: The Stanfords as Collectors and Patrons of Art, 1870–1906.* Palo Alto, CA: Stanford University Museum of Art, Stanford University, 1986.

Painter, Gerald Leroy. *The Tie That Binds: Grenville M. Dodge and the Building of the First Transcontinental Railroad.* Northfield, VT: Norwich University Press, 1985.

Palmquist, Peter E., and Thomas R. Kailbourn. *Pioneer Photographers of the Far West: A Biographical Dictionary, 1840–1865.* Palo Alto, CA: Stanford University Press, 2000.

Panzer, Mary. *Mathew Brady and the Image of History.* Washington, DC: Smithsonian Institution Press, 1997.

Phillips, Ray. *Edison's Kinetoscope and Its Films: A History to 1896.* Contributions to the Study of Popular Culture. Westport, CT: Greenwood Press, 1997.

Prodger, Phillip, and Tom Gunning. *Time Stands Still: Muybridge and the Instantaneous Photography Movement*. New York: Iris & B. Gerald Cantor Center for Visual Arts at Stanford University / Oxford University Press, 2003.

Ramsaye, Terry. *A Million and One Night: A History of the Motion Picture*. New York: Simon and Schuster, 1964.

Rayner, Richard. *The Associates: Four Capitalists Who Created California*. New York: Norton, 2008.

Rinhart, Floyd, and Marion Rinhart. *The American Daguerreotype*. Athens: University of Georgia Press, 1981.

Robinson, David, Stephen Herbert, and Richard Crangle, eds. *Encyclopedia of the Magic Lantern*. Kirkby Malzeard, UK: Magic Lantern Society, 2001.

Robinson, John. *The Octopus: A History of the Construction, Conspiracies, Extortions, Robberies, and Villainous Acts of the Central Pacific, South Pacific of Kentucky, Union Pacific, and Other Subsidized Railroads*. New York: Arno Press, 1981. Originally published 1894 by Bancroft, San Francisco.

Rodowick, David N. *Gilles Deleuze's Time Machine: Post-Contemporary Interventions*. Durham, NC: Duke University Press, 1997.

Rosen, Philip. *Narrative, Apparatus, Ideology: A Film Theory Reader*. New York: Columbia University Press, 1986.

Rossell, Deac. *Living Pictures: The Origins of the Movies*. Cultural Studies in Cinema/Video. Albany: State University of New York Press, 1998.

Sabin, Edwin L. *Building the Pacific Railway: The Construction-Story of America's First Iron Thoroughfare between the Missouri River and California, from the Inception of the Great Idea to the Day, May 10, 1869, When the Union Pacific and the Central Pacific Joined Tracks at Promontory Point, Utah, to Form the Nation's Transcontinental*. Philadelphia, London: J. B. Lippincott Company, 1919.

Sandweiss, Martha A., ed., and the Amon Carter Museum of Western Art. *Photography in Nineteenth-Century America*. New York: H. N. Abrams, 1991.

Schimmelman, Janice Gayle. *American Photographic Patents 1840–1880: The Daguerreotype & Wet Plate Era*. Nevada City, CA: Carl Mautz Publishing, 2002.

Schivelbusch, Wolfgang. *The Railway Journey: Trains and Travel in the 19th Century*. New York: Urizen, 1979.

Shaw, Jonathan, Eadweard Muybridge, and Harold Eugene Edgerton. *Time/ Motion: Photographs by Eadweard Muybridge, Harold Edgerton, and Jonathan Shaw*. Stockport, UK: Dewi Lewis / Birmingham Library Services / Birmingham Museums and Art Gallery, 2003.

Sheldon, James L., and Jock Reynolds. *Motion and Document, Sequence and Time: Eadweard Muybridge and Contemporary American Photography*. Andover, MA: Addison Gallery of American Art, 1991.

Sobieszek, Robert A., Frederick Scott Archer, Louis Désiré Blanquart-Evrard, and Albion K. P. Trask. *The Collodion Process and the Ferrotype: Three Accounts, 1854–1872.* The Literature of Photography. New York: Arno Press, 1973.

Solnit, Rebecca. *River of Shadows: Eadweard Muybridge and the Technological Wild West.* New York: Viking, 2003.

Souriau, Paul, and Manon Souriau. *The Aesthetics of Movement.* Amherst: University of Massachusetts Press, 1983.

Stanford, Leland. *Government Loans on Real Estate: Speech of Hon. Leland Stanford, of California in the United States Senate, Dec. 19, 1890.* Washington, DC: 1890.

———. *Pacific Railroad: Speech of Hon. Leland Stanford, in the Constitutional Convention of the State of Nevada, on Wednesday, July 13th, 1864.* San Francisco: Francis, Valentine, 1865.

Stanford University, and Eadweard Muybridge. *Semi-Centennial Celebration in Commemoration of the Motion Picture Research Conducted by Leland Stanford 1878–1879: With the Assistance of Eadweard J. Muybridge, John D. Isaacs, J. D. B. Stillman,* 1929.

Starr, Kevin. *California: A History.* New York: Modern Library, 2005.

Stillman, J. D. B., and Leland Stanford. *The Horse in Motion as Shown by Instantaneous Photography: With a Study on Animal Mechanics Founded on Anatomy and the Revelations of the Camera, in Which Is Demonstrated the Theory of Quadrupedal Locomotion.* Boston: James R. Osgood, 1882.

Thomas, Alan. *The Expanding Eye: Photography and the Nineteenth-Century Mind.* London: Croom Helm, 1978.

Tissandier, Gaston. *A History and Handbook of Photography.* The Literature of Photography. New York: Arno Press, 1973. Originally published in London, 1878.

Tosi, Virgilio. *Cinema before Cinema: The Origins of Scientific Cinematography.* London: British Universities Film & Video Council, 2005.

Trachtenberg, Alan, and Eric Foner. *The Incorporation of America: Culture and Society in the Gilded Age.* American Century Series. New York: Hill and Wang, 1982.

Tutorow, Norman E. *The Early Years of Leland Stanford: New Yorker Who Built the Central Pacific Railroad.* Ithaca, NY: DeWitt Historical Society of Tompkins County, 1969.

———. *The Governor: The Life and Legacy of Leland Stanford, a California Colossus.* Vol. 1. Spokane, WA: Arthur H. Clark, 2004.

———. *Leland Stanford: Man of Many Careers.* Menlo Park, CA: Pacific Coast Publishers, 1971.

Virilio, Paul. *The Vision Machine.* Bloomington: Indiana University Press, 1994.

———. *War and Cinema: The Logistics of Perception.* London: Verso, 1989.

White, Richard. *Railroaded: The Transcontinentals and the Making of Modern America.* New York: Norton, 2011.

Williams, Linda. *Hard Core: Power, Pleasure, and the "Frenzy of the Visible."* Berkeley: University of California Press, 1989.

—————. *Viewing Positions: Ways of Seeing Film.* New Brunswick, NJ: Rutgers University Press, 1995.

INTERNET SOURCES

Bancroft Library, University of California, Berkeley. "Lone Mountain College Collection of Stereographs by Eadweard Muybridge, 1867–1880." Online Archives of California. http://www.oac.cdlib.org/findaid/ark:/13030/tf6t1nb6w7/.

Herbert, Stephen. *The Compleat Eadweard Muybridge.* http://www.stephenherbert .co.uk/muybCOMPLEAT.htm.

Kingston Museum. "The Eadweard Muybridge Bequest." Kingston upon Thames website, http://www.kingston.gov.uk/brose/leisure/museum/museum _exhibitions/muybridge.htm.

National Museum of American History. "Freeze Frame: Eadweard Muybridge's Photography of Motion." Virtual National Museum of American History. http://americanhistory.si.edu/muybridge/index.htm.

University of Pennsylvania. "Eadweard Muybridge, 1830–1904, Collection, 1870– 1981." University Archives and Records Center. http://www.archives.upenn .edu/faids/upt/upt50/muybridgee.html.

PHOTOGRAPHY BY EADWEARD MUYBRIDGE (CHRONOLOGICAL LISTING)

Catalogue of Photographic Views Illustrating the Yosemite, Mammoth Trees, Geyser Springs, and Other Remarkable and Interesting Scenery of the Far West by Muybridge. San Francisco: Bradley & Rulofson Gallery, 1873.

The Pacific Coast of Central America and Mexico: The Isthmus of Panama, Guatemala, and the Cultivation and Shipment of Coffee, 1877.

Panorama of San Francisco from California Street Hill. San Francisco: Morse's Gallery, 1877.

The Attitudes of Animals in Motion. A Series of Photographs Illustrating the Consecutive Positions Assumed by Animals Performing Various Movements: Executed at Palo Alto, California, in 1878 and 1879, 1881.

Animal Locomotion. An Electro-Photographic Investigation of Consecutive Phases of Animal Movements. 1872–1885. 781 plates, 11 vols. Philadelphia: University of Pennsylvania, 1887.

Descriptive Zoopraxography: Or the Science of Animal Locomotion Made Popular. Philadelphia: University of Pennsylvania, 1893.

Animals in Motion: An Electro-Photographic Investigation of Consecutive Phases of Muscular Actions. London: Chapman & Hall, 1899.

The Human Figure in Motion, an Electro-Photographic Investigation of Consecutive Phases of Muscular Actions. London: Chapman & Hall, 1901.

ADDITIONAL RESOURCES

While more than eighty libraries and museums in North America and Europe own photographs by Muybridge, the municipal archive of his hometown, Kingston, England, holds most extant primary sources on his life. Stanford University houses most of Leland Stanford's papers.

Bancroft Library
University of California, Berkeley
bancroft.berkeley.edu/info

Beinecke Rare Book and Manuscript Library
Yale University
library.yale.edu/beinecke/

The British Library
bl.uk

California Historical Society
californiahistoricalsociety.org

California State Library
library.ca.gov

California State Railroad Museum
csrmf.org

Cinémathèque Française
cinematheque.fr

George Eastman House
International Museum of Photography and Film
eastmanhouse.org

Kingston Museum and Heritage Service
kingston.gov.uk

Library of Congress
loc.gov

National Archives & Records Administration
archives.gov

Royal Academy of Arts
royalacademy.org.uk

Smithsonian Institution
Washington, DC 20560
americanhistory.si.edu

Society of California Pioneers
californiapioneers.org

Stanford University
Cantor Center for Visual Arts
museum.stanford.edu

Stanford University
Special Collections and University Archives
Palo Alto, CA 94305
library.stanford.edu

University of Pennsylvania
Rare Book and Manuscript Library
library.upenn.edu

University of Pennsylvania
University Archives and Records
archives.upenn.edu

Victoria and Albert Museum
vam.ac.uk

ILLUSTRATION CREDITS

Titles of illustrations are transcribed from the photographic prints or from the catalogue of the library that houses the image.

ABBREVIATIONS

E.M.: Eadweard Muybridge, Edward Muybridge, E. J. Muybridge, or Helios
BL: The Bancroft Library, University of California, Berkeley
KM: By permission of Kingston Museum & Heritage Service
LCP: Library of Congress Prints and Photographs Division, Washington, D.C.
SA: Iris & B. Gerald Cantor Center for Visual Arts at Stanford University
SU: Dept. of Special Collections and University Archives, Stanford University Libraries

iv E.M., *Athletes. Swinging Pick. Plate 110*, 1879, from *The Attitudes of Animals in Motion*, 1881. KM.

iv Alfred A. Hart, *The Last Rail Is Laid. Scene at Promontory Point, May 10, 1869*. Alfred A. Hart Photograph Collection, SU.

2 E.M., *Horses. Running. Phryne L., Plate 40*, 1879, from *The Attitudes of Animals in Motion*, 1881. Courtesy National Gallery of Art, Washington.

6 E.M., *Panorama of San Francisco from California Street Hill*, 1877. Eadweard Muybridge Photograph Collection, SU.

8 *Stanford Family Trio*, 1881, photographer unknown. Stanford Family Photographs, SU.

11 E.M., *Drawing Room (Pompeian Room)*. Eadweard Muybridge Photograph Collection, SU.

16 E.M., *"Abe Edgington," owned by Leland Stanford; driven by C. Marvin, trotting at a 2:24 gait over the Palo Alto track, 15th June 1878*, 1878. LCP.

17 Walter Keyte, *Muybridge Apparatus at Kingston Library*, ca. 1931. Walter R. Miles Research concerning Eadweard Muybridge, SU.

21 E.M., *Man on Horse*, ca. 1879. Lantern slide. Muybridge Collection. KM.

23 Lawrence & Houseworth, publisher, *South Park looking from 3rd St. east toward 2nd St.*, 1866. Roy D. Graves Pictorial Collection, 1905.17500 v.10:199—ALB. BL.

23 *Smith & Wesson Army No. 2, .32 Rimfire*. http://commons.wikimedia.org/wiki/File:Smith_%26 _Wesson_Army_No_2.JPG.

30 *Cottage at Yellow Jacket Mine*, n.d., photographer unknown.

32 Charles L. Weed (attributed), *U.S. Grant, Mariposa Grove, portrait of Edward Muybridge at base of tree*, 1872. Muybridge, Eadweard—POR 4. BL.

35 C. B. Gifford, *San Francisco. Bird's-eye view*, ca. 1864. LCP.

37 E.M., Logo for Helios Flying Studio (detail from *Grand Masonic ceremony of laying of the cornerstone of City Hall and Law Courts, 22nd February 1872*, verso), 1872. Lone Mountain College Collection of Stereographs by Eadweard Muybridge [hereafter "Lone Mountain Collection"], 1971.055:1124—STER verso. BL.

38 E.M., *North Point Dock*, ca. 1868. Lone Mountain Collection, 1971.055 v. 1:301—ALB. BL.

40 Lawrence & Houseworth albums, *Montgomery Street, San Francisco, instantaneous*, ca. 1866. Gift of Florence V. Flinn. The Society of California Pioneers.

43 E.M., *Residence of James Rogers at Watsonville, California*, ca. 1879. LCP.

46 E.M., *The Flying Studio, Photographer's Equipment in the Field*, 1867. Lone Mountain Collection, 1971.055 v.1:114—ALB. BL.

46 E.M., *Little Grizzly Fall*, 1867. Lone Mountain Collection, 1971.055:1336—STER. BL.

47 E.M., *Kahchoomah, Wild Cat Fall, 30 feet high*, 1868. SA; Elizabeth K. Raymond Fund.

48 E.M., *Charon at the Ferry*, 1868. Zelda Mackay Collection of Stereographic Views, 1905.16011—STER. BL.

49 E.M., *Sawing section of the original, 98 ft. at base*, 1868. Zelda Mackay Collection of Stereographic Views, 1905.16057—STER. BL.

49 Larry S. Pierce, *American Optical Co., Scovill Mfg. Co., props.: Philadelphia Stereoscopic Box*. http://www.piercevaubel.com/cam/images/amoptphiladelphiastereo5x8a719.jpg.

51 E.M., *Contemplation Rock, Glacier Point*, 1872. Muybridge Stereographs of Yosemite Valley, 1867–72. Courtesy, California Historical Society, FN-18893/CHS2009.176.tif.

53 *Sacramento City; K Street, looking west from Masonic Hall*, from *Stereoscopic views of Sacramento, California. 1865. Stereograph*. Robert Dennis Collection of Stereoscopic Views, Miriam and Ira D. Wallach Division of Art, Prints and Photographs, New York Public Library, Astor, Lenox, and Tilden Foundations.

54 *Theodore D. Judah*, 1848, photographer unknown. Daguerreotype. Courtesy of the California History Room, California State Library, Sacramento, California.

62 *Front view of house, Leland and Jane on stoop*, ca. 1868, Alfred P. Hart. Stanford Family Photographs, SU.

65 Henry T. Williams, *New trans-continental map of the Pacific R.R. and routes of overland travel to Colorado, Nebraska, the Black Hills, Utah, Idaho, Nevada, Montana, California and the Pacific Coast*, 1877. Library of Congress Geography and Map Division, Washington, D.C.

65 Alfred A. Hart, *East portal of summit tunnel. Western summit. Length 1,660 feet*, ca. 1866. LCP.

67 E.M., *The "Heathen Chinee" Prospecting*, 1868. Courtesy, California Historical Society, FN-04470/CHS2009.138.tif.

68 Lawrence & Houseworth albums, *Wood Train and Chinamen in Bloomer Cut*, ca. 1866. Gift of Florence V. Flinn. The Society of California Pioneers.

74 E.M., *Savings and Loan Society, Clay Street*, 1869. Lone Mountain Collection, 1971.055 v.1:340—ALB. BL.

76 E.M., *Effect of Earthquake in San Francisco, 21 Oct. 1868*, 1868. 1984.021:1—CDV. BL.

76 E.M., *Pierce's House—Hayward*, 1868. 1958.021 v.1:231—fALB. BL.

78 E.M., *Pom-pom-pa-sus (Leaping Frogs)*, 1868. SA; Elizabeth K. Raymond Fund.

78 E.M., *Tu-loch-ah-nu-lah (Great Chief of the Valley)*, 1868. SA; Elizabeth K. Raymond Fund.

79 E.M., *Yo-wi-ye (Nevada Fall), 600 feet fall*, 1868. 1962.019:32—ffALB. BL.

82 E.M., *Fort Tongass, Alaska*, 1868. 1905.17137:143—PIC. BL.

84 E.M., *Cemetery with cloud effect*, 1875. Lantern slide. Muybridge Collection. KM.

84 E.M., *Cemetery without cloud effect*, 1875. Lantern slide. Muybridge Collection. KM.

85 E.M., *Moonlight effect on bay*, 1868. Lantern slide. Muybridge Collection. KM.

85 E.M., *A Study of Clouds*, 1868. Lone Mountain Collection, 1971.055 v.2:536—ALB. BL.

87 E.M., *Long Ravine Trestle and Bridge—113 feet high, 878 feet long—looking east*, 1869. Lone Mountain Collection, 1971.055:766—STER. BL.

88 E.M., *San Jose train depot*, ca. 1869. Lone Mountain Collection, 1971.055 v.1:267—ALB. BL.

88 E.M., *Buffalo skulls beside Central Pacific track*, ca. 1869. Lantern slide. Muybridge Collection. KM.

89 E.M., *Shoshone Indians at Corinne, Utah*, 1869. Lone Mountain Collection, 1971.055 v.2:754—ALB. BL.

90 Unidentified artist, American, 19th century. Possibly by Silas Selleck, American, 1827–1885. Sitter: Eadweard J. Muybridge, American, 1830–1904. *Eadweard. J. Muybridge*, ca. 1869. Photograph, albumen print. Image (oval): 8.6 x 5.5 cm (3⅜ x 2³⁄₁₆ in.). Mount: 10.6 x 6.3 cm (4³⁄₁₆ x 2½ in.). Museum of Fine Arts, Boston. Source unidentified, 1991.435. Photograph © 2012 Museum of Fine Arts, Boston.

93 Bradley & Rulofson studio, *Flora Downs*, ca. 1868, from *Brandenburg Album of Bradley & Rulofson "Celebrities" and Muybridge Photographs*, 1874.

96 E.M., *View of Mills Seminary (now Mills College), Oakland, California*, 1873. Albumen silver print mounted on cardboard. 39.1 x 54.2 cm. PH1986:0014. Collection Centre Canadien d'Architecture / Canadian Centre for Architecture, Montreal.

97 E.M., *Convicts quitting work, State Prison, San Quentin*, ca. 1870. Lone Mountain Collection, 1971.055:1682—STER. BL.

99 Alfred A. Hart, *The Last Rail Is Laid. Scene at Promontory Point, May 10, 1869*. Alfred A. Hart Photograph Collection, SU.

101 Thomas Hill, *The Last Spike*, 1881. Oil on canvas, 96 × 144 in. Courtesy California State Railroad Museum.

103 E.M., *Stump of Fossil Tree. Petrified Forest near Calistoga*, ca. 1872. Courtesy, California Historical Society, FN-10785/CHS2012.961.tif.

104 E.M., *Display of Paintings*, ca. 1870. Lone Mountain Collection, 1971.055 v.6:5—ALB. BL.

105 Carleton E. Watkins, *Woodward's Gardens, San Francisco*. Watkins Views of San Francisco, Yosemite, and Monterey Photographed, 1876–90, 1987.029:2—PIC. BL.

105 E.M., *The Heathen Chinese Giant, 8 ft. high, at Woodward's Gardens*, ca. 1870. Lone Mountain Collection, 1971.055 v.2:614—ALB. BL.

105 E.M., *Animals at Woodward's Gardens*, ca. 1870. Lone Mountain Collection, 1971.055 v.2:595—ALB. BL.

107 E.M., *South Park*, ca. 1873. Lone Mountain Collection, 1971.055 v.2:628—ALB. BL.

109 E.M., *Lighthouse at Punta de los Reyes, Coast of California*, 1871. http://commons.wikimedia.org/wiki/File:Point_Reyes_Lighthouse_1871.jpg.

109 E.M., *Sea Lion Islet*, ca. 1872. Lone Mountain Collection, 1971.055:1003—STER. BL.

112 Bradley & Rulofson studio, *Leland Stanford Portrait*, ca. 1880. Stanford Family Photographs, SU.

112 E.M., *Stanford Residence, North Facade*, 1872. Stanford Family Photographs, SU.

113 E.M., *Sacramento, Residence of Leland Stanford, Dancing Hall, 94 feet in length, looking west*, 1872. Courtesy of the California History Room, California State Library, Sacramento, California.

117 Stephen William Shaw, *Portrait of Edwin B. Crocker*, 1873. Oil on canvas. Crocker Art Museum, E. B. Crocker Collection.

118 Charles Nahl, *Sunday Morning at the Mines*, 1872. Oil on canvas, 72 × 108 in. Crocker Art Museum, E. B. Crocker Collection.

119 E.M., *Mrs. Stanford lines up a shot on the billiard table*, 1872. Stanford Family Photographs, SU.

121 John P. Soule, *Race course, at Sacramento*, from *Stereoscopic views of Sacramento, California. 1870*. Stereograph. Robert Dennis Collection of Stereoscopic Views, Miriam and Ira D. Wallach Division of Art, Prints and Photographs, New York Public Library, Astor, Lenox, and Tilden Foundations.

124 John Cameron, *The California Wonder Occident, owned by Gov. L. Stanford*, 1873. Lithograph, Currier and Ives, publisher. LCP.

124 Thomas Kirby van Zandt, *Goldsmith Maid Driven by Budd Doble*, 1876. Crayon and ink wash underdrawing on canvas. SA; Stanford Family Collections.

127 *Smith & Wesson #2 revolver*, photographer unknown. National Rifle Association. National Firearms Museum, NRAmuseum.com.

132 Bradley & Rulofson studio, *William Herman Rulofson and Family Group at His San Francisco Home*, ca. 1880. Courtesy, California Historical Society, FN-25940/CHS2009.183.tif.

134 Bradley & Rulofson studio, *Eadweard Muybridge*, 1872. Janet Leigh Collection.

134 E.M., *Leland Stanford, 268 feet high, 82 feet in circumference*, 1872. Lone Mountain Collection, 1971.055:1552—STER. BL.

137 E.M., *California Theatre and Pacific Music Hall*, ca. 1870. Lone Mountain Collection, 1971.055 v.1:384—ALB. BL.

138 E.M., *The Cliff House*, ca. 1870. Lone Mountain Collection, 1971.055:1632—STER. BL.

140 E.M., *Captain Jack's Cave in the Lava Beds*, 1873. Lone Mountain Collection, 1971.055:1602—STER. BL.

141 E.M., *One-eyed Dixie and other Modoc Squaws*, 1873. Lone Mountain Collection, 1971.055:1625—STER. BL.

142 E.M., *Flora Muybridge*, 1874. Collection of Leonard A. Walle. (Does not appear in the electronic edition due to rights issues.)

148 G. Frederick Keller, *The Curse of California*. Cartoon, from *The Wasp* [San Francisco], Vol. 9, No. 316 (19 Aug 1882). F850.W18 v.9:316, 8/19/1882. BL.

152 E.M., *Nob Hill mansions, San Francisco*, 1877. Pictorial Collection, 1946.011:1—ALB. BL.

153 Alfred A. Hart, *Car Stanford; Built at C.P.R. Car Works, Sacramento, Cal.*, 1882. Stanford Historical Photograph Collection, SU.

153 *Jane L. Stanford*, ca. 1870, photographer unknown. SA; Stanford Family Collections.

153 Astley David Middleton Cooper, *Mrs. Stanford's Jewel Collection*, 1898. Oil on canvas, 50 × 75 in. SA; Stanford Family Collections.

156 E.M., *Calistoga Springs, Grotto of Petrified Wood*, 1874, from *Stereoscopic Views of Lake, Napa & Sonoma Counties, California (1872–1874)*. Stereograph. Robert Dennis Collection of Stereoscopic Views, Miriam and Ira D. Wallach Division of Art, Prints and Photographs, New York Public Library, Astor, Lenox and Tilden Foundations.

171 *Childhood home of Edward Muggeridge, Kingston, UK*. Photographed by the author, 2010.

173 *Edward Muggeridge*, ca. 1850, photographer unknown.

174 *Susanna Norman Smith*, ca. 1860, photographer unknown.

179 *Lovekyn Chapel (Queen Elizabeth's Grammar), Kingston, UK*. KM.

184 *Coronation Stone, Kingston, UK*. KM.

187 H.R. Robinson, *The transatlantic steam ship* Liverpool. Lithograph, ca. 1840. LCP.

195 Lawrence & Houseworth albums, *The Court House, Napa City, Napa County*, ca. 1866. Gift of Florence V. Flinn. The Society of California Pioneers.

203 *Leland Stanford Sr.*, 1848, photographer unknown. Stanford Family Photographs, SU.

209 *Jane and Leland Sr.*, 1850, photographer unknown. Stanford Family Photographs, SU.

213 *Stanford & Smith store, Michigan Bluff, CA*, ca. 1853, photographer unknown, from George T. Clark, *Leland Stanford: War Governor of California, Railroad Builder and Founder of Stanford University* (1931).

215 *The Huntington & Hopkins Store, K Street, Sacramento*, ca. 1855, photographer unknown. The Mariners' Museum, Newport News, VA.

220 *Governor Stanford, DuPont Street between California and Pine, San Francisco, July 4, 1863*, photographer unknown. Courtesy, California Historical Society, FN-08549/CHS2012.940.tif.

225 Front page, *New York Illustrated News*, 12 Nov 1853, illustrator unknown. Beinecke Rare Book and Manuscript Library, Yale University.

228 Charles Meryon, *San Francisco panorama*, 1856. Engraving. Library of Congress Geography and Map Division, Washington, DC.

233 *Famous Fort Gunnybags of the Vigilantes of '56*, 1856, photographer unknown. Jesse Brown Cook Scrapbooks, 1996.003:85a—fALB. BL.

236 E.M., *Le Count Bros. & Mansur's Stationery Establishment*, 1872. Stereographic Views of San Francisco Bay Area Locations by Eadweard Muybridge, ca. 1865–79, 1971.069:38—STER. BL.

240 *Butterfield Overland Mail Co./Concord Carriage*, ca. 1860, photographer unknown. Wells Fargo Corporate Archives, San Francisco.

240 *Butterfield Overland Mail Company map*, ca. 1860, mapmaker unknown. Smithsonian National Postal Museum.

244 Lawrence & Houseworth albums, *Napa City, from the Court House, looking east*, ca. 1866. Gift of Florence V. Flinn. The Society of California Pioneers.

244 Lawrence & Houseworth albums, *Napa City and Churches, Napa County*, ca. 1866. Gift of Florence V. Flinn. The Society of California Pioneers.

266 London Stereoscopic and Photographic Company, *The Nave of the International Exhibition, from the Western Dome*, 1862. http://commons.wikimedia.org/wiki/File:1862_expo.jpg

272 Stock certificate, the Ottoman Company, London, 1865. Collection of Stephen Herbert.

282 E.M., *Weeding and protecting the young coffee plant from the sun. Antigua*, 1875, from *The Pacific Coast of Central America and Mexico; the Isthmus of Panama; Guatemala; and the Cultivation and Shipment of Coffee Illustrated by Muybridge*, 1876 [hereafter *The Pacific Coast . . . by Muybridge*]. Courtesy of the California History Room, California State Library, Sacramento, California.

282 E.M., *Group of alcaldes at Santa Marie*, 1875, from *The Pacific Coast . . . by Muybridge*, 1876. Courtesy of the California History Room, California State Library, Sacramento, California.

283 E.M., *A roadside scene, San Isidro*, 1875, from *The Pacific Coast . . . by Muybridge*, 1876. Courtesy of the California History Room, California State Library, Sacramento, California.

283 E.M., *Reception of the Artist*, 1875, from *The Pacific Coast . . . by Muybridge*, 1876, SU.

285 E.M., *Hacienda Serigiers*, 1875, from *The Pacific Coast . . . by Muybridge*, 1876, SU.

285 E.M., *Planting the seed at Las Nubes*, 1875, from *The Pacific Coast . . . by Muybridge*, 1876, SU.

286 E.M., *Plaza of Antigua*, 1875, from *The Pacific Coast . . . by Muybridge*, 1876. Courtesy of the California History Room, California State Library, Sacramento, California.

286 E.M., *San Rafael orphanage: Exterior view, with staff and children (boys)*, ca. 1872. Eadweard Muybridge Photograph Collection, SU.

289 E.M., *Self-portrait*, ca. 1885 / Eadweard James Muybridge, photographer. Thomas Anshutz Papers, Archives of American Art, Smithsonian Institution.

292 E.M., *Hall*, 1878. Eadweard Muybridge Photograph Collection, SU.

293 E.M., *Library*, ca. 1878. San Francisco History Center, San Francisco Public Library.

298 E.M., *General view of Palo Alto Stock Ranch*, 1881. LCP.

299 Thomas Hill, *Palo Alto Spring*, 1878. Oil on canvas, 87 × 138 in. SA; Stanford Family Collections.

301 E.M., *Panorama of San Francisco from California Street Hill*, 1877. Five of eleven photographs, plus captioned key. Beinecke Rare Book and Manuscript Library, Yale University.

308 E.M., *"Occident," owned by Leland Stanford; trotting at a 2:30 gait over the Sacramento track, in July, 1877*, 1877. SA; Stanford Family Collections.

311 G.W. Peters, *Kearney Speaking to the Workingmen on Nob Hill, San Francisco, October 29, 1877*. Illustration, from Ira Brown Cross, *The History of the Labor Movement in California* (1935). Ira Cross: California Labor Notes, 1815–1960, BANC MSS C-R 12, Box 1:4. BL.

312 E.M., *Camera and shutter (side view). Plate B*, 1879–80, from *The Attitudes of Animals in Motion*, 1881. KM.

314 A: E.M., *General view of experiment track, background and cameras. Plate F, 1879*, from *The Attitudes of Animals in Motion*, 1881, SU. B: *Apparatus for filming a galloping horse*, 1881, illustrator unknown. Visual Resources Collection, Yale University Library.

316 E.M., *"Occident" Trotting at a 2:20 Gait*, 1878. SA; Stanford Family Collections.

320 E.M., *Athletes. Posturing. Plate 115, 1879*, from *The Attitudes of Animals in Motion*, 1881. KM.

322 E.M., *Leland Stanford, Jr., on his Pony "Gypsy"—Phases of a Stride by a Pony While Cantering*, 1879. Lantern slide. SA; Stanford Family Collections.

325 E.M., *"Nimrod" pacing, maquette for a zoopraxiscope disk*, ca. 1879. SA; Stanford Family Collections.

327 Bernard Alfieri, *Muybridge's zoopraxiscope*, ca. 1956. KM.

331 G. Frederick Keller, *The Retribution Comet*. Cartoon, from *The Wasp* [San Francisco], vol. 7, no. 258 (8 Jul 1881), cover. F850.W18 v.7:258, 7/8/1881. BL.

333 Jean-Louis-Ernest Meissonier, *Leland Stanford*, 1881. Oil on canvas, 13 × 17 in. SA; Stanford Family Collections.

344 Waléry Studio (Paris), *Leland Stanford Jr.*, 1881. SA; Stanford Family Collections.

347 E.M., *Eadweard Muybridge's outdoor camera house, 36th and Pine Streets, Philadelphia*, ca. 1885. Eadweard Muybridge Collection, University of Pennsylvania Archives.

348 E.M., *Two women shaking hands and kissing each other, plate 444*, from *Animal locomotion: an electro-photographic investigation of consecutive phases of animal movements*, 1887 [hereafter *Animal Locomotion*]. Wellcome Library, London.

349 E.M., *Walking, saddle; female rider, nude; plate 583*, from *Animal Locomotion*, 1887. Wellcome Library, London.

350 E.M., *Woman, sitting and smoking, plate 247*, from *Animal Locomotion*, 1887. Wellcome Library, London.

351 E.M., *Stages of men wrestling*, from *Animal Locomotion*, 1887. Wellcome Library, London.

352 E.M., *Walking, ascending step, using shovel, using pick*, from *Animal Locomotion*, 1887. Eadweard Muybridge Collection, University of Pennsylvania Archives.

358 *Leland Stanford, Rutherford Hayes*, ca. 1885, photographer unknown. Stanford Family Photographs, SU.

364 *Thomas Edison*, ca. 1890, photographer unknown. U.S. Dept. of the Interior, National Park Service, Thomas Edison National Historical Park, West Orange, NJ.

366 William K. Dickson, *Monkeyshines*, 1889. Filmstrip. U.S. Dept. of the Interior, National Park Service, Thomas Edison National Historical Park, West Orange, NJ.

370 *Leland Stanford, about 1890*, photographer unknown. http://commons.wikimedia.org/wiki/File:LelandStanford1890.JPG.

373 *Zoopraxographical Hall, World's Columbian Exposition, Chicago*, 1893, photographer unknown. Courtesy of the California History Room, California State Library, Sacramento, California.

378 *Edison's Kinetographic Theater (the "Black Maria"), Edison Manufacturing Company, West Orange,*

NJ, ca. 1893, photographer unknown. U.S. Dept. of the Interior, National Park Service, Thomas Edison National Historical Park, West Orange, NJ.

379 William K. Dickson, *Edison's kinetoscopic record of a sneeze (Fred Ott's Sneeze)*, 1894. LCP.

381 *Peter Bacigalupi's San Francisco Kinetoscope and phonograph parlor, Market Street, San Francisco*, 1894, photographer unknown. U.S. Dept. of the Interior, National Park Service, Thomas Edison National Historical Park, West Orange, NJ.

388 *Edwin S. Porter directs "A Country Girl's Seminary Life And Experiences," Edison Studio, Bronx, New York, 1908*, Henry Cronjager. Courtesy Margaret Herrick Library, AMPAS.

389 *Portrait of Muybridge*, ca. 1900, photographer unknown. Walter R. Miles Research concerning Eadweard Muybridge, SU.

390 *Interior of Harris and Davis's Nickelodeon Theater, Pittsburgh*, ca. 1905, photographer unknown, from *Moving Picture World*, 30 Nov. 1907.

INDEX

Page numbers in *italics* refer to illustrations.

ABOUT THE AUTHOR

Edward Ball is the author of four works of nonfiction, including the bestselling National Book Award–winning *Slaves in the Family*. Born and raised in the South, he lives in Connecticut and teaches writing at Yale University.